Mrs. John W. C̶_____

17676

THE
FORTY-FIRST YEARBOOK

OF THE

NATIONAL SOCIETY FOR THE STUDY OF EDUCATION

PART I
PHILOSOPHIES OF EDUCATION

Prepared by the Society's Committee

JOHN S. BRUBACHER (Chairman), MORTIMER J. ADLER, WILLIAM C. BAGLEY,
FREDERICK S. BREED, HERMAN H. HORNE, WILLIAM H. KILPATRICK,
WILLIAM McGUCKEN, and EDWARD H. REISNER

Edited by

NELSON B. HENRY

Distributed by
THE UNIVERSITY OF CHICAGO PRESS
CHICAGO 37, ILLINOIS

Published by

THE NATIONAL SOCIETY FOR THE STUDY OF EDUCATION

5835 KIMBARK AVENUE, CHICAGO 37, ILLINOIS

The responsibilities of the Board of Directors of the National Society for the Study of Education in the case of yearbooks prepared by the Society's committees are (1) to select the subjects to be investigated, (2) to appoint committees calculated in their personnel to ensure consideration of all significant points of view, (3) to provide appropriate subsidies for necessary expenses, (4) to publish and distribute the committees' reports, and (5) to arrange for their discussion at the annual meetings.

The responsibility of the Yearbook Editor is to prepare the submitted manuscripts for publication in accordance with the principles and regulations approved by the Board of Directors in the " Guide for Contributors."

Neither the Board of Directors, nor the Yearbook Editor, nor the Society is responsible for the conclusions reached or the opinions expressed by the Society's yearbook committees.

Published February, 1942

First Printing, 3,000 Copies
Second Printing, 600 Copies, June, 1943
Third Printing, 1,000 Copies, November, 1943
Fourth Printing, 1,000 Copies, December, 1945
Fifth Printing, 1,000 Copies, April 1, 1947
Sixth Printing, 1,000 Copies, September, 1947
Seventh Printing, 1,000 Copies, January, 1948
Eighth Printing, 2,000 Copies, June, 1948
Ninth Printing, 3,000 Copies, May, 1949
Tenth Printing, 3,000 Copies, May, 1950
Eleventh Printing, 3,000 Copies, June, 1951

Printed in the United States of America

OFFICERS OF THE SOCIETY

FOR 1941–1942

Board of Directors
(Term of office expires March 1 of the year indicated)

WILLIAM C. BAGLEY, *Chairman* (1942)
Columbia University, New York, New York

WILLIAM A. BROWNELL (1945) *
Duke University, Durham, North Carolina

W. W. CHARTERS (1945) *
Ohio State University, Columbus, Ohio

FRANK N. FREEMAN (1943)
University of California, Berkeley, California

BESS GOODYKOONTZ (1944)
Office of Education, Washington, D. C.

GRAYSON N. KEFAUVER (1942)
Stanford University, Palo Alto, California

GEORGE D. STODDARD (1944)
State University of Iowa, Iowa City, Iowa

RALPH W. TYLER (1943)
University of Chicago, Chicago, Illinois

NELSON B. HENRY (*Ex-officio*)
University of Chicago, Chicago, Illinois

Secretary-Treasurer
NELSON B. HENRY (1942)
University of Chicago, Chicago, Illinois

* Elected for three years beginning March 1, 1942.

THE SOCIETY'S COMMITTEE ON
PHILOSOPHIES OF EDUCATION

MORTIMER J. ADLER, Associate Professor of the Philosophy of Law, University of Chicago, Chicago, Illinois.

WILLIAM C. BAGLEY, Professor Emeritus of Education, Teachers College, Columbia University, New York, New York.

FREDERICK S. BREED, Associate Professor of Education, University of Chicago, Chicago, Illinois.

JOHN S. BRUBACHER (*Chairman*), Associate Professor of the History and Philosophy of Education, Yale University, New Haven, Connecticut.

HERMAN H. HORNE, Professor of Education, New York University, New York, New York.

WILLIAM H. KILPATRICK, Professor Emeritus of Education, Teachers College, Columbia University, New York, New York.

WILLIAM McGUCKEN, S.J., Professor of Education, Saint Louis University, Saint Louis, Missouri.

EDWARD H. REISNER, Professor of Education, Teachers College, Columbia University, New York, New York.

iv

EDITOR'S PREFACE

The Yearbook for 1942 could not be appropriately presented without mention of the distinguished editorial services of Dr. Guy M. Whipple, Secretary-Treasurer of this Society from 1915 until his death last August and Editor of twenty-six of the forty yearbooks heretofore published. While the content of these volumes is the work of hundreds of zealous members of the profession, Dr. Whipple's technical skill and consistent adherence to high standards of workmanship have recorded their conspicuous imprint upon this widely accredited series of professional publications. It is an enviable privilege to succeed him in these offices and to record in this preface the acknowledgment of a professional obligation of long standing for his effective contributions to the plans and purposes of this organization.

The Forty-First Yearbook follows the plan of presentation of many previous yearbooks of the Society in the respect that it consists of two parts printed as separate volumes. It is unique in the sense that the two parts were from the beginning planned as companion volumes designed as scholarly expositions of the concepts of different schools of thought with respect to two fundamental issues in educational theory and practice. These issues pertain to the ultimate purposes of education in a democratic society and the nature of the learning process.

The projected aims of a social enterprise, even though they may be defined in terms of scientific knowledge, are the expression of a choice of alternatives. The final determination of such aims is the motive of philosophy. The effective methods to be employed in realizing selected objectives may most assuredly be disclosed through laboratory and other experimental techniques. Thus, in education, the issues involved in the determination of what knowledge is to be acquired are resolved by reference to the philosophical concepts with which the purposes and results of schooling are to be reconciled, while the methods by which this knowledge may be attained are to be sought in those refinements of experience achieved by the science of psychology in the testing of different theories of human learning. The companion volumes constituting the Forty-First Yearbook of this Society render noteworthy service to the profession of education by providing authoritative commentaries on the educational implications of varying viewpoints among influential schools of philosophy and psychology.

The plan of this Yearbook grew out of the discussion of a suggestion by Dr. Bagley that provision be made for a yearbook affording a comparative treatment of the philosophical systems underlying present-day educational theories. Dr. Bagley's plan for such a yearbook was outlined in a letter to Dr. Whipple dated December 8, 1938. The proposal was presented to the Board of Directors at the meeting in Cleveland in February, 1939. The discussion of the proposed plan developed several suggestions by different members of the Board, including the suggestion that the effort be made to provide a companion volume affording similar treatment of psychological theories underlying educational procedures. The Board requested Dr. Bagley to meet with a preliminary advisory committee consisting of recognized leaders in the several schools of philosophy for the purpose of considering the possible development of a yearbook in this field. Dr. Freeman was requested to confer with a like committee with respect to the proposed volume in the field of psychology. Funds were appropriated to defray the expenses of these committee meetings.

When the Board met at St. Louis in February, 1940, Dr. Bagley presented a report on the deliberations of the advisory committee on philosophies of education. Varying opinions were expressed by the different members of this group. This report was supplemented by the reading of a letter from Professor Brubacher, one of the members of the advisory committee, in which the value of a yearbook in this field was stressed and the outline of a plan for its development was presented. The Board then invited Professor Brubacher to arrange for a conference with other interested persons in the field with the view of preparing recommendations pertaining to the content and organization of the volume as well as the personnel of the yearbook committee. The report of this group was presented to the Board and approved at the meeting held in Washington in May, 1940, and Professor Brubacher was requested to serve as chairman of the committee.

Dr. Freeman's report of the conference regarding the proposal for a yearbook treating different viewpoints in psychology was also discussed at the February meeting of the Board. Different opinions concerning the proposal had been expressed by different persons participating in the advisory conference, and the project was not recommended by the group as a whole. Professor McConnell, one of the members of this advisory group, favored the proposal and presented an outline of a possible yearbook for the consideration of the Board. This plan was approved and Professor McConnell was invited to serve as chairman of the committee. The members of this committee were appointed at the May meeting of the Board.

The necessary appropriations for the work of these two committees were voted at different meetings of the Board of Directors as the requirements of the committees were ascertained. Additions to the original membership of the committees were made as work on the Yearbook progressed. Some difficulties were encountered in the effort of the committees to bring the two projects to completion in accordance with the desire of the Board to present companion treatises on these topics in the same yearbook. The work of the Committee on Philosophies of Education is herewith presented as Part I of the Forty-First Yearbook. Part II, entitled the *Psychology of Learning,* is presented in a separate volume.

Nelson B. Henry

TABLE OF CONTENTS

ix

CONTENTS

xi

PHILOSOPHIES OF EDUCATION

INTRODUCTION
PURPOSE AND SCOPE OF THE YEARBOOK

JOHN S. BRUBACHER

Associate Professor of the History and Philosophy of Education
Yale University, New Haven, Connecticut
and Chairman of the Yearbook Committee

As everyone knows, education is a discipline of many component parts. These parts have become more and more highly differentiated as the discipline has grown in importance and extent. The differentiation, or specialization, however, has not always taken place evenly in all directions at the same time. Method of instruction or the composition of the curriculum, for instance, has undergone much greater improvement in some periods of educational history than in others. So it is with the philosophy of education in the present century. Probably now as never before, students of education are engrossed with the problems which perennially concern philosophy.

Doubtless a variety of factors have produced this result. Preeminent among them, however, must be the muddled times in which we live. Certainly nothing throws one on the resources of philosophy more certainly than perplexity and doubt as to what ends and means should control inside and outside the school. Confusion here has been chiefly compounded of innovations from the bearings of science on education together with the full impact of industrialism on the schools and the calling in question of a long-accepted political ideal of education. This being the case, no period could have been timelier than the present one for the National Society for the Study of Education to devote one of its Yearbooks to a consideration of philosophies of education.

How to compose the difficulties presented by such conflicting forces as those indicated requires comprehensive thinking about fundamentals. Numerous partial proposals have been made. Educational literature is full of such suggestions, that is, suggestions which deal with this or that fractional aspect of the many-sided problem of education. In recent decades, however, there has been a persistent striving to find solutions in the light of inclusive theory. Piecemeal solutions are

3

good as far as they go but unless each is seen in relation to others there is considerable danger of unsuspectingly working at cross purposes, thus adding to the already mounting confusion.

The persistent endeavor to find a common denominator of consistency in the theory underlying educational practice has already resulted in the emergence of several major systems of educational philosophy. To date most of the books published on philosophy of education have been expositions of some one of these systems. "An Introduction to Philosophy of Education," either as a main or a subtitle, generally has meant an introduction to the educational philosophy of the author rather than to the field in general.

Far too many educators have only been acquainted with some one of these systems, the one in their local schools, perhaps, or the one which obtained where they were professionally prepared. Recently, however, there has been a movement to correct this professional astigmatism through the comparative study of educational philosophies. Sourcebooks in the philosophy of education were one of the earliest indications of this trend. Among treatises on educational philosophy comparison has been effected in two main ways. One tendency has been to lay various philosophies down in separate chapters and to compare them as chapter succeeded chapter. Another has been to select a number of critical areas in educational thought and practice, and to compare the different philosophies as to their contribution in each field.

Each approach has obvious advantages — and disadvantages. Under the latter point it might be listed that the sourcebook lacks continuity; that the first sort of treatise at best is a rendition second hand, consequently running the risk of failing to represent some viewpoints with the persuasiveness of a sympathizer; and that the second sort of treatise may fail to set out each point of view adequately in its systematic entirety. The instant Yearbook is a continuance of the trend toward a comparative study of educational philosophies, but with an endeavor to avoid these shortcomings.

In order to avoid any refraction of philosophical light through the prism of someone else's treatise, leading representatives of the major divisions of educational philosophy have been invited to speak directly to the reader in the central chapters of this Yearbook. For the open-minded reader this should provide an unparalleled opportunity to come to his own conclusions intelligently and independently. For those interested in getting the clinical case record of contemporary philosophical issues in education, the initial chapter provides an appropriate historical perspective for the expositions of the several philosophies treated in the five following chapters. The final chapter presents a review of these expositions in the form of a comparative analysis of the major points at issue.

At one stage of the planning of the Yearbook it was hoped to have each contributor address himself to the same minimum selection of problems in the philosophy of education. The intent of this plan was to make sure that the different philosophies would openly and unmistakably clash at the important points of disagreement and that the student of such problems would be facilitated in finding out the major options open to him for resolving these difficulties. Of course, no contributor was to be limited to this list; he could treat of as many more problems as space permitted. Fortunately or unfortunately this plan failed of adoption because the Yearbook Committee not only failed to reach an agreement on which problems should be selected, but could not even agree as to what constitutes a problem in the philosophy of education. Consequently, it was decided to permit each contributor to expound his school of educational philosophy in the way that seemed to him most adequate, leaving it to the chairman of the Yearbook Committee to achieve as much of the earlier purpose as possible in the concluding comparative chapter.

Five main schools of educational philosophy have been selected for comparison in this Yearbook — pragmatism, realism, idealism, Aristotelianism, and scholasticism or Catholicism. These have been chosen because of their generally admitted prominence in contemporary educational thought and practice. Doubtless other points of view exist and might have been included. Especially is this true of shades of opinion inside and even crossing the categories already mentioned. There being easily imagined and understood limits to the size of such a book as the present one, it was decided to open it only to viewpoints that have a wide vogue in educational literature and practice at the present time.

Although these variants of basic differences of outlook could not each have its own champion, a conscious endeavor has been made to provide against disregarding them altogether. This has been done as part of a general precaution to prevent the exposition of any single school of educational philosophy being too narrowly the point of view of the one chosen to expound it, and his alone. The expositions presented here are intended to be *representative* of a school of thought,

not of an individual. To achieve that end, each contributor submitted
his manuscript, before putting it in final form, to the review of two sympathetic critics. One of these has been an educational philosopher and
the other someone in general philosophy, but both belonging to the
contributor's own broad school of thought.

Finally, a word of introduction, if that be necessary, for those
selected to represent the various schools of educational philosophy.
Pragmatism, or experimentalism, is represented by William H. Kilpatrick, professor emeritus at Teachers College, Columbia University.
Except for John Dewey, Professor Kilpatrick is second to none in the
influence he has exerted on the theory and practice of American
Schools. Since the other contributors all sharpen their viewpoints by
comparison with the experimentalist position, it seemed advisable to
have this contribution appear first. Following is the standpoint of
realism, expounded by Frederick S. Breed of the University of Chicago. The appearance of his *Education and the New Realism* easily
nominated him as the leading man to make this contribution. The
idealistic viewpoint is presented next by Herman H. Horne of New
York University. His *Philosophy of Education* and *The Democratic
Philosophy of Education,* if one were to mention no other of his writings, give him front rank in this category of educational thought.
From the University of Chicago also comes the sponsorship for the
philosophy of education based on Aristotelian principles. Wide attention has been called to this view because it has been espoused by
President Hutchins of that University. Professor Mortimer J. Adler,
who has been closely associated with President Hutchins in expounding this doctrine, represents it in this Yearbook. William J. McGucken,
S.J., dean of the school of education at St. Louis University, writes
for Catholicism. Highly regarded by his order and by Catholics generally, he is also author of *The Catholic Way in Education.* Professor Edward H. Reisner, also of Teachers College, Columbia University,
who writes the first chapter, is especially fitted for the undertaking
because he is fortunately a philosopher *and* a historian. The concluding comparative chapter is contributed by the chairman of the Yearbook Committee.

Because the Yearbook Committee has been anxious to have the
chapters on the different schools of educational philosophy appear as
representative as possible and because to that end each contributor has
asked one or more other members of his school of thought to give his
chapter a critical reading before publication, acknowledgments are in

order to the following people whose willingness to read the manuscripts is the best guarantee the Yearbook has of being representative and not merely personal conclusions of the individual authors: to Professors George Axtelle and Howard Lane of Northwestern University for reading the chapter on pragmatism or experimentalism; to Professor Henry M. Sheffer of Harvard University for reading the chapter on realism; to Doctors Louise Antz and Marie C. Swabey of New York University for reading the chapter on idealism; to Presidents Stringfellow Barr of St. John's College and Robert M. Hutchins of the University of Chicago, Deans J. L. Haggerty of St. Mary's College and Jerod Smith of Marquette University, Professors R. J. Belleperche of John Carroll University, Ruth Byrns O'Meara and A. C. Pegis of Fordham University, and Robert Slavin of Catholic University for reading the chapter on Aristotelianism; and to Professors Bakewell Morrison, S.J., and William L. Wade, S.J., of St. Louis University for reading the chapter on Catholicism or scholasticism.

CHAPTER I

PHILOSOPHY AND SCIENCE IN THE WESTERN WORLD; A HISTORICAL OVERVIEW

EDWARD H. REISNER
Professor of Education
Teachers College, Columbia University
New York City, New York

In this Yearbook there are presented five important world-frames, or philosophies, within each of which the meaning of education is to be considered. These philosophies are (1) the Aristotelian, (2) the Thomistic, (3) the modern, or absolute, idealistic, (4) the realist, and (5) the pragmatic, or instrumentalist.

Of these the Aristotelian and Thomistic are not only the oldest, but probably the ones accepted by the greatest number of people in the Western World today. Absolute idealism was an extremely important way of viewing man and his universe during the nineteenth century, and some of the most significant of the current conceptions of good education were initially stimulated by it. Realism also has been influential historically in educational thought and this is particularly true if Herbart can be classified under this philosophical designation. Realism has entered upon a new phase of importance with the restatement during the twentieth century of the realistic position. Moreover it is very closely related to the pragmatic philosophy in that one may accept much of the pragmatic discussion of the nature of truth and goodness and retain the metaphysical position of realism. The pragmatic, or experimentalist, philosophy has been mainly concerned with the problems of knowing and ethical relationships, and has generally avoided any effort to define for itself what could be called a metaphysical system.

Among them, these world-views pretty well fill up the entire history of man's sophisticated thought about the universe in which he has lived, especially in the Western World. Many volumes have been written dealing with this story as a whole, or even with small parts of it, so obviously the present effort to exhibit on a time-line so much of the entire history of philosophy as is represented in the great systems of

9

thought to be considered, must be highly selective. As the basis for
such selection I propose to consider these various world-frames in relation to the general intellectual milieu in which they came into existence and prospered. In other words, I shall consider these philosophies
with respect to their consistency with the science of their heyday and
as in some very real sense depending on that science and growing out
of it.

I. The Aristotelian World-Frame

From the vantage point of the twentieth century, the philosophy of
Aristotle seems almost to have filled the classical and medieval past,
because it is the world-frame which represents for us the effective historical tradition. However, it is easy to overestimate the prevalence
and the influence of Aristotle before the work of Albertus Magnus and
Thomas Aquinas in the thirteenth century placed him at the center of
the intellectual structure of Christian theism. Not to overlook the materialistic philosophy associated with the names and works of Democritus and Lucretius, there were even in the idealistic classical tradition
at least two philosophies which were important, or shall we say successful, rivals of that of Aristotle. The views of Plato, particularly as
developed in the teaching of the Neo-Platonists, were tremendously influential in the ethical, religious, and philosophical life of the early
Christian centuries, and may be said to have furnished great aid to St.
Augustine in his elaboration of a theoretical support for his Christian
belief. Hardly less important in supplying a tie between Greek philosophy and the Christian religion was the Stoic world-view, from which
came particularly the triune conception of the nature of God.

It was, however, the philosophy of Aristotle which in the long run
proved to be the most authoritative intellectual counterpart of a mono-
theistic religion. It was the science of Aristotle which proved to be the
convincing description of the universe of stars and living things and
inorganic matter. In short, it was Aristotle, as philosopher and scientist in one, who provided a world-frame which not only held together
in meaningful consistency, but which supplied an irrefutable system in
which the Christian religion and its values found a secure and logically
demonstrable place. It is hardly less important to note that the fundamental conceptions of the Aristotelian world-frame held their own for
at least three centuries of important scientific advance after their distinctively Christian implications had been seriously weakened or altogether discredited within the intellectual tradition. Many of the funda-

mental Aristotelian scientific concepts remained authoritative even among scientists until the nineteenth century. And it is only fair to say that Aristotle's conception of the world continues in its main aspects to seem reasonable and true to the millions who have not effectively built into their experience the new facts and formulas of modern science and of historical research.

In a very real sense Aristotle approached his world as many persons do today. His was a bare-handed, naked-vision interpretation. It was undertaken without the aid of telescope or microscope, without any knowledge of chemistry or electrophysics, without possession of the facts only of late brought to light regarding the intricate processes of heredity, biological evolution, cellular body structure and the physiological economy of living organisms. It is equally important to note that in Aristotle's thinking there was not available the concept of change taking place in indefinitely receding time, stretching back for the history of the earth alone some two billions of years and for the universe as a whole lost in the mist of nebulae.

As a man of good sense, Aristotle started with a given world. The fact that that world existed demanded that it should have been brought into existence by some adequate cause. Furthermore it was a world which very obviously operated according to order and system, for while there was a ceaseless process of change going on, that change occurred within clearly defined limits. Nature had its inner controls, its orderly arrangements. The ceaseless flow and ebb of life followed patterns which were changeless and secure.

The explanation of such a world would have to provide for (a) the process of change and becoming within set limits and (b) the element of ultimate causation and orderly control. The first necessity was taken care of by Aristotle in the form-matter concept and the second by the hypothesis of Pure Form, beyond and above the world of process and change, but operating upon it and within it.

For Aristotle, the form-matter concept embraced the two poles of absolute potentiality and perfect actuality. Matter was nothing, but it was the ground of everything in the world of nature. It was sheer stuff — formless, inert raw material to be worked over into things. Form was the principle of order, of patternedness, of creativeness, and of intelligence. The world as one sees it is the result of the interplay of these two opposite, but complementary, factors. Each relatively fixed manifestation of nature, such as sparrow, oak tree, and man, followed the process of its own form's subduing matter to itself in the creation of the individual thing. The forms were eternal and unchanging. They were the limits of the process of change and becoming — the bulwarks of order and continuity in the world of nature.

There can be no doubt that Aristotle's form-matter hypothesis was an outstanding stroke of genius. It was the master-concept for the understanding of the universe which ruled the science of the Western World for many centuries. If the concept was a philosophical one it was nevertheless the support of the ruling scientific tradition. It bore the same relation to the intellectual world before the seventeenth century that Darwin's evolutionary hypothesis did to that of the late nineteenth century or Einstein's theory of relativity to that of the present. *But it was hypothesis!* Aristotle's form-matter concept was a stupendous ' as if,' which for a very long time was a satisfactory master-formula. It was consistent with all that men knew about nature and was an extremely useful hypothesis of description and understanding. But, notwithstanding, it was just Aristotle's guess, posited upon all that he knew and the best that he knew. The ultimate difficulties connected with it were (a) that he knew nothing, really, about the constitution of what we may still call matter, and (b) that the apparent changelessness of the forms was proven illusory by evidence discovered more than twenty centuries after his death.

Aristotle's cosmology seems convincing even today to the man who simply stands upon his two feet and looks into the heavens with unaided vision. The earth is the center of things. As the word *earth* would imply it is the most material of all the bodies which meet the eye, for in Aristotle's interpretation, the farther up and away from the earth, the more ethereal were the denizens of the middle distance, until out beyond the sphere of the fixed stars there was no matter whatsoever. There abode the Pure Form, the great epitome of all the lesser forms, which partook of its absolute nature. There was reason, knowing and ruling all the categories of nature. There was the great First Cause, the Prime Mover, the Absolute Knower, independent of the world, but acting upon it and endowing it with movement, development, order, and reason.

Every living thing had its soul, but man's soul alone was endowed with self-conscious reason. Man was a rational animal. In that respect he stood out above all the rest of animal creation and participated, at a great distance, to be sure, in the quality or characteristic of the Pure Form, which Aristotle discussed under the heading of theology. In his own thinking man could recognize and follow the concepts which were the structurings of nature — could classify individual things according to their kind. Truth was achieved when the pattern of thinking corresponded with the structure of reality. Accordingly, truth could correctly be considered as something absolute. For the same reason, thinking was an exercise in classification rather than a process of discovery. In such an intellectual dispensation, it would be correct to say with President Hutchins that truth was " always and everywhere the same."

While it is true that his metaphysical systems and his formal logic represent a very important — probably the dominant — part of Aristotle's intellectual influence, it is easy to underestimate the experimentalist method which he used so freely. In many fields of natural science Aristotle was a close observer and faithful recorder of facts, from which he made cautious generalizations. His studies of rhetoric and poetry were based upon analysis of the wealth of experience available to him in those fields in the Athens of his day. His observations on politics followed upon the collection of numerous constitutions of ancient states and took into account the circumstances of the communities in which these basic laws were operative. Even his formal logic was built upon an extensive study of syllogistic arrangements and propositions, to discover which among them were sound, and a part of his logical theory dealt with the logic of discovery.

It is in the field of ethics, however, that Aristotle's experimentalist bent is most clearly seen. While he employed his chief metaphysical principle when he said that the good life must be one lived according to reason, the content with which he filled in the formal pattern consisted of the values and attitudes of the Athenian aristocrat of his times. Aristotle did not, like Plato and even more Plato's later disciples, attempt to reduce the good life to the asceticism and severity which is implied in an extreme devotion to the exercise of the rational faculty. Aristotle was a humanist — a humanist in terms of Athenian comfort and good taste. Reason being the culmination, or apex, of man's nature, its exercise was the highest manifestation of human living. But man was not only a rational animal, he was, according to Aristotle, an animal of varied needs, all of which could be legitimately taken care of within the pattern of the good life. Over and above the high satisfaction that came from the intellectual life, there were other goods gladly to be accepted — goods of social esteem, of normal biological functioning, and of downright creature comfort. For the proper use of the materials of experience in leading the good life, man's reason was the guide toward the 'golden mean,' the umpire between excess and deficiency, the mentor showing the way of solid advantage and good taste. In terms of the ultimate values represented in Aristotle's pattern of the good life one sees the background of the Greek world — its sophistication, its luxury, its social stratification, its contempt for manual labor, as well as its devotion to things of the mind and its flair for good taste and beauty. If Aristotle's formal pattern for the good life was to live according to reason, its detail was provided out of the habits, the prepossessions, and the prejudices of the rich, well-born, educated Greek of the third pre-Christian century.

II. Christian Theism

Christian theism is the resultant of a fusion, during the first three centuries of our era, of the Judeo-Christian religion with certain key-concepts of Greek philosophy. This fusion could take place because the world-frame of that great historical religion had in the later stages of its evolution become strictly monistic. Its God was the great first cause, the creator and governor of the universe, in whom mankind, formed after his image, live and move and have their being. In common with many other cultural movements of the age, this religion had accepted the notion of man's eternal life after his physical dissolution. It is readily seen that a close parallelism existed between the Judeo-Christian religion, which had developed within the frame of poetry and ethical insight, and, making allowance for variety and divergence among them, the philosophies of Plato, Aristotle, and the Stoics. On the ethical side, Christianity developed on sternly ascetic lines. It was distrustful of the bodily appetites and even of the ordinary interests of the world of business and politics. In this, too, it was not alone, but had the support of later Platonism and of Stoicism.

By the beginning of the fourth Christian century, the Christian religion and the ruling intellectual concepts of the Graeco-Roman world had run together, with the result that the religion had acquired an intellectual frame and justification. In other words, Christian theism was at once good science and inspired religion. The religion of the Judean shepherd and the Man of Galilee had become a theology acceptable to men of learning.

It was at the Council of Nicaea (325 A.D.) that the principal theological tenets of Christianity were formulated and officially adopted. During the nine hundred years which followed that event, the church performed important social services and developed its institutional and religious forms in a living relationship with its cultural environment. During that period matters of the intellect were secondary and such doctrinal evolution as took place occurred without reference to any clearly conceived philosophical formulas. When, in the eleventh and twelfth centuries, men of active mind began to concern themselves with the logic of Christian practice and belief, they were only in very incomplete possession of any of the philosophical systems which in the first three Christian centuries had provided the intellectual sources of Christian theology. It was, accordingly, a matter of prime importance that the complete works of Aristotle became known in the universities of Europe in the latter part of the twelfth century. Christianity at this time was subject to competition from Mohammedanism, from Manichaeism and from the critical questioning of scholars in the universities of Christendom who were conscious of certain problems, even of discrepancies, within the body of Christian belief and practice. It is true that Aristotle alone had not provided the philosophical elements in Christian theology, but his prestige in every field of learning was so great and his philosophy in its main bearings was so apt for the task of Christian apologetics that he rapidly became the chief support of the church canon. Many medieval philosophers participated in this task of logically justifying Christian doctrine in terms of Aristotle's philosophy, but it is St. Thomas Aquinas who represents the culmination of these efforts and with whose name the thirteenth-century restatement of Christian theology is preëminently connected.

Aristotle's principal philosophical conceptions entered into St. Thomas' system. The form-matter hypothesis became basic to it. God was seen as pure form, the great first cause, the governor of the universe, the source of all good and truth. Man as a rational animal belonged to the system of eternal forms and thus was the bearer of immortality. In the cosmological and the teleological proofs of the existence of God, advanced with so much certainty by St. Thomas in his *Contra Gentiles*, the argument follows lines of logic which are clearly Aristotelian. Thus, it was possible to find impeccable intellectual justification for some of the principal tenets of Christian belief.

However, thirteenth century theism was much more than a metaphysical system. It was also the religion expounded in a book contributed to by many hands and representing a spiritual evolution covering many centuries. Furthermore it was an institution which had been developing for many centuries after the books comprising the canon had been written and had taken on forms of worship, articles of belief, and a system of administration which were unknown to the founders. All of this ran beyond Aristotle. Much of it was inconsistent with his philosophical principles and his ethical values. Accordingly, St. Thomas accepted two areas of authority — one of reason, over which Aristotle ruled, and the other of faith, for which the Bible and the Divine sanctions of the living church were sponsors.

It will thus be seen that the Aristotelian and the Thomistic philosophies were in no sense identical. The latter included the main points of the Aristotelian metaphysics and scientific theory, but its ethical system was quite different from that of Aristotle. Moreover, in accepting so extensive and diverse a body of divine authorities, which were to be accepted with unquestioning fidelity, as did Thomism, the clean-cut, orderly logic of the Aristotelian system was lost. A further difference lies in the fact that many primitive, nonscientific or prescientific views were included in the body of fact to be explained, and defended, by the Christian apologist of the thirteenth century. St. Thomas' fame and influence rest upon the impressive effort which he made to harmonize and unify the details of a historically developing tradition and institution with the main positions of a close-knit philosophical-scientific system.

III. The Beginnings of a New World Outlook

1. Modern Science and the Aristotelian-Thomistic World View

While it is true that even within the scholastic tradition there were attacks made upon the philosophical system of St. Thomas Aquinas, which had become authoritative and official within Christendom, nevertheless it was the development of a new activity of scientific observation and generalization which eventually weakened the hold of that system upon the minds of the intellectuals. The succession, Copernicus, Kepler, and Galileo, recalls the heavy blows dealt in the late sixteenth and early seventeenth centuries to Aristotle's cosmology. The earth was proved to be, not the center of the universe, but a planet revolving about the sun. Its orbit was not a perfect circle, as good logic would require of an all-wise Creator, but elliptical. The stars were not fixed in a great, all-compassing crystalline sphere, but took their way through endless space. By such new facts the Aristotelian-Biblical cosmology was discredited and much more of Aristotle's physics, which had been deductively arrived at from original theoretical assumptions, was shown by direct observation and experimentation to be unsound.

The definitive culmination of this early modern period of scientific discovery came with the labors of Isaac Newton and his theory of gravitation, which gave a new and authoritative law of nature and sent
Aristotle's cosmology into the limbo of discarded hypotheses.

In spite, however, of these punishing blows, the philosophical core
of the Aristotelian-Thomistic system retained its prestige. The mind-
matter hypothesis remained standard within the new scientific setting
throughout the eighteenth century, and the best intellects of the time
continued to believe in a world created and governed according to purpose and design by an omniscient, all-powerful Creator. Thus the
main properties of the theistic world-frame persisted intact. Men of
science could believe in the soul of man as the bearer of the immortal
life and in God, the ' spirit, infinite, eternal and unchangeable in his
being, wisdom, power, holiness, justice, goodness, and truth.' During
that same period they continued to think of the world as a short-term
affair, created all at once only a few thousand years in the past and
destined to be discontinued at a not-too-distant future time.

The most significant differences in intellectual outlook brought
about by the new science of the seventeenth and eighteenth centuries
lay within that area which St. Thomas himself had been unable to
bring under the Aristotelian formulas, namely, the realm of faith. Generally speaking, it was that part of the Christian world-frame which
had developed historically, as a product of everyday experience and
feeling rather than as the outcome of philosophic-scientific thought,
which lost standing with the members of the intellectual class. They
could continue to believe in God, according to the rather cold formulas
of rationalism, but they had difficulty with the Bible as the revelation
of God. The anthropomorphism of that Book, its prescientific prepossessions, its heavy dependence on the miraculous, the intricate metaphysical puzzles of some of its key theological concepts, even the direct
contradictions of strict scientific evidence contained in its pages, made
its position, to say the least, ambiguous. In the same way the authoritative role of organized religion, whether that of the Church Universal
or of one of the dissenting beliefs of the Protestant revolt, lost its logical connection with the world-frame as St. Thomas had conceived it.
For the most part the intellectuals of the eighteenth century continued
to believe in a world created and governed by an all-wise, all-powerful,
and benevolent spirit, God, and in man as sharing in God's rational
and moral nature and thereby destined to eternal existence.

2. A New System of Human Values

Before passing on to consider later additions to man's knowledge which caused reëxamination of fundamental philosophical concepts, it is desirable to consider a thoroughgoing shift in the system of human values which occurred in the latter part of the eighteenth century. It may well be believed that one of the sources of this new value system lay in the progress of representative government during the period under consideration. With or without democratic political forms, changes in the circumstances of human living bring about changes in institutional and legal arrangements, but with the acceptance of the concept that legislative bodies representing the will of the people have the function of consciously modifying those laws and institutions in the interest of public welfare, the dynamic of social change is not only consciously recognized, but is elevated into a major principle. The early parliamentary governments were undoubtedly mainly concerned with making social change to the advantage of the upper classes, but the principle could not for long be constrained within such narrow objectives. Men became possessed by the idea of making over human institutions in the direction of greater human good. Thus, the concept of upward social movement, of human progress, came to displace the older concept of social status. Unsatisfactory institutional arrangements not only could be changed, but should be changed. The social order was not as it was because God had willed it to be so, but because man, by his lack of vision and his indifference, had consented to its inadequacies.

Hand in hand with this new attitude toward social institutions had gone a new hopefulness regarding the possibility of human betterment as based on the new controls over nature which the new science had either provided or promised. By this means man had gained new instrumentalities for combating the deficiencies of his existence. Science had unlocked the secrets of nature and thus had provided the necessary resources, to be more fully realized in the future, to be sure, against poverty, disease, and famine.

Thus had come about in the more sensitive and philanthropic minds of the late eighteenth century a radical change in ethical outlook. They had recovered a faith in the possibilities of the good life *within this world*. The old attitude of submission to the curses which afflict human existence had given way to a doctrine of attack. Poverty, disease, famine, war, political tyranny, oppression and exploitation of the weak, ignorance, superstition, and intolerance — all these human ills existed in the world not because God sponsored them, but because man allowed them to continue.

It is hardly too much to say that the change in the locus and the character of human values which is suggested above represents the beginning of a new ethical and religious era. In a very real sense it exhibited a return to the faith and optimism of the Hebrew prophets, who placed their ideal of ultimate human welfare and happiness within the world of experience. Their kingdom of heaven was to be on this earth. In the same way, the social vision of the eighteenth-century philosophers was not of a kingdom of perfection beyond the bounds of space and time, but of a renewed, regenerated society, in which institutions would favor universal justice and welfare and in which human beings might develop the divine virtues of intelligent goodwill and friendly coöperation for ends of common welfare.

IV. Toward the Modern World

1. Some Centuries of Philosophic Tinkering

While the scientific advances of the seventeenth and eighteenth centuries profoundly affected the prestige of the Christian theistic world-view, they did not displace the more basic hypotheses of Aristotle. Philosophers continued to work on the assumption that Aristotle's mind-matter hypothesis was sound. They accepted his conception of the changeless character of the genera, species, and forms which gave the law of order to living and inorganic nature. They believed in God, the Great First Cause and the guarantor of system, meaning, and purpose in the world. They also built into their thinking the notion that man, in his possession of a soul and a rational faculty, was definitively separated from the lower animals — not separated from them only in degree of mental ability, but in actual quality of being. Within these boundaries, with a few exceptions which this account must neglect, the philosophic tradition from Descartes to Kant operated.

In the long view the progress of philosophic thought in the modern world has not lain with the philosophers at all, but with the scientists who provided the philosophers with the new data and new fundamental assumptions. From this premise, Dalton, Lavoisier, La Place, Lyell, Liebig, Darwin, Clerk-Maxwell, Pasteur, and Curie have been more important in establishing a new world-outlook than have the technical philosophers who make up the subject matter of the histories of philosophy. It was the scientists who suggested new guesses about the nature of reality which came to seem more reasonable than those proposed by Aristotle. Indeed it was the scientists who took great areas of experience, which had been the playground of speculative thinkers, out of the realm of speculation and placed them in the realm of demonstrated fact.

However, before trying to show how the scientists have compelled us to move out into a new world, it is important to note a contribution to the description of mind which was made by a succession of thinkers from Hobbes to Locke. It is further noteworthy that much of this contribution was made in the spirit of scientific description rather than in terms of philosophic speculation. Hobbes made the beginning with his shrewd insights into the processes of association and Locke carried much farther the description of the way in which experience is built up. To be sure, Locke's assumption that the mind at birth was a *tabula rasa*, an empty slate, has been shown to be false in the light of more recent psychological knowledge, but his procedure in showing how experience comes into the mind, how it is retained, how it is recombined with new data, how general ideas are built up, how patterns of thinking come into operation, was scientific in method and in spirit. He was, for the most part, concerned with mind as a phenomenon rather than as an entity, with descriptions of the processes and development of experience, rather than with metaphysics. The Frenchmen, Condillac and Helvetius, contributed to this influential strand of psychological science, and Bishop Berkeley, though primarily concerned with a metaphysical theory, rendered important service with his *New Theory of Vision* in showing how the perception of space was a complicated process of interpreting various sense cues. Two other Englishmen, Hartley and Priestley, carried the analysis of the association of ideas still further, and, in addition, suggested the physiological counterpart of the nerve cells and connective tissues of the brain with the repertory and interrelationship of ideas.

The associationist tradition added enormously to the realistic analysis and description of mental processes. Indeed, in the end it was so successful in substituting pattern and process of ideas for the concept of an over-all mind that it tended to develop its own metaphysical conception, as in the case of the German philosopher, psychologist, and educator, Herbart. The ideas themselves became entities, combining in the patterns which make up human consciousness, with the ego reduced to the status of a kind of home base, without real quality or further significance. When this had occurred it was evident that the associationists had 'played out their string.' Scientific psychology had to wait for further progress, until biology could provide it with new basic assumptions which in turn would bring new insights.

While it may truthfully be said that the philosophers of the seventeenth and eighteenth centuries did not make much positive progress in their treatment of the philosophical concepts of mind and matter, it may be added that they considerably disturbed the easy certainty which men had enjoyed with reference to them. John Locke had undertaken an analysis of matter which resulted in his declaring that we really know nothing about its nature beyond the sensations we get from a material object. Matter was only an abstraction of human thinking. Do as much as we can, we can never penetrate beyond the testimony of the senses regarding that which may underlie them. But Locke did not make a great deal of his skepticism regarding matter. He unexpectedly turned to the conclusion that there was just as much warrant for believing in spirit as there was for our complete faith in the reality of matter. In effect he said we believe in matter although we know nothing about it, therefore, knowing at least as much about spirit, which is exactly nothing, there is no less warrant for positing the existence of spirit.

A Scotchman, David Hume, extended Locke's analysis, but instead of ending up with Locke's double faith he came out with a double skepticism. He held that there was no warrant in experience for pretending that we know anything really about either mind or matter. All we have is a series of sensations and images extended into meanings and theories which go far beyond anything the data justify. Hume had nothing positive to suggest by way of relief for the obvious paradox which his thinking had precipitated. One might no longer believe in the theoretical concepts which had for so long served to explain experience and yet experience seemed to be constituted according to the no-longer-acceptable generalizations.

To meet this impasse, Immanuel Kant, in the last quarter of the eighteenth century, proposed a solution of the main problem involved. His primary purpose was to find some way of explaining why the natural world, in our experience of it, held together in an orderly, reliable manner and why the individual's own experience possessed unity and self-identity. His findings substantiated the validity of scientific method and the confidence exhibited by men in their practical dealings with the objective world, but they wrote ' finis ' to the kind of thinking which had been the stock in trade of the philosophers since the time of Aristotle.

Kant drew a sharp distinction between the world of experience and the world of 'things-in-themselves,' which latter represented an un-acknowledged holdover in Kant's mind from the kind of thinking which his method repudiated and the validity of which it denied. Without attempting to follow the Kantian argument, it may be said that Kant found a formula which justified men's confidence in the orderly opera-tions of the world of experience, which is severely limited by the fact that its data always and inevitably start with sensations. All sensa-tions coming to the mind are compelled to submit to certain conditions which are imposed by the nature of mind itself. The structure of mind makes it inevitable that all experience should be set in time and space relationships and that it should exhibit orderly and necessary condi-tions and modes of operation, such as are represented by the category of cause and effect, to give but one example. The experience thus built up was a world of phenomena. As long as we keep within the world of phenomena, the rules of order hold. The scientist may proceed with perfect security, the practical man with confidence, because experience, as experience, is constituted according to certain infallible patterns. But there is no warrant for anyone to extend his thinking beyond that closed-in area which begins with sense perception and ends with the elaboration of the data which come through the senses.

It is easily seen that the Kantian critique shuts out from man's ex-perience the 'things-in-themselves,' but most of the concerns of phi-losophy lay in that banned territory. By the terms which Kant laid down, the mind of man could not say anything, could not know any-thing, about matter in the abstract, about mind as absolute something, nor about the genera, species, and forms of the Aristotelian and ration-alist tradition — not even about God. In effect, Kant said that philos-ophy had all along been trespassing in an area which was forbidden it by the very constitution of man's thinking apparatus. Man's think-ing was valid within experience, but philosophy had been, from time out of mind, slipping across the deadline of its competency. Philos-ophers had thought they were thinking when they were only guessing, or wishing, or something else equally unrespectable in good intellectual circles.

It may not be forgotten that, in his *Critique of Practical Reason,* Kant himself conducted some high, wide, and fancy operations among the things-in-themselves, but in so far as the vogue of rationalism is concerned he had dealt a lethal blow. The easy confidence which phi-losophers had had in their right to pass from the realm of experience, in which their thinking had validity and warrant, into the realm of pure forms, which was beyond the jurisdiction of their thought processes, was forever undermined. Kant's critical philosophy was the end of an era of human thinking. It put up a sign, " Road Closed." Philosophers could and would try to find other ways to their objectives, but the way of Aristotle could no longer be followed.

2. The Idealistic Detour

In the history of philosophy a great deal of attention is customarily given to the way around the Kantian impasse which was followed by the modern idealistic school. Its most creative participants were the Germans, Fichte, Schelling, and Hegel, and these were followed in later time by the Englishman, Thomas Hill Greene, and the American, Josiah Royce. This philosophic position is important for education because it provided the world-frame for such important educators as Fichte, Froebel, Felix Adler, and William Tecumseh Harris. Furthermore, it established certain presuppositions regarding the nature of mankind and of the child which operated powerfully and with benign influence upon educational thought and practice in the nineteenth century. For that reason it deserves appraisal in even so limited a sketch of the history of thought as this.

The idealists who followed Kant took the position that the Kantian ' things-in-themselves ' were not only unknown, but useless for any understanding of reality. Accordingly, they ignored the ' things-in-themselves ' and built a world-frame out of a new patterning of experience. For Kant, the focus of the world of experience had been the individual mind, in which operated certain universal categories. The idealists thought of all experience as the content and being of a universal mind. The universe was to them a self, striving for realization. The heavens and the earth were the outward thrust of his Being. Mankind was the instrumentality for the realization of his moral purposes. All of the physical world as it could be described by the scientist, all human existence as it could come under the scrutiny of the historian, all of human aspiration in the fields of art, ethics, and religion, were parts of the Universal Being. They were at once the objectification of his inner purposes and the necessary contributing complement of those purposes.

The idealist found his need for perfection and completeness satisfied not in positing a pure, abstract form lying beneath appearances, but in endowing the phenomenal world with a soul and making these phenomena the objectification and expression of the inner spirit. While the modes of thinking which were dependent upon Greek rationalism conceived of God as a perfect being outside the world of nature and mankind, the modern idealism imbued nature with a living soul, making it not so much an artifact of God as the objectification of God himself. Instead of being a lawmaker for mankind, God was realized in the moral actions of mankind and only therein. He was as much dependent upon the human individual for the expression of His own inner strivings and purposes as man, on the other hand, was dependent upon God for the impulse to moral activity. The individual man thus became a partner of God, rather than a very inferior subject dependent upon divine light and guidance. By this transposition man's ethical life became, in effect, a coöperation with God.

In estimating the quality of absolute idealism as a mode of thinking about the whole of reality, it is easily seen that it makes use of a great many unproved assumptions. If the Aristotelian philosophy had employed a number of unverified ' as if's,' the idealists employed a great many more, but with some important differences. Aristotle assumed certain controlling factors which were in some sense above and removed from experience, while idealism took tremendous liberties in establishing patterns within experience, patterns which they saw to be there, which they said were there, but for which they had no warrant except their own imagination.

As one reads today the works of Fichte, Schelling, and Hegel one has difficulty in understanding how their own generation took them so seriously, for we can hardly think of any system of speculation which demands greater credulity than do theirs. The explanation of their popularity probably is to be found in the fact that idealism was congenial to the intellectual climate of their generation. It was a time when the intellectual class in Germany had for the most part accepted the Kantian criticism of the traditional rationalism. The intellectual world had also recovered its historical sense and had begun the Herculean labors which in the nineteenth and twentieth centuries were to make available so informing an account of the history of the earth and of mankind. Man had caught the idea of evolution — evolution of the universe in terms of the nebular hypothesis of La Place, evolution of organic species in terms of the theories of Erasmus Darwin and Lamarck, evolution of the institutional and moral life of mankind in terms of the concept of progress and the indefinite perfectibility of mankind. Moreover, with the sweeping advances being made in natural science, their minds were oriented toward the variety, richness, and intricacy of the world of experience. It was a sophisticated age, and idealism reproduced that sophistication. If its assumptions were unjustified they were at least in the grand manner and in accord with the ruling intellectual interests of the time. It played up to the reigning interest in the world as it was described by science; it utilized the growing knowledge of history; it accepted the conception of gradual evolution of nature and human institutions; it took unto itself the notion of human progress and the upward march of humanity to undreamed of heights of welfare and happiness. With so much in its favor, it is easy to understand why a few unproved assumptions — even a few cartloads of unsupported guesses — did not interfere with the popularity of idealism during the first third of the nineteenth century. After all, if a man's heart is in the right place, why not give him a little leeway with regard to his facts!

The vogue of idealism, however, was short-lived. The great metaphysical systems of German idealism had hardly been constructed before the intellectual temper of Europe became positivist. To men of 1800 it had seemed thoroughly respectable that philosophers should indulge in those dizzy flights of the metaphysical imagination which eventuated in the various systems of idealism. The intellectual of 1850 was interested only in the facts — the facts of science as demonstrated in the laboratory and the facts of history as arrived at through workmanlike research. To such an intellectual temper the easy play of metaphysical imagination seemed childish and unwarrantable.

V. Philosophies of the New Science

1. Modern Science Ushers in a New World-Frame

It has been held in this paper that many of the basic assumptions which Aristotle made about the universe persisted into the latter part of the eighteenth century. His cosmology, to be sure, had been superseded as a result of the scientific discoveries of the seventeenth century and much of his physics had gone into the discard at the same time. The eighteenth century had even become skeptical about the validity of his twin concepts of mind and matter. It was, however, only with an amazing expansion of man's knowledge of nature in the nineteenth century that any new and positive substitution could be made for certain of the Aristotelian hold-overs.

One of the most important differences between the nineteenth-century world-frame and that of the seventeenth and early eighteenth century was the tremendous expansion of the time-line. The nebular hypothesis of La Place (1799) had implied the very great age of the celestial world and this theory was substantiated, at least as far as the age of the earth was concerned, by geological discoveries which culminated in the publications of Sir Charles Lyell. The acceptance of the age of the earth as two billion years in itself requires no small reconstruction of one's thinking about reality, while the calculations of modern astronomy in putting some stars so far away from the earth that it takes millions of light years for light to come from them to the earth creates a mental setting worlds removed from even that of Isaac Newton.

It was against the concept of a world some thousands of millions of years old that Charles Darwin reduced to sober scientific hypothesis the early nineteenth-century ' hunches ' that the variety of living forms to be found on the earth had evolved from simple organisms. By the careful collection of data, Darwin showed the evolution of certain species and set forth his theory that all the species of living things upon the earth had come from some distant unicellular ancestor. Slight variations of individuals had proven advantageous for their survival, which meant that they would reproduce themselves according to their special character. In the course of long periods of time the variations thus produced and conserved could account for the multiplicity of living forms which inhabit the earth, the water, and the air. While much has been learned about heredity since Darwin's day, this theory, substantially as he proposed it, has been generally accepted, and enters into the experience of every educated modern person. It is unnecessary to say that with Darwin's theory, the Aristotelian concept of changeless genera, species, and forms which eternally set the limits for the reproduction of individual things was no longer tenable. The universe of changeless order had become a universe of endless change.

In no other particular does modern science differ more radically from that of Aristotle than in its description of matter. For Aristotle, matter was inert stuff, a pure principle of negation. For modern science, it is electric energy.

The process of scientific discovery whereby this profound discovery of the nature of matter was made is too long and technical to be treated here. Suffice it to say that it is the story of the advance in chemical and physical science. The late eighteenth century saw the beginning of the process of breaking down undifferentiated matter into its atomic constituents and the nineteenth century not only isolated some ninety-odd chemical elements and established the table of atomic weights, but also linked up the entire kingdom of living things with the quantitative description of chemical process and function. The lore of the atom was enormously extended through the investigations of the electrophysicist in the twentieth century when the inner structure of the atom was laid bare and the relationship between atomic structure and chemical quality was established. Incidentally, it had been proven by scientific process that the chemical constitution of the sun and the most distant stars was identical with that of the inorganic substances on the earth, thus eliminating another of Aristotle's theoretical positions.

Probably science has not as yet reached the limit of its knowledge about matter, but at least enough is now certain to discredit completely the conception that matter is inert stuff, mere filler, to be manipulated by some principle of activity and purpose. Not only is matter energy, activity, it is patterned with reference to action and reaction with other matter surrounding it. That same matter enters into the constitution of every living thing. It is the source of human activity, raw force which supports every good deed and noble aspiration of mankind — not to mention every naughtiness as well.

The interplay between the progress of modern science and the reconstruction of the concept of mind is likewise an extremely long and complicated story. Accordingly, only one phase of that interconnection can be suggested here, namely, the recognition of mind as a function of biological survival which is present in every animal organism from the simplest to the most complex. Even so humble an unicellular animal as amoeba has a multiform awareness of its environment and specialized responses to it. Without special organs, without differentiated nervous structure, amoeba knows and reacts. That adjustment to its environment is accomplished by what, for amoeba, is 'mind.' As we follow upward the hierarchy of animal form, there is seen to be increased differentiation of tissue for specialized and improved contact with the environment, more varied response of the organism, more complicated nervous structure, but the fundamental function of mind as an instrumentality of survival remains. The continuity of the animal phyla exhibits no break in the succession upward from amoeba to man. Man's mind, in common with that of all animals, is a biological phenomenon performing a biological function. It may be a better mind than that of any other animal, but it is not separated from the other units of the animal series by some generic, absolute difference which sets man apart in the animal kingdom.

The recognition of mind as the biological function of adjustment between the organism and his environment puts an end to a lot of troublesome problems which have endlessly baffled philosophers. For some centuries philosophers recognized a special branch of their craft which dealt with the problem of knowledge and was called epistemology. The primary puzzle in this field for centuries was how mind, which is unextended spiritual substance, could come into contact with extended material substance. Stated in such terms, there is no answer to the problem, as an examination of the history of philosophy will show. There is no answer because the basic assumptions of the problem are invalid and unreal. But when mind is seen as the means of contact of an organism with its environment, the problem is not so much solved as made nonexistent. For any living animal is *ipso facto* in touch with its environment. It is just made that way — made with the equipment of awareness and response, which from the beginning is in operation. Knowing is a natural phenomenon just as the opening of a door by means of a photoelectric mechanism is a natural phenomenon. In such a setting, the problems of epistemology become the subject of scientific description and cease to be metaphysical puzzles.

Within the naturalistic setting of an organism in its environment, the concept of truth is likewise thrown into a new orientation. Provided with the possibility of multiple response, the organism, when its action is impeded, tries first one movement and then another. In the higher stages of mind the stores of memory and powers of constructive imagination allow the organism to lift its 'trial and error' reactions to a more sophisticated level in which projected ideational patterns are operative in the meeting of difficulties and the solution of problems. The test of the worth of any such projected trial program of action or intellectual judgment lies in its value in resolving the difficulty and allowing full speed ahead. Truth is no longer a relationship which describes success in putting individual units of discourse into more comprehensive conceptual classifications, but one which describes success in eliminating stoppages encountered in an ongoing experience.

The orientation of the problems of ethics, likewise, is profoundly changed by the new description of mind. The concept of 'the good' is placed squarely within the area of experience. In its most limited aspect, 'good' represents an immediate favorable or accepting attitude on the part of the living organism of some presented object or action-pattern. With the inclusion of conscious social relationships in the pattern of choice, which for the most part is the area of 'human' as opposed to sub-human experience, ' good ' appears as the description of conduct which is socially approved. But, in all events, the meaning of good is derived from and inheres within a context of experience. It is in no sense a successful reproduction in human conduct of an ideal pattern of the good which exists in some way independent of and superior to the halting and imperfect efforts of human beings to follow a rewarding way of life. Ethical values are a function of experience — not a derivative from some transcendental concept of the ' good.'

2. Realism and Pragmatism, or Instrumentalism, as the Philosophic Counterparts of the New Science

At an earlier point in this chapter it was said that the philosophy and the science of Aristotle represented a consistent unity. His basic assumptions about the nature of reality and the knowing process were not only philosophy, as dealing with the ultimate problems, but also science — the best science which was available under the existing limitations of man's knowledge. Aristotle's barehanded, naked-vision interpretations were a work of intellectual genius. They seemed so right that they ruled men's thinking for many centuries. But with the development of artificial means of extending man's vision, with the advances in chemistry, physics and biology, with the vast additions that have been made to man's knowledge of the past of the earth and of human history, a new body of science has been created which departs radically from the science of Aristotle and which has necessitated the elaboration of new philosophical formulas. In the large, modern realism and pragmatism, or instrumentalism, represent the philosophy of the new science. They frankly accept the world described by scientists and experienced by living organisms as reality. They refrain from positing a reality beyond the world of experience to explain or justify experience. Likewise, they refuse to bind the world of experience into desired meanings with the aid of self-made and self-willed speculative patterns imposed upon the world which science reveals and describes.

The changes from the fundamental Aristotelian hypotheses, which were compelled by the new knowledge made available in the last few centuries, have already been discussed in earlier sections of this chapter. There remains to be made an attempt to distinguish between realism and pragmatism, or instrumentalism, mainly, this writer thinks, because the pattern adopted for this work has set them apart. Certainly they are much alike — alike in their common acceptance of the new understanding of reality which modern science has achieved. Both accept a world which exists independent of the individual knower — a world which existed long before there was any sentient organism to be aware of it and which will continue long after the conditions which created sentient beings will have disappeared. At the same time, both schools recognize the experience of sentient organisms — their knowing, the modifications which they make within the world, their manipulation of natural forces to their own ends, social institutions which they establish to further the ends of their living, the ethical standards which they set up and come to serve, all that they have created of beauty, and all their religious aspirations — all these are acknowledged by both the realist and the instrumentalist as significant and real parts of the world.

The chief difference between the two schools of thought lies in a difference of emphasis. The pragmatist has been indifferent to the problems of being, or metaphysics, and has confined his interests to the analysis and description of experience, particularly to the problems of knowing and conduct — to the conceptions of truth and goodness. And yet the pragmatist accepts the same world as that which the realist invests with the quality of ultimate reality. Would it not be fair to say that the pragmatist would be a realist if he took the trouble to deal consciously and directly with the problem of being?

Some distinction between the two schools lies further in their treatment of the meaning of truth. For the realist, truth lies in the faithfulness of the idea in the mind of the knower to the reality which is the object of knowledge. Truth, for the realist, lies more in a fact relationship, divorced from the pattern of utilization by an organism. To the realist it seems to be a piece of presumption that the whole texture of relationships within the world should be subordinated to man's attempts to understand or make use of them. On the other hand, the instrumentalist replies, while the world wags on quite independently of the knower, it is only when the awareness of an organism enters the scene that any such relationship as truth is created. The sun emits its energy in ways that are the ways of physical reality and which have no concern whatever with the process of knowing. Knowledge arises only when a sentient organism becomes aware of the sun, either as a gross phenomenon subject to description in terms of the mythological imagination or as the object of description in terms of the best scientific insights available. As between sun and earth, even as between sun and man as passively warmed and preserved by the sun, there is no question of truth. Truth, in this instance, is purely a conception which relates to man's success in understanding and describing the movements and the processes of the sun. In a more comprehensive sense, the instrumentalist insists that truth is a meaning which develops only in connection with the contact of a knower with the world of experience. Truth is the conventional designation for those awarenesses, those theoretical explanations, those practical trial judgments, which are sustained by the further events of experience.

With this effort to exhibit the interplay of the newer modes of philosophic thought with the new and currently authoritative science, the objectives which were announced for this chapter have been accomplished. It will not seem gratuitous, however, if one raises the question as to the effect of this new intellectual alignment upon the religious experience. In an earlier connection it was shown how the formulae of Aristotelian science and of Greek idealistic philosophy, in general, closely coincided with the world-views which had been independently arrived at in the historical Judeo-Christian tradition. In that happy situation religion enjoyed the support of the best intellectual authorities. With the development of the newer scientific outlook, that support has been removed from the traditional religious world-frame because the new science has provided different architectonic patterns for the world-frame and has withdrawn its support from some of the concepts upon which the religious tradition depended. Does this mean that religion is no longer possible?

In the writer's opinion, man's quest for values and his devotion to them will persist, and that, it seems to him, is the most important element in the religious consciousness. Necessarily, a new world-frame within which these values may exist and be fostered will have to be accepted by those who have entered fully into the new world which science has described. However, it is to be expected that a new religious orientation will be developed, as indeed it already has been developed in many individuals, which will be not only consistent with the newer and authoritative intellectual outlook, but immediately and eagerly responsive to the human values and ethical insights of each succeeding generation of mankind.

VI. WORLD-FRAMES AND PHILOSOPHIES OF EDUCATION

The main task which was assigned the writer has now been completed, that task being the placing on a time-line of the five philosophies which enter into this Yearbook. However, it seems desirable to discuss briefly the relation of these philosophies to education.

The presumption has been too easily accepted that there is a unitary correspondence between a metaphysical principle and a philosophy of education which might be thought of as logically derivable from it. It is the opinion of the writer that such unitary relationship cannot be substantiated, and that from a given metaphysical core a considerable variety of educational philosophies may be and actually has been developed.

To illustrate this position, it may be recalled that in many ways there was a close family relationship among the philosophies of Plato, of Aristotle, and of St. Thomas Aquinas. In one degree of explicitness or another, these philosophies accepted the contrast between the creative forms and passive matter. They also gave assent to the conception of some over-all, guiding, planning form which was at once the meaning and controlling principle of all reality. And yet, an examination of the ethical philosophies and the philosophies of education which are developed by Plato, Aristotle, and St. Thomas, respectively, discloses a wide divergence. Plato had never worked out satisfactorily in his own mind the relationship which exists between form and matter, and he assigned a role of perfection and separateness to the factor of form which placed a decidedly negative and low appraisal upon all of experience which was touched to its disadvantage by matter. The result in terms of knowledge was that Plato had little respect for any grade of knowing except what was to him the very highest, namely, the direct knowledge of ideas gained through a process of dialectical reasoning. His political thought, particularly as shown in the *Republic*, reflects the disillusionment of the dispossessed Athenian aristocrat. In the field of ethics, also, the influence of Plato's sharp division of ideas from everyday experience was indicated by his low estimation of the biological urges of the individual and of the practical everyday concerns of the economic life, resulting in a kind of bluestocking Puritanism in his ethical outlook which denied a great deal that lent color and satisfaction to normal human existence. Those limitations of his theory of knowledge, of politics, and of ethics were definitely involved in Plato's *Republic* and specifically in his discussion of education under the Republic.

Aristotle, in sharp contrast with Plato, had found a very satisfactory way of relating the creative form to passive matter in his conception of potentiality and in his emphasis upon the passage of unformed matter into the finished thing. For Aristotle the process of change and becoming was thus given status and the forms were involved in the actual process of phenomenal experience. In observing Aristotle's system of ethics we see that while he gave definite priority to reason as the highest exercise of human faculty, he nevertheless had a great deal of respect for the general texture of human feeling and desire within which the process of reason served as guide. As was said in an earlier connection, Aristotle was definitely experimentalist in his acceptance of the idea of the golden mean and in his description of the good way of life as resulting from the adequate management and superior utilization of the possibilities of life. As a result, Aristotle's ethics is not nearly so severe and privative as is that of Plato.

Aristotle's attitude toward knowledge was likewise much more sympathetic with the phases of knowledge and thinking intermediate between conceptual knowledge and opinion. Unlike Plato, Aristotle was much interested in the means of persuasion, and one of his most famous works, the *Rhetoric*, deals with this phase of human activity which Plato completely despised and of which he had no good whatever to say. We do not have a record of Aristotle's complete philosophy of education because the greater part of his treatise on education, which constitutes the concluding part of the *Politics*, has been lost, with the result that outside of his famous theory of catharsis and his strong emphasis upon habit as being the objective of education, rather than mere knowledge, we do not know Aristotle's ideas in that field. However, it may be presumed that they would exhibit somewhat the same experimentalist attitude as is found in his *Ethics* and in his *Politics*.

To go to the third of the great philosophers mentioned as accepting the same general metaphysical outlook, it may be said that St. Thomas Aquinas was influenced tremendously in his total philosophy by the historical tradition of Christianity. He accepted the Christian virtues in place of those which Aristotle believed in, and his world-frame had in it profoundly important elements which were derived from the Bible and the historical tradition of the early Christian centuries. It is unnecessary to belabor the point that Christian theism involves a great deal more than a metaphysical core and, even though the metaphysical core accepted by St. Thomas was that which had been elaborated centuries before his time by Aristotle, it would be a grave error to identify the ethical values and the educational counterpart of those values as accepted by St. Thomas with the same as set forth by Aristotle.

Resulting from this discrepancy between the total world-frame of any philosopher and the metaphysical core at its center, it becomes clear that philosophies of education are related to the total world-frame of any philosopher rather than exclusively and unitarily to a metaphysical principle. In other words, one cannot draw a philosophy of education out of an abstract metaphysical system because a philosopher, as human being, elaborates upon the metaphysical principle in creating his total world-frame, and he does so in terms of his own time and place and personal preferences.

In further development of this point, it might be shown that within the world-frame of Christian theism alone there has been a very great variety of educational patterns. St. Jerome, in the fourth Christian century, presented a distinctive conception of education decidedly different from the educational system which was in actual operation during the middle ages. The system of instruction developed by the Jesuits had its own quality as influenced by the needs and circumstances of the post-Reformation period. Christian education under middle-class Puritan auspices in England and in the New England colonies in turn reflected a new emphasis which was definitely related to the maturing capitalistic system of economics. In the seventeenth century John Amos Comenius, operating strictly within the theistic tradition, described a system of education which exhibited many of the enlightened aspirations of eighteenth- and nineteenth-century democracy. And it might be added further that in the twentieth century there are educators who are able, within the world-frame of Christian theism, to accept and to embody in educational thought and practice the greater part of that which goes by the name of progressive education in our day.

The thesis which is here being maintained is that one would have difficulty in establishing a unitary relationship between any given metaphysical position and the educational consequences which are ostensibly drawn out of that metaphysical position. The position is taken that the detail which implements any given metaphysical formula is affected in particular by the personal attitudes and preferences of the individual making that application and in general by historical elements of experience which are quite independent of any metaphysical position whatsoever. This thesis has been illustrated with a number of examples out of the various philosophies which have had at their core the form-matter concept which dominated philosophy from Plato's time down at least to the end of the eighteenth century. It might equally well be shown that out of the general metaphysical position of absolute idealism, which had its day from the latter part of the eighteenth century to almost the middle of the nineteenth, the same contrariety of outcome is exhibited.

Fichte, for example, the first in the classical succession of absolute idealists in Germany, adopted a set of social values and attitudes which causes him to be recognized as one of the founders of modern socialism. He was extremely liberal in his social philosophy, and in his educational thought he established a system of democratic values. It is undoubtedly true that in opposition to this socialistic and democratic quality of his ethical and educational thought, Fichte, as one of the great theoretical nationalists of the early nineteenth century, introduced factors which were in conflict with democracy. However, whether democratic or nationalistic, the filler of Fichte's world-frame was contemporary and, perhaps it might be added, personal with him. The metaphysical vehicle of his thought was empty until it was filled in with matter of experience. His choice of patterning and his adherence to certain social values took place in processes of knowledge, thought, and feeling which lay in the realm of actual experience rather than in the realm of a metaphysical absolute.

A second great idealistic educator, Friedrich Froebel, operated within the species of absolute idealism sponsored by Schelling. It is true that there were considerable differences in detail between the metaphysical systems of Fichte and Schelling, but the family resemblance of their thought is clear and, for purposes of this discussion, they may be taken together. The great educator representative of Schelling's idealism, namely, Froebel, was among the most liberal democratic thinkers of his generation. The kindergarten, of which he was the founder, became suspect during the fourth and fifth decades of the nineteenth century in Prussia, as being a subversive influence inimical to the established conservative and monarchical order. Transplanted to the United States, Froebel's educational thought and practice were so consistent with the free political ideology of this country that they were acceptable with little or no modification as part of progressive educational thought following the Civil War.

The third exhibit which might be introduced to show the variety of social, ethical and educational positions which apparently grew out of and certainly were sponsored under the auspices of the philosophy of absolute idealism, is the social system championed by the greatest of all the German idealists, Hegel. Hegel was definitely on the conservative side, in sharp contrast with Froebel. It is sufficient for our purpose to indicate that conservatism by recalling that, for Hegel, the culmination of the vast architectonic evolution of the absolute in political terms was the reactionary Prussian state of 1830. This conclusion of Hegel's, that the world process of social evolution had culminated in the illiberal social philosophy and the restrictive institutions of the early nineteenth-century Prussian state, is about as good an example as could be found of the way in which personal predilections or environmental influences actually determine choices in the field of ethics. The metaphysician, playing with his grandiose system, tends to betray himself as the *deus ex machina* whose personal judgment of values creeps into the pattern which ostensibly is absolute and independent of human intervention, but which actually represents his personal preferences.

It might finally be added that the twentieth-century Italian fascist, Gentile, under the sanctions of a revived and modernized absolute idealism, described and defended a system of education which admirably serves the purposes of a most illiberal and reactionary social philosophy.

If these illustrations are accepted, it will seem evident that out of one basic metaphysical formula many varieties may be born. In the case of absolute idealism this will be easily recognized as inevitable, because, as was pointed out in an earlier section of this chapter, the absolute idealist accepted experience as the concrete expression of the absolute and patterned that experience according to the current intellectual and ethical environment and further modified it in terms of his own personal predilections and loyalties.

Turning to experimentalism as a philosophy, one would expect a variety of ethical and educational positions developed under such auspices, for experimentalism is the philosophy of experience, and no one would expect anything else than that the opinions of any individual would be related to the times in which he lives and to his personal background and preferences. The experimentalistic philosophy has had only a very brief history and during that time has been dominated by men who have, in general, been liberal in their social philosophies and in their systems of personal values. For that reason it might appear that there is a unitary relationship between experimentalism and the kind of education which up to now has developed under its auspices. However, it is quite possible that different social circumstances and different environments might profoundly modify the choices made under the aegis of experimentalist philosophy.

Within the paragraphs immediately preceding, an effort has been made to introduce a note of decided caution against attributing any given educational position to any given metaphysical formula. Metaphysical formulas are abstract and are therefore empty until they are filled in with a content which is and must be drawn out of experience. For that reason, the interpretations or applications of any metaphysical formula change with the passage of time and the alteration of human circumstance. It is true that there is a very close relationship between an educational system and an elaborated, filled-in, philosophy or world-frame, yet that elaboration and that content are scarcely matters of metaphysics at all, but matters of time, circumstance, and personal choice of values. For this reason the claim that a system of education is unitarily dependent upon a system of metaphysics is without support.

To some it may seem an admission of defeat to assert that it is impossible to draw our theories and practices of education out of some system of absolute truth. On the other hand, to the writer, it seems to be a matter of good omen that the essentials which enter into systems of ethical values and of education are a derivative of experience. It seems a matter of congratulation that metaphysical systems are shown in the progress of history to have been responsive to new content as prompted by the changing circumstances of human existence and by the new insights of sensitive human beings. It is highly improbable that all of us will be satisfied with the same intellectual formulas, but there is more reason to believe that men of goodwill may lay hold in our changing social order upon the same system of human values. If such be the case, the prospect of uniting the forces of good conscience and goodwill in support of a system of education which will lead to better social arrangements and to more secure and richer personal living is good indeed.

CHAPTER II

PHILOSOPHY OF EDUCATION FROM THE EXPERI-
MENTALIST OUTLOOK

WILLIAM H. KILPATRICK
Professor Emeritus of Education
Teachers College, Columbia University
New York City, New York

The philosophy of education as seen by the present writer stands on a foundation of general philosophy and exists to help conscious education manage itself better than otherwise it would. The philosophy of education especially undertakes to render this help (1) by criticizing the assumptions used by educators, (2) by helping to clarify educational aims, and (3) by evaluating critically the various educational methods as these bear on the selected aims.

Education as herein conceived involves two interrelated aspects, the psychological and the institutional. The psychological turns on the central fact of learning. How past or prior learnings are essential to effective living is everywhere seen and accepted. That present or current learning is equally essential to present effective living is but little understood or accepted. How these things are so and how the child accordingly learns what he lives, will form a considerable part of the present discussion.

The institutional side or aspect of education means, in general, the conscious effort of older and more experienced persons to influence for good the learning of the less experienced ones under their charge. Since, however, as was intimated above and will later appear more fully, the child will learn what he lives as he accepts it, the effort of the older ones to influence the child's learning has to be directed to his living. But here the influence, if it is to be good, has to be indirect; for the quality of living, like that of mercy, is not strained. It must come as the child's own inner (and outer) response to the situation as he sees and feels it. What these things mean for the proper management of the school will come later.

Education as consciously directed assumes, among other things, the actual world of experience in which older and younger live together. If

39

the older are to lead the younger wisely, they must have a defensible conception of the good life as well as an understanding of the necessary conditions for living such a life. These will involve an understanding of the group culture which supplies the structure of group living, as this in turn constitutes the means through which the infant builds his self-hood and the youth grows to maturity.

Any adequate educational program will thus be concerned to help each individual child grow up from his state of initial dependence into full participation in the richest available group life, including in a democratic country a full share in the active management of group affairs. Such an adequate program will go on further to an active effort to improve the group culture, for, as matters now stand with us, only thus can the good life be brought effectively to the underprivileged members of our group and in best degree to all. The foregoing general statement will perhaps suggest the main heads of the discussion which is to follow.

I. The World of Experience

In times past many efforts have been made to discuss such things as the essential being of the universe. The effort here to be made will be less ambitious, limiting itself instead to such matters as seem necessary for the management and improvement of the educational process, but this broadly conceived.

1. The Nature of Knowledge

Any human knowing, of whatever degree or kind, must go on within human experience. Whoever asks any question about knowing asks it out of his own experience as this has gone forward within the social setting of his group. The noun *experience* as here used is to be taken as the inner object of the verb *to live* (as a human). In the sentence, "They fought a battle," the noun *battle* does no more than state more explicitly what was already given in the content of the verb *fought*. So, here, the noun *experience* simply states, possibly more explicitly, the content of the process of human *living*.

Many seem to think of experience as merely a private affair, such that no one can really know of another's experience or share in it or learn anything materially useful from it. A different view is here taken. Each person able to share in such a philosophic discussion as this has come to be what he is, as will be brought out more explicitly in a moment, through growing up within a social group possessed of a very considerable body of more or less common culture. The language one uses, the distinctions one makes, the questions one discusses and the more spiritual or human values felt to be at stake, are both possible and desirable precisely because of one's participation in the group culture as this manifests itself in shared experience with others. Each one is, in any defensible sense of what *is* means, largely a social product. One's experience comes to him in and through the contributions of the common culture. He not only shares this culture with others, but it is this sharing which allows him to have such experience at all. Moreover, the typical human purpose is inherently social in character and must go forward in a social setting, for no one liveth to himself and we, the members of any group, are, in fact, all members one of another.

The process of experiencing, since it is a process of living, implies organism and environment — often better stated for us here as person and situation. Life everywhere is a continual interactive process between organism and environment. Man alone has experience in the full sense, for man alone is in any full sense self-conscious. A person faces situations made in part by the way he sees the environment. The formation of selfhood goes forward only by increasingly shared communicative living within a social group in which the older members have already achieved a more adequate selfhood.[1] The resulting characteristic of selfhood is a being able to think of itself in terms of what it knows of others and to think of others in terms of what it knows of itself. Only such a self-other compounded being can think of itself as persisting through its successive experiences, or as an effecting agent, or as accountable for what it does, or as responsible for the consequences of its behavior. All such considerations we include here under the term *self-conscious behavior*.

The normal adult human is such a self-conscious being. He thus not only recognizes signs of impending events (dogs do this much), but he has also learned how to consider the meanings of such signs apart from specific instances of their use (as a dog cannot). He invents names (words) for these meanings, and then discusses them with others. From these and other analogous abilities flowing from his self-other constitution, man has been able to invent and use tools and, especially significant for our present purposes, to note uniformities amid the changes and shifts of life's affairs. Through describing in words these observed uniformities in such terms as *fire burns, stones fall, winters*

---

[1] See the author's *Selfhood and Civilization: A Study of the Self-Other Process.* New York: Macmillan Co., 1941.

come and go, man has during the long years been accumulating much practical knowledge. However, before the time of the Greeks such knowledge was not very critically held.

With the Greeks, there came for the first time in any full or critical sense what may be called cultural self-consciousness. Each tribe had previously known its own customs, to follow them and to insist that all tribal members obey them. And many tribes, or other more advanced groups, had known that other tribes or groups had somewhat opposed customs. But it was the Greeks who first became critically conscious of such, and proceeded to ask which of such opposed customs were right, and whether any could claim to be right, or whether the term *right* has any distinctive or valid meaning, whether in fact all such were not simply matters of accident of custom. Thus arose among the Greeks consciously critical philosophy — so great a contribution that western Europe and the modern world in general have counted this critical inquiry to be perhaps our surest sign of intellectual civilization. It was in this way that the Greeks asked about knowledge and recognized explicitly and critically what man had long uncritically known, that some opinions are better founded than others. But there was more to come.

Beginning now some five hundred years ago, man began to build further on this Greek foundation. Galileo and others embarked on the plan, in our phrase, of putting questions to nature. The wise men before that day had thought, partly from tradition, partly by untested deduction, that a five-pound ball of iron, for example, being five times as heavy as a one-pound ball of iron, would fall five times as fast. Galileo, from his actual observations, had come to conclude otherwise and so taught. Conflict thus arose. Upon Galileo's insistence, so the story goes, they tried it out. Galileo was proved right; the tradition was proved wrong. But more than the specific question of falling bodies, there was therein developed a method of study destined to shake the world.

It was thus that modern experimental science began. Discoveries followed, slowly at first, but in time faster and more sure. At length in the realm of physical nature, man began to feel that not only was there no other basis available for finding out what to think and expect, but that his knowledge in this realm was surer than any other knowledge available to man. This attitude received further impetus from the certain discovery that Euclid's geometry is not the only logically possible one, but, *mirabile dictu,* that there are three parallel but divergent geometries such that no mathematician is able to prove that Euclid's is logically any truer than the other two. This remarkable discovery greatly spread a growing skepticism as to the existence of self-evident truths and consequently as to the validity of a priori reasoning.

This experimental approach to knowledge, when further studied, allows us to side-step many old puzzles, which, it seems, are unnecessary in any practical use of knowledge. If there is any other kind of knowledge or any other access to knowledge, some traces of such should appear in experience. Any such traces would call for study by this experimental method. If the results of this study should seem to contradict either the experimental method itself or the results otherwise reached by experimental methods, then the experimentalist would be called upon either to explain such results by his method or to revise his method — or to admit his failure thus far to deal with them. Einstein's relativity presented such a case. It was in direct opposition to much hitherto taught on the basis of experimental science; but the revision of the Newtonian outlook into the Einstein outlook, while raising problems not yet fully solved, is still counted a victory for science, and not a defeat. It was accomplished by the use of scientific methods.

This scientific type of knowledge is thus never final, but always open to possible revision. The demand for such revision may come on the basis of a closer discrimination of results than any hitherto made or it may come from new data not hitherto taken into consideration. In either way, the older explanations no longer suffice; in either way, an advance in scientific knowledge may be effected. From these and other like considerations, we can say that knowledge in the realm of the physical and allied sciences is now more extensive, more accurate, and more usable than had ever before been thought possible.

Epistemology, the study of how knowledge is possible, is a term often used in connections like this. For the experimentalist, the practical question of epistemology is *solvitur ambulando*. So far as concerns finding experimentally-determined knowledge, it is a fact. This method does it; it does furnish usable knowledge. The experimental method furnishes an ever increasing amount of ever more usable knowledge. No alternative plan or proposal is, in comparison, worthy of consideration. If anything attempted by man has established itself, this has.

2. Knowledge and Value: Experimentalism as a Philosophy

There will be those to say that whatever validity attaches to the discussion just finished depends on the distinction between science and philosophy, that the two realms are fundamentally different, that the methods of the former can have little or no bearing on the latter — no more, that is, than to set certain problems which the latter must consider. The aim of the discussion at this point is to see whether the method developed in science may not, by extension, prove useful also for philosophizing.

In the last quarter of the nineteenth century certain men in America, building, of course, on the efforts of preceding thinkers, began to explore the possibilities of extending a kind of generalized scientific method to all human inquiry, including specifically the ethical and the philosophical. Peirce led off, James and Dewey followed.

Science itself in its own thinking had for quite a while been moving in the direction of process as opposed to entities. Tyndall's *Heat as a Mode of Motion* (1863), for example, was one sign of the trend. Clerk Maxwell's epoch-making work on *Electricity and Magnetism* (1875) greatly pushed forward the stress on process.

In line with this trend Peirce proposed, in effect, that any term shall mean its consequences in experience. If two terms lead to the same results in experience, they mean the same thing. If a term leads to no specific experience consequences, it means nothing. Such a conception not only gives an operational definition to terms, it also limits inquiry and knowledge to experience, to actual on-going experience. The philosophic proposal, then, is to study experience and to find therefrom what man can find as to what to think and to value. On this basis, terms attain validity according as they indicate observable distinctions within experience, distinctions on which other phases of experience seem to turn, such distinctions, of course, as different competent observers can verify and accept in the same sense. Relations thus are relations observed within experience. Propositions are propositions asserting relationships observable within experience.

Three conceptions seem to belong together here to make up the experimentalist outlook: (1) the conception discussed just above, that ideas mean only their consequences in experience; (2) the conception that experience, at least of the kind we are interested in, is essentially social in origin and predominantly social in purpose; and (3) the conception that we find out what to expect in life by studying experimentally the uniformities within experience. If we put these three conceptions together we have a point of view at least promising for the study of any and all human experience. If such a method of attack should, as an hypothesis, not only explain the already generally accepted positions in social-moral outlook, but also go on further to help us make advances in the study of philosophy and ethics and do these things better than do alternate proposals, then we can claim to have found a promising method of philosophizing. It is this outlook and method which is herein called *experimentalism*.

Our concern here is to see how the experimentalist outlook, as thus defined, furnishes the philosophic guidance needed by the educator for conducting his work. The problem of morals or ethics affords perhaps as crucial a test as any; and the answer, if it is to be satisfactory, should give not only specific guidance in actual teaching, but should furnish, in addition, adequate background on which to build a satisfactory unified life and character.

3. The Problem of Morals

Three basic questions will perhaps sufficiently open up the main problem: (1) How shall we determine what is to be accepted as morally right? (2) On what foundation stands the moral obligation to do this right? (3) What, psychologically, can effect the discharge of this duty? The third question is, to be sure, only partially philosophical, but even so it seems to belong in the picture at this point. The discussion of these questions may seem a bit involved, but we shall expect to consider them all before we finish.

Since we are, in this whole discussion, primarily concerned with education, it may be well to begin there. The writer recently visited a kindergarten. He asked about teaching the children to ' take turns ' in the swing or on the slide. The answer given was that it is usually necessary to take positive steps to teach this, especially with children who live in homes as the only child. For such, to wish to swing usually meant a move to take the swing even though another child was at the time swinging. Conflict naturally ensued. ' Taking turns ' was then explained and enforced, with short ' turns ' at first so that the plan might seem a real ' taking of turns ' and not a mere indefinite postponement. Under adult guidance the children came, in time, to see this plan of taking turns as both fair and effective. Most of them would then insist upon all following the plan and would themselves help to teach it to the newcomers.

Here we have in essence the answer to the problem of morals. Certain children could, at first, see no other way than to go and take whatever they might wish at that moment. These children were persons, however, not mere animals. They had, as suggested above, previously built themselves as persons on a self-other basis such that within their range of experience they understood others in terms of what they had first seen in themselves and understood themselves in terms of what they had previously seen in others. Possessed thus of such self-other compounded personalities they could (1) understand at least measurably how the others also felt about the wish to swing and could in like measure see the necessity, therefore, of finding some plan to accommodate all; and (2) they could see with a clearness, increasing with practice, how taking turns furnished a fair plan — a plan that, in effect, treated all alike. Successful use of the plan would tend to strengthen both insight and acceptance. The chance, too, to teach the newcomers would give varied satisfactions and so further help the children to fix the acceptance of the plan in themselves as individuals and, at the same time, in the group as a continuing body.

In what has just been said there are implicit the beginnings in these children of a goodly number of ethical conceptions. It will be useful to name and comment upon some of these. That the instance deals with children makes it easy to stress the fact of beginnings, with the implication of further growth in the conceptions themselves both as regards boundary or content and also as regards internal complexity and interrelationships. For any conception is a general idea which should take due account of all the experienced particulars included within it. From this consideration every conception should, theoretically, always be growing, though in practice many cease to show significant growth after a while.

Regard for others and fair play (or justice as an ethical equality of treatment) are perhaps the most significant moral conceptions to be found in this instance of taking turns. The only-child had dealt but seldom with others of his own level. His life had failed to present many varied instances for taking his equals into account. He had, therefore, not learned to consider other children as proper recipients of regard as to their happiness. The swinging conflict brought more clearly to his consciousness than before (1) how he feels in connection with this one of his own wishes and (2) that others feel much the same way when they have the same wish. He further felt (3) actual conflict between equals and (4) at least a beginning need for a real solution to the problem. With the ' taking-turns ' solution presented to him, he began (5) to see it as a solution based on (6) a beginning notion of fairness or justice or ethical equality of treatment. The ' acceptance of this solution to act on ' would grow with practice, as might also, under proper guidance, the attitude of regard for the rights and feelings of others and the acceptance of fair play (or ethical equality of treatment) as a proper characteristic of group life.

A third moral conception, less obviously present in the instance given, is regard for the common good, the attitude of accepting responsibility to support what makes for the common good of the group. As the older children in the group, themselves having accepted 'taking turns' as the approved way of interactive behavior, supported this plan for the group as a whole, they were in a beginning sense learning to accept responsibility for the common good. This would grow yet stronger as they sought to teach this way to the newcomers, for people learn (as we shall later discuss) whatever they accept to act on. It is for this reason that wise teachers try to have their pupils understand *what* they do, as well as its *why*, because the pupils will learn both to do and why so to act as they hold these in mind when they act. In this way, they include these things consciously within what they accept to act on. If these older children could be led to accept not only taking turns as the approved way of behaving in this group but also to think of this as really the best for all concerned, then they would more surely be building acceptance of the common good in their own characters. Of course, here as always, teachers have to be on their guard against children doing certain things merely to please the teacher. If this happens, it is probably immoral attitudes, rather than moral, that are being built. Cant is easily learned, and many teachers are highly successful in teaching it. But at least a beginning toward conscious acceptance of the common good is possible even in the kindergarten.

Certain moral implications for the teacher of these children may be pointed out in this connection. It must be clear to discerning teachers that all they do, or fail to do, with the children has some sort of educative effect. Since education affects life for good or ill, the teachers then are under moral obligation to see that all they do is the best possible for the lives of these children and for the future lives of all others whom these children will probably influence. These considerations call for a word or two on the conception of the good life and its interrelation with morals.

4. Morals and the Good Life

The 'good life,' as here used, is the 'life good to live,' as good music is music good to hear or a good apple is an apple good to eat. What do we mean by *good* in the phrase *music good to hear?* How do we find

out what music is good to hear? More generally, how did man get to
where he now is in music? What is the final test of music? Possibly,
if we answer these questions for good music, we shall get a start on
answering them also for the good life.

As for music, we may believe that, historically, men began by noting
that some sounds, as such, are pleasanter to hear than others. In time
man hit by chance upon what we call musical sounds, continuing notes
from the same source, made first perhaps by the human voice or perhaps by blowing over a reed. Practice would make some man expert
in producing such pleasing sounds. Varying ways of making this early
music would be accumulated and handed down. Geniuses would from
time to time appear. New musical instruments were thus contrived and
new musical forms invented. But always the test was and is in the
hearing. Good music is music good to hear. Tastes may differ, but
music to be counted good must have backing from hearers, backing from
respectable numbers, but more especially the backing of respectable
opinion. The best music is that which best stands the test of being
heard and approved, widely approved by those most competent to
judge.

And it is much the same, *mutatis mutandis*, with the good life. Men
early rated some kinds of experience as better than others, better in
and for living purposes. It is uncomfortable to be too hot, and uncomfortable to be too cold. Hunger annoys; so does thirst, and illness, and
danger. Quarrelsomeness is bad; peace is better! To say it generally,
men have wants, the satisfaction of which gives the first approximation to the good life.

But the mere satisfaction of original wants supplies only the raw
material of the good life. Wants get in one another's way. Adjustments become necessary. A want gratified in a certain degree or under
one set of circumstances brings lasting satisfaction; satisfied in other
degrees or under other conditions, it may bring regret. To satisfy certain wants in certain ways interferes with other people's happiness and
so causes resentment and possible retaliation. All these things mean the
necessity of working out ways of behavior that bring the greatest net
good life to all concerned. It is an abiding problem in history. Conditions may change, so that new solutions become necessary. Old solutions may also go out of date because different and better solutions are
contrived. The history of ethics, as that of music, shows its geniuses,
men of superior sensitivity to the moral problem along with superior
insight and creativeness in finding moral solutions.

The moral problem, then, is the problem of what to do in the face of conflict among the actual values of life. It may be a conflict of values conceived of as lying primarily within the life of any one person; more usually it is a conflict between the values of different people. To say the same thing in other terms, the moral problem is the problem of finding within the situation that holds the conflict a course of action which promises the greatest net of the resulting good life to all concerned. If, as suggested above, the conflict lies primarily within the life of one person, then it is a problem of making his life the best possible, usually a problem of adjusting present wishes and future needs. But if, as is more usual, the conflict lies between the aims and values of different persons, then the problem is to find a course of action which promises the greatest net good life to all concerned.

What constitutes moral obligation was perhaps sufficiently implied in what has just been said. Once the solution to a moral problem has become apparent, the moral obligation follows at once: to accept that solution for action, both inwardly and outwardly, and put it accordingly into operation. What has just been said will seem to some too brief a statement of so important a problem. They will wish to know more explicitly about this moral obligation and perhaps fear to leave it no better safeguarded than seems here indicated.

How moral obligation arises from the appropriate social setting can be studied from history and anthropology, and currently in the psychological development of our own children as was illustrated with the above discussion on ' taking turns.' A study of data from these varied sources seems to lead to the conclusion that a ' sense of obligation ' does in fact arise naturally out of normal human relationships. As has already been suggested, some ways of behavior manifestly make for satisfactory living better than do others. Boas says that, within any given group, murder, theft, lying, and rape are taken as wrong and universally forbidden.[1] Men thus set up customs and, often, explicit laws to control admittedly hurtful conduct.

In the degree that a custom or law has been well established, children, under the teaching and demands of their elders, will build a ' sense of ought ' in connection therewith. The steps for this seem as follows: (1) the child builds a sense of ' agency ' as he learns to effect movements at will; (2) he next develops a ' sense of accountability ' as parents and other elders hold him consistently to account for doing or

[1] Franz Boas, *Mind of Primitive Man*, pp. 205 f. New York: Macmillan Co., 1938 (revised).

not doing certain things; (3) following upon ' agency ' and ' account-ability,' as the child grows older he will accept ' responsibility ' not only for following the pattern to which he has been held to account, but also for helping others, especially those younger than himself, to obey the same pattern; (4) this ' sense of responsibility ' carries with it — perhaps consists essentially of — the ' inside ' or subjective feeling of ' ought.' So much for the way in which the ' sense of ought,' conscience, arises. It is the normal psychological response to feasible social demands when these are held and insisted upon with high consistency by the surrounding group.

The ethical validity of such demands, for us who live in a critical culture, is, of course, an entirely different matter. Improvement upon what we may have at any time is for us a constant aim; and this extends to most, if not all, aspects of life, including proper ways of behaving. Ethical validity comes under such circumstances not from consistency of existing social approval but from the social validity of the specific ethical demand. Does the demand follow the best available social solution to the specific problem? Does the proposed conduct, so far as we can tell, make best for the good life for all concerned? In the degree that the answer to these questions is ' yes,' in like degree does the proposed conduct carry moral obligation for us.

Three conceptions are here involved in successive logical sequence: (1) the highest conception we have, at the time, of the good life; (2) the highest adequacy of the proposed conduct (as against alternative proposals) to bring this highest good life to all on the highest conceivable basis of justice; (3) the moral obligation to accept this most adequate available conduct as binding and so to put it into operation.

The state of the culture of any given group will affect the moral conduct of the group. Plato was so shocked by the conduct traditionally attributed to the gods that he proposed to forbid the use of these stories in his schools. We, in turn, are so shocked by some practices current among the men of Plato's day that we do not ordinarily mention them in our school textbooks. Any history of morals will, over a sufficient length of time, show growth and development in respect to the conception of the good life, though not a uniform advance in all respects; hindering conditions may arise as we see in the world today.

The term *justice* used in the second of the three conceptions given above is especially illustrative of the changing ideas due to different cultural conditions. In aristocratic societies justice generally allows certain greater privileges to the upper classes than to the commonalty. Breasted holds it to the especial credit of the Egyptians that they first, about 3500 B.C., were able to put all men, ethically, on the same basis.[1] The early Hebrew code was tribally centered; " Thou shalt love thy neighbor as thyself " meant then " neighbor " and not stranger or foreigner. Jesus gave it a broader interpretation. " An eye for an eye and a tooth for a tooth " was again an earlier conception. In fact, we may say that justice and proper ethical treatment are two conceptions that advance together, as they are practically two ways of saying the same thing.

An analysis of the act of moral deliberation will throw further light on the general problem of morals and the relation thereto of the good life.

Suppose a situation such that I am in doubt as to what I ' ought ' to do. The following steps will indicate a feasible procedure for answering as best I can: (1) I examine the situation to see what ' live option ' alternatives are available; (2) I develop as best I can the future consequences to be expected if the respective alternatives were acted upon; (3) holding my decision in suspense as best I can, I expose myself as impartially as I can to the respective pulls of these contrasting sets of probable consequences; (4) one set will (in general) win out over the others; that path becomes therein my choice. A word or two may help to clarify the analysis.

(1) I must take pains to find in fact all reasonable alternatives to consider. Otherwise I may unwisely overlook the really best path. To be surer I may talk the matter over with others, or sleep over it, or read up on the subject.

(2) In developing the possible consequences I call on my own past experience and any available help I may find. Depending on how much seems at stake, I must give serious thought to the matter.

(3) This step, culminating as it does in the fourth step, will test my character to the depth. If I am a careless sort of person, I will rush hastily to a choice, led by whatever emotion happens to be uppermost. To have formed the settled habit of acting thoughtfully is the mark of the higher character. As I attend in succession to each elaborated content of values involved, I weigh each such against my organized set of life's values — my ' philosophy of life,' that is, if I hold my values critically. However well or ill-made one's system may be, each one does have his own system of values and they do choose for him (if his habit of control over his emotions permits) what course he will pursue.

(4) When under the fourth step one path of developed values proves

---

[1] James H. Breasted, *The Dawn of Conscience.* New York: Charles Scribner's Sons, 1933.

strongest and I move along that path, say along alternative *C*, then I am by definition said to *choose C* in preference to *A* or *B* or *D*. But the verb *to choose* is merely descriptive of what has happened: under the conditions as seen and felt by me, I, being the kind of person I then was (seeing and feeling as I did), felt most the pull of *C* and so followed path *C* in preference to paths *A* or *B* or *D*.

An older day used the word *will* here as if somehow ' my will ' of its own accord took charge of me and carried me along path *C*. Moderns avoid the term *will* as misleading. At best or at most, it means that the whole organism is thought of as moving in one direction rather than along any alternative direction, and as doing this perhaps in spite of persisting internal tendencies in opposition. We may thus speak of a ' strong will,' meaning that the person does in fact ' make up his mind ' definitely and, having so done, moves insistently in that direction in spite of difficulties and oppositions, whether internal or external.

It may be added as an anticipation of later discussions, that, while men do not as a rule fully live up to their own best insights, still their choices do tend to improve with their insights. So that, historically considered, the long-run ethical view is encouraging rather than the contrary. The chief difficulty seems to be that discoveries and inventions change conditions so that new moral situations arise and the solutions to these naturally take time to develop.

5. Origin and Nature of Value

It becomes necessary to show how value is explained on the threefold basis proposed earlier as constituting the experimentalist outlook. Life for any organism consists precisely of the continual interaction between organism and environment. In any particular instance, something has happened within or without the organism — or perhaps better between organism and environment — to stir the organism to action. Looked at from ' within,' this stirring appears as want, wish, inclination. Looked at from ' without,' it appears as movements. These movements are not haphazard, but on the whole tend to change things in the direction of meeting the want. The hungry animal makes movements that tend to find food. In the case of man such movement may not only tend to find food, but may be intended to do so. All organisms are goal seeking; man can set up his goals consciously and seek them deliberately.

In such a situation of seeking in answer to felt wants, we say that anything which satisfies a want is by definition a *good*, a psychological good. But wants or goods may conflict: I want to buy this motor car but I also am saving to buy a house. Which shall I do with what I now have on hand? But still more, I help my mother meet her expenses and now the doctor is advising for her a costly operation. Three wants thus confront and stir me; each, if only it did not conflict with the other two, would, if satisfied, be a good, a clear, definite good. But as I am situated, there is clear conflict; I must choose which I shall do. The process of choosing we saw above. It is essentially a process of weighing these alternatives against each other; relative values which they are to hold, under the circumstances, must be assigned.

So weighed, the three previously separate *goods* now become for me, under these circumstances, comparative values. I have weighed each against the other on the scales of my philosophy of life — on the basis of the man and character I propose by this act to be and become. For I am making my philosophy of life as I am building my own character by the successive choices I make. What I accept to act on, *that* I build at once into character, *that* — if I think straight — I must tell myself and the world, is the kind of man that I propose to be. Thus do human values come out of human choices, choices that build character at the same time that they assign values. Thus do choices and values cut, both of them alike, as deep as morality itself can go.

6. Certain Philosophic Principles Stated

A peculiar difficulty about the stating of social or philosophic principles is pertinent here. Ordinary science is perhaps relatively free from this difficulty, but anyone who tries to state a general social or ethical principle finds difficulty in both stating it in terse and clear language and at the same time allowing for the exceptions that logically must be understood in connection. The sixth commandment, for example, says, " Thou shalt not kill." This is terse enough, but is it clear? " Kill what? " it might be asked. In India, one would most likely get the answer, " Not to kill any living creature, not even a fly." In this country most people would say, " Not to kill men." But are men never to be killed? Is the command an absolute? Most people say not; most would except capital punishment and also the extreme of personal self-defense and even a war of national defense. Not a few will say impatiently of such questions that all this is quibbling, that everybody knows what the commandment means. Certainly it is true that the central nucleus of this sixth commandment is as clear as it is important in human affairs, even though certain exceptions can be pointed out on the fringe. But it is equally clear that for most people the commandment as stated is no absolute; it does admit exceptions.

In the sense just discussed the effort will here be made to state certain philosophic principles relating especially to ethics. They are stated as explicitly as the writer can, with the warning that they hold without exception only in the central region of application. On the outside edge, many will find questions and exceptions. In fact, it seems that only in this sense can one state any general principles in human relationships. Conceptions are, in fact, thus made and principles are so applied in action. The following principles are thus stated here.

(1) Each person is to be treated always as *end* and never merely as *means*. In this ethical respect all men are to stand equal.

(2) Conversely, each person is under moral obligation so to act as, negatively, not to hurt the good life of others and, positively, to foster the good life for all.

(3) The more honestly and carefully study is carried on by different individuals and groups, the more likely will they reach like results.

What is *good* study is itself to be determined by other study. We begin where we are and examine the results of our study so as to improve our methods of study.

(4) The free play of intelligence stands as our final resource to tell us what to do — intelligence playing freely upon experience in any and all of its content, including the use of intelligence itself.

(5) We know no absolute principles; that is, none which now stand properly above criticism or which may not conceivably be modified, perhaps in intent, perhaps in application, as new conditions arise.

(6) From all the foregoing, democracy follows as the effort to run society on the combined basis of the good life and ethics, as these are managed coöperatively by the members themselves.

Some words of comment and explanation regarding these principles may prove helpful. Perhaps the chief way of treating a person as an *end* is to allow and help him to set up ends and purposes, to make choices and decisions, for himself. We contrariwise treat him as means when we refuse to let him decide for himself and instead use him merely or primarily as instrumental to our ends and purposes.

Principles (1) and (2) set clear limits to purposes and choices. Each person has liberty only in so far as it is consistent with the like liberty in others. We must all live together as persons, mutually respecting each other as *ends*. Some have proclaimed it as a great and novel finding that equality limits liberty. Of course it does; but more than limiting liberty, equality defines liberty. The great problem of morals in our complex interdependent society is how to find and establish such social arrangements as give the maximum feasible of freedom, but a freedom that simultaneously respects the rights and feelings of others and all on a basis of ethical equality.

It is a proper question as to how the principles stated above were arrived at and what validity they possess. As here stated they represent the writer's choice and wording of the criticized experience of mankind. According to J. H. Breasted, as we saw earlier, the first principle was originally conceived by the Egyptians some 3500 years B.C. The wording here given is, of course, largely that of Immanuel Kant. Principles (3), (4), and (5) are philosophic principles that have come to the world chiefly as a result of modern scientific thought. It is, of course, true that as here stated they go far beyond what is ordinarily called science.

The phrase ' criticized experience of mankind ' as used above will of course cover a wide range, from an extreme at one end of results universally accepted alike by common sense and science to the extreme at the other end of faiths over which men today fight, and not always in words only. On this scale the six principles here under consideration belong *toward* the latter extreme, some would say that certain of them belong at this extreme. Does this mean that with regard to them the argument is a toss-up? That the considerations pro and con are so nicely balanced that one is free to accept or reject simply ' at will '? That the controlling factor as to whether one does in fact accept or reject is simply the way one happens to feel at the time? Or simply the way one's personality has by chance been conditioned by his natural glandular secretions or by the accident of the group in which he is born and the consequent chance indoctrination he has thus got?

To all these questions, except the concluding one on indoctrination, the writer himself would return an emphatic ' no.' In his opinion all six of the stated principles are the survival of the fittest of a long, long period of critical consideration with a clearer and clearer emergence of competent thought favoring all the principles substantially as stated. In this respect, however, it is true that the six break up, historically and otherwise, into three groups.

The first two — relating, respectively, to the proper treatment and conduct of persons, are essentially ethical in character. It is hardly too much to claim that for three thousand years they have increasingly received the highest moral and religious approval. The present denial of them by the existing despotic and totalitarian powers may be astonishing but, so far as this writer can see, such denial has, on its side, nothing but brute force to offer in opposition.

The third, fourth, and fifth principles — relating, respectively, to like results from study, to the free play of intelligence, and to the denial of absolutes — stand, both as to content and as to history, on a different footing. They are rather intellectual and philosophic than ethical in character; and they are too new in history to have won as yet the same degree of support as the first two. The writer himself believes that they are more easily proved, that is, they are less matters of faith, than are the first two; but they conflict basically with so much that has so long been accepted that the matter of indoctrination referred to above becomes one important factor in opposition to their acceptance.

Another important weight in opposition is that these three principles demand a greater faith in man and his intelligence than many seem able to give in a world so greatly troubled as now. For such people the phrase ' retreat from reason ' seems apt and fitting. Amid a sea of troubles these faint-hearted ones seek security in many varied forms of external authority. Hitlerism offers one such authoritative escape and many have accepted it; a priori metaphysics offers another such escape, and authoritative theology still another. Such escapes, however, seem but eddies on the stream of time, remnants only of what men once widely accepted.

The sixth principle, the statement in behalf of democracy, has its roots mainly in the first two and, accordingly, in a long past, but as a system of government, democracy is mainly modern, so modern in fact that most of the world has never yet given it a serious trial. Of all six, democracy (considered as an ethical outlook) stands, for the writer, as perhaps the surest instance of a faith, though a faith that even so has good history to back it. This history, supported by the ethical basis of the first two principles, establishes democracy — for the writer and, he believes, for many other millions in the world today — as a faith worthy of all acceptance, worth dying for if need be, that through it those who are to come after us may live more surely as persons can and should.

A word about principle (4), the free play of intelligence, may clear up certain misconceptions. First of all, intelligence is not simply innate as certain psychologists have seemed to hold. In any ordinary instance of effective intelligence there are two components at work, one innate, the other derived from the culture. The innate component differs, as all may see, from person to person; but so far as we know and believe, it has not changed appreciably in the race within a good many thousand years.

The other component of intelligence, the cultural, calls for a further word. That this has along certain lines increased appreciably within known history seems certain. It appears from our best authorities [1] that European man, after he became *homo sapiens*, went for some 25,000 years without improving upon his chipped stone implements. Then he learned better and for 10,000 years ground and polished his stone implements, meanwhile learning how to use fire. By the end of this time he learned from the use of fire how to smelt copper and tin and so made bronze instruments. These he continued to use for 1000 years, when he learned how to smelt iron. This improvement in invention rate while impressive is still not to be compared with our current rapid rate of discovery and invention. The question then becomes insistent as to how this rate of discovery has been so greatly increased, seeing that man is born now not appreciably more intelligent than during those early 25,000 years. The answer seems clear: Men have accumulated during the succeeding ages not only knowledge of processes but methods of inquiry. The result illustrates the definition sometimes given to the culture as communicable intelligence. We have in fact within a few hundred years built and spread scientific intelligence. We have learned far better than previously how to question and how to discover and invent. Possibly, let us hope, we may soon begin to effect a like advance in social intelligence.

Along another line, some have been troubled lest naming the free play of intelligence as our final resort for thought and act means either an effort or a willingness to reduce life solely to the intellectual. Nothing of the sort is meant. Thinking, or the effective use of intelligence, must deal with any and all content of life. Some of this experienced content may relate to things as material as stone or steel; other content may be as spiritual as a hope, or a fancy, or a sense of duty. Thinking must deal with all. Some hopes, for example, are feasible to pursue, others not. Which are feasible and which not, that is not for the hope as such to say. Thinking based on pertinent data must decide. It is

---

[1] For example, Henry Fairfield Osborn, *Men of the Old Stone Age*, pp. 18, 261, 501. New York: Charles Scribner's Sons, 1916 (second edition).

the same also with fancies. And the same with impulses to duty. Some impulses felt as duties may be mistaken and should not be obeyed; others are justly felt and should be obeyed. It is again for thinking to decide, not the impulses as such. But the thinking, in order to be able to decide, must be a thinking familiar in the area and sensitive in social and ethical matters.

Along still another line, others have asked whether the individual is to be his own judge in the thinking that he does. The answer is that no one is to be free to think just what he may wish. In the degree that thinking merely follows wish, in like degree does it cease to be thinking. Thinking must follow the meanings honestly sought and got from the situation itself, seen of course in the light of previous pertinent studies. But even so, one's mere individual judgment does not suffice. As the late Justice Holmes well said, " Truth is something I cannot help believing." One is morally bound not to be satisfied with results that he does not honestly believe would be independently upheld by further impartial study, as good as or better than his. Truth is no private matter, nor indeed is it merely man-made. It is man-contrived, but contrived from what is found. Properly speaking, man is free to think only what the facts carefully studied will admit or demand.

The third stated principle — that adequate study by whomsoever done will produce like results — is another instance of belief inductively supported even though the word *proof* as used by scientists is too strong to assert. The statement itself is, of course, little more than a variant form of the fourth principle on the free play of intelligence. Both are abundantly illustrated and verified in particular instances, so much so that we seem justified in accepting the principle to live by at all times unless and until sufficient contrary evidence should accumulate to call the principle in question.

Statement (5), denying absolute principles, will meet with opposition from various sources. But the opposition seems to spring rather from the wish to believe than from independent inquiry to find out what to think. The more common instances offered of absolute principles are either definitions or truisms, not principles in the full sense. " Thou shalt do no murder," for example, is little more than a definition. *Murder* is by definition *unlawful killing*. To say, " Thou shalt do no unlawful killing," is to express a truism; for if it is unlawful, it shouldn't be done. Some will ask — perhaps facetiously — whether statement (5) is not itself an absolute and so self-contradictory. This inquiry would seem to go along with the assertion one sometimes hears: There are exceptions to all rules, including this one. But even so, the statement as it appears seems sufficiently guarded to stand unchanged.

The final principle, that relating to democracy, is perhaps better conceived as a definition of democracy than as a principle regarding it. It is, however, still true that what we understand by democracy does come to have an admittedly strong hold upon us as soon as we admit the preceding principles.

Finally, lest some misunderstand, let it be stated explicitly that in none of the foregoing is there any claim that mistakes may not attend the effort to run life on the bases of democracy, ethics, and intelligence. The contrary is probable. The claim, however, is made that, so far as we now know, men can do no better than to work along the general principles here laid down. No alternative known to man promises better results. That these precise formulations are permanent as given is not claimed. That even the best formulation now possible will last forever unchanged seems improbable. But it does seem possible — probable, this writer believes — that future development in this area will grow out of such principles as these rather than deny them precisely.

7. A Novelly Developing Universe

Before leaving the World of Experience, a word about change seems called for.

In the Platonic-Aristotelian outlook, as commonly held in the past, change had small place in important matters. Specifically, on that point of view, fundamental principles never change. With such a point of view conservatives, whether of wealth or of social position or of doctrine, have usually found themselves in general accord. For all such, change is, on the whole, a bad word indicating something like degeneration. As the popular hymn had it, change and decay went together: " Change and decay in all around I see."

This general attitude to disparage change was common until recently. In fact, until very recent times as history goes, even the idea of progress seemed beyond the ken of man. Not until the eighteenth century could man clearly conceive it. Marcus Aurelius, for example, said in the second century A.D., " Our children will see nothing fresh [or novel], just as our fathers never saw anything more than we " (*Meditations*, xi, 1). Backwards or forwards, the content of history was the same to him. Of course, the conception of general or all-inclusive net progress has its difficulties, but progress along specific lines is clearly established. Our means of communication, for example, have progressively improved for now a century. Our surgery is increasingly better. Transportation has improved wonderfully.

But a more fundamental aspect of change than any of the foregoing concerns us here. In times past many have seemed to hold that the whole future was already fixed in advance. As Omar Khayyam put it,

> Yea, the first Morning of Creation wrote
> What the Last Dawn of Reckoning shall read.

Some called it fate, others predestination, still others scientific determinism; but the resulting state of affairs was the same for all and thus, as Pope had it,

> Heaven from all creatures hides the book of Fate,
> All but the page prescrib'd, their present state.
> — *Essay on Man*, Ep. I, line 77.

William James, it seems, was the first to conceive clearly a view of the universe in opposition to this universal predeterminism. As he saw things, such a determinism nullifies the very notion of purpose and effort. On the common-sense view, herein accepted, any instance of conscious effort or action is an attempt to shape the course of events. If one could really believe that each event is already determined in advance, the whole point of thought and effort would fail: Why try when the event is already fixed? So, following James, men have increasingly accepted the idea of a ' universe with the lid off,' that the stream of affairs develops novelly, a mingling of new with the old and familiar. And the actual event is precarious — we never know just how our efforts will turn out. It is on this basis that John Dewey has said, " All action is an invasion of the future; of the unknown. Conflict and uncertainty are ultimate traits." [1]

From this point of view man's creative part becomes a highly significant fact in history. In our own day the ever-increasing round of discovery and invention has so forced the fact of change on man that he is at long last compelled to take it into account. Change, rather than stability, has become the chief characteristic of social life. The social sciences, including education, must, as we shall later see, give great prominence to the ever-changing character of life.

---

[1] *Human Nature and Conduct*, p. 12. New York: Henry Holt & Co., 1922.

II. The Group Culture

Our second great topic as suggested at the outset relates to the culture. By the group culture we mean all those transmitted results of prior human experience and contrivance through which the group now carries on its life. This includes, especially, language, customs, tools, institutions, knowledge, distinctions, ideals, and standards. Any distinct cultural aggregate, we cannot doubt, has come only gradually into existence, requiring all told the hundreds of thousands of years during which man has lived as man on earth.

How completely we are dependent on our culture for the lives we now live becomes obvious as soon as we begin to think about it. But little would be left to life as we now know it if there were taken away all that comes to us through the use of our transmitted tools, institutions, and knowledge — not to mention language and our socially transmitted distinctions, ideals, and standards. Little would remain to us beyond the primordial impulses of animal nature. Hunger, for example, we should still feel, and soon very acutely; but what to eat, how to find it or prepare it — not to speak of serving it — these would all go. And if they went suddenly, probably almost all of us outside the tropics would starve to death before we could procure enough to eat.

The more distinctively human aspects of life are, if possible, even more completely dependent on the culture. Literature, for example, could not be conceived until long after language had become a sure human possession. Morals, similarly, could become a matter of concern only as customs were at work; and the study of ethics could come in any full sense, we feel fairly sure, only after more critical thinking had begun to arise. Breasted is of the opinion that man had been making tools of warfare possibly a million years before conscience had reached the point of considering each human as a person entitled to moral consideration irrespective of social status.[1]

How international law and order are still lacking from our culture in any effective sense is only too sadly evident as we look at the world today. Equally true is the need for such law and order if men are to live decently with one another. In any specific instance, as we now see, the absence of order brings most forcibly to mind the part that order can and must play if life is to be good. For many centuries we have been developing domestic law and order, that is, law and order within our several countries — and the gains have in historic time been great.

---

[1] *Loc. cit.*, pp. ix, 406.

Now the next step to be taken seems surely some effective form of world order. Without it our effective culture is awry.

How the culture molds the individual to its general model is easy to see. Each babe — innocent of the culture, so far as it knows — is born into an already existent group possessed of its specific culture. Through increasing participation in the living thus going on about him, the child builds his selfhood. As we saw earlier, he thus learns the language of his parents, their customs, and (at least at the first) their ways of thinking and judging, including both their ideals and their prejudices. It is through this process that the baby in Japan becomes Japanese and the baby in France becomes French. It is the culture that does it, and not any peculiar racial heredity.

1. Learning the Group Culture

It is the bearing of the culture on education that here concerns us. Children must learn the essentials of the group culture or they cannot live the group life. The culture thus sets the first great task of education. But we must say in immediate connection that if the culture sets the aim of education, it is psychology that fixes the method. The two are, in fact, far more intimately related than most think, so much so that it seems dangerous to separate them at this point even for discussion. A brilliant Britisher gave us a half century ago a promising lead for keeping them together. Said W. K. Clifford, " It is the peculiarity of living things not merely that they change [that is, behave] under the influence of surrounding circumstances, but that any [such] change . . . is not lost, but retained and, as it were, built into the organism to serve as foundation for future action." [1]

From this we may see both how the child learns the culture and how to state the correlative aim of education. The child shares in the life of the family and neighborhood; he must do so, his existence depends upon it. This surrounding life goes on, as we saw, in terms of the culture. The child in living this life lives it as shaped and permeated by the cultural contribution. What is thus lived is not lost, as Clifford says, but retained, built at once into the child's organism, into the very structure of his being, to serve as the foundation for future action.

The task of education and the relation of method to this task becomes now clearer. The original and primary aim in education, so felt by responsible parents and teachers in every conscious age, has been

---

[1] W. K. Clifford, *Lectures and Essays,* p. 54. London: Macmillan Co., 1886 (second edition).

that the child shall increasingly learn to live the life of the group and to accept appropriate responsibility in connection therewith. Following Clifford, we see the method inherent in the process. The child learns what he lives, and what he learns he builds at once into character there "to serve as foundation for future action."

We may anticipate the subsequent discussion on learning and say that the conclusion just stated must be the capital rule for us who would guide the learning process. If the child is to learn anything, he has first of all to live that very thing; it has to enter actually into the content-stream of his life. If it is a feeling he is to learn, he has first to feel it in his life, feel it as his own appropriate response to something then happening in his life. If it is a thought, an idea, that is to be learned, this has to arise in the learner's mind as an appropriate response on his part to a situation calling it forth. If it is a moral decision that he is to learn, he has to live that moral decision in his own life; that is, he must in some actual life situation — probably in several successive situations, to ensure strength of learning — make this decision as his way of meeting each situation where the decision is pertinent. If the child is to learn the culture, he must live it in his own life as his way of living that life.

2. Learning the Culture in a Static Society

What has just been said would hold alike in both static and dynamic societies, but there are significant differences between the two which we should study, since we are now living in the transition from the static to the dynamic.

In those older days when our society was largely static — a state of affairs predominant until about a century ago — each generation so nearly repeated the preceding that parents could teach their children the ways of living which they had learned from their parents, and the children growing up could expect in turn to do the same with their children. Under such conditions most young people learned to live the life of the group in the apprenticeship of home and trade. The family of that day was a highly complex economic institution; and children grew up, in the relatively large families of those times, performing from even tender years whatever they could to help the family life and work.

If it were a farm family, as was true of most early American life, the girls helped the mothers especially inside the home and the boys worked largely with the father outside on the farm. Little effort, out-side of living itself, was needed to ensure that the children learned

through living. The actual demands of family life furnished both opportunity and incentive. Even when the boy was apprenticed to a trade
outside his own home, he probably lived in the home of his master and
learned his trade in personal contact with actual work. If he did a bad
job, his individual output showed it; and the result was there to be seen
and judged by those who worked with him.

As children thus grew up, they inherently lived what they were to
learn, and they learned it under the concrete life situations which both
called it out and tested it. It was a life they could easily see as one
working whole. Even the social problems of government and church
were discussed at home and in the immediate neighborhood. So that
for the most part life itself as necessarily lived in the static society
sufficed to teach the young people how to share effectively in the group
life.

3. Learning the Culture in a Dynamic Society

With the coming of modern industry, based as it is on science and
bringing in its train very rapid social changes, there have come great
changes in the educational problem. Family life is greatly altered.
Hardly at all is the typical modern family an economic institution.
Instead of raising and making what it consumes, it now buys nearly
everything it uses. Even the wheat farmer will sell his wheat and buy
his flour, and this, perhaps, already cooked as bread, and mayhap even
already sliced. Children now, instead of being economic assets, are in
general economic liabilities. Instead of home being a place where children live and work together with their parents most of the time for
twenty-four hours a day, children are now off at school and play most
of the waking hours; and father is likely to be away from home nearly
every day, and mother away much of the time. However much we may
deplore it, the home in general is not and cannot be the educative influence it once was, while surrounding social life has become both so complex and remote as to be hard to understand. Under these conditions
the school, as a kind of residuary social agency to take care of our
culture, has been compelled to take on, in a new sense and degree, the
increased difficult task of inducting youth into social life. The essential cultural contribution to life must be learned; the school inherits this
new duty in connection with these social changes.

Those, then, who object to the modern type school with its activities
and excursions and community study and socially useful projects are
simply refusing to look facts in the face. Many of these objectors demand that the ' race experience ' be taught, but they refuse to see that

their old-style school work cannot effectively teach the living culture. Likely enough, many parents could use the home more educatively, and surely enough many years of thoughtful effort will yet be necessary before administrators, teachers, children, parents, and citizens have come to an adequate understanding of an effectually best way in which to teach the essential culture. But it cannot be successfully denied, first, that the cultural contribution has to be lived if it is to be learned and, second, that the old-type school cannot supply the needed living of a changing civilization. The modern type education is but the conscious effort to meet and solve the problems so set. Civilization is impossible save on the basis of the culture. The young have to learn the common essentials of civilization, and they can learn these satisfactorily only on a basis of living them.

4. Education and a Changing Civilization

But a changing world makes greater demands on education than merely learning how to live now, greater even than how to live under the changing conditions as we now know them. The unknown future makes a different kind of demand. The world of affairs is clearly changing more rapidly in our day than ever before, and the stream of events always develops in novel fashion. The future becomes thus even more uncertain than hitherto. Some things we can, to be sure, in reason foretell: Seasons will recur; children will be born, grow up, live out their time, and die; people must eat; institutions of some kind will survive; people will continue to read and argue and act. But who can foretell what specific significant events will happen, what new problems will arise? Twenty years ago who foretold this war? Who can now foretell what Europe, or the world, will be like in another twenty years?

We have to prepare our youth to live amid conditions yet to come, amid conditions now unknown to us. We cannot teach them the answers to their problems — we do not even know what their problems will be, let alone the answers. We have then to get our young people ready to meet that unknown future.

As we think of this task of our schools, we can name certain things which with reasonable certainty they must work to get. (1) For one thing, we can work for the practical adaptedness of our children within the concrete world about them. This much goes without saying. School life must be concrete. (2) For another, we must care for each child's personality adjustment as we have never done in the past. In fact, many of the older type schools have so blindly sought their formal and artificial subject matter requirements as to damage greatly the personalities of many school children. Those of lesser gifts have especially suffered — a treatment that is simply inexcusable cruelty. Amid the greater stresses of modern social life, regard for personality adjustment becomes increasingly urgent. (3) There are certain social-moral attitudes and habits for which we must work in season and out. In addition to such older virtues as truth-telling and honesty, we must work for an effective regard for the rights and feelings of others on terms of justice and fair play; and for an ever broader and deeper acceptance of effective responsibility for the common good. Unless we can more effectively secure these two attitudes, the future looks dark; for any solution to the strategic problems of a better economic system and an enduring peace turns largely upon the active presence of these ethical attitudes. (4) A rapidly changing civilization brings ever new social problems. For some time now, it seems, such problems have been appearing faster than we could solve them. Each such unsolved problem represents that much social strain. We face the mounting danger of an increasing load of unsolved social problems. Under this stress various European countries broke, and dictators took over. So far the democracies have fared better but we dare not face the risk. We, too, can break. We must solve those problems.

As matters stand, it is not certain that we have available sufficient intelligence to solve our more difficult problems. It seems probable that many among us fall short both of sensing the problems and, even more, of understanding the solutions. Probably, too, even the best among us lack as yet ideas adequate for the solution of the most difficult of these problems. The answer to this situation is that we must build social intelligence. We have in the past century or two built and spread scientific intelligence. We must next build social intelligence and spread it effectively among our people.

III. The Learning Process and the Work of the School

Learning is herein seen as far more closely interrelated with the process of living than most among us have thought. Such a conception remakes the school at the same time that it puts character building into the heart of the educative process.

1. Living and Learning

By learning is meant the state of affairs when some part or aspect of experience stays with one to influence pertinently one's further experience. It appears undoubted that such learning is not only going on all the time that one is alert and active, but that its presence and work are necessary to give coherence to experience itself as well as to allow intelligence a chance to serve within experience. How these things are true, an illustration or two will perhaps make clear.

Let the first illustration be a conversation. *A* and *B* are talking, and earnestly enough for the conversation to clear up for both a situation which each had previously but partially understood. Let us see how learning attends the conversation and what it does there.

First *A* speaks. Now *B* must, as *A* speaks, learn what *A* says; otherwise, he (*B*) cannot reply pertinently to *A*. But *A*, when he speaks second in reply to *B*, must take into account what he (*A*) had himself first said at the opening of the conversation. So *A* as well as *B* learns what *A* first says and learns it as he is saying it.

Clearly the same things hold when *B* first replies to *A;* and so on, indeed, on both sides as *A* and *B* each further addresses the other. Learning is taking place continually as the conversation advances; and this learning is absolutely necessary or the conversation would break down. The conversation, as an experience, thus owes its coherence to the fact of learning and to the work the learning does to weave each new phase of the developing experience pertinently into the preceding experience so as to make a developing unity of the whole. In the same way, learning is necessary to give intelligence a chance to act pertinently during the conversation, for intelligence can find opportunity to deal pertinently in any developing situation only as the user of the intelligence himself holds in mind what has been happening so that the next step can be appropriately (intelligently) directed.

So far then as this conversation is concerned and so far further as we count the experience typical, that far are we ready to write *Q.E.D.* to the thesis set forth at the outset. The assertions there made as to the place and function of learning seem justified. Lest, however, some should think of learning as predominantly an ability to recall in memory and therefore count it a merely intellectual affair, we need to consider learning in connection with other kinds of experience. Let us then next consider the emotional.

Suppose the *A* and *B* of the conversation above reported had previously been long-time friends, but that on this occasion *A* had brought to the conversation some feeling of painful resentment at the way *B* had seemed on a previous occasion to disregard his (*A's*) rightful feelings on a certain matter. Suppose further that *B* was able during this particular conversation to clear up the misunderstanding to *A's* entire satisfaction, so much so that A's resentment was now quite gone and in its place had come even some doubt as to whether he had not himself been too hasty in imputing evil to B. Under such circumstances there would arise in A not only the now resumed friendly feelings for B but, besides, an added contentment that it was so. And these new feelings would abide with A to make him think and speak and act differently because of them. He would, for example, give B an unusually hearty handshake as they parted. He would, as he walked off, recount to himself how glad he was that the matter was now cleared. He would explain to their mutual friend C how the misunderstanding had occurred and how everything was now quite all right between them.

But these feelings arising in A are themselves instances of learning: They are parts or phases of experience which stayed with A after they had first been lived to affect pertinently his further experience. Therefore they constitute learnings as truly as did the remembered words and ideas of the conversation. We learn then our feelings as truly as we learn ideas.

It is further possible that both A and B, as they thought back upon the painful experience, should have decided each to be more careful of such matters in the future. If so, and if the decisions so made stayed with the men to influence pertinently what they further did, then these decisions would likewise fall under the definition of learning. And learning is seen to include in fact all the content that life can show; any part or phase can remain to influence pertinently further living. This is no treatise on psychology, so it will suffice to state briefly in the next few paragraphs what elsewhere should properly be shown in greater detail.

The content of life consists psychologically of what happens to us and what we do in response. But what happens to us is responded to by us as we take it to be, as we accept it to act on. Hence, for learning purposes, we can say that life for us consists of our responses, our responses to what happens about us; and that we learn these responses as we accept them to act on. It is clear regarding the new feelings which A learned, (1) that they were his responses to the new situation as explained by B and (2) that he (A) learned these feelings as he accepted them. This is also equally clear with regard to any decisions either A or B made in retrospect. Such decisions (1) were their respective responses to what had happened and (2) were learned as they were respectively accepted to act on.

We may then sum up the discussion on learning as follows: *Each*

*one learns his responses, only his responses; he learns all his responses
as he accepts them to act on, some to do, others to ignore; he learns his
responses in the degree that they are important to him and in the further degree that they are interrelated with what he already knows.*[1]

Since what is learned is one's reactions and since each one reacts to
situations as he understands them, it follows that each item learned is
learned in its relations as then experienced. If the item learned represents one's reactions to a broadly related, thoroughly understood situation, it is learned thus broadly related. Also, since what is learned
stays with one to affect pertinently his further living, each item learned
does thus in some degree permeate further living — it permeates it in
the degree that it was learned and in the degree that it proves pertinent
to the further living.

It thus appears that each item learned is by the act and fact of
living-learning-living related both to past learnings and to future (pertinent) learnings. That learnings thus stay with one to affect pertinently further living means then, finally, that *what we learn we therein
build at once into character.*

If we put together these two italicized statements on learning, we
see (1) that each child learns what he lives; (2) that he learns it as he
accepts it in his own heart to act on; (3) that he learns it in the degree
that it is important to him and in the degree that it has meaningful
connections with what he already knows; and, finally, (4) that what
he learns he builds at once into character.

If these things be true, and they are hard to deny, then the quality
of the child's living as he understands and accepts it becomes the most
important fact for conscious education, namely, that the child (and the
youth and the adult) shall live the quality of living fit to be built into
character.

Let it be noted carefully, as was discussed on page 63, that if the
child is to learn an idea, that idea must (before it can be learned) spring
up in the child's mind as his response, his thinking response, to a situation which he confronts. I, as teacher, may help that particular idea
to arise in his mind, but he learns it as an idea only as it constitutes
his response to the situation which calls it forth. I can help him, but I
cannot simply hand him an idea and tell him to learn it.

It is the same way with any particular moral attitude. If this

[1] For a fuller discussion of this conception of learning, see the author's *Group
Education for a Democracy*, pp. 4–12 (New York: Associated Press, 1940); and
his *Selfhood and Civilization*, pp. 140–58 (New York: Macmillan Co., 1941).

youth is to learn it, really learn it as his moral attitude, then it must (before he can learn it) arise for him as his response to a moral situation which he feels. I, as parent or teacher, cannot compel it. In fact, if I try to compel a moral attitude or other moral response which the child does not himself feel and accept as his own personal moral response to the confronting situation, I not only fail to teach that moral response, but I may instead be calling forth reactions of resentment against me, against morality and duty, against home or school. If I do call forth such resentments and this youth accepts them as his responses, then I am by so much to blame for the bad character this youth builds at that point.

There is no more serious thought to confront the parent or teacher than that the child, the pupil, the learner, learns only and exactly his responses and learns them as he accepts them in his own heart to act on. It is the quality then of the child's day-by-day living that counts. For that living he will learn and will build into character. It is the quality of that living for which we, his elders, must constantly work. That defines our task.

Some will immediately ask whether this doctrine of learning means that we, parents and teachers, have to abdicate. Because the child will learn only what he accepts, does that mean his elders have no part to play? Should we never refuse or command?

The answer to all these is " No." It means none of these things. I may have to refuse my child what he wishes. I may have to require these schoolboys to do what they do not wish to do. But it does mean that when I decide to refuse or to command, I must know what I am doing. I must know that my child or my pupil or my student will learn, not necessarily what I wish him to learn, but what he responds, as he accepts his response. In other words, refusing and ordering cannot constitute the steady diet of moral education. Rather do they represent emergency efforts on my part, the least evil of the many ways in which I might try to deal with this difficult situation.

In other words, since the child will learn his responses as he accepts them, I must work indirectly. I cannot directly control his responses or his acceptances. I must try other ways than compulsion. I hold my power of compulsion as a last resort, but not my main reliance. It is the living of the group at which I must work. In the degree that this is fine and good, in like degree may I hope it will call out fine responses from the members of the group. All of which is to say that many teachers and parents have misconceived the task of the school. We cannot follow their misconceptions if we plan to succeed.

2. Building Mind and Character

An older view took mind as a faculty that had two possibilities: (1) it could acquire knowledge which it then held as a man may hold silver dollars in his hand or in his pocket; (2) it could as a faculty be trained by having to work with difficult material so that it could thenceforth think better about anything that minds can deal with. The first of these possibilities has received some support from the over-emphasis on native ability by our mechanistic psychologies. The same mechanists deny the second possibility.

The position herein upheld is different from both traditionalists and mechanists and in both respects. As here conceived, the building of minds or character is conditioned by three observable attributes of learners: (1) each organism inherits the dispositions to be stirred to action and accordingly to pursue goals; (2) each inherits its own peculiar degree of innate intelligence (i.e., differing from person to person); and (3) in accordance with (1) and (2) some individuals are more resourceful than others in pursuing goals and some are natively more able than others at learning.

The first most important use of these endowments for action and learning is to build selfhood, which each normal child does on the self-other process previously discussed. The child is able to accomplish this in the present high degree because he grows up in a social group that has accumulated a high-grade group culture during the preceding centuries. He thus builds his selfhood on the group model. The process continues throughout active life, but is developed to a significant degree within a few years after birth.

The second most important use of these endowments by each person follows the achieving of effective selfhood, and consists in accumulating and organizing through learning the results of one's personal experiences. We have already discussed how learning saves and organizes one's experiences. Here we are concerned to point out that the organization of these saved-up and interrelated experiences constitutes a kind of unity for which we may use any one of several names. We call it *character* when we are thinking of *what kind* it is in comparison especially with the analogous organization in other people. We call it *mind* when, by abstraction from the whole, we are considering especially the meanings that enter into the whole, the

meanings and their organized interactions among themselves, with
only subsidiary and implied consideration of the connections of these
meanings with emotion, habits, nerve connections or other nonmean-
ing constituents of the whole. We call it soul (in a nontheological
sense) when by analogous abstraction we select out for emphasis the
organization of emotional responses and their relations with each
other, especially the finer-made and the more admirable of one's emotional responses.

In the sense thus discussed each one builds out of his experience
— which in turn makes essential use of the group culture — his selfhood, his mind, his effective intelligence, his soul, and his character.
It is the business of conscious education to supervise and aid in the
best possible building of these.

3. Mind, Meanings, ' Transfer '

It may be well to elaborate somewhat upon what was said above
about mind so as to take account of what is often called the problem
of 'transfer of training.' The wording of this phrase is unfortunate,
being question begging, since it assumes the theory of specific $S \rightarrow R$
bonds. If learnings were always specific trainings, as this theory
held, it would indeed be a problem to explain how any such training
could be 'transferred' to a new and different situation.

This problem of 'transfer' arose a generation ago in protest against
the then widely held Platonic-Aristotelian doctrine of formal discipline. This theory assumed entity faculties (Platonic forms as opposed to content) as reason, memory, neatness, and the like. It held
that the faculty could be trained (disciplined) to an improved state
of effectiveness and that the improvement being of the form (the
faculty) would apply then equally to any proper content of that
faculty. Both common sense and scientific observation deny such a
theory, but it still holds considerable sway especially in some liberal
arts colleges and secondary schools where subject-matter departments
are hard put to it to defend their vested interests.

What position to take on this so-called problem of transfer often
turns, interestingly enough, upon the accepted theory as to the nature
of mind. In the position here maintained only inductive studies can
settle the question of 'transfer'; and the theory of the mind must fit
the facts so disclosed. It thus appears that the basis of mind, or
thinking, is not the faculty; that is no more than a reification of observed processes made before scientific observation was well devel-

oped. Nor can a satisfactory basis be found either in the specific S → R bond or in the 'conditioned reflex.' These are more modern efforts to reduce thinking to some nonthinking basis. The more satisfactory basis seems to be meaning. This term admits two senses, one of which man shares in degree with the lower animals; the other is peculiar to man as a self-conscious being. In the first sense, a certain call will *mean* feeding to hogs or a cloud will *mean* rain to man. In this sense, the sign as a neuter noun is the subject of the verb *mean*. In the second and higher sense, the verb *mean* has a personal subject, as a speaker *means* (intends) what he says. That is, he (1) foresees the probable effect his words will have (as meanings in the first sense) and (2) intends (*means*) his words to have that effect. Because man can mean in this second and higher sense, he can study the meanings (first sense) of his terms and make them more exact and otherwise more usable. The term *mind*, as was brought out above, includes the organized aggregate of all one's meanings with all their interactive relations with one another, on the one hand, and all their connections with emotions, impulses, habits, etc., on the other hand. Such a mind is of course in process of continual building and rebuilding during the whole period of one's competency.

The key to the problem of 'transfer' seems to be found in the conception of generalization. Certain authors have discussed this as if it were made by finding and uniting into a single simple whole the common elements of the individual objects of a class. This may be a proper exercise in the older logic, but it is not the psychological process followed in life for use in transfer. My conception of a dog has not been so formed, but includes rather all my various experiences of dogs with some notion of their probability of reappearance; it even includes the negation of certain possibilities. Thus I may think of dogs as possibly black, white, brown, tan, spotted, but never purple or green. I may further think of dogs as varying in height from about four inches to about forty inches, but never four hundred inches. The concept organizes into one visible whole all my experienced and related particulars.

From another angle the conception begins as a generalization, and the user learns later what content to expect in connection with it. Thus a child having learned to recognize a cat, called a lion, " big kitty." The signs used by the child for the recognition of a cat did in fact carry so far as to include the lion. He started here with a generalization too wide for ordinary adult usage (whatever scientific opinion may say) and was probably told, " No, not a cat, a lion." In more general terms, any word (sign) means for its user whatever range of content it may have for him. For one who has lived in China, that name carries a greater content than for one who has never visited the country. Bagley's well-known instance of training in neatness illustrates this principle for the problem here under discussion.[1] Two groups worked alike on arithmetic papers and each sought neatness. One restricted its attention to the fact that they were dealing with arithmetic papers; the other thought, not arithmetic papers, but written papers (of any kind). Both gained in the neatness sought; but in the one case, the gain was restricted to arithmetic papers, while the other gain extended to all types of written work.

Still another type of effective generalization is found in Judd's instance of the boys learning to throw a dart at a target under water.[2] All the boys learned by trial and error practice how much allowance to make for refraction when the target was ten inches deep. Half of the boys were then taught the scientific formula for refraction and how to work it in general. When all the boys were again brought before the target, this time only six inches under water, those who had been taught the theory quickly made the necessary adjustment, while the others took about as long the second time as they had the first.

In one word, then, the problem of so-called transfer is the problem of thinking. Whatever helps one to broaden and extend the meanings one gets from experience is helping him to face new situations more effectively. The meanings acquired and used furnish the key with which to face the unknown future.

4. What Kind of School?

The character of the school will vary according to the educational theory that governs. For us here, since children and youth learn what they live, the school must be a place where living goes on, the best and finest type of living we can help our young people to create. They will live. It is our part to work on that living in any way older people can to make it as fine as possible. At this point some conventionally minded ones who have difficulty with new ideas will ask with mingled

---

[1] William C. Bagley. *The Educative Process,* pp. 265–83. New York: Macmillan Co., 1905.

[2] Charles H. Judd, " The Relation of Special Training to General Intelligence," *Educational Review,* XXXVI (June, 1908), 28–42.

doubt and imagined triumph, "Well, haven't children always lived in school? What do you mean 'they must live'?"

It is true that our children have stayed alive until school was out; the old-fashioned schools didn't kill their bodies. But for many it did nearly kill their minds and their spirits. Not for all, for there have perhaps always been some capable enough to live and flourish in spite of what was done to them. And always, too, there have been teachers better than their times. But for most, if not for all, the older type school did fail to develop the most educative kind of living. What we wish is a school where the highest quality of living possible to be attained is the dominant aim.

What kind of living is fine enough to be built into character? It must of course be good, rich, wholesome living, suited to the age of the young people, the kind in which they can feel purposes of their own and pursue such purposes, alone at times but more often in groups. The more eagerness they can feel, the better; though over-excitement is to be avoided. What they undertake must be difficult enough to challenge them, but not so difficult as to bring discouragement. In and through it all they must be building, under wise teacher guidance, ever higher standards with which to judge what they do. Possibly, the more desirable single quality to life is that it shall in and of itself sprout ever further and finer living. Morally, they must learn ever better to accept responsibility for their acts — to think ever better before acting and wish for others what they would wish for themselves.

As they thus live, tempting opportunities will arise at times to override the rights and feelings of others. Usually this will be thoughtless, but the teacher must be alert to what is impending and help all concerned to think it through. As a rule, such thinking will suffice to bring the finer responses to the fore and the danger is over for the time. Fortunately too, each victory of this kind makes other like victories easier.

But there are still other kinds of living, as for example the esthetic. Almost the same discussion will hold here. The children must be free to work at things that involve the esthetic. The resourceful teacher can suggest fruitful experiences. After the school is in good running order on a basis of purposeful living, there will be no lack of esthetic opportunities. And the observed results show here, as with the moral qualities, that the activity type of school will show more of creative drawing, painting, music, dancing, and writing, as it will show more of truth telling and better honesty. These things come because the children on the whole like them, but even so, they come successfully only as the teachers work for them.

Many who read of this type of school get troubled over the fate of the ' old line subjects,' spelling, reading, writing, arithmetic, and the like. For answer we may say that excellence and exactness therein is, so far as desirable, simply another phase of good quality living. We must work for these qualities too; and again the actual figures show the fears unnecessary. The activity schools show as good subject-matter knowledge and skills as do the old. For my own part, I think the new type school should do better at the defensible old line skills. So far, however, the available figures seem to show only as good. One set of figures, we are told, however, does support the better results of the new along subject-matter lines, and that is the report of the Aikin Committee.[1] If the thirty schools listed in this report be arranged in the order of ' progressiveness,' the lowest six are about average as compared with American secondary schools in general and their graduates in college show average results. But the six highest of the thirty on the ' progressive ' scale have their graduates showing up in college appreciably better than corresponding graduates of otherwise equal ability from otherwise equally good schools. The point is that the school must include intellectual and other ' old line ' excellencies within the desired quality of living for which they are to work. If they do so work, they can get it. But they work for it in different fashion.

5. Curriculum and Curriculum Making

How shall we understand the term curriculum? It is the whole living of the pupils or students so far as the school accepts responsibility for its quality. We are thus back again to living and its quality.

But many will not be satisfied with such an answer. To them it seems evasive. They wish to know how much of this or of that is to be taught to the pupils and in what order. Here let me speak for

---

[1] W. M. Aikin, " Some Implications of the Eight-Year Study of Secondary Education," *Bulletin of the National Association of Secondary-School Principals,* XXV (February, 1941), 29–36.

For further studies of the comparative results of activity schools, see J. Wayne Wrightstone, *Appraisal of Experimental High School Practices* (New York: Teachers College Bureau of Publications, 1936) and the same author's *Appraisal of Newer Elementary School Practices* (the same, 1938).

myself. Later I will notice that variant answers are returned by other experimentalists.

In the sense formerly understood by subject-matter requirements there is not much that I should care to name in advance that must in the end be learned and still less should I wish to state when it will be learned. I know that there is a considerable body of common knowledge and common skills that any decently educated group will show; but I don't believe that naming this body in advance is the helpful way to begin.

I would have the school start with its children wherever they are and help them, first, to get wholesome and vigorous living under way. Then, I should have the school work at all time, in season and out, (1) to raise as best it could the quality of living at each age level; (2) to make this actual living grow up into all-round living — including the growing up into the best phases of current social life — as all-round as the school can manage, not to interfere with the high quality of living otherwise; and (3) to develop the creative aspect of living as the finest single test of success, that these children may grow in the actual ability to think up good new things to do, in the wish so to do, and in the effective ability to do them wisely, all things considered. If we can get our schools to work honestly and zealously along these lines, I believe we shall get better results of every defensible kind than can be attained on any other basis. Such a program may be called the *emerging curriculum*.

There are good school people, experimentalists, I mean, who will perhaps agree substantially with everything given in this particular presentation except for this interpretation of the emerging curriculum. This they fear to risk because of the wish to prescribe in some manner or degree what shall be learned. I respect the honesty and the sincerity of these people and many of them I count very good school people, but for myself I still hold to my opinions as here expressed.

6. Classification of Pupils

For myself I would group children according to social age. The word *promotion* and what it stands for would drop out. I strongly oppose X, Y, Z grouping as unnecessary and as cruelly degrading to the Z group. I would have no separate subjects taught, as such, in the elementary school and, accordingly, no departmentalized work there. Such divisions in operation so cut across living at that level as to sadly deaden it.

In the secondary school I would continue for at least half the school day this nondepartmentalized, all-round, life-core living-learning under one teacher as in the elementary school. In preference, the seventh-grade teacher would have, say, three-fourths of the pupils' time with the other one-fourth given to such specialization as may be deemed wise. This three-fourths I would gradually diminish to one-half in the twelfth grade.

I would use no textbooks as such, but instead all sorts of reference books. Many of these would need to be prepared for varying age levels. I would give no marks in either elementary or secondary school, and send no regular report cards, especially of a kind intended to compare one pupil with another. I think all such seriously hinder the kind of living the school exists to foster.

7. Teaching Democracy

As was earlier brought out, democracy is very intimately interrelated with ethics. On the basis of the theory of learning set out above, our young people can learn democracy only as they live democracy. It cannot be taught by indoctrination for that is an essentially undemocratic process. Our schoolrooms must then become living democracies as far as is feasible with children and youth. It may further be added that the schoolrooms can hardly be living democracies unless the school systems are themselves living democracies.

IV. Education and the Improving of Life in Society

From one point of view everything thus far said finds its application under the head of improving life. From another point of view each thing here to be said could have been included at some point, possibly without undue strain, to round out the preceding discussion. It does, however, seem desirable to provide a separate heading under which to treat certain items in a way to bring the whole discussion to a rounded close. A philosophy of education must contemplate a philosophy of life.

1. The Relation of the Individual to Society

In all the preceding it has been at least implicit that no human individual can realize his personal life to the attainable fullness apart from others. His actual life is from beginning to end dependent to an essential degree on what others contribute. To begin with, his organic existence springs from his two parents. And once thus begun, he remains, during some years, quite dependent on these same parents, or their substitutes, for his continued existence; without the food and other care they supply he would surely die.

This much, it may be rejoined, the brute animals do for their young. But in a further way, quite beyond the brutes, the young of humans are dependent for their well-being on others. The culture, which is peculiar to man, conserves the accumulated prior human achievement and, through the medium of shared family and community living, gives it to each on-coming child as he partakes of and in this living. Utilizing this cultural contribution, he becomes, through the essentially social self-other process, the cultivated, self-conscious, intelligent, and moral personality which alone can live the truly human life.

And, as if these dependencies were not enough, the normal human being of today is in still other ways further dependent on others for his well-being. Division of labor seems essential to our well-being. No one of us actually provides for himself all the food, clothing, shelter, and other goods wherewith he lives; on the contrary, each one of us, for the most part, works mainly at just one line of service and with the income from it buys the most of what he uses. In these various ways each human individual is dependent on society for essential parts and aspects of the good life he may live. And the more fully he lives beyond the merely animal life, the more fully is he thus dependent.

The same dependence can be stated in another way, namely, in terms of the institutions furnished by the culture, including also in particular the safeguarding institutions of law and order. In order to live well together in the various ways implied above, we must as we pursue our varied purposes adjust our behavior appropriately to each other. We can define social institutions, broadly, as the mutually understood ways of correlative appropriate behavior by means of which the individuals of a social group effect their interactive living. Institutions thus defined constitute an essential part of group life. The fitness of such institutions to carry satisfactorily the burden of social intercourse becomes accordingly a matter of essential concern to all the members of the group. On the proper working of their institution depends their daily well-being.

It is possible, and desirable, to broaden what has just been said to include the whole of the culture. Any specific culture in order to be in good working order must have its various parts and aspects work so fittingly together as to form an harmonious working whole. History shows instances in the past where various specific cultures have approximated such a state of satisfactory working harmony. With us, however, this is not true at the present time. The Industrial Revolution has brought rapid change, but not even or uniform change. Different parts of our culture have grown at differing rates. Some parts have grown very rapidly; the industrial, for example, and all that goes with it — the making and using of goods. But other parts have changed more slowly, especially those features of the culture that uphold values already imbedded in the status quo. Specifically, as among the parts that resist change, can be named all those institutions which uphold existing privilege, whether of wealth or social position or of institutional arrangements, and the theories of right and wrong and other philosophic conceptions which facilitate the defense of the imbedded values.

If change in one part of the culture had but slight bearing elsewhere, men might contemplate change with little concern. But some changes are so far reaching in their consequences and so resistless in their inevitability that social stability is threatened unless and until corresponding and compensating or corrective changes are effected in the group culture. Our industrial changes are of this threatening character. One dare not ignore them. We must make further changes to bring the social structure in line with them, or most serious danger threatens. The philosophy sketched in the early pages of this chapter is one effort to bring the inclusive theory of life abreast of the fundamental social and intellectual changes already effected by science and industry. But further institutional changes are demanded. To understand better what further changes are now needed, we must look further into the character of the economic problem.

2. The Nature of the Economic Problem

As we study the world-wide effects of the Industrial Revolution we find the situation for this country has been different from what has obtained in the older settled parts of the world. Here the fact of abundant lands, easily available to settlers, made a capital difference to the poorer people. In the older countries the lands had, so to speak, already been all taken up, held largely in fee tail; the poorer people could never hope to become land owners or otherwise rise in the world. In both parts of the world the bulk of the common people lived from agriculture, with the village or neighborhood handicrafts enlisting the next most considerable number. In this country, however, the very poorest — if only they had physical health and the will to work — could hope in our early days to become independent land owners and their children could hope to rise to any height of wealth or position.

And the economic independence was as true as was the political or social. Production was, under those early conditions, predominantly for consumption, for home consumption, not for sale. Each farm family, using the neighborhood mill and blacksmith shop, raised and made at home nearly all that the family used. On the actual frontier, buying might be limited to gunpowder, salt, and iron goods; the rest was provided at home. With the passing of the frontier more would be bought; but even so, production for home use was still the dominant rule. In those early days each American family was in most respects literally independent; the prevailing economy made it possible.

Thus arose the American dream, as J. T. Adams calls it, the vision of a society of free men, democratically governed and possessed of real equality of opportunity where each could hope by the combined family efforts to start from nothing and still effect the good life for self and loved ones. And up to the coming of the great industry the dream was no mere dream, but in large measure an actuality — an actuality for those here on the grounds and a reasonable hope for other millions yet in Europe.

But the underlying conditions of the American dream as thus once held have passed away. For one thing, the free lands are now gone; the frontier ceased to exist in the 1890's. For another thing, America has ceased to be agricultural; 90 per cent of our population in 1790 lived on farms, now only 30 per cent. But most of all, production for consumption has now practically ceased even for the 30 per cent still on farms, and obviously so for the 70 per cent who work for wages and salaries. The farms are now no longer separately self-sufficient. Increasingly does the great industry sell to the farmers what formerly they themselves made — soap, lights, clothing, household implements, and even foodstuffs. As the farmers have thus increasingly bought, so must they increasingly sell. In this way do the farmers now in fact join ranks with all wage and salary earners who buy all they use.

But all who buy what they use must sell in order to buy — must sell goods and services to get wherewith to buy. And this makes all these people economically dependent: If they would sell, there must be a market for what they would sell. They thus become dependent on ' business conditions,' and these conditions vary, good at times, bad at other times; at the worst, as in 1932–33, very bad. When business conditions are thus bad, goods and services can hardly be sold — at best they may be sold for less, at worst perhaps not at all. Mills thus shut down, workers lose their jobs. We saw this in the late depression, and we all suffered together in it. Some suffered much worse than others, but all suffered. Our common dependence on the proper working of our economic system was thus proved, and to the hilt. It cannot be denied that we are now all tied together. The dependence of each on the society of which he is part has become a crucial fact, strategic to any satisfactory life.

This economic system upon which we have become thus dependent grinds out very unequal results — unequal as regards different periods of time, unequal as regards different persons affected. The unequal results as regards time we call ' the business cycle.' So far this proves a veritable juggernaut, unpredictable and uncontrollable. The unequal treatment of persons has become now intolerable. A system that can produce more than it can dispose of, and yet leaves millions stranded — such a system cannot be defended. And the effects of the mad pursuit of wealth on the spiritual life of all are, if anything, worse than the unjust treatment, bad as that is, of the underprivileged. Since institutions are man-made, the problem becomes one to be coped with by the conscious thought and effort of all concerned. Moral obligation demands it.

3. Common Dependence, Common Responsibility

Moral obligation, we saw earlier, applies in any situation where a number of people are so related that what one does affects the welfare of the rest. Men have, of course, known this for a very long time and have made moral codes accordingly; but eighteenth-nineteenth century individualism led many, under the *laissez-faire* doctrine, to restrict the doctrine of moral responsibility to merely negative applications: One should not damage others, but one was under no positive obligation to help others. Under *laissez-faire*, it was literally each man for himself and the devil take the hindmost; and the effect of this teaching is still lamentably widespread.

But moral theory could not rest content on so negative a basis. Each person must be held responsible for the consideration of all the possible consequences of his acts, constructive as well as destructive.

The extension to include constructive acts within the moral purview is as inevitable as the development of mathematical thought from arithmetic to algebra; the scale of moral obligation cannot be restricted to the negative side only, it must include also the positive. Each one, before he acts, must forecast the contrasted probable consequences from all the possible alternates and must choose that course of action which best promises to bring the good life to all concerned and this, as far as it is humanly possible to effect it, on a basis of ethical equality for all concerned. And, it may be added, this enlarged doctrine of moral responsibility is no modern innovation. It represents, on the contrary, the emergent outcome from the best thinking of the acknowledged moral and religious leaders of all ages.

It is in this way that we all become morally responsible for the working of our economic system. We cannot stand idly by and see distribution fail so badly while production can do so much. We must take our institutions of distribution in hand and remake them to the point where they can be ethically defended and where the highest conception of the good is really fostered. With production put to work as effectively as it now can be, we should be able not only to banish poverty but also to bring reasonable comfort to all. With wealth no longer the main aim, the good life can be really sought.

It is no proper part of this work to tell how to remake our economic system. Possibly no one now knows the proper steps; probably it will require decades of thoughtful experimentation to find out. But the obligation to work at it remains. And it is not simply our material welfare that is at stake. All other aspects of life are involved. One instance will perhaps suffice to show what is meant. When a man cannot find work, try as he may, his morale suffers; the life of his family is strained and their morale weakens; his children suffer humiliation in school. Such undeserved misfortune is an intolerable cruelty; and this is but one instance of the evils of our unbalanced industrialism.

4. What Can Education Do?

We saw earlier how mankind has, through the cultural accumulation, built actual effective intelligence, particularly in the realm of natural science. We need now to build social intelligence to enable man to grapple more effectively with these resistant social problems. The schools, it would seem, can have a real part in this effort. One thing the school can do is to lay a foundation of social knowledge by having the pupils and students study their communities and undertake socially useful work along with others in the community. A more directly intellectual attack on the building of actual social intelligence is to have the pupils and students, especially as they advance in years, study social problems, trying to understand our society and its strength and its weaknesses. One especially important phase of such social study is to work at difficult current problems, necessarily of course in a manner suited to the age level.

As soon as this study of controversial issues is raised there come forward many who are opposed. It is true that local political problems may easily become too personal for free study. But the deeper problems of civilization have to be studied and our citizens must become intelligent about them. To oppose the honest study of such problems is in effect to deny democracy. To wait until the young are grown is too late to begin such study. Too many minds will by that time be set in family prejudices; and, further, the cares of this world and the influence of riches, or of poverty, will too often prevent an honest and open study. Moreover, one must study live issues if one is to learn how to attack unsolved problems. Merely to study dead issues, prior solved problems, does not give the practice needed.

There are of course precautions necessary in this connection. The teacher is there to teach, not to indoctrinate the pupils with his views. Good teaching here is mainly teaching how to study efficiently and how to conclude logically. The teacher's aim must be to make of his pupils and students capable, independent thinkers. He must be very much on his guard lest those under him build dependence on him. Ordinary teaching founded on the older conception of authoritative knowledge has too often made pupils and students study to please the teacher, study to give him back what he wants. This is mis-education, ineffective, and anti-democratic.

But the good teacher can avoid such evils. He can aim clearly at reliable methods of study and concluding. It will often be wise to keep his own opinions in the background, especially with the younger ones lest they do build a hurtful dependence on him. If the schools will do their part, we can hope for a great increase in social intelligence among our people. Already it seems true that a larger proportion of our people are studying and thinking than ever before. If we can ever once get popular thinking off the old static-logic basis and onto an effective dynamic basis, the outlook for a better world is bright. For the first time in history we can now create enough to maintain all without denying any. We can, if we will, now move forward from an economy of scarcity to an economy of plenty. If we can do this wisely, the moral and spiritual advance can be even greater than the economic. In all of this, wise teaching can play a very effective part. Possibly without such teaching it may never come.

V. CONCLUSION

Thus ends the effort to exhibit the working of an experimental philosophy of education. This philosophy, in one word, is the method of modern science so generalized as to deal with all aspects of life. It starts with experience as we meet it in the varied phases and aspects of living. We are already living and in this we are already using a very considerable social inheritance. We watch life as it thus goes on and note that some features are less satisfactory than others. From this we project ideas for improving life; and we try out these proposals, watching meanwhile the results so as thereby to correct and improve our proposals. As we continue this, we build ideals of the good life and ideas as to how to act with a view to the better attainment of these ideals.

Also as we study experience we find a certain factor at work that we call learning, and we see further that this can be so directed as to help effectively in the pursuit of the good life. We further find, contrary to much previous thinking, that present learning is an essential ingredient of present on-going experience. And still further we find that each child learns what he lives, learns it as he accepts it to act on and live by, learns it also in the degree in which he lives it and counts it important; and, finally, we see that what the child learns he builds at once into character.

With such a conception of learning in relation to living and character building, we conclude that school should be a place in which the best possible living shall go on; for out of this living the child builds his character. Since, further, the child learns exactly what he accepts to act on, it follows that our part as teachers is but indirect. We cultivate and encourage the best quality living, but we cannot command it. The children learn their own responses to what happens to them and about them. We work to help them make these responses as fine and wholesome as possible. But our success with our pupils is attested by their growth in the ability and disposition to bring forth from within ever richer and finer living. In a democracy it is self-directing personalities that we try to build, the kind that can carry forward life ever more successfully in a developing world. Such a world calls for the experimental outlook and an experimentally directed education.

REFERENCES

BODE, BOYD H. *Fundamentals of Education.* New York: Macmillan Co., 1921. Pp. xi + 245.

BODE, BOYD H. *How We Learn.* Boston: D. C. Heath & Co., 1940. Pp. 308.

CHILDS, JOHN L. *Education and the Philosophy of Experimentalism.* New York: Century Co., 1931. Pp. xix + 264.

DEWEY, JOHN. *Democracy and Education.* New York: Macmillan Co., 1916. Pp. xii + 434.

DEWEY, JOHN. *Experience and Education* (Kappa Delta Pi Lecture). New York: Macmillan Co., 1938. Pp. xiv + 116.

DEWEY, JOHN. *Experience and Nature.* New York: W. W. Norton & Co., 1929. Pp. xi + 443.

Educational Frontier (William H. Kilpatrick, editor). Chap. II, " The Social-Economic Situation and Education," pp. 32–72, and Chap. IX, " The Underlying Philosophy of Education," pp. 287–319, written by John Dewey and John L. Childs. New York: Century Co., 1931. Pp. 325.

KILPATRICK, WILLIAM H. *Education for a Changing Civilization.* New York: Macmillan Co., 1926. Pp. v + 143.

KILPATRICK, WILLIAM H. *Selfhood and Civilization: A Study of the Self-Other Process.* New York: Macmillan Co., 1941. Pp. 244.

CHAPTER III

EDUCATION AND THE REALISTIC OUTLOOK

FREDERICK S. BREED
Associate Professor of Education
University of Chicago
Chicago, Illinois

I. INTRODUCTORY CONSIDERATIONS

A distinguished American savant once declared that the most interesting thing about a man in his beliefs; and, he might well have made the same observation about a nation, for beliefs represent the net result of thinking, the outcome of human reactions to the world. They body forth the forms of things to come; they bear the patterns of our personal behavior; they determine the direction of our thrust into the enveloping darkness. They are the creeds and the dogmas, the theories and the hypotheses, the philosophies and the religions for which men live and for which they sometimes struggle even to the uttermost.

1. Need for Educational Preparedness

It is trite to say we live in a world of warring ideologies. Yesterday men battled to the death for religious faiths; today they wage relentless war for social creeds and dogmas. From the present raging conflict of ideas the teachers of the schools are by no means disengaged, for educational and social ideologies are always intertwined. Educational institutions are merely a species under the genus, social institution; they are part and parcel of the general social fabric. Moreover, it is accepted as axiomatic that the creed that permeates the state shall be the creed that permeates the school. No philosophy of education can therefore confidently aspire to general acceptance in the United States of America that does not square with democratic principles. This is acknowledged even by the radicals, else why have they so blandly and fatuously offered the now floundering doctrines of Engels and Marx to our populace as democratic political philosophy raised to the nth degree?

The idyllic days of Calvin Coolidge and the fabulous twenties are behind us. The greatest breakdown of the modern world's political and economic structure is with us. The greatest threat to the existence of democratic government in the world is hanging over us. We are in the toils of a vast social revolution. We are witnessing the decay of many social institutions that have served their day and generation and are now no longer adequate. We are confronted with the need for reorganization and reform, but, first of all, with the need for understanding. We have been challenged and have been found wanting. We have been found wanting not only in material defense; we have been found wanting in mental defense as well. As a people we have had neither the arguments nor the armaments to repel totalitarian attack. The painful discovery of these deficiencies explains the feverish rush of preparation under way today in these United States. It explains the flood of literature, the endless stream of articles, books, and pamphlets on the subject of democracy and education, the drive for psychological preparedness within and without the school. It explains in part the general urge toward a more progressive program of instruction in the public schools, with stress on social understandings. It explains the project of which this chapter is a part, for in the general search of the public mind and heart, there has been increasing demand for light on fundamentals, on basic principles, on the essential meaning of education and the democratic way of life. This demand for social clarification explains the revival of the philosophy of education as a subject of study for prospective educators after its years of somnolence, dilution, and dogmatic suppression.[1]

2. Interest in Fundamentals

The revival of interest among educators in the fundamental generalizations upon which to build for the future has already been attended with important gains. It has shown that the conservative education which reigned in the roaring twenties under the banner of science needed only to be questioned to pass a poor examination — poor for the reason that its implicit faith had never been made suffi-

---

[1] As an indication of revived interest, it might be mentioned that members of education faculties offering courses in the philosophy of education in American colleges and universities met in Philadelphia in February, 1941, to discuss their problems and form an organization. The organization will be known as the Philosophy of Education Society.

ciently explicit. Small wonder, then, that to certain reformers it bore, in one respect, a strange resemblance to the doctrine of divine right, a doctrine that served as a superb foundation for a potentate only until some annoying skeptic pried beneath the trappings of the throne. But here the parallel comes to an end. While kings have been dethroned by the collapse of the doctrine on which they leaned for support, the science of education is promised a new dispensation by the exploration of its underpinning, for the logical framework of an objective approach in education is now being disclosed.

When a progressive group in the bewildered thirties moved forward on the basis of certain pragmatic principles, recourse of their critics to philosophy was unavoidable, for obviously it was impossible to understand without philosophy that which is philosophical, or to be intelligently critical of that which was not understood. Now as the profession plows more deeply into fundamentals, it gradually becomes more enlightened regarding the scope of a progressivism based on instrumentalism. Indeed it has already been rescued from the delusion that Dewey's instrumentalism is *the* philosophy of education, or *the progressive* philosophy of education, or even *the democratic* philosophy of education. The realization dawns that this outlook is but one of several well-recognized ways of looking at life and education, and that, by its own criterion of truth, it must stand or fall according as it works in human affairs. Idealism, realism, and scholasticism, each centuries old, also continue, in one form or another, to appeal to many whose thinking dips below the surface of things, presenting points of identity one with another and with instrumentalism, and points of difference that lead to vital differences in application, each furnishing an organization of knowledge and a general intellectual orientation that may serve as a design for education and for life. The serious student is therefore increasingly inclined to weigh his theory of education in relation to a set of more comprehensive generalizations appropriately labeled ' a philosophy of life.'

3. Can Philosophy Help Education?

From what has been said it may be inferred that the writer is not suffused with sympathy for educators who carry the banner of philosophy without its substance, or for those who deride the ' thin intellectuality ' of philosophy and avoid its fundamental problems as irrelevant and superfluous. Whatever the writer's philosophic attainments may be, his respect for such attainments in others has never been hampered by the suspicion that generalizations which he does not comprehend must therefore be mere verbalisms, conceptual impostors that circulate in the field of thought without denoting anything genuinely real. After making light of philosophy, the foes of the subject proceed to make the 'philosophy of education' so light that then, if ever, does intellectuality deserve the name of thin. This is not to say, however, that technicalities in epistemology, logic, and metaphysics always have important bearings on education. No more do all the technicalities of psychology or biology. Our belief is rather that, where philosophical conceptions do have important bearings, the relation to education is not often enough understood and indicated, and so a metaphysical technicality stands out like a passion without a purpose. This is the principal danger where competence in philosophy is not coupled with an equally competent grasp of the underlying problems facing the educator.

Many competent philosophers admit their lack of close acquaintance with the problems of education, as readily as educators in general admit their lack of special attainment in philosophy. One would, therefore, not expect philosophers or educators of the type mentioned to point out the important relations between the two fields, and indeed examination of the books of these individuals bears out one's expectations. When a luncheon conversation recently touched on the increased interest of educators in philosophy, a logician of note modestly inquired how the study of philosophy aids in the solution of educational problems. By way of example he was informed of certain educators who, influenced by the doctrine of the relativity of truth, assert that truth properly conceived is here today and gone tomorrow, and therefore needs to be given little attention in curriculum construction. They decline to make truth an important determining factor in the child's education. They prefer to make the personality of the child determinative and to exalt his demands over the demands of truth, in the spirit of the doctrines that the truth is that which is satisfactory to the child and that the problem approach in teaching is vitiated when the solution of a problem is fixed in advance. This simple statement sufficed to bring a quick expression of attitude. Our logician friend immediately enrolled himself on the side of an educational philosophy that combats such heresy by promulgating views more closely resembling his own!

II. Temper of the Realistic Mind

1. Definition of Philosophy

If the sense herein attached to the term philosophy has not been made sufficiently clear by implication in the foregoing paragraphs, that sense may now be more definitely suggested. In agreement with Bertrand Russell and numerous other modern philosophers, we regard philosophy as continuous with science, not separate therefrom. As here defined the subject has neither materials nor methods peculiar to itself, but employs the materials and the methods of science. It differs from science, however, in the degree of generality of its problems. Philosophers of this type are interested more than most scientists in the fundamental conceptions of the different sciences and in the relations among the sciences. Thus they put themselves in a better position to attempt a general integration of human knowledge. Indeed, in the present unity-of-science movement one observes a coöperatively organized attempt to achieve just such an integration.

Philosophy in this sense is empirical; it is objective; it is experimental. It not only consistently absorbs the techniques of scientific experimentation, but has also successfully adapted the tools of logistics and semantics to its purposes — tools of a type long regarded as the special, if not the exclusive, instruments of rationalism. It is an empirical–rational outlook, and has been christened the ' scientific philosophy ' by one of its most distinguished exemplars, Bertrand Russell.

Since we regard philosophy as innocent of an ambition to unscrew the ' unscrutable,' and confine it to the modest ambition to achieve a better organization and interpretation of verified knowledge, we anticipate no widespread opposition to the definition stated. Thus defined, philosophy is hardly more than a stubborn attempt to think our world consistently. If, however, the reader still insists that the ambition described seems too much like a quest for the unattainable, one may suggest that both scientists and philosophers have fruitfully pursued this quest, and such research as that of Russell and Whitehead on the relation between logic and mathematics will amply illustrate the possibilities.

2. Impressive Revival of Realism

It is the aim of this chapter to throw a ray of light on education as seen from the point of view of the philosophy described. Since the days of Aristotle it has been unnecessary for realism to apologize either for its existence or for the character of the arguments adduced in its behalf. This philosophy has persisted through the centuries with varying fortune, but seldom has it been at a loss for brilliant supporters. In the present generation it has had an impressive revival, and today numbers among its adherents many of the most prominent thinkers of our time. The revival of realism in America stems from events in the early years of the present century, after pragmatism had made a successful attack on the stronghold of absolute idealism and, following a period of destructive criticism, had undertaken to become constructive in its own right. But as soon as certain pragmatic principles were laid bare for public inspection many of the best philosophic minds began to show distinct signs of metaphysical uneasiness. Particularly was this true when the early pragmatists laid down their doctrine regarding the nature of truth. William James declared that the notion of truth was pivotal in pragmatism; whereupon the realistic critics quite generally replied that the pragmatist's conception of truth was the feature of pragmatic philosophy they could tolerate the least.

It was Bertrand Russell, I believe, who said that both of these philosophic strains trace their origin to William James, and anybody who has made a reasonable acquaintance with the thought of James will know that, though a doughty champion of pragmatism to the end, he also continued to play with the idea of remaining a realist as well.[1] This in itself is a fact of some significance, for it at once suggests a large area of agreement between the two philosophies. But after the death of the founder — even before — devoted followers began to diverge on the differences between the two philosophies, differences which James had never reconciled, and which have not to this day been reconciled, even though the masterly work of Whitehead has made a contribution in this direction by adopting much that is precious in pragmatism while avoiding its anti-intellectualism and, withal, remaining fundamentally realistic.

3. Basic Principle of Realism

One of the first questions my ' fratres pedagogical ' pose, after noting my enthusiasm about something that has been a matter of no considerable moment in their academic lives, goes like this: Now exactly what, in a few well-chosen words, do you mean by realism? One of course does not venture to comment in their presence on the general

---

[1] Professor Dewey refers to his own philosophy as "naive realism," and is opposed to the "presentative realism" defended in this chapter.

prevalence of philosophic illiteracy, or to suggest that a professor in a modern institution of learning might expect his colleagues to read his books. Why bother with the books, might come the embarrassing rejoinder, when everyday familiarity with the author has already advertised both his intellectual limitations and his perversities? Nevertheless, where ignorance is bliss, it is not always folly to be wise. So, what others have attempted to do in volumes of print we rashly and patiently undertake to do in a few pages.

A recent reviewer, noting that the writer seemed to be gathering prestige for his doctrine by identifying certain distinguished persons with the philosophy of realism, has properly reminded his readers that identity of name in this case does not mean identity of view. What he meant was that realists differ one from another in certain respects and, he might have added, are even aligned in different schools. This, of course, is readily admitted. For example, Santayana and Lovejoy belong to the school of critical realists; Montague and Perry have been identified with the school of neorealists. There is nothing in this situation that is disconcerting to the writer, however, for he is much more interested in the resemblances than in the differences among these groups, much more interested in the principles that bind them together than in those that hold them apart.

The principle above all others that unifies the realists is known in brief as the *principle of independence*. The term refers to a fundamental feature of the process of knowledge, a region in which most important differences in philosophic outlook take their origin. To precipitate the fundamental issue, let the reader pose the question to a realist: Can a thing *be* without being humanly known? Or ask him: Can anything exist *independent* of our knowledge process? His answer will be in the affirmative. But the instrumentalist answers the same questions definitely in the negative. A realist does not believe that the process of knowledge is constitutive of its objects. Whereas the instrumentalist believes that objects are created by acts of cognition, the realist believes that they are disclosed by such acts. For the realist, becoming known is an event that happens to things assumed to exist prior to and independently of the act of knowing. According to this interpretation, knowing is a process mediating an external relation between an organism and another existent. Both sides believe that intelligence is a name for a particular kind of function or reaction, and both are therefore in full harmony with functional psychology, even behavioristic psychology, after the latter has been rescued from the narrow physical and biological limitations with which Watson hemmed it in. They differ, however, in their interpretation of what takes place in the noetic, cognitive, or intellectual response. Does one attribute to intellectual activity an impression or prehension of the preëxistent? If so, he is a realist. Does one attribute to this activity the creation of the existent? If so, he is not a realist.

After turning this definition over in mind, the mood of the questioner may perhaps be expressed in the more or less withering query borrowed from the adolescent vernacular: "So what?" Such a response would probably mean that he doubts the utility of such an epistemological technicality as the foregoing and challenges us to demonstrate the educational implications, if any, of the realistic interpretation of the knowledge process. Accordingly, we suggest that such a skeptic consider the rest of the chapter as an attempt to meet this challenge. Also, it may be added in sincere modesty, that since no one has yet worked out the educational implications of modern realism in any fullness, much will remain to be done after the present chapter is completed. If we can but establish a presumption in favor of the value of further inquiry in this direction, and possibly, in certain quarters, be accepted as the bearer of a message not lacking in significance for education in the democracy regenerate of tomorrow, our gratification will naturally know no bounds.

III. KNOWLEDGE AND THE EDUCATIVE PROCESS

1. Theory of Knowledge Basic in Education

Just as the region of epistemology marks the birthplace of philosophic theories, so also does it mark the birthplace of important educational theories. Epistemology is nothing but the philosopher's disconcerting terminology for theory of knowledge; and whatever else education deals with, knowledge certainly has been its central interest through the centuries. Note how the educational and spiritual leaders of men have been captivated by the conception of truth — and even more by the conception of Truth. Not in all quarters today does the capital T bring added veneration, or the truth of science suffer beside the Truth of God. That in itself precipitates a problem of knowledge on which contributors to the Yearbook will expand and divide. It is the problem of absolute as against relative knowing. But regardless of the division of opinion on the scope of relativity in the field of knowledge, the disputants will quite generally agree that sound knowledge provides a most important objective for the curriculum of the schools, in the broad sense of the doctrine that we shall know the truth and the truth shall set us free. However, before objection is taken to this statement from certain viewpoints represented in the present volume, let us hasten to add that knowledge must be more clearly defined before assent can be expected from some of the pragmatists or indeed from many of the realists — a situation, incidentally, that tends to confirm the strategic nature of theory of knowledge in education as well as in philosophy.

If the term ' knowledge ' is used to denote the static end results of the knowledge process, if it refers to the propositions, conceptions, generalizations, or abstractions in which the cognitive activity of others presumably more competent has eventuated, and if these end results in propositional form are logically organized and embalmed in printed form for ready use in so-called subjects of study, to be memorized and re-cited at the beck and call of a school teacher, educators of pragmatic leaning will have none of it. They emphasize the process rather than the product of the knowledge quest, certainly rather than the product of the quest of someone other than the learner. Indeed, they become so absorbed in the process that in unrestrained and irresponsible moments some of them pooh-pooh the truths of subjects as of small consequence in a program of instruction. They rivet their attention instead on the growth of the pupil's personality, on the development of understandings in his experience, on the progressive solution of problems that occur in his personal life from day to day. And if a conservative critic presumes to identify subject matter as he understands it with the ' understandings ' mentioned, the pragmatic educator at once makes it clear that even here he is looking at affairs dynamically, and that ' understandings ' are regarded as acquired dispositions for desirable reactions to life situations, not as acquired ability to repeat items of subject matter or expressions of truth on demand.

In the foregoing, the progressives and conservatives alluded to are not mere men of straw. They can be found functioning in the flesh by anyone who takes an observant stroll into the classrooms of the nation's schools. Admittedly, however, they are not typical. They are not meant to be typical. Enlightened conservatives and progressives are not so one-sided in their educational treatment of knowledge. Nevertheless, even the best representatives of these opposing theories differ much in emphasis, one group being more concerned with the logical product, the other with the psychological process of cognition. The worst offenders, on the one side imbued with a mossy and musty traditionalism, on the other inspired with a reckless and superficial radicalism, are the victims of a restricted vision. After abstracting from extremists who are either creatures of habit or of blind devotion to an unknown god, the liberals who remain can profit from an adjustment of their perspective through a comprehensive grasp of the knowledge process. They need what we all should seek — a balanced view of education based upon a better recognition of basic factors in the knowledge process; for education is primarily an organized means of facilitating this process in the schools. Indeed on such breadth of view the writer largely depends for the resolution of certain important conflicts in contemporary educational theory and the retention of certain indispensable values now ignored by one or the other of the contending parties.

2. What Value in Conservatism?

May we interject a word at this point to forestall an objection? There are so many educators who talk and act as if conservatism is an outmoded attitude devoid of reason that we may profitably spend a moment examining this view. These educators are about as intelligent as the member of the profession who dubs every liberal a radical. Naturally, if one's social interest is totally confined to the preservation of the *status quo,* if he learns nothing and forgets nothing, if what was good enough for grandpapa is good enough for him, then we do not condemn the progressive element for looking askance at him. But, as is common in the heat of debate, the disputants too often reject a point urged by their opponents even when it has the force of truth. Just say in these critical times that Hitler has the shrewdest sense of political timing in Europe, or attribute any other outstanding merit to him, as an intelligent person might to His Satanic Majesty, and many well-meaning folk will regard you as a suitable subject for incarceration in the local bastile. But to the writer there is no progress without conservation. Professor Kandel has said he is a conservative because he is a progressive. He evidently has respect for the best problem solutions achieved in the past, and also holds the way open to better solutions in the future. Conservatism, as we shall use the term, means a healthy respect for the human values realized to date. It maintains that these values represent our most precious social inheritance. Its respect is not thereby lessened for the source from which these blessings flow — the process of inquiry and reflection. The conservative believes that educational prosperity is like business prosperity; it demands attention to profits as well as to processes of production. If we support the constant need for inquiry and the improvement of social institutions, including the educational, if we remain truly open-minded toward proposals to improve these institutions, ready always in true scientific manner to examine the evidence and decide accordingly, most of the responsible progressives will have no quarrel with us.

In what we shall say about the process of knowledge, the realistic position will be compared frequently with instrumentalism,[1] in order not only to clarify by contrast at critical points, but also to sharpen the issue between a philosophy that has captured the interest of many forward-looking educators and another that has been widely implicit in educational practice but less explicitly analyzed.

IV. Realism versus Instrumentalism

1. Agreement on the Problematic Approach

Both of the philosophies mentioned are of the experience type. Thinking, knowing, learning are used as terms applying to phases of the stream of human experience. Idea and object are also terms applying to aspects of the process of knowledge. The conception of an ' experience continuum ' is borrowed from the Jamesian notion of the ' stream of consciousness,' wherein action proceeds by a series of ' flittings ' and ' perchings,' as James said without committing the literary atrocity of a mixed metaphor. ' Flittings ' is evidently but a picturesque phrase for reactions that take place when the individual grows uneasy on his ' perch.' Situations that provoke the reactions, the instrumentalist calls problematic. In their original novelty, such situations are the natural stimuli for intellectual reactions; once become familiar, they are the natural stimuli for habitual reactions. Problematic situations are therefore to be regarded as the natural point of departure for thought, ideation, intellection — all three terms referring to the same process, which is none other than the knowledge process.

Now a realist can accept this account in its entirety if he is permitted to supply his own interpretation of the statements made. But as soon as this is supplied, the affections of the instrumentalist will be quite completely alienated. Take the problematic situation, to begin

---

[1] By instrumentalism is meant, here and hereinafter, the form of pragmatism to which Dewey holds. It takes its name from the fact that ideas are regarded not only as instrumental in adjustment, but also as instrumental in creating the qualities of objects.

with. Pragmatists frequently hark back to James and quote with approval his description of the preliminaries of intellectual life in an infant as a big buzzing confusion. This is accepted as a passable picture of a problematic situation in almost anybody's psychology. Essentially, the idea is that life is a process of getting into confusion of this same general type, though not always so accentuated, and getting out again, or trying to. The function of thinking is ' designed ' to release one from such embarrassing moments. One thinks in order to find a way out, and, of course, because a way out has not already been charted in previous experience and preserved by habit.

Let us take another example, this time from the life of an adult. The experience in question was that of the writer emerging from a state of anaesthesia after a surgical operation. In the first few moments of ' returning consciousness ' his world consisted of an abyss of darkness engulfing a feeling of pressure. Nothing more. There was no appearance or thought of other objects inhabiting the darkness, not even of a body inhabited by the sense of pressure. Just an experience such as a primitive polyp might have, or a quivering jellyfish, or a half slumbering alligator, when prodded from without. Then gradually this rudimentary world was enlarged and enlivened when to the sense of pressure was added a sense of pain. It is difficult to state just when a feeling of inquiry about the situation entered the picture, or whether any suspicion arose that this was not exactly the normal state of the writer's intelligence, but certainly a degree of reflection appeared before the pressure and the pain had been located at the point of a surgeon's incision in a body identified as the writer's own.

2. Are Objects Creations of Intelligence?

The two sides in the controversy agree that knowledge of objects has its inception in such problematic situations, that an object of knowledge may be described as an organization of qualities in a particular location at a particular time, and that these qualities come to be known through reactions to the situation. A little reflection will show that, so far as we know, any object, such as a nugget of gold, is the totality of its qualities. One says gold is yellow, gold is heavy, gold is malleable, and so on. Each statement is an expression of an idea, of a thought, of a judgment, an item of knowledge, if you will, and each is an expression of a quality. Neither the realist nor the instrumentalist posits a material substance, a basic ' matter,' in which such qualities inhere like epithets stuck in a substrate. For each, an object bears some resemblance to the surprise package which is really nothing but wrappings. A critical realist believes that the qualities are the effects of unknown causes. A neorealist believes that they are in part or altogether ingressions from a world without. The instrumentalist believes that the qualities of objects are instituted by the creative activity of man's intellectual operations.

According to the philosophy most commonly used as a foundation by educators styling themselves ' progressive,' the objects that are accepted about us, the facts which are referred to as physical, are not really independent existents; they are *prior* creations of the mind of man. According to this conception, said objects once built up from problematic beginnings are subject later to the rapid rehabilitation of habit. In every instance they have been constituted by our experience, of our experience, for our experience; and further than that deponent saith naught.

A dissenting critic [1] quotes the following comment on the instrumentalists, and seems to regard it as a curious misrepresentation, whereas the writer still regards it as quite a satisfactory characterization:

I reiterate, the notion of a world independent of man in the ordinary geological sense is absolutely lacking in the furniture of their minds. Science, together with all its objects of knowledge, is regarded as entirely within human experience. Its laws and objects are the conceptual products of human thought, shaped from immediate experience. The ' external ' world of natural science is put down in the calendar of such philosophers as a gratuitous fancy, an unnecessary assumption.[2]

To support his criticism, this critic italicizes portions of a passage from Dewey. The passage is artfully written and likely to deceive the unwary. It reminds one of the heretical minister of the gospel who retains his pulpit by virtue of the orthodox interpretations of his vocabulary in the pews. Listen:

That stones, stars, trees, cats and dogs, etc., exist independently of the particular processes of a knower at a given time is as groundedly established fact of knowledge as anything can well be.[3]

[1] Alfred L. Hall-Quest, " Education and the New Realism," *Educational Forum*, III (May, 1939), 495–501.

[2] Frederick S. Breed, *Education and the New Realism*, p. 100. New York: Macmillan Co., 1939.

[3] John Dewey, *Logic: The Theory of Inquiry*, p. 521. New York: Henry Holt & Co., 1938.

The objects mentioned, the instrumentalist believes, " exist independently of the particular processes of a knower at a given time," they are part of the capital with which any new cognitive enterprise starts, but they are not given from without nor is their existence posited outside his personal experience. They are simply accepted as earlier constructions within the knower's experience and used as points of departure for the only kind of knowing Dewey believes in, namely, what James defined as knowledge-about. These objects 'have emerged.' Note well the language. They have emerged as creations of the knower's intelligence. Once created, it would be, of course, a " waste of energy to repeat the operations by which they have been instituted [created] and confirmed," as Dewey says.[1]

It is easy to understand the appropriateness of the term ' generative ' for this theory of the knowledge process. It is also easy to understand how a thinker who denies that existents are given or determined from without must provide for their generation from within. Finally, it is easy to see how the theory comes to be used as the foundation for a radical movement in creative education.

With a great French stylist the instrumentalist says, in effect, " We make our world, and when we die we take it with us." That is, erase the human race and you erase the world that humans know.

3. Two Outlooks on the World

This solution of the world problem is thoroughly inacceptable to a realist, but it grows naturally out of a basic presupposition with which the instrumentalist starts his philosophizing, namely, his radical empiricism. This is a canon of fundamental procedure according to which he admits for consideration into his scheme of thought anything that is experienced and rejects therefrom anything that is not experienced. The program is highly positivistic and in the spirit of the law of parsimony. Its outstanding value is methodological and negative. It prevents the inclusion of unnecessary substances and faculties, questionable entities, mysterious bugaboos and spooks in the instrumentalist's system of thought. But, according to the realist, the principle is too stringent in its exclusion. While eliminating dispensable elements, it also eliminates the indispensable. It achieves metaphysical nicety at too great a cost, a chronic disease in the realm of philosophy. Since

---

[1] For a more complete reply to critics of the writer's position, see the article entitled " The Road to Objectivity in Education," *School and Society*, LII (August 10, 1940), 81–86.

the principle of radical empiricism and the principle of independence are mutually antagonistic, logically contradictory, there is no hope of reconciling the two philosophies in their present form. And for either philosophy to abolish its fundamental assumption would be to abolish itself.

For the present, then, the two ways of looking at the world will continue in opposition. Instrumentalism is solipsistic in character, suffering from the rigors of a radical and parsimonious methodology, flouting the intuitions of common sense regarding the existence of an external world, and attributing creative power to the intelligence of man to supply the data of knowledge that an amputated cosmos can no longer supply. And with the exaggeration.of human power goes the flattery of human hopes. The drift of such a philosophy is to inspire its devotees with quixotic schemes of educational, political, and economic reform. The world that man has made, he can quite easily unmake, they tend to believe, as if man were the measure of all things. The more radical exponents of this philosophy, outdoing the more sober and responsible adherents, have been accountable for most of the romantic adventures in ' creative education.' They have been responsible for encouraging the heresy that truth is a fetish of conservatives designed to keep a long suffering world in its accustomed groove. They have been responsible for shaking the confidence of teachers and pupils in the fundamentals of the democratic way of life, and for holding up the Russian model as a pattern for a more beautiful society.

In comparison with the instrumentalist, the realist is generally regarded as a somewhat more conservative individual, and probably is. He is somewhat more conservative because he has more respect than the instrumentalist for the truths of science. He has this greater measure of respect because he believes the laws of science rest on something much more stable than the facts of human behavior. Human behavior is a factor in their discovery, but, to him, an idea or a plan of action achieves the stamp of truth the way a penny wins in a matching game — by conformity with something external to itself and not of its own creation. To every idea nature seems to say, in effect, " You're matching me." The laws of the physical world thus become more than mere assertions regarding the qualities and interrelations of thought creations. They are statements, including mathematical formulas, reflecting the nature and interrelations of independent existents — a vast concourse of entities with which our personal entities must live, and about which they must know if they would live effectively.

Realism is a gospel not devoid of discipline in the sense of external pressure — even accepting the idea of compulsion from without, a factor in method so dreaded and derided by certain educational extremists. The teacher operates not only *in loco parentis*, more fundamentally still he operates *in loco naturae*. Most of us justifiably criticize a pedagogue guilty of arbitrary compulsion. But how about rational compulsion — restraining diminutive Bobbie from jumping out the upstairs window because nature has a way of taking such a diminutive individualist for a ride to earth fast enough to give him a perfectly good headache? The basis of discipline in life is nothing more than the requirements implicit *in rerum natura*, the demands of the laws of nature.

There is probably no better place than this to comment on the related 'interest' doctrine in education, a doctrine that has been vigorously exploited by liberals and reformers in the past, and has been commonly regarded as in direct opposition to the disciplinary theory. Frequently in liberal circles it masquerades in the name of the project method. Though the terminology may be new, the instructional procedure is often based on the assumption that immediate interest is an index of correct educational approach, the basis, indeed, for the selection of both the material and the method of instruction. It is unlikely that many educators look forward to this type of program as one of the unrealized Utopias in education. However, the writer was no little astounded recently, when, after expressing definite doubts of this eventuality, he was seriously asked, " *Is* the doctrine of curriculum-making by the pupils really nonsense? " Literally applied, this doctrine cannot exclude the activity of jumping out upper-story windows as a curriculum exercise, if such is the choice of the children. How the either-or thinkers needlessly embroil themselves in a logical stew over this situation, when all they need to do is to assume the both-and attitude and make the issue one of emphasis or degree, rather than of kind!

4. Direct and Indirect Interest

A sane progressivism has for some time taken cognizance of two types of interest, spoken of variously as direct and indirect, intrinsic and extrinsic, or immediate and mediate. Immediate interest is a response to an object as an end in itself. Mediate interest is a response to an object as a means to an end. Situations to which one attends are either intrinsically or extrinsically attractive. One can favor the intrinsically attractive in school and in life, and avoid as completely as possible that which is attractive only extrinsically, but if one expects to get on in his world, complete avoidance of the extrinsically interesting is obviously not the policy to be approved. Since no pupil ever consciously responds to a situation without interest of one or the other sort, one can still say that the school must operate entirely on the basis of *interest*, but one should also observe that discipline as defined above is not thereby excluded, for it appears in the guise of mediate interest. A pupil who fails to find arithmetic in itself attractive lacks immediate interest for the subject. If he desires to become a civil engineer, and we show him how absolutely essential mathematics is in the engineering profession and he thereupon devotes attention to that which makes no direct appeal to him, he is moved by mediate interest. And no different in principle is the case of another pupil lacking in arithmetical interest who is inspired to effort by a threat of punishment.

The reader should note that with either type of interest the impulsion to do the arithmetic comes from within, is the pupil's own, and that the difference lies in the attending circumstances. It is these circumstances that make the difference in method. For years many of our best educators have grown increasingly partial to direct interest and have advocated educational readjustments to enable pupils to do more and more of their school work on the basis of this type of interest. In general, psychology has supported this mode of approach, and its greater humaneness has been no small factor in its favor. Lastly, it seems more in harmony with the principles of democracy. This does not mean that a child will be permitted to avoid an important line of action that is not directly agreeable. Reason is here substituted for the rattan. The pupil is given a glimpse of a higher wisdom. Laying on of arguments takes the place of laying on of hands. The general assumption is that if a thing is worth doing, a good teacher can prove it; and, if so, an intelligent class, like an intelligent community, will approve it. It is the doctrine of consent. A teacher employing this doctrine must know his objectives and must, like a real statesman, carry the electorate for his cause. Not that a democratic state or a democratic school dispenses with more severe pressure or compulsion, or even punishment. It merely reverses the old order and makes these measures the exception rather than the rule, retained for special cases and emergencies. " The best way of dealing with the few slackers or trouble-makers in our midst," says President Roosevelt, " is, first, to shame them by patriotic example, and if that fails, to use the sovereignty of government to save government." The protest against the immoderately authoritarian character of the common American school grows apace, based on the conviction that education for life in a democracy is not best attained in the atmosphere generated by a fascistic schoolmaster.

Before leaving the subject of discipline, it may be interesting to note that the term is often applied to the pressure put on a child who is disinclined to face the unpleasant, or to a kind of training designed to increase his general ability to face the unpleasant. But in each case the root of the problem lies in the fact that man must face a reality not always made to his liking. In handling this problem some psychiatrists are as amusing as the extreme advocates of freedom of expression in education. Products of their doctrine, shielded and pampered and indulged, turn up in their clinics ' unadjusted ' because they have never learned to face reality. When remedial treatment for this deficiency is prescribed, it is not to be regarded as an exception to sound progressivism, but as expiation for an accumulation of sins. It is a concession to wisdom rather than to folly. Freedom is acknowledged as the first principle, but discipline is acknowledged as an indispensable supplement. Madam Montessori professed to operate on the basis of the first principle alone; Mr. Dooley, on the basis of the second. How agreeably our risibilities are stirred at Mr. Dooley's proposal to throw theory of value into reverse and, consequently, theory of education, with his famous pedagogical masterpiece: It doesn't make any difference what a boy studies just so he doesn't like it.

V. In Defense of Realism
1. The Principle of Independence

Several questions now intrude to thicken the plot of the chapter and complicate matters for both author and reader. Is there any proof that things can exist without being known? If such things do exist, how can they be known? Can there be a common world of knowledge without a common world of sense? How can an instrumentalist escape solipsism; that is, the theory that the world is nothing more than his personal experiences? After weighing these queries thoughtfully for a moment, it will be a relief to the reader to reflect that this chapter has a space limitation of 40 or 50 pages. Fortunately for him, the external requirements imposed by the committee in charge, like the laws of the cosmos in general, provide external conditions in accordance with which we must labor and to which, therefore, we must adjust, with the best grace possible, if we would get on with our project. There is an invitation to be constructive but within certain general limitations. Such is the gospel of life in a realistic world.

The realist is frank to admit that if anything is unknown, it cannot at the same time be known, and hence, on the basis of direct knowledge, the truth of the principle of independence cannot be asserted. But the realist does not claim to prove its truth in this impossible way. The principle is not an established generalization from fact. It is an assumption, a presupposition, one of those propositions or generalizations based on experience, but regarded as in the nature of an hypothesis. Indeed, realism in its totality is an hypothesis. So is instrumentalism. If the objection to the assumption is that it includes too much, the answer is that the radical-empirical assumption of the instrumentalist includes too little. The realist is a fellow close to common sense and to the common man in his attitude toward knowledge. He observes things coming into his ken, then going out, or so it seems, without suffering any significant modification as a result of such experiencing. The big brightly colored parasol that shades a corner of the porch across the Himmarshee Canal at this moment, seems to enter my experience as I look up at it, then to depart therefrom as attention returns to my writing without being materially affected by the act of perception. And the chair upon which I sit does not seem to vanish from the world when I lock up the apartment and saunter toward the beach. Only philosophers of a peculiarly pale cast of thought ever get so estranged from the common mood of mankind that they can believe this piece of furniture vanishes in any way but from the mind of the observer. Experience is a double-barreled term, implying the *experiencing* and the *experienced*. The first denotes the activity of thought; the second, its content. The *content* of experience is the original of all that is referred to as subject matter in education, and, according to the view here expounded, is not manufactured by mental functioning. And within particular psychological functions the conclusion is the same: Always there is the act of perceiving and something perceived, the act of remembering and something remembered, and similarly with other functions.

2. Activity versus Content

In times of emotional stress and general befuddlement, anybody may be excused for losing his bearings in a moment of indiscretion or indigestion, for getting out on a limb occasionally instead of sticking to the trunk of the tree. During the nineteen-thirties certain extremists became so eager in their campaign to substitute an activity curriculum for the traditional subject curriculum in the public schools that they unfortunately maneuvered themselves into an unenviable position. They were correct in demanding *more* emphasis on activity, but not in demanding *exclusive* emphasis. I still recall a meeting of professors of education during that period, in which this issue came to a head when an advocate of activity asserted that content can be ignored, in line with the theory that both the means and the ends of education are activities — a theory that embodies just enough truth to be dangerously misleading. Yet, if one accepts the physical theory that all is energy, then what *does* become of content? The dilemma for the activist, however, is just as puzzling when he is challenged to exhibit a case of activity apart from content. Even Dewey has never done so, nor will he. But he has never claimed to. For him, activity is an ineffable ultimate assumed as the mysterious source from which all objects and ideas somehow blossom forth.[1] His theory is essentially that mind gives form to something that is without form and void. Similarly, with Whitehead and his vibratory world, activity is always an inference from a situation in which items of content undergo change in spatial-temporal relationship. One experiences patches of color, refers to these as objects or terms, and posits activity as the explanatory or causal principle in interpretation of the change observed.

It is amusing to note, as we pass, what happens to the instrumentalist's radical empiricism and logical consistency at this point. The realist has been criticized for the assumption of independent existents, for transcending the limit permissible in an experience philosophy. But note that basic preëxistent activity is likewise assumed by the instrumentalist with no greater warrant, and in apparent violation of his radical empiricism.

The writer has no great quarrel with the concept of activity in the instrumental pragmatism of Dewey or in the organismic realism of Whitehead, so long as it remains a postulate. One can be more positivistic than either of these philosophers, devoting himself to the study of terms and their relations in experience, in the Carnap manner. But if one frets for a theoretic explanation of terms and their changing relationships, desires more than a factual record of events in experience, there seems to be no more satisfactory postulate than that of

---

[1] Ralph Barton Perry, *The Thought and Character of William James*, II, 522–23.

activity. If so, it appears to the writer that Whitehead has offered the most plausible theory in suggesting that content, in last analysis, is found in the *form* of activity, or, to use physical terminology, in the patterns of vibration in this ' vibratory world.' All the so-called stimuli of the psychologist, the original materials of knowledge, seem to be reducible to vibratory terms, and the patterns of vibration such as those of sound and light, the forms of undulation, are well known to physicists. If the reader will but consider for a moment that the external world is represented by most of us largely in visual terms, and that these terms quite obviously have their source in light radiations of varying rate that impinge on the retina of the eye, he can hardly avoid one of the most truly fascinating and mystifying problems of knowledge: Can events of the physical world be known directly? Are the basic facts of knowledge events that are common to the physical and psychical world? One who answers these questions affirmatively has the basis for a ' common world of sense,' and, then, of knowledge, for while the mentality of a solipsistic creature is by definition isolated completely, that of a creature in a realistic world may come to know what is in the mind of another by perceiving what the other perceives.

Note, now, the different interpretations that are attached, from these different viewpoints, to what has been referred to as a problematic situation. Remember that out of a nebulous indeterminate experience, out of a state of confusion, a nondescript commotion, if you will, predicates are developed by intellectual activity, ideas are formed, ideas that are described by the instrumentalist as operational in character because they are regarded as plans of action or behavior. The realist, in the presence of a problem, is just as much interested as the instrumentalist in the question, " What in the name of Heaven shall I *do?* " but he is also tremendously interested in the question, " What in the name of Heaven *is* that? " His interest in the second question, true, is often, though not always, subsidiary to his interest in the first. The instrumentalist seldom stresses the query, " What is that? " as the central theme of inquiry, after the manner of William James, for he believes " that " which problematically confronts him is not yet what comes to be known. His language is reminiscent of Gertrude Stein and the cult of the unintelligible, for he seems to say: If anything is anything, it is something that it is not yet.

3. Analysis of a Problem Situation

The realist, however, looks at a problematic situation as an indistinctness that may disappear like a fog, as research proceeds. A problematic situation is like an indescribable stimulus that looms ahead on the horizon. As the situation develops, something in the nature of a pattern appears in the problematic locus. Later the forms of trees appear, then trunks and limbs, leaves and cells, followed by evidence of the existence of molecules and atoms, protons and electrons, if the process of investigation or knowledge development is sufficiently prolonged. You see, we are still building on the belief that knowledge of the world is fundamentally the disclosure of the preëxistent, the presentation of independent events or entities of the physical world.

Here we come face to face with the much discussed method of analysis advocated by the realist as a fundamental path of approach to the secrets of the universe. . . . We make our world? . . . Ah, no, on the contrary, we seem to find it! The method of analysis is simply a process of probing into problematic situations, a probing which fundamentally consists in selective reaction to or appropriation of the smallest elements possible. Microscopes but facilitate our prehension. The research of physicists on the nature of atoms, on the constitution of protons, or that of the bacteriologists on microbes and viruses, filterable and nonfilterable, are examples of exploration on the frontier of the infinitesimal.

4. Relative Stability of Knowledge

Instrumentalism is often called a philosophy of change, and well it may be. Most instrumentalists are irked by a man like President Hutchins, who stresses the relatively permanent elements of experience and the importance of acquiring knowledge of such elements. The Newtonian law of gravitation remained unmodified for two centuries, and, even after Einstein attached an amendment, the old law remains valid for all general purposes. How does the instrumentalist explain this degree of stability? How does he explain the regularity with which the sun appears above the brow of yon high eastern hill, the constancy with which sugar dissolves in my tea, the consistency with which any object retains its complement of qualities? How explain the consistency with which the same organization of qualities persists from perception to perception of an object that we refer to as the same? Since no characteristics can be imputed by an instrumentalist to the problematic situation out of which an object develops, they must be attributed to the nature of the inferential process. Thus it becomes more evident than ever that, instrumentally interpreted, the earthly footstool of humankind and the blue canopy of heaven are but elaborations of the mind, a dreamworld of our fabrication, and that ' education is reconstruction of experience ' in the sense that out of the crude experiences of childhood a richer experience is actually and gradually created.

5. Operational Character of Ideas

Something had better be said at this point about the operational nature of ideas, lest we neglect to say it elsewhere. This is a favorite notion of pragmatists and of progressives who build upon this philosophic platform. Bridgman [1] has in recent years carried the conception over into physics and others will be found adopting it, for the range of application is as broad as the range of ideation. But before going into abstractions, let us glance for a moment at the problem in a concrete setting. Suppose I show you a nugget of gold and ask you to state what you know about it. You look at it and say, " It is heavy." Fine. Now we have before us an expression of an idea. The expression is not the idea, of course; it is a symbolic representation. The idea is the thought sequence, not the symbol sequence, and it is a plan of action in the sense that it outlines in experience what will happen when one lifts gold or places it on a jeweler's balance. Any idea of an object is interpretable as a sketch, plan, forecast, or anticipation of the consequences of a human reaction to it. It is a case of knowing-about, which is relational in character. It points in the direction of that which is to be experienced. It expresses a relation of intentional reference. The reaction mediates between or connects that which is experienced directly as yellow, rough, and of a given shape, and that which will be experienced when one lifts the nugget, namely, the heaviness. It is a typical case of a relationship among terms.

Education may be defined as behavior training, but there is no possibility of proper behavior training without regard to the content of experience, the terms that enter into relation. Indeed, who ever heard of a plan of action or a pattern of behavior, or a pattern of any kind, devoid of items of content? What, otherwise, could a pattern

[1] Percy Williams Bridgman, *The Intelligent Individual and Society* (New York: Macmillan Co., 1938); also, *The Logic of Modern Physics* (New York: Macmillan Co., 1929).

consist of?　Content is always implied in a behavior situation.　You may know how to test weight, but knowledge of the operation includes *what* you are weighing.　If now you insist on growing metaphysically more subtle, and assert that the qualifications of my terms are in turn reducible to plans of action, and that ultimately the world is nothing but a system of relations intersecting at certain points in space and time, I could protest that your being my neighbor may be a quality dependent on an external spatial relation, but that it is more difficult to reduce the intrinsic redness of a rose to the status of a mere relation.　Nevertheless even color may be a configuration of light vibrations, light a configuration of corpuscles, and so on to the simplest organic units or entities.　The discussion now begins to remind one of the familiar jingle,

> Big fleas have little fleas
> upon their backs to bite 'em,
> Little fleas have littler fleas,
> and so *ad infinitum.*

But if we may trust Whitehead's intuition, the way of analysis is probably not the way of an infinite *regressus.*　If so, our analytical quest may terminate in organisms or entities not further analyzable. Thus content is as solidly intrenched as these entities.　In any case it is as real as the forms of experience, or, if activity is postulated, as the forms of activity.

6. Can the Independent Be Known?

In passing, we cannot ignore the logical problem, How can the mind establish relations with anything independent of mind?　If one thinks of the mind as a class of experiences, of your mind, for example, as the constellation of your experiences at this moment, things that have never previously entered your mind may now be admitted as simply as citizens previously outside the order may be admitted to the Odd Fellows.　The question really is, Can a thing assume a new relationship?　In a pluralistic and realistic world, assumption of such relationships is not only the very beginning of knowledge, but the essence of change — of progress and of retrogression.　The whole realistic position depends first on the doctrine of independence; second, on the doctrine of external relations.　It appears logically sound.　Can it command a semblance of scientific support?

If there are any supporting data, they will not be found in the kind of psychology which has been predominant during the last generation, for the general trend of this psychology has been to leave the student in a dualistic frame of mind, to leave him with the old mind-matter dichotomy on his hands, and a representative theory of knowledge in possession of the field. Psychological facts may have some correspondence with physical facts, according to this view, but what can be said regarding their resemblance? Correlation does not imply resemblance. The dualist therefore finds himself in the position of one, the door of whose dwelling place is closed to the outside world. There is a knock at the door. Since the door cannot be opened, the knower does not sense the physical cause directly, but is aware of a psychological effect called a sensation or perception. In other words, a ' stranger ' knocks without, and, as a result, there are produced those spectres of an inner world, sensory and perceptual ' states of consciousness.' But consciousness as a substance no more exists for the opponents of this view than matter as a substance. It exists only as a relation of meaning, of intentional reference, between a given experience and one anticipated. The experience that is interpreted, accordingly, is not a state of consciousness, not if consciousness is thought of as a spiritual medium in which the contents of mental life, such as sensations, are immersed. Sensations are regarded rather as prehensions or selections of existents that dwell in the environment. That which is sensed is a form of experience that can appear equally well inside or outside the human mind, mind being regarded as a manifold of such contents and their relations. This is the import of the doctrine that the physical and the psychical intersect, overlap, in sensation. It means that ' physical ' events can be directly apprehended.

7. What Is a Physical Fact?

How is direct apprehension of the physical possible? Much depends on one's conception of the physical. The ' philosophy of organism ' attributes feeling to every object throughout the actual world. Whitehead insists, again and again, that there are no vacuous entities, no actualities completely devoid of experience. We know experimentally that certain one-celled organisms can learn. Beyond that we face the problem of infraconsciousness. Said James, lecturing to a class of students: " Even that chair may have some dumb, dead, dull sort of consciousness." In similar vein, Whitehead [1] says of the sim-

---

[1] Alfred North Whitehead, *Process and Reality*, p. 268. New York: Macmillan Co., 1929.

pler entities: "There is thus some direct reason for attributing dim, slow feelings of causal nexus, although we have no reason for any ascription of the definite percepts in the mode of presentational immediacy." This amounts to saying that every organism from an electron to a human personality may be thought of as having its objective and subjective aspects. It is well to note, in this connection, that "Those elements of our experience which stand out clearly and distinctly in our consciousness are not its basic facts." Visual experience does not seem the most typical of our fundamental background of feeling. The appetitive elements, emotional drives and impulsions seem more fundamental and primordial; they also seem to resemble physical experience more closely, the experience of causal efficacy, a type of vector feeling that can be thought of as embodying the first intimations of ideation.

As stated earlier in the chapter, one may begin, as Dewey does, by attributing to intellectual activity the forms which experience takes as exemplified in the structure of the objects perceived. According to the view of Whitehead, however, activity is not only inherently experiential, but also possesses form in its own right, prior to entering the human mind. Thus the forms of things may be imported into our experience as aspects of the things themselves. Physiology interposes no difficulty so far as the neural transmission of the forms of vibration is concerned. The mechanism of a sense organ acts much like the transmitter of a telephone. Vibrations are transferred from one medium to another, from the atmospheric to the electrical and back again, without compromise of identity. Likewise, vibrations of sound may as easily be carried in the form of neural impulses to the central nervous system without loss of character. The cases of telephone and human organism seem all the more alike when one takes into account the electrical character of the neural impulse as found in the investigations of Professor Frank Lillie. Then, if one rounds out his theory by taking into account the integrative action of the central nervous system, first painstakingly investigated by Sherrington, and, in general, regards said system as a mechanism of reception and of reaction to impulsions from without, including in the concept of reaction the organization of impulsions, one lays the foundation for a truly objective theory of cognition and of education.

Not that all form in experience is thus imported from without. One is too familiar with erroneous forms and attributes imparted from within, of psychological integrations that have no discoverable counterpart in the environment. The constellation known as the ' Big Dipper ' is a psychological, not a physical, integration; while the units of the solar system, soundly integrated in fact, are not perceived as integrated. This is the problem of truth and error, to be dealt with presently.

8. Differentiation and Integration of Experience

For the moment we must explore in somewhat greater detail the possibility of presentations from without. This problem is indissolubly tied up with the highly controversial function of perception. If theory of knowledge is the birthplace of philosophies, perception is probably the chief bone of contention within this field. In simple phrase and quite untechnically, what we have been saying amounts to this: The experience called a sensation is the experience of that which touches us. In this apparently simple cognitive process we seem to sense an impulsion directly. Experiments on tapping are enlightening in this connection. If the taps are not more than 2 or 3 per second, they are felt as separate and distinct experiences. When, however, the rate is increased to 600 per second, the series of tactual impulsions is experienced as roughness. Is roughness a quality given from without or one created from within? The instrumentalist maintains, of course, that it is an intellectual creation. To him it is an integral or unified experience unanalyzable into tactual sensations. In this contention the Gestaltist supports the instrumentalist. The realist dissents. In education the pragmatic attitude manifests itself in extreme or exclusive emphasis on the *whole child,* on integration of the learner's personality, and in adverse criticism of educators who have assiduously devoted themselves since 1910 to analysis of the child mind into detailed contents and their connections or relations.

The writer has no adverse criticism of the increased interest in integration of personality as an end in education. He sides with liberals in the belief that a desirable outcome of our instructional endeavors has been dangerously overlooked by the profession. On the other hand, he believes just as strongly that a progressivism which turns its back on analytical technique, on measurement of specifics, on the details of diagnostic analysis, is committing a regrettable and unnecessary blunder. There is no real reason for an either-or attitude in the presence of this problem. One may rationally believe in integrations, configurations, *Gestalten,* and also in the reality of the components found in the analysis of such integrations. For example, the realist has not abandoned the notion that a perception is a complex of sensations, or that a chemical compound is a combination of elements. At bottom, the two theories on this point are but adumbrations of the fundamental presuppositions of the opposing philosophies. The belief that hydrogen and oxygen exist in water would violate the doctrine of radical empiricism. Acceptance of their existence in water creates no difficulty for the realist, for it is congruent with his fundamental assumptions.

9. Exaggerations in the Gestalt Theory

Many Gestaltists pursue their theory with such one-track devotion that all experience is assumed to be figured. As an illustration of the relation between sensation and perception in a configuration, between constituent elements and the figured whole, Woodworth cites a weather map, which is describable as a pattern of barometric readings. The readings are analogous to component sensations, the total pattern to the derived perception. The reasoning would be the same for the perception of a chord composed of simpler auditory elements. Other examples will readily suggest themselves, such as the composition of forces in physics, where two lines of force operating at a given angle on a point exert a force in the direction of the diagonal. In certain configurations of sounds and colors, observers can be trained to differentiate the components, which tends to show that the components continue to function in the compound or integration. The realist is not disconcerted by the argument of the opposition to the effect that the qualities of water are very different from the qualities of the hydrogen and oxygen that are supposed by chemist and realist alike to compose it. He admits all this. He accepts the view of the chemist, however, that the bonds between two elements like H and O, the relations into which they enter, affect their behavior. When two hydrogen atoms unite with an oxygen atom, the whole thus formed, the configuration known as a molecule, now quenches thirst when quaffed, whereas neither of the components could so perform in single blessedness. One could just as well cite the young blade who, after marriage, figures no longer wildly in night-club episodes, but in company with his wife tamely washes dishes, plans the household budget, and even saunters off to church on Sunday morning. We marvel at the transformation from September-Morn to Sunday-morn devotion. It is explained by taking account not only of the elements yielded by analysis, but also of the relations that have entered the picture. In the bonds of matrimony with his wife former qualities of the young man, like those of oxygen in union with hydrogen, have dropped into obscurity. Moreover, the realist agrees with the chemist that two elements in a given relation often exhibit types of behavior, qualities if you will, that separately they show no signs of possessing. The realist, accordingly, accepts both the existence of the elements yielded by analysis and also the reality of the integrations analyzed. Moreover, he believes in hierarchies of integration, in the integration of integrations. He holds that educational growth may be appropriately described as the achievement of important integrations of knowledge, attitude, and feeling. Indeed, he regards his absorption in educational philosophy as a drive in the same direction. He believes that one's philosophy of education, properly conceived, is essentially a comprehensive integration of a thousand specifics and more or less inclusive integrations of knowledge, an educational weather map based on the reports of scientific observers.

10. Résumé of the Discussion of Realism

The process of knowledge, the act of knowing, has now been discussed from its origin in a problematic situation to its consummation in answer to the general question, " That is what? " It has been described as a form of reaction of the organism to a problem situation. The question of content is answered by an organic response. In temporal sequence comes first selective reaction to forms of activity that do not depend on knowledge for their existence. These are directly prehended by the neural mechanisms of the organism, and transmitted to the central nervous system. Integration of impulsions takes place as a result of the connective activity of the organism, selectivity and connectivity being the chief aspects of its intellectual operations. Integration, as Sherrington long ago suggested, consists of the coördination of impulsions successively occurring and the coördination of impulsions simultaneously occurring. Selection of items of content and their interconnection — these seem to be the basic processes denoted by the term, intelligence. If the theory outlined is valid, all the processes of thought from the simplest association to the most complex generalization, can be described in terms of the simpler functions mentioned.

There are thoughtful readers who may regard this picture of the cognitive process as mechanical and materialistic. Realism is frequently associated with materialism. But such an identification in the present instance seems obviously without support. The view presented is as completely experiential and as completely devoid of inert and vacuous substance as modern idealisms and pragmatisms. It assumes that the world, known and unknown, is constituted of experiential content.

VI. THE NOTION OF TRUTH

1. Truth as a Quality of an Idea

Now comes in natural course the query that was lifted to world prominence in the fateful trial of the lowly Nazarene: What is truth? It would be an elaboration of the obvious to say that the problem posed by Pontius Pilate is related in some way to the knowledge process, that truth is a kind of knowledge. If, in alignment with the empirical school, we abstract from the question of supernatural knowledge, we can continue on common ground with our instrumentalist friends by confining the discussion to natural knowledge. Beyond the obscurities of our limited vision there are possibilities of knowledge untold, perhaps even of perfect knowledge, but the knowledge we possess seems to rest on a natural foundation, subject to the frailties of human nature. We may remain still further on common ground, if we define truth as confirmed natural knowledge. The term ' true ' then denotes a quality of a belief, the quality exemplified by its workings, or, in the favored phraseology of the instrumentalist, by its consequences. We can also agree that an idea or belief is an intraorganic event, and even a plan of action. It is a plan of action, it is operational, in the sense that it is an actual partial reaction to a situation, and by this token usually embodies features of the complete reaction and outcome. A part does duty for the whole in our thinking, even as a symbol. The anticipatory aspect of the idea, its pointing towards the more to which it refers, probably resides in the experience of transition, a type of relation which is obviously present.

A true idea in its pattern sketches faithfully, and in its symbolic representation expresses accurately, what will happen as the plan unfolds. If, in looking at the nugget of gold used previously as an example, one says, " It is malleable," one is describing, as suggested before, what will happen if one reacts in a certain way to that which one designates as gold. The thought of its malleability is this anticipatory reaction to the visual presentation. It may be referred to as an idea or as a judgment. The verbal statement is a symbolic representation of the idea or judgment. This statement may be called a proposition, although the term, ' proposition,' is often applied to the original judgment instead of to its verbal expression, just as 'term' is used at times to denote that to which a word refers rather than the word itself. Confusion can be avoided by recognizing, in line with the present trend in logic, that a word is a symbol to be constantly distinguished from that which it symbolizes or signifies.

No serious conflict arises between the two theories of truth until the workings or consequences are examined. At this point the realist insists on pressing his analytical method. He invites the instrumentalist to state in what the satisfactory workings, the satisfactory consequences, consist. He suggests that an idea works when the pattern it carries fits a pattern which it later *finds*. Change the last word to *makes* and the instrumentalist concurs. Let the word stand with its implication of discovery or disclosure of the preëxistent, and he dissents. You see the instrumentalist's theory of truth is consistent with his notion of the creativity of intelligence, the constructive and reconstructive power of the knowledge process. As one looks upon the Black Hills of South Dakota from a certain coign of vantage, he will see a crotch in a mountain side that marks the spot where the lode was discovered that has since become the famous Homestake gold mine. When a prospector once looked out upon this scene and said, " There is gold in them thar hills," what later made his idea true? Was the truth not established by the disclosure of something that matched the content of the idea? In other words, something in the mind *corresponded* to something *discovered* in the mountain. This is the realist's criterion of conformity, and, observe it well, a reflection again of the principle of authority. This criterion is employed by Whitehead and stated as follows:

Along the 'historic route' [of percipient occasions constituting a personality] there is the inheritance of feelings derived from symbolic reference: now, if feelings respecting some definite element in experience be due to two sources, one source being this inheritance, and the other source being direct perception in one of the pure modes, then, if the feelings from the two sources enhance each other by synthesis, the symbolic reference is right; but, if they are at variance so as to depress each other, the symbolic reference is wrong.[1]

Later the same author describes the test as one of ' comparison ' or ' correlation.'

Realism holds with common sense that a basis for the truth of the prospector's idea was slumbering in the mountain side, needing but to

---

[1] Alfred North Whitehead, *Process and Reality*, p. 275.

be unearthed, not to be mentally manufactured. But as we urged before, since the instrumentalist cannot logically entertain the notion of such antecedent existence without forsaking a presupposition, he holds to the presupposition, turns his back on common sense, and says, in effect, that the truth of an idea depends on whether or not acting upon it produces the result forecast in it. According to this notion the great problem of truth is completely in the grip of man. Where else? The idea projected as well as the consequences of the idea are the products of his personal invention and construction. It is not therefore unfair to say that this criterion of truth is reducible to personal satisfaction, or in a popular educational phrase, personal integration. It is therefore subjective and individualistic. The instrumentalist is backed into this corner because nothing prior to an act of personal creation can be assumed as a determinant of that which is created except previous personal creations. That is, nothing of the kind can be assumed by a *consistent* exponent of this philosophy. Since nothing is given from without, everything must be created from within, and truth becomes a matter of congruence of elements within the human mind. There is, of course, no objection to the notion of internal congruence, intellectual or emotional. This is exemplified every day in the consistency and inconsistency of ideas, in emotional balance and imbalance. But the realistic opponents of the instrumentalist outlook recognize still another type of consistency in the establishment of truth — that between ideas and things given from without.

2. Effects of the Instrumentalist Criterion of Truth

At this juncture a positivist may suggest that in the practical search for truth the difference between the opponents makes little difference in the results obtained. This, however, has not been clearly demonstrated. The difference in outcome will mainly stem from a difference in attitude. He who denies the existence of God spends little time in prayer. He who denies the existence of external reality gives little heed to its effect on his fortunes. Contentment with that which is personally satisfactory, an indisposition to acknowledge the true though unpleasant, a predisposition to think that human beliefs in themselves are freighted with all the potentialities of good and ill for mankind — this is a drift of the instrumentalist mind. A careful reading of the most intelligent instrumentalists reveals again and again their anxiety about the limitations to human action inherent in a realistic philosophy. In the bowels of their being there is a deep hankering for a surpassing freedom. Mankind, they seem to assert, must not be shackled in a slavery to things. Mind is not within nature, they insist; nature is within mind. Which leads me to repeat:

The pieces of the world picture within our observation are fragmentary, and temperament as well as logic determines how the puzzle will be completed. Wishful thinking beclouds the vision of the philosopher as well as that of the commonest man. The instrumentalist attributes lordly power to the spirit of man, for what can stay the hand of man the creator? He rejects realism partly because it fails to confirm his estimate of human nobility; because it denies to man a habitation in the company of the gods. The external pressure of the cosmic process, as viewed by his opponents, stirs his bones with deep anxiety. In such a cosmos he would be too largely at the mercy of the elements, the impressive mass of which gives him a sense of insignificance, a philosophic headache. "Human life *must* be more fortunate than that," he whispers encouragingly to himself. "It *is* more fortunate than that," he firmly decides. "I'll say it is," he adds with a touch of real evangelism, and so delivers his flattering message to a receptive world.[1]

3. Appreciation and Deprecation of Subject Matter

The process of knowledge eventuates in certain verified propositions that constitute the body of truth so revered by conservatives and so discounted by many who have lost their bearings in their ultramodernity. Radicals naturally belittle truth. It has a stabilizing influence that offers resistance to their revolutionary ambitions. The subjugated minions of Hitler and the nimble legions of Mussolini are marshalled in a desperate conspiracy against the citadel of truth. The same iconoclastic zeal has flared up ominously in certain educational reformers. Having defined truth as relative, they have jumped to the fantastic conclusion that it is of negligible educational importance. Finding certain traditions objectionable, and truth a component of tradition, they prepare to throw out the baby with the bath. It would be unfair, perhaps, to charge that the sins of the pedagogical father have been visited upon the social inheritors of his doctrine, that the excesses of certain professed followers of Dewey are faithful in their reflection of paternal qualities. Yet Dewey is to a degree responsible, even if somewhat misinterpreted through exaggeration. The drift to which we refer finds its roots in the pragmatic emphasis on the dynamic rather than on the static aspects of life, on function rather than on form. Dewey's attitude toward science is fundamentally il-

---

[1] Breed, *op. cit.,* pp. 119–20.

lustrative of his position in this regard. He realizes, even if many of his followers do not, that science may be defined either as a mode of acquiring knowledge or as a body of knowledge acquired. His forays into logic, however, are concerned with the procedure of research, the technique of experimentation, the mode of arriving at conclusions, and not with the conclusions themselves. Scientific method is identified with the process of reflection, or of cognition as seen through instrumentalist eyes. Educators, accordingly, are admonished to adopt this emphasis in the schools, if they would redeem education from the errors of a checkered and unenviable career. Even the developments in modern symbolic logic strike no responsive chord in Dewey's instrumental bosom, though these techniques have won the favor and support of Russell, Whitehead, Tarski, Carnap, Sheffer, and many others known as competent contributors and authorities in this field. And the achievements of the mathematicians seem to be no more significant to Dewey than those of the modern logicians. To him these gentlemen are birds of a feather playing with the dead precipitates of the knowledge reaction, playing with term-to-term relationships, playing with the remains of dynamic reflection after the spirit of reason has flown.

4. The Instrumentalist's Emphasis on Method

Recently Dewey [1] contributed a statement on the unity of science that appears side by side with chapters written by exponents of this new movement. While those most responsible for this movement are concentrating on content, on the organization of the findings of science, Dewey dismisses the central problem of his philosophic colleagues with faint praise, and advocates a unity of science in terms of a unity of attitude toward a coöperative effort to bring about the ' universality of scientific method.' He laments, as usual, that " scientific subjects are taught very largely as bodies of subject matter rather than as a method of universal attack and approach." The " method of universal attack," he believes, is the " method of free and effective intelligence." When he moves over into the educational arena, he often disparages the demands of subject matter in the schools and advocates more complete reliance on a training in methods of thinking.[2]

Elsewhere he maintains the same general position:

---

[1] *International Encyclopedia of Unified Science*, I, 1, pp. 29–38.
[2] See John Dewey, *How We Think*, Preface. Boston: D. C. Heath & Co., 1933. Pp. vi + 224.

We are brought to the question of method. In ancient science the essence of science was demonstration; the life blood of modern science is discovery. In the former, reflective inquiry existed for the sake of attaining a stable subject-matter; in the latter systematized knowledge exists in practice for the sake of stimulating, guiding and checking further inquiries.[1]

Later on in the same work he says, " But in the practice of science, knowledge is an affair of making sure, not of grasping antecedently given sureties."

5. Liberal Attitude toward Subject Matter

Liberal minded educators eagerly reaching out for better methods of instruction have, in considerable number, interpreted these statements of Dewey to mean that the acquisition of knowledge should be purely incidental to its use in practical activities. For such teachers subject matter is not an end, but a means. It functions only as, if, and when it can be used to further a pupil's purpose or facilitate his solution of a problem. Dewey's statements are misleading because they convey the impression that modern scientists are no longer devoting their efforts to obtain stable findings, when the reverse is true. Indeed, reliability of results is still one of the central objectives of science. Moreover, even if one admits that the chief function of knowledge, systematized or otherwise, is guidance of human action, it should still be obvious that it is not sufficient for this purpose that some compendium on a library shelf contain the knowledge needed, or even that recipes of unknown origin be taken for application from such a source. The heavy pragmatic stress on *application* of knowledge to the neglect of its *development* apart from incidental acquisition, has led many estimable folk in the educational profession to believe that a problem or project specifically designed to eventuate in the acquisition of subject matter, in the comprehension of an idea, in the achievement of a concept or generalization, represents the prostitution rather than the prosecution of an education. But is it not crystal clear that the problem of development versus use is really the familiar problem of liberal versus vocational study, of pure versus applied science — a problem whose roots descend into the field of value, where knowledge in the one case is regarded as intrinsically valuable, in the other extrinsically? The two types of value differ as ends differ from means, and few who are competent to judge would deny that, in

[1] John Dewey, *Experience and Nature*, p. 152. London: Norton, 1929.

general, the first is the more fundamental. The significant point, however, is that the two types issue from different aspects of human behavior and are as fundamental as are the demands of curiosity and utility, respectively, in our everyday lives. Though one is spoken of as theoretical and the other as practical, the difference resolves itself into a difference in the type of problem confronting the personality.

When integration of personality is fully understood as an educational aim, it will be found to include a balanced view of things as they are, a systematic and consistent body of ideas about the world in which we dwell. Consistency and comprehensiveness of grasp do not just come to one. Neither does systematic arrangement of the furniture of the mind. Both must be sought. Both must be included in the objectives of instruction. The traditional subject curriculum is overgrown with moss, but subject matter, the fundamental truth that has accrued from the historic stream of human experience, remains among the transcendent aims of education, to be achieved indirectly, yes, and directly as well, but in any case to be achieved. Dewey is apparently aware that many educators have confused reform of the subject curriculum with neglect of subject matter and have become so engrossed in method that content has seriously suffered. These extremists he takes to task in a recent book, as if he himself were in no way responsible:

It is a ground for legitimate criticism, however, when the ongoing movement of progressive education fails to recognize that the problem of selection and organization of subject matter for study and learning is fundamental.[1]

This defect in ' progressive ' procedure, this sin of omission, has probably led, more than anything else, to the vigorous opposition of the essentialists, for to them the truth of science, the best authenticated knowledge, ranks among the most precious elements of our cultural tradition, and thus merits exalted rank among the essentials of the school curriculum. The essentialists have performed a genuine service to education by making a defensive stand on this important ground.

There is a tremendous need today for a scholarly attempt to put the main pieces of the knowledge puzzle together and find out what they spell. Mr. Dewey is continually at work on the integration of his own personal knowledge, and should more clearly recognize a similar need in the rest of us. In some ways, indeed, it is not impossible

---

[1] John Dewey, *Experience and Education*, pp. 95–96. New York: Macmillan Co., 1938.

that our need for an improved integration of knowledge will seem more conspicuous to him than to ourselves! The menace of authoritarianism does not inhere in a progressive but always tentative systematization of knowledge, any more than it inheres in the apparent changelessness of Dewey's philosophy of change, or the relativity of all doctrines but his doctrine of relativity, or the persistence without shadow of turning of his radical-empirical principle, or the perdurability of his operational criterion of truth. If these are not dogmas, one gets no hint of it from his undeviating adherence to them for over a generation.[1]

The ' dogmas ' of pragmatism and of modern realism are of course the presuppositions that constitute the foundation of an empirical and scientific approach to the problems of life. Professor Mortimer J. Adler took the initiative in a recent renewal of educational warfare at the University of Chicago by delivering a slashing attack on modern college professors, attributing to their empirical minds the disorder in contemporary education and the disunity and chaos of modern culture. Special significance is attached to the attack because Professor Adler openly aligned President Hutchins of the University of Chicago with his Thomistic outlook, confirming a community of intellectual interest that has long been a matter of common knowledge on the Chicago quadrangles.

The clash between Adler and his opponents may be reflected in the form of a dialogue:

" Common to the various forms of positivism," said Adler, " is an affirmation of science and a denial of philosophy and religion."

" Not a denial of philosophy and religion, but of your definitions," answered the professors who believe in philosophy as one with science in both method and basic material.

" Knowledge is of two kinds, natural and supernatural," said Mr. Adler.

" Supernatural? " inquired the professors with lifted eyebrows. " Prove it."

" Knowledge is of two kinds, relative and absolute," said Mr. Adler.

" Absolute? " queried the professorial skeptics. " Let's have a sample."

" Values transcend science," said Mr. Adler.

---

[1] Much less does one get a hint of it from Brubacher's vigorous article entitled, " The Absolutism of Progressive and Democratic Education," in *School and Society*, LIII (January 4, 1941), 1–9.

" No, even values are grist for the mills of science," responded the recalcitrant professors, with a perceptible glint of empirical dogmatism in their eyes.

Every reader who has taken as much as an introductory course in philosophy should recognize this argument as something not altogether new, as having much in common with philosophic disputation at the turn of the century, when William James went forth to do battle with the fearsome Goliath of absolute idealism and put an irreparable dent in its head with no more formidable weapon than a despised empirical slingshot. Later, during the generation that followed, empiricism invaded the most hidden recesses of philosophy, as Adler implied.

But this does not mean that Mr. Adler is not a voice crying in the wilderness. Forget his scholasticism, his supernaturalism, and he still remains a prophet of the disaster that will overtake a divisive individualism, a flabby liberalism, and an impotent skepticism. He appears to be saying the hour of decision has arrived: One cannot build a program of education on the right to doubt; one must also believe. He demands a more intelligent, a more definitely purposeful, organization of higher education. With Hutchins he would set up, among other things, definite academic machinery for the exploration of fundamental concepts in various areas of knowledge and of the interrelations of these concepts, in the hope of gaining a clearer picture of things as they are and, then, of education as it ought to be. Such a program may have the sanction of medievalism, but it also has a logical place within the confines of modern empiricism as an extension of scientific thought in the direction of greater generality. Indeed, a large group of ' positivistic ' philosophers are already occupied on an international scale with this project, a movement which is known as the unity-of-science movement.

The organization of a university is based on the organization of knowledge. The first will improve as the second improves. Can the second be improved by research directed to this specific end? The group of scholars referred to above answer this question in the affirmative. Who are better qualified to judge?

VII. The Bipolar Theory of Education

1. A Proposed Synthesis

The functionalists in education, better known as activists, have a program designed to remedy a situation generally admitted to be deplorable. Others have long talked about the traditional emphasis on material and memory, to the neglect of method and the intellectual life. The progressives now propose to do something definite by way of reform. If they have become too exclusive in their devotion to method, it may equally be said that the conservatives have been too exclusive in their devotion to subject matter. If many of the progressives have failed to recognize the values inherent in the verified outcomes of the thought process, certainly many of the conservatives have failed to recognize sufficiently the value of training in the process itself. The writer ventures to propose an educational program in which the chief values of both the method and the material of knowledge will be synthesized and conserved. In this program the problem approach seems psychologically and philosophically inescapable as the foundation of educational method. This approach is not only psychologically defensible; it is also politically defensible, for it is perfectly congruent with the basic principle of a democratic society, namely, respect for individuality. Respect for individuality demands that the instructional approach, in so far as possible, should be through problems experienced by the learner. It does not mean that the accidental interests of children should determine the direction of education. These interests furnish only the point of departure. The teacher who said, in reply to a visitor's question about the nature of the program for the morning, " I don't know what it will be; the children haven't come in yet," is not a suitable soul for a berth in the school under description. In this school the teacher's function will not be that of an inert or impartial observer, but that of an intelligent guide, one who will direct the process of learning in the light of both the present status of the learner and the important ends to be achieved.

2. A Criticism of the Synthesis

In opposition to this view, a critic has urged that such a plan of education violates the spirit of the problem approach " by fixing in advance outcomes of active educational attempts to solve problems." His position rests on a misconception of the range of freedom in a democracy and its schools. He is evidently frightened by the bogie of authoritarianism. His ardor for subject matter has been definitely dampened, like Dewey's, by the fear that respect for truth may degenerate into subservience to authority. Possibly, too, he is tainted with a brand of pragmatism which holds that a belief of an individual is true if the individual is satisfied with it. In any case the critic is a victim of the exaggerated individualistic emphasis found in instrumentalism. The different position of the writer can be easily set forth in an example. Assume a youngster, unacquainted with the process of multiplication, facing the job of determining the extent of his riches after coming into possession of four big nickels. Though the outcome, the solution of his problem, is fixed in advance, this fixing in no way violates the essential spirit of the problem approach to education, unless one decides to go in for creative multiplication and accept as a solution to the problem any product that tickles the child's fancy. The example is simple but significant, for the study of every problem, including the most scientific investigation, proceeds on the same principle. Man proposes, but nature disposes. The child projects, but the teacher directs. This is the essence of the definition that teaching is the *guidance* of learning.[1] The test of truth is conformity with something not of one's own creation, and the content objectives of a good curriculum are but selections of values thus attested.

3. Liberalism and Authority

Liberalism is ever intent upon the springs of human progress. Freedom and tolerance and open-mindedness are but outgrowths of this fundamental attitude. The objectivity of scientific method forever disqualifies it as a doctrine for dictators and qualifies it for the label of liberalism. It is the eternal foe of unreason and untruth, arbitrariness and irrationality, prejudice and superstition. But art is long and so is science, and from the schools and scholars of the world there is absorbed but slowly the leaven of a better way of thought, the leaven of the scientific outlook and approach. All the more honor, then, to every member of the teaching profession who helps to spread the gospel of the scientific method, a gospel that is acting as an impelling motive in the current resurgence of liberalism in American education. The present chapter is meant to lend its full support to this forward trend as one observes it in the stress on intellectual training, problem solving, thinking ability. Not, then, that we love this emphasis less, but that we love the emphasis on the content of knowledge more. We would have the child improve the selection and the organization of his knowledge as well as the accuracy and general efficacy of his thinking. One may not

---

[1] Professor Bode comments on the teacher whose individualistic theory makes bootlegging the only possible mode of entry for her directive genius. To such a teacher we are saying, " Let not your heart be troubled. Prohibition is repealed."

be able as a theorist to have two masters, but he certainly can have two friends. The weakness of the position of certain admirable liberals in education is, as previously intimated, that phases of the educative process which are complementary have been regarded as antithetical. The error is a sin of omission, more than of commission, and derives mainly from too exclusive reliance on the principle of individualism, single-minded devotion to the principle of liberty, undue trust of the pupil's immediate interest. Respect for individuality is indispensable, but it is not enough. It provides a full foundation for neither the schools of a democracy nor the state of which they are a part.

There is another principle to which many refreshingly progressive spirits give lip service but pay a scanty and grudging respect. This is the principle of authority. Since the principle of authority seems to contradict the principle of liberty, some well-intentioned progressives propose to build without it, though a larger number proceed as if it were a case of making judicious compromise with a necessary evil. But this principle of seeming Satanic origin turns out to be one of the fundamental factors in adjustment. It springs from the *other* in life — the other person, the other entity, the animate and inanimate neighbors with which one makes his peace or wages war. Knowledge is but a revelation of their devious ways, and such knowledge therefore becomes the supreme guide for our adjustment to them. With regularity the fundamental factors of adjustment boil down to two — organism and environment, individual and society, purpose and possibility, personal interest and external demand, or, if you prefer, freedom and authority. It is the problem of freedom *and* authority rather than of freedom *versus* authority, for the two are complementary. They furnish the basis for a theory of instruction, indeed for a theory of government in the broadest sense, to which the term 'bipolar' seems appropriate.

The writer's criticisms are not to be interpreted as a total war on the activity movement, but only as a foray against certain excesses. More than appears, perhaps, he is tremendously interested in preserving precious features of this movement. (Few controversialists exaggerate the strength of their opponent in public.) The chief weakness of the activistic extremists may in general be characterized as an inadequate sense of fact, a sentimental retreat from reality and the values inherent in our common culture. They err in the extremity of their liberalism, as the rock-ribbed conservatives err in the rigidity of their respect for tradition. Think of an educator condensing the essential message of a book, if not of a lifetime of educational activity, in the ominous passage, " Modern society has reached the stage in its evolution when it aggressively imposes its institutions on the individual."

The battle with the progressive extremists is definitely drawn between defenders of mental content internally produced and defenders of mental content externally supplied; between those whose criterion of truth is the satisfaction of man and those whose criterion includes also the satisfaction of fact; between the champions of education as the creation of environment and the champions of education as adjustment to environment; between advocates of a morality sanctioned by the natural propensities of the individual and advocates of a morality that in addition is sanctioned by the demands of a self-existent social world; between those whose theory of freedom ignores the necessity of external restraint and those who foresee disaster in ignoring such restraint; between believers in an education determined alone by the inner tensions of a personality and believers in outer as well as inner integration.[1]

VIII. FOUNDATION OF EDUCATIONAL MEASUREMENT

1. Testing in Traditional Schools

The attack on the outmoded subject curriculum first degenerated, in certain activist quarters, into an attack on subject matter as a negligible factor in education, and, in its more recent emphasis, on educational measurement as an effete support of subject matter. The writer carries no brief for the conventional measurement program in its entirety, and makes no offer to underwrite or wash away its sins. There has naturally been a close relation between the prevailing curriculum and standardized tests, because the latter were devised to fit the organization of instruction which the test technicians found in vogue. The testers have made few pretensions as curriculum experts. They have adapted themselves to a situation for which they were not responsible. Their spirit has been, " Tell us what your objectives are

---

[1] It is a pleasure to note that the philosophy of the ' progressive extremists ' and that of the Progressive Education Association need no longer be confused. In a recent publication bearing its official approval, the Association rejects the view that individual value, child-centeredness, though primary in a democracy, is sufficient in itself for the conduct of education, and fully recognizes the factor of social value, the control of social ends, as well. The writer heartily commends this publication to students of educational theory. It is entitled, *Progressive Education: Its Philosophy and Challenge,* and can be obtained from the Progressive Education Association, 221 W. 57th Street, New York.

and we shall try to measure the degree to which they are being attained." And in the same tradition, the eight-year study sponsored by the Progressive Education Association has been conducted. This is not to say that the practices of conventional measurement sufficed for this study, but that the departures therefrom are attributable to differences in objectives of instruction rather than to differences in principles of measurement. The conventional school and conventional measurement, it was believed, emphasized habituation to the neglect of intellection, acquisition of skills and information to the neglect of improvement in the thinking process. The liberals in charge of the measurement program in progressive schools have accordingly found the toolhouse of measurement decidedly lacking in instruments suitable for measuring certain important achievements. The next step in advance was therefore the extension of the measurement program, rather than its discontinuation.

The principles of measurement march on. The movement will be accorded special support in its forward drive by a philosophy that is objective rather than subjective, for objectivity is the soul of science. It will be given special support by an outlook that is also analytical in its approach, for analysis is everywhere an indispensable phase of scientific technique. Finally it will be accorded special support by a philosophy that absorbs without strain the conceptions of both qualitative and quantitative analysis, for there can be no hope of more than an abortive science of education if the quantitative treatment of data is regarded as a futile aspiration. Reports of observations, such as, " The day is warm," " The burden is heavy," " The boy is tall," have their scientific importance, though purely qualitative. When, however, one is able to report the amount of each quality, saying how warm, as 97.5° F., how heavy, as 91.75 lb., and how tall, as 5 ft. 11 in., then only does one enter the portals of a maturing science. It is the ambition of science to describe events in respect to both quality and quantity. It conceives of every quality as exhibiting the more-less dimension, of possessing extensive or intensive magnitude, and therefore possessing that which is the natural object of quantitative investigation.

2. Objective Basis of Measurement

The objective basis of educational and psychological measurement is to be found, first, in the environmental source of the original content of knowledge, and, second, in the conception of intelligence as a type of organic reaction. Some of the items of content, like some of the intellectual reactions of the organism, are so largely intraorganic as to be appropriately called covert instead of overt, but, from the standpoint of the mind, objects both overt and covert are regarded as belonging to the environment.

The activity of intelligence consists of the selective reactions by which data of the external world are received and the connective reactions by which they are associated, integrated, and interpreted in experience. In terms of a language made popular in recent investigations, these two phases of intellectual behavior seem to constitute the fundamental factors of mental life. They seem to be revealed by analysis of the other more complex functions of the mind.

Most of the testing of educational achievement, and even of intelligence, features connectivity, the process of learning, and stresses but slightly the factor of selectivity; yet abstraction is a process of selection, and ranks among the most significant behaviors of man. Learning bulks large in achievement tests, with sparse attention to the activity by which learning takes place. In general, test items in the leading standardized tests can be understood as verbally presenting problem situations to which the pupil is invited to make response, commonly by writing, checking, or underscoring a word. The response indicates in the main whether a child can reproduce problem solutions reported by others in books. It indicates whether or not the pupil has correctly made a given connection in experience. Thus intelligence tests and achievement tests measure little besides what has been learned. Their community, the degree to which they measure the same thing or things, is about 90 per cent.

There is no theoretic obstacle in the way of measuring objectively the activities that constitute the problem-solving process, from observation and collection of data, through the tabulation and interpretation of data, to the summarization of results and the formulation of conclusions. The profession does not yet fully sense the need for this advance, but the need will soon be appreciated. Provision will be made for better intellectual training in the schools, after which will come provision for its evaluation. Subject matter will differ for different fields, but the methods of reflection will be essentially the same. Content and process in psychology, terms and relations in logic, subject matter and method in education mark the ends of analysis as they do the objects of measurement, for they rest on the irreducibility of activity and form in experience.

IX. The School and the Social Order

1. Fundamental Principle of Democracy

Not long ago I received a letter from a student at New York University stating that he was writing a doctor's dissertation on the philosophical bases of the activity movement and requesting me to indicate my reaction to the following statement made by an eminent educator:

> As to idealism or realism, I am personally unable to make my peace with them. I do not believe that it is possible to formulate an acceptable philosophy of democracy on any such basis as these philosophies provide. Progressive education must go pragmatic if it is to have a future.

Implied in this statement is a fundamental premise to which we have already acknowledged allegiance, the premise, namely, that in the United States of America one's educational theory cannot be seriously regarded unless it is consistent with the principles of a democratic state. Our first task in the defense of realism against the charge of this educator is therefore to come to some understanding, if possible, concerning fundamental principles of democracy. On this point we should be able to agree with former Chief Justice Hughes and many other American statesmen that the first principle of democracy is *respect for individuality*. This is the source of the emphasis on individual liberty in a democratic state, and on individual interest in schools properly designed for such a state. In fact, freedom of speech, freedom of press, freedom of assembly, and freedom of religious belief are nothing more than corollaries of the doctrine of liberty, logical implications of respect for individuality. Of these essential liberties both instrumentalism and modern realism are staunch defenders. In fact there is no difference between their starting points in educational and political theory. In each the point of departure is individual freedom, initiative, spontaneity, interest.

The realist has therefore no quarrel with a child-centered school if it is not child-circumscribed. He does not object to the school that makes integration of personality its central objective, if the aim is comprehensive enough to include external as well as internal integration. He can even absorb the individual-growth objective into his system, if growth receives its direction from social as well as from individual demands. This is but to emphasize the bipolar character of the modern realistic theory. It would be difficult to find a better illustration of this doctrine than Dewey's description of the relation between the child and the curriculum, written in 1902. Said Dewey at that time:

> The child and the curriculum are simply two limits which define a single process. Just as two points define a straight line, so the present standpoint of the child and the facts and truths of studies define instruction.[1]

2. Excesses of Individualistic Emphasis

The unrestricted emphasis on individualism by some Dewey disciples is due in part to the excesses of their philosophy, in part to the excesses of their interpretation. Consider the educator of progressive allegiance who queried, " Do we need to pay any attention to truth? Isn't it here today and gone tomorrow? " This, one observes, is an exaggeration of pragmatism's doctrine of the relativity of truth, but quite a natural exaggeration. The doctrine of relativism, coupled with the doctrine that one's facts and ideas are the creations of one's intelligence, and that other doctrine that truth is determined not by conformity to something externally given but by the consequences of one's reactions, may well be construed as implying the self-sufficiency of individual sanctions in education. Just stop momentarily and weigh the practical educational implications of the following remark of Dewey's:

> The attempt to bring over from past objects the elements of a standard for valuing future consequences is a hopeless one. The express object of a valuation-judgment is to release factors which being new, cannot be measured on the basis of the past alone.[2]

The attempt to bring over from the past a standard for valuing future consequences does not seem so hopeless as Mr. Dewey makes it out to be. In fact there is no other standard. The behavior of any entity, personal or physical, can be predicted only on the basis of its past performances, and prediction thus founded, indispensable to accurate evaluation, is one of the major objectives of scientific research. It is regrettable when one in his progressive zeal becomes so intent on keeping the gateway to new truth open that he seems to disparage the truth already achieved.

Modern realism accepts the bipolar interpretation of the philosophy

---

[1] John Dewey, *The Child and the Curriculum,* p. 16. Chicago: University of Chicago Press, 1902.

[2] John Dewey, *Essays in Experimental Logic,* pp. 378–79. Chicago: University of Chicago Press, 1916. Pp. vii + 444.

which Dewey offers to educators, rather than the one-sided interpretation offered by those of his followers who are outdoing him in their individualistic emphasis in education. Moreover, the trend in human affairs at this moment is not in the direction of greater individual freedom, but greater individual control. The drift toward license and *laissez faire* has been severely rebuked on the political and economic fronts, even though it continues to be nursed along by the radical fringe in education. The radical theory fails to take account of the truly external determinants of human conduct, the ways of behavior of the physical and personal entities that surround the individual and constitute what is known as his environment. One may dream of a world devoid of compulsion and of obedience to law, but the fulfilment of such a dream is certainly more remote today than it seemed yesterday, and, except for romantic personalities that find their solace in a retreat from reality, it is as a goal that dimly glows at an infinite distance.

After some years of wandering in the wilderness, educators are becoming more and more convinced that individual interest, freedom, or liberty furnishes no complete foundation for either the schools or the government of a democracy. Liberalism in state and school means acceptance of the principle of freedom linked with the principle of authority. Freedom is here defined as exemption from external determination of conduct. The principle of equality, which conflicts at many points with the principle of freedom and which is now receiving much needed attention in America, rests, of course, on the rights of others, the recognition of which automatically places a curb on individualism. The attitude of tolerance so essential to liberalism and the democratic way of life derives its chief justification from the rights of others, their right to be heard, particularly, and introduces into democratic social relations an essential note of duty and responsibility. In a word, the demands of external entities, physical and personal, furnish the foundation of an inescapable factor known as discipline in life.

3. Authority of Truth and Tradition

The principle of authority asserts itself in the guise of the much used and abused conception of tradition. Truth, as was suggested, constitutes an important element of the general social tradition. Constitutions and statutes, institutions and conventions, customs and manners, precedents and prejudices, all are elements of the general fabric of this tradition. It embodies the problem solutions of the past, some of them reflecting the solidity of the findings of science, some of them reflecting the insubstantiality of mere convention, prejudice, or even superstition. They show, for better or for worse, how the conflicts in social experience, the problems of daily life, have been met. Since the findings of social science are, in general, more in dispute than those of physical science, the voice of authority in politics and economics is not so forceful or compelling as that in natural science. But even there the best is not fit object for reckless mockery, else the work of our hands today is held in contempt tomorrow. This may be a healthy attitude for an undergraduate clearing his slate for constructive thinking, like one who iconoclastically remarked to the writer that morality is mere convention: as if " Thou shalt not kill " and " Thou shalt not steal " had no rational foundation in social experience! The ultimate democratic appeal is to the evidence for authority and to the capacity of the community to understand the evidence when presented pro and con by competent leadership.

The fact that the demands of authority are subject to the approval of a majority of the individuals of a given age in a democracy before they are enforced is no proof that individual impulse holds the key to the treasures of the world. It may hold nothing but the key to the treasuries. A burden of taxation necessary to pay our collective debts does not derive its justice from the consent of the governed or lose its avoirdupois just because it is bravely shouldered. When Margaret Fuller decided to accept the universe, it offered her no special inducements. And so with democracy and the schools of the same. A fundamental query today is, " Will the sovereign people pay the price of social salvation? " The champions of democracy believe it will.

4. Defects of Our Present Democracy

The foundation of this belief is deserving of more consideration than it ordinarily receives. There is plenty of evidence that it has been neglected or bungled by many schools and other educational agencies. Otherwise there would not be so many bewildered youth sincerely wondering, as was the case in France, whether democracy in the present crisis is truly deserving of support. Democracy has been taken for granted by our population to such an extent that knowledge of its foundation has been wanting. In lieu of knowledge, the ' sugar daddy ' conception of Uncle Samuel has captured the imagination of millions, and their dear old *pater familias* is fondly pictured rich beyond the dreams of avarice, as fabulous in generosity as he is in resources, surrounded by a prolific progeny blessed with precious rights but burdened with few duties. It is an individualistic dream, a burst of romantic fervor without a basis in reality. Like a tidal wave it has swept through America with its depredations of the privileged and the under-privileged, its lawlessness and crime, its graft and political dishonesty. This is the democracy that conscientious youth despise. This is the democracy from which the Lindberghs fled. Could youth but see that concessions to the freedoms that wrought the terrible Lindbergh tragedy are violations rather than applications of the principles of democracy, they could unite in a sweeping crusade for the clarification of demo-cratic principles and their proper application. A youth organization, free of political-party affiliation, friend of fundamental human rights, foe of the unsocial everywhere, could make a tremendous contribution to the democratic cause. The cure of our social ills is not to be found in submitting to " The Wave of the Future," as if the totalitarianism of Adolf Hitler were cosmic in its proportions, as if Hitler were a man of destiny and democracy were doomed to destruction. Neither logi-cally nor practically do we face the dilemma of a decadent democracy or a corporate state. We do not face this dilemma logically, because de-mocracy must be tried before it can be condemned. And, practically, we seem to remember that there was another man of destiny who swept through Europe like a scourge and was checked in his ambitions of con-quest because a few hardy souls like the Duke of Wellington did not succumb to the spell of the Napoleonic legend nor approve the pur-poses behind it.

5. Faith in a Defensible Hypothesis

Can it be shown that the democratic way of life surpasses others designed to supersede it? There is needless hesitancy in facing this question. To the scientific and empirical mind there is no absolute certainty about any of the great philosophies, any of the great religions, any of the great political ideologies. Youth has absorbed and distorted the trend of this thinking and has become increasingly skeptical, as Mr. Adler laments. The simple faith of the common people in God, or home, or native land becomes the pitiful object of derision and disdain to these sophisticated youth. And in the extremity of their skepticism the sense of values tends to disappear. They forget that even the values of science are not matters of absolute certainty, but of relative cer-tainty; that knowledge varies in degrees of certainty; and that intelli-gent use of knowledge consists in selection and application according to this degree. Here is the foundation for the curriculum of the schools and the legislation of the state; here is the foundation for conclusions and beliefs in any area — a foundation in verified knowledge.

Value, in the last analysis, rests on the facts of human interest. Man is interested in the validity of thought, and so arises logical value. He longs for a power beyond himself that makes for righteousness, and so arises religious value. He is interested in the harmonies of human experience, and thus aesthetic values come to life. He is interested in everything that contributes to the intellectual development of his kind, and so arises educational value. Knowledge of the facts of human preference or selection serves the usual guidance function of knowledge, tilting the balance of opinion toward one or another economic policy, political plan, educational objective. The popular vote in a democracy is an approximate measure of value, the basis of which, according to this theory, is empirical.

The foundation of democracy is natural; not, to our knowledge, supernatural. It rests on generalizations from fact, not presumptions of omniscience. ' Clear and distinct ideas ' that are advertised as compelling in their authority because fresh from the faculty of *Reason* and the citadel of *Truth*, are no more impressive than the capital letters that linger on as a literary tradition in philosophy. Even the assumptions and presuppositions, the fundamental premises which thinking uses as a springboard in any field, are at bottom derivatives from particular items in experience, from the facts of experience. There seem to be no self-evident truths in the field of term-thing relationships. The democratic faith is a political theory or hypothesis. Its central objective is the enhancement of human welfare, the most satisfactory integration of human interests. What better aspiration can be proposed for a state? Respect for individual demands and respect for social demands are fundamental principles of democracy because they seem designed to contribute better than any others to the realization of the greatest welfare for the greatest number. The great virtue of the individual principle is progressive. In the spirit of science and the liberal outlook, it provides for the open door to truth. It operates on the theory that many heads, other things equal, are better than one; that the preferences of the many, in the long run, are more accurately and safely indicative of social value than the preferences of a privileged few, to say nothing of a privileged dictator. It keeps the springs of human spontaneity and invention open to tolerant consideration.

The principle of social demand is the principle of conservation. It acts on the apostolic injunction, " Hold fast that which is good." It means respect for institutions until out of the secret depths of individuality comes the inspiration for a better way. The constitution of the United States is respected as a distinguished solution of a complex problem by a convention of intelligent statesmen, but it is also regarded as subject to change to fit changing conditions, as indeed the constitution in itself provides.[1]

6. Balance between Freedom and Authority

Now a final word of assurance for those who expect the writer at any moment to stretch out a rigid right arm in the Nazi salute. Such an expectation would be the natural reaction of an all-or-nothing mentality, one of those not uncommon minds obsessed with an either-or complex even when confronted with a both-and situation. Objection to individualism, they say, must mean authoritarianism. The world in which we live, they likewise argue, must be one either of permanence or of change: it cannot partake of both aspects. They rush to the conclusion that activity is the all-pervasive educational principle and content nothing but a philosophic fiction. In the same single-track perversity they look upon subject matter as a nonessential, even pernicious, control in education and propose to erect their curricular edifice exclusively on pupil interest. This is the gospel of Jean Jacques Rousseau, exhumed and dusted off, then dressed attractively in modern habiliments, as if it were the resurrection and the life.

The bipolar view proposed as a guide to education is proposed as well for our orientation throughout the general area of social relations. It begins with respect for individual demands, but it includes respect for social demands. It accepts the spirit of the doctrine that man proposes, but God disposes. It asserts that liberty should be supplemented by authority in both school and state; that liberty left to itself is anarchy; that authority heedless of individual demands is totalitarianism. It believes that democracy maintains itself in a flexible middle ground, where it seeks the most effective balance between two complementary factors. " There comes a point in the organization of a complex society," says Chief Justice Stone, " where individualism must yield to traffic rules and where the right to do as one wills with one's own must

---

[1] The Tugwellian theory that the state is a function of the school and the opposing theory that the school is a function of the state are simply ways of emphasizing respect for freedom, on the one hand, and organization, on the other. It is the writer's contention that a theory of interaction, of flow and counter flow between school and state, offers a more rational foundation for social action.

bow to zoning ordinances or even to price-fixing regulations. Just where the line is to be drawn between individual liberty and government action for the larger good is the perpetual question of constitutional law." Thus, the central problem of both political and educational theory seems to be the discovery of the proper emphasis to place on each of these two inescapable principles. Education can no more travel on one alone than can a cart on a single wheel.

REFERENCES

BODE, B. H. *Progressive Education at the Crossroads.* New York and Chicago: Newson & Co., 1938. Pp. 128.

BREED, FREDERICK S. *Education and the New Realism.* New York: Macmillan Co., 1939. Pp. xx +237.

BREED, FREDERICK S. "The Road to Objectivity in Education," *School and Society,* LII (August 10, 1940), 81–86.

Contemporary American Philosophy. 2 vols. (George P. Adams and William P. Montague, eds.) New York: Macmillan Co., 1930. Pp. 9–450; 9–447.

DEWEY, JOHN. *The Child and the Curriculum.* Chicago: University of Chicago Press, 1902. Pp. 40.

DEWEY, JOHN. *Experience and Education.* New York: Macmillan Co., 1938. Pp. xiii + 116.

JAMES, WILLIAM. *Some Problems of Philosophy:* A Beginning of an Introduction to Philosophy. New York: Longmans, Green & Co., 1911. Pp. xi + 236.

The New Realism: Cooperative Studies in Philosophy. New York: Macmillan Co., 1912. Pp. xii + 491.

PERRY, RALPH BARTON. *General Theory of Value:* Its Meaning and Basic Principles Construed in Terms of Interest. New York: Longmans, Green & Co., 1926. Pp. xvii + 702.

PERRY, RALPH BARTON. *Present Philosophical Tendencies.* New York: Longmans, Green & Co., 1912. Pp. xv + 383.

PERRY, RALPH BARTON. *The Thought and Character of William James,* as Revealed in Unpublished Correspondence and Notes together with his Published Writings. 2 vols. Boston: Little, Brown & Co., 1935. Pp. xxviii + 826; xxii + 786.

RUSSELL, BERTRAND. *Sceptical Essays.* New York: W. W. Norton & Co., Inc., 1928. Pp. 11–256.

RUSSELL, BERTRAND. *Scientific Method in Philosophy.* Chicago and London: Open Court Publishing Co., 1915. Pp. 30.

SANTAYANA, GEORGE. *Winds of Doctrine:* Studies in Contemporary Opinion. London and Toronto: J. M. Dent & Sons, Ltd., 1926. Pp. vii + 215.

WHITEHEAD, ALFRED NORTH. *Modes of Thought.* New York: Macmillan Co., 1938. Pp. viii + 241.

WHITEHEAD, ALFRED NORTH. *Process and Reality:* An Essay in Cosmology. New York: Macmillan Co., 1929. Pp. xii + 547.

WHITEHEAD, ALFRED NORTH. *Science and the Modern World.* New York: Macmillan Co., 1926. Pp. xi + 296.

CHAPTER IV

AN IDEALISTIC PHILOSOPHY OF EDUCATION

HERMAN H. HORNE
Professor of Education, New York University
New York City, New York

I. IDEALISM AS A PHILOSOPHY

The title of this chapter is too ambitious for the space allotted to it. 'Idealism,' 'philosophy,' and 'education' are three large terms. If brevity were only the soul of wisdom as well as of wit!

1. Definition of Terms

Philosophy is the mind of man wrestling with the universe. Sometimes the mind takes a fall, and begins to wonder what we really know (skepticism). Sometimes it takes a worse fall, and concludes we cannot know anything (agnosticism). But all science represents partial successes of the mind in wrestling with selected portions of the universe. And such partial successes urge the mind of man on to inquire concerning the nature and meaning of the whole (world view or *weltanschauung*).

Idealism is the conclusion that the universe is an expression of intelligence and will, that the enduring substance of the world is of the nature of mind, that the material is explained by the mental. Idealism as a philosophy stands in contrast with all those systems of thought that center in nature (naturalism) or in man (humanism).

Idealism as a philosophy has its characteristic answer to all the main questions about our world. What is it *to be?* Or, what is *being?* Take the example, "The apple is red." The copula 'is' links the subject, 'apple' with the predicate, 'red.' But suppose there is no predicate and we have only the statement, "The apple is." What does 'is' mean now? Philosophers differ as to the meaning of 'is,' 'are,' 'to be.' In grammar the verb 'to be' is irregular; this may suggest that the being of the universe is complex and not easy to define. The problem of the nature of being is called by the technical term *ontology.* And to say it abruptly, according to idealism, *to be* is to be experienced by an absolute self. There are different forms of idealism but

139

into these we will not go as yet. Continuing our idealistic answers: To what is the order of the world due? The order of the world is the problem of cosmology, and idealism holds that the order of the world is due to the manifestation in space and time of an eternal and spiritual reality. What is knowledge? Knowledge is the problem of epistemology, and idealism holds that knowledge is man thinking the thoughts and purposes of this eternal and spiritual reality as they are embodied in our world of fact. What is beauty? Beauty is the problem of aesthetics, and idealism says that the beauty of nature which man enjoys and the beauty of art which man produces is the perfection of the infinite whole of reality expressing itself in finite forms. And what is goodness? Goodness is the problem of ethics, and idealism holds that the goodness of man's individual and social life is the conformity of the human will with the moral administration of the universe.

These highly abstract statements will become clearer as the argument advances. They suggest to us now that education and its philosophy need to be understood against a universal background of meaning and purpose, and that they are not simply man's puny efforts at progress in a neutral and alien universe.

Education should be thought of as the process of man's reciprocal adjustment to nature, to his fellows, and to the ultimate nature of the cosmos. In this process the individual both adjusts himself to his world and, in a lesser sense, his world to himself. He learns to know the ways of nature and in a measure to control her ways. He learns what his fellows require of him and how to work with and to influence them. And he learns, if his education is at all complete, to sense his kinship with the responsive heart of reality, to feel himself at home in the universe, and not an orphan or an alien in his world. Not only the individual, but human society itself, is becoming increasingly adjusted both to the kind of world in which it lives and to itself, despite all appearances to the contrary in the mutual antagonisms of its parts.

An idealistic philosophy of education, then, is an account of man finding himself as an integral part of a universe of mind.

But why say the universe of reality partakes of the nature of mind? Why be an idealist? In answering this question we shall not first undertake to show why the leading differing philosophies of naturalism and humanism in their varied forms (realism, pragmatism, etc.) are held to be inadequate. Rather, we shall come to the heart of the matter at once and say what the reasons are for accepting idealism.

If these reasons are convincing, they will of themselves provide the answer to opposing systems.

2. Living and Thinking

First, let it be observed that we probably live our way into a system of thinking rather than think our way into a pattern of living. This means that living is more influential in determining thinking than thinking is in determining living. All the acquired habits of childhood and early adolescence give a certain trend to our thinking, so that when the study of the various philosophies begins we are already predisposed to accept a certain one and to reject the others. Thus, children reared in a strictly scientific home tend later to accept naturalism, those reared in a strictly ethical and social home tend later to accept humanism, while those reared in a religious home tend to accept idealism.

While it is true that life determines thought rather than thought determines life, it is also true that thought does to some extent determine life. Once the issues of philosophy are squarely raised and faced during or after the period of adolescence, thinking begins to influence our beliefs and our conduct.

Or course, much thinking is rationalizing, that is, giving the best reasons we can for continuing to hold the views we have. The writer of this section may of course be mistaken in the personal judgment that he would be willing to surrender his belief in idealism if any other philosophy had in it as much inner consistency, harmony with known fact, inspiration for effective living, and practical guidance. However, it is possible to think objectively without rationalizing, whether we end by retaining or by modifying our old beliefs. It is further to be recognized that, if we continue to grow with the years, there is a constant interplay between actions and beliefs, each modifying to some extent the other.

3. Grounds for Accepting Idealism

What, then, are the grounds for accepting an idealistic interpretation of the universe? There are several. They do not demonstrate the validity of idealism, but they indicate why idealism is a reasonable philosophy to hold. They may be rejected one by one, yet they have a certain cumulative force when taken together.

a. *Mind is the principle of explanation.* There is no denying this fact. It is our minds that raise problems, face problems, and seek the solution of problems. We think with our minds, using our bodies as aids. Mind is the explainer. Mind as the explainer is real. Mind, the real explainer, cannot consistently regard itself as unreal. Neither can mind, the real explainer, consistently say that anything else than itself is more real than itself. For this supposed thing other than itself, supposed to be more real than itself, is *itself a conception of mind.* The very conception of something other than mind is itself a conception of mind. Even the famous 'thing-in-itself' of Immanuel Kant is a concept made by the mind. We live, and move, and have our intellectual being in a world of mind. There is no adequate denial of this fact.

Of course, be it said, this is just another case of Professor Perry's "ego-centric predicament," that our thinking of something external as mental does not prove it to be mental. True enough. But this same predicament forever makes it impossible for the mind to prove itself unreal, or even less real than the supposed nonmental thing alleged to explain it.

Perhaps it should be said at this point that what we mean by mind is just what we introspectively know ourselves to be. We think, we feel, we purpose; we know what we think, feel, and purpose; we are selves; we are self-conscious; we are egos in relation to other egos. And we claim that the universe is of the nature of mind because we cannot consistently claim anything else. It is not only *with* mind but also *by* mind that we explain, that is, by concepts framed by the mind. Mind, subjectively used and objectively applied, is the sole principle of explanation.

Why then do not all nonidealists recognize the validity of this argument and accept idealism? Because they have not been conditioned to the idealistic way of thinking; because, though the argument is interesting, perhaps persuasive, it is not convincing to them; and because they have other principles of explanation to propose than that of mind.

b. Mind is not matter. Matter occupies space, mind does not occupy space. Space itself as we conceive it is an idea in our own mind. Whatever else space is, in addition to an idea in our own mind, may (reasoning by analogy) very well be an idea in the universal mind. Matter has weight, but the mind has no weight. Weight itself as sensed or conceived by us is a sensation or an idea in our own mind, and whatever else weight is beyond our own mind may very well be (reasoning by analogy again) an idea in the universal mind. Occupying space and having weight, matter of course has dimensions, but the mind has no dimensions; it is neither long nor short, neither thick nor thin, neither broad nor narrow. But all these dimensional qualities are, as we conceive them, ideas in our own minds; and again whatever else they are beyond our minds may (again reasoning by analogy) very well be ideas in the universal mind. St. Augustine was arguing in the fourth century (*De Quantitate Animae*) that the soul is not corporeal since it has conceptions of the incorporeal, e.g., the mathematical point.

The mind that thinks matter cannot itself be matter, and matter, being unintelligent, cannot think itself. Mind has a remembered past and an anticipated future, and matter in its continuing existence neither remembers nor anticipates. The mind has meanings; it knows what it means to say and do; but matter has meaning only for a mind that knows it and sees its relationships, and has no meaning to itself. The mind experiences pleasures and desires to repeat them, experiences pains and desires to avoid them, but matter is insensate and feels neither pleasures nor pains. The mind has conscience, a sense of right and wrong, and experiences satisfaction in doing the simple right and experiences remorse in doing the devious wrong, but matter is indifferent to right and wrong. The language of ethics is inapplicable to the reactions of matter. The mind possesses, or may possess, a knowledge of the truth, but matter, though it may be known, itself knows nothing. Mind perceives the qualities of the world, such as colors, tones, tastes, odors, but matter, though it may be composed of waves, perceives no qualities. For these reasons and many others of a like import, we must conclude that mind is too qualitatively different from matter ever to be regarded as matter or as a product of matter, though matter may be regarded as objectified mind, or mind in its 'otherness,' as painting objectifies the thought, feeling, and purpose of the artist.

c. Mind comes from mind. Like comes from like. Mind is too unlike matter to be a derivative of matter. But finite minds may be derived by heredity from finite minds, and the presence of any finite minds at all in the stream of time may very well be due to the self-manifestation of an infinite mind, just as the universal law of gravity manifests itself in every falling body, or as the sun that shines for all is mirrored in every dewdrop.

The idea is sometimes expressed that despite the dissimilarity of mind and matter, mind might yet have come from matter by a proc-

ess of 'emergent evolution.' Interesting illustrations are given of
how new substances arise out of preëxistent conditions which do not
prefigure what is to come. Thus, common table salt, though derived
from sodium and chlorine, has qualities neither of these possesses.
And water, regarded by Thales as the principle of reality, is derived
from two gases neither of which has the properties of water, which will
devour the flames of its own constituent gases. But there are three ob-
jections to the view of emergent evolution that mind comes from
matter. The first is that based on the principle of Aristotle that every
potentiality is based on a preceding actuality: without *energeia*
no *dunamis*. There must be a realized actual mind before there
can be a potential derived mind. There must exist a reservoir of
universal mind before any streamlets of mind can trickle through
matter.

Second, there is no evolution, emergent or other, without previous
involution. Nothing more can come out of the egg of potentiality
than went into its making. From nothing comes nothing. From the
nonmental comes only the nonmental. If mind eventuates, then mind
originated. It is both common sense and reason to hold that if mind
is itself and not matter, then it came from mind and not from matter.
Without involution, no evolution.

Third, evolution itself would appear to be a purposive process.
There is a suitability about the environment for the production of organisms. In this sense the environment itself is biocentric. There is
a suitability about living organisms for the appearance of mind. In
this sense the organic world is itself psychocentric. There is at least
an immanent purposiveness in the evolutionary process which eventuates in life and mind. Every event in the process has its antecedent
cause and its consequent effect. The cause is not only efficient but
also final. The end is a purposive outcome of the process. Emergent
evolution itself is the outcome of an immanent design or intention.
This immanent design in time really is not self-explanatory but implies an eternal and universal purpose.

For these three reasons, then, we hold that no process of emergent
evolution, unless mind is at its basis, could produce mind out of
matter and that, consequently, mind must be thought to come only
from mind.

It may be objected that we should adopt a functional view of
mind and hold that the mind is a function of the brain, or of the
total living organism in relation to a problematic environment. This

is the naturalistic view of mind. In its cruder materialistic form in the eighteenth century (Moleschott, De la Mettrie) the view was held that the brain secretes thought as the liver secretes bile. But bile is material and we have seen that mind cannot be held to be material. At this point the striking analogy fails. But the very notion of the mind as a function of the brain or of the living organism is itself one of the conceptions held of mind. The mind that can formulate such a conception to describe and explain itself is more than the conception it formulates. The producer is greater than the single product. The mind as the explainer is the source of the concept of mind as a function. Recall the argument for the first position above, that mind not only explains, but is the very principle of all final explanation. Other philosophies use mind to explain by reference to some other reality than itself but do not make mind the principle of explanation. This is not to deny that much thinking is 'operational' in character, but rather to assert that operational thinking is not the whole story of mental activity and reality.

Again, it may be objected that it sounds as well to say matter explains mind as it does to say mind explains matter. But the objection is specious. It presupposes that mind and matter are convertible terms, or have interchangeable reality. Our argument could not allow this to be the case, seeing that 'matter' is a concept of mind and that it is stultifying to claim any equivalence of value in the two, or that the greater value inheres in nonmental matter.

Again, it may be objected that such common facts of experience as the existence of the vermiform appendix or the pineal gland indicate a mechanical rather than a teleological explanation of natural phenomena. Two things are to be said here. The first is that these now supposedly purposeless things may yet have purposes in the organism of which we are unaware, or may come to have them, as color-blind people have an advantage over those with normal vision in detecting camouflage. Geographers know the uses of the Sahara Desert. The taking over of new functions by an older part of the organism is not unknown; e.g., when the left brain is injured, the right brain may assume some of its functions, as in speech. But even apart from the question of the possible usefulness of such 'vestigial remains,' and on the supposition that such parts are now useless, they are nevertheless mute witnesses to the fact of their former utility. They once served a purpose, even as shells of the seashore were once useful to their owners. We need not be surprised that purpose, as it shapes matter to its own ends and moves on to new ends, should leave behind a record of ' outgrown shells.' Such a record does not prove mechanism or disprove purpose so much as it proves that purpose is on the march in time.

d. *There can be no object without a subject.* An object is always an object of thought. The subject is a thinker. The thinker thinks an object. The thinker may think itself and thus make itself its own object. Whatever the thinker thinks about becomes for him the object of his thought. An alleged world of objects without a thinker to think them is a self-contradiction. The proposition that without a subject there is no object is true of all thinkers whatsoever. The world exists for the finite thinker only as he thinks the world. If he thinks the world exists when he is not thinking of it, it exists for him as this independent thing which he thinks it to be. The transition is easy in thought from the world as the object of finite thinking to the world as the object of infinite thinking. The world then would exist in itself as the object of infinite thinking just as it exists for us as the object of finite thinking. And because thinking the world and the will to have a world go together as phases of the mental process, man has a world because it fulfills his purposes to have a world. Even so, we may suppose, the world exists in itself as it is thought and willed, that is, ordered and sustained, by the universal mind whose thought the world is and whose purpose the world fulfills. This line of argument is epistemological. It holds that the kind of world we know suggests that it is itself the expression of a universal intelligence in whose image our own intelligence is cast. On this point a historian of philosophy writes:

These doctrines, in which the *subject* and the *object* are for the first time opposed to each other, exaggerate a highly important truth — the truth that reality is not something external to the thinking and feeling subject: that the feeling and thinking object is a coefficient in the production of the phenomenon; in a world, that thought — whether it be transformed sensation or something else — is one of the principles of things, one of those primary conditions of reality for which philosophy has been seeking, a principle which it divined in the logos of Heraclitus, the One of Pythagoreanism, and the *nous* of Anaxagoras. Thought *not only strives* to reduce things to a unity, it *is* the unifying principle itself, that which unifies and measures reality; it is, indeed, the measure of all things.[1]

---

[1] Alfred Weber, *History of Philosophy*, p. 42. New York: Charles Scribner's Sons, 1925.

e. Man has an inalienable conviction that personality is reality.
He may deny it, but in denying the reality of personality he is paying tribute to the apparent worth of personality. It is that which has value in itself, that for which other values exist, and that which is deserving of respect above all things. By personality is meant the quality or state of being a person; and by person is meant a self-conscious center of experience. A person knows himself as an individual, as responsible for his acts, and as responsive to the claims of his higher nature upon him.

Now personality, like mind, must have an origin adequate to explain it. Such categories as chance, mechanism, necessity, evolution, emergent evolution, or all of these together, are not an adequate explanation of the origin of personality in the stream of time. Personality might conceivably be in the line of descent from the super-personal but it could not be in the line of ascent from the impersonal, for the same reason that a stream cannot rise higher than its source. The personality of man and the values inherent in it proclaim an infinite mind that thinks the universe in personal terms. But to think the universe in terms of an original Person expressing himself in finite persons is idealism as a philosophy. The final test of the value of any economic, political, social, or educational system is the effect it has on individual personality.

There are different kinds of idealism but they all stress the reality of personality, though in unequal degrees. We have both subjective idealism and objective idealism. Subjective idealism is the view that only persons exist, that there is no world of material existence between persons, that ideas of the external world take the place of an existent external world. Objective idealism maintains that there is an external world of nature but that it exists in space and time as the expressed thought and purpose of the universal mind. Subjective idealism stresses the exclusive reality of persons while objective idealism stresses the manifestations of the universal mind both in the realm of nature and in finite persons.

We have also personal and absolute idealism. Personal idealism stresses the independent reality of each person, both finite and infinite. Finite persons are held to fall outside the conscious life of the infinite, to exist in their own right and not as included thoughts of the infinite. Personal idealism reaches its conclusions through emphasis on the ethical consciousness. Absolute idealism, on the other hand, maintains that all reality, including finite person, exists as experienced by the absolute, that finite persons live, move, and have their being within an absolute whole of experience. Absolute idealism reaches its conclusion through recognition of the fragmentary character of all finite experience which implies a whole, and also through emphasis on the unifying relations which must bind all persons together. Absolute idealism is careful not to ascribe personality in anthropomorphic terms to the infinite but insists that finite personality has its fulfillment, that is, its complete realization, in the infinite. Absolute idealism is fearful lest the emphasis on the mutual independence of all personalities lead to the conception of a finite deity.

Thus the concept of the reality of personality is bound up with the conception of idealism that reality is of the nature of mind. All forms of idealism hold that reality is personal or it is that which by thinking makes personality possible. Man's conviction that personality is real is warranted by idealism as a philosophy.

Some readers may be interested to know whether objective idealism is the same as pantheism. It is not. Both systems of thought are forms of theism but there the resemblance ends. In the system of pantheism the divine essence is distributed through all things as their sole reality, and what is apparently other than this divine essence is illusion. God is all and is held to be impersonal. In the system of objective idealism, all things exist as content of the absolute experience. They exist as willed and as thought. All is not God, but all is God's. The absolute experience is properly conceived as an infinite person, fulfilling and surpassing all that can be meant by a finite personality.

f. Man also has the conviction that he is a free moral agent. This conviction is justified, if idealism be true. It is also justified, be it said, by that form of pragmatism held by William James. Man may seek to convince himself by scientific ratiocination that he is not a free moral agent, but his sense of being such remains with him nevertheless. Man denies his own freedom through some concept of his own, like determinism, mechanism, causation, and the like. But these concepts were devised by man to assist him in understanding and in controlling for his own purposes the course of nature. They are themselves the evidence of man's mental creative freedom. Man shows his freedom in applying his own concept of determination to his own behavior; he does not have to do so; he does so because he wills to do so. He is like the boy who says " q " when he says " I shan't say ' q '."

But a world in which personality has freedom is an idealistic world, a world of the nature of mind, a world in which mind explains matter but matter does not explain mind, a world in which personality counts for most as it reshapes conditions to meet its own purposes. If reality is of the nature of mind and mind's nature is to reveal and express itself, then man's conviction that he is a free moral agent is justified.

g. *Idealism as a philosophy supports this belief of man, that man's self is immortal.* Man as a race has had the intuition that he was not born to die. This intuition implies an idealistic world. If reality is of the nature of mind, is personal, then the destruction of selfhood is paradoxical and self-contradictory. The immortality of the self of man is one with the view that the origin of mind is mind. The question of the origin of mind looks backward, the question of the survival of mind looks forward. In each case the answer is the same if reality is of the nature of mind. Man lives because mind is real and man will live because mind is real.

The evidence for man's immortality lies in the rationality of the universe. All progress in scientific knowledge is evidence that the world is intelligible, understandable, amenable to law. But if the death of the body, which is itself a creature of mind, meant the death of the mind too, then mind would not be the reality after all. But in a rational world whose order expresses mentality, it would be sheer waste and contradiction to destroy what mind had produced. The belief in man's immortality is a logical consequence of accepting the reality and universality of mind in our world.

Idealism has its own theory of the relation of mind and body. " The mind is form and doth the body make," wrote Edmund Spenser, expressing both a Platonic and an Aristotelian viewpoint. The mind makes the body as the tool of the mind, as the means of communication in space, as the instrument for the expression of purposes in time. The body being effect and mind the cause, the death of the body leaves the mind free to utilize another means of expression and communication.

Idealism is not averse to receiving experimental evidence through psychical phenomena, or otherwise, of the soul's survival of bodily death but it is not dependent upon such evidence for its belief in the immortality of personality. Man's intuition of his own immortality suggests idealism, and idealism would warrant the belief in man's immortality.

h. *Man has the conviction that the ends of justice are met,* that there is a moral world-order, that no man can flout the moral law and ' get away with it,' that in the end there is a return of the deed on the doer, that the law of cause and effect holds in the moral world, that the consequences of doing right have survival value, that the consequences of doing wrong are self-destructive. In the inner world of personal ex-

perience, if not always in the outer world of criminals and courts of
law, these ethical convictions of mankind are justified over and over.
These convictions are fully warranted and sanctioned by an idealistic
interpretation of the universe. The good is just the nature of absolute
reality, and moral evil is the opposition of man to the very nature of
reality. A moral world-order is itself a phase of an idealistic interpretation of the universe. The absolute fulfills the ethical demands of
men.

Idealism as a philosophy is not committed to the idea of an unending
heaven or everlasting hell for good and wicked souls. It is enough that
souls are on their way toward their chosen destiny. Conceivably, good
choices would be increasingly satisfying and evil choices increasingly
unsatisfying. The influence of these consequences might well work,
even against the laws of habit, to bring all souls finally into allegiance
to the good. On the other hand, there is nothing to exclude the possibility that evil souls might continue to choose their own degradation,
at the cost of suffering to themselves and God. In either case the ends
of justice are met and the moral order of the world maintained.

   i. *The religious intuitions of the race suggest some form of idealism.*
Man's religious nature is as natural, profound, and significant as any
other quality of his being, such as the logical, the aesthetic, the ethical.
All races of mankind have their characteristic religion. It is rare for
any anthropologist to claim for any primitive group of people the entire absence of all religious beliefs and practices. There is something
about religion that meets a profound need of man and that makes a real
demand on the universe that it be worshipful and responsive. It is
man's religious intuition that the world is a spiritual order just as it is
his ethical intuition that the world is a moral order. This does not
prove that the world is what man intuits it as being. But it does prove
that the universe, which made man what he is, made him religious. If
the universe were only a machine, it would be logical to expect man to
be only a machine. But man is a worshipping being, and so it is natural
to hold that the universe is in some sense worshipful. The environment
of man has made him a religious being. Man is probably made in the
image of his Maker. The universe itself must have in it that fulfilment
which the nature of man, the child of the universe, demands. These
conclusions would not follow with such conviction if religion were a
sporadic or sportive response of man to his world. But it is elemental
and universal. There is water for gills and fins, there is air for lungs
and wings, there is earth for feet and crawling things. By analogy it

is easy to suppose that there is a Spirit answering the spirit in man and that spirit and Spirit can meet. Ours is the kind of world in which religions flourish. They have survival value. They meet a need. They indicate the correspondence of man with his fashioning environment. If there is this correspondence, then indeed reality is of the nature of mind and spirit.

  j. There have been great minds in the world which have championed each of the leading divergent philosophies. It is the logical fallacy of *argumentum ad hominem* to claim that a view is acceptable because great minds have accepted it. But one can conclude that if one finds some of the greatest minds of the race have accepted idealism then *one may not justifiably reject idealism without giving it due consideration.* The distinction of the supporters of idealism lend it some presumptive evidence. And among some of the great minds of the race in the western tradition which have accepted idealism in some form as a philosophy of life are Plato, St. Augustine, Thomas Aquinas, Berkeley, Leibniz, Fichte, Schelling, Schopenhauer, Hegel, Lotze, Carlyle, Emerson, T. H. Green, Borden P. Bowne, Edward Caird, William Wallace, D. G. Ritchie, John Watson, F. H. Bradley, Josiah Royce, Benedetto Croce, Giovanni Gentile, J. S. Mackenzie, A. E. Taylor, Bernard Bosanquet, G. H. Howison, Sir Henry Jones, Mary Whiton Calkins, J. E. Creighton, J. A. Leighton, May Sinclair, E. S. Brightman, Marie C. Swabey, R. C. Lodge, W. E. Hocking, Hilda Oakeley, R. F. A. Hoernlé, R. T. Flewelling. It would take many years just to read what these have written. These names are many, significant, and important and because of them we are not warranted in rejecting idealism hastily. Similar tests could of course be made of the opponents of idealism, leading to a similar conclusion, that these philosophies too must not be hastily rejected. Other writers in this volume will speak for these. The study of philosophy is valuable, not because it gives us the final answers to our questions, but because it gives us the possible answers. Final answers to open questions are narrowing, possible answers are broadening.

  At this point we turn from the general exposition of idealism as a philosophy to its application in the field of education. In so doing we shall follow in the main the general plan of this book and, omitting other weighty matters, refer in some detail and in the order given to the following five matters: the learner and his learning, the curriculum, the methods of teaching, the interest of society in education, and the objectives of living and educating.

II. Idealism as a Philosophy of Education

1. The Learner and His Learning

What or who is the learner? Certain philosophies, consistently with their content, phrase the question concerning the nature of man, " What am I? " [1] Different philosophies prefer to phrase the question thus: Who am I?

a. The Naturalistic View. The learner is not just a certain grouping or organization of atoms, each atom being composed of its constituent electrons, positrons, neutrons, etc. This view reduces the learner to a *what* or a *somewhat*. It is the view that must logically be taken by all naturalistic philosophies, whether materialism, energism, or positivism. ' Naturalism ' as a philosophy holds that nature is all, and by ' nature ' is meant the total series of events in space-time moving according to inviolable law. If the matter that occupies space is held to be reducible to atoms, we have ' materialism ' (Democritus). If atoms are further reduced to energy, electrical or other, we have ' energism ' (Ostwald). If man's science of this natural world is held to be the only correct view of the universe, we have ' positivism ' (Comte).

According to ' naturalism,' not only is the pupil a grouping of atoms but his reactions to the actions of his environment are mechanical. He is really a machine.

This view is inadequate because it omits consideration of the pupil as a living, conscious being who has intentions, desires, purposes, feelings, thoughts, and decisions of his own. It holds the pupil to be of the same essence as the earth upon which he treads. It omits the essential distinction that the earth (we suppose) does not know it is being trod upon, but the pupil knows it. A teacher who accepts naturalism as a philosophy may, while in the act of teaching, actually regard his pupils as nonmechanical and unpredictable in their responses but he will not be logically consistent.

b. The Realistic View. Neither is the pupil just a nervous system in a physical body responding selectively to the stimuli of his environment. This is the view of modern realism, not Platonic realism, not scholastic realism. It is the view of that modern realism which holds that the most real things are those that appeal to the senses, that the object which we sense is more real than our sensation of it, that the real

---

[1] Cf. the title of the volume by the neorealist, E. G. Spaulding, *What Am I?* New York: Charles Scribner's Sons, 1928.

object is independent of our sensation of it or of any knowledge of it, and that we know the object as it is. This is the view of current ' neorealism ' (R. B. Perry), not the view, however, of the ' critical realists ' (Durant Drake) who hold with Kant that we do not know the real object but only its appearances and that these appearances are of course dependent on the knower. In accordance with the view of ' neorealism,' the pupil is a series of mechanical reactions to selected stimuli. The nervous system itself does the selecting.

Neorealism has the advantage over naturalism of emphasizing the distinction between living and nonliving bodies and between conscious and nonconscious bodies, but its view of the pupil is inadequate because it treats his reactions as still mechanical, though selective. In the view of idealism, the pupil is a creature whose own consciousness is one of the determinants of his behavior, instead of being merely a living body with mechanical responses to stimuli selected by the needs and interests of his nervous system. Consciousness is not that ' epiphenomenon ' described by Huxley which is without effect upon the chain of events. Instead, consciousness itself is a useful addition to the organism. The fact of its presence is an indication of the need of the organism for it, and the fact of its continuance is witness to its utility and efficacy. As in the case of the teacher who accepts naturalism as a philosophy, the attitude toward his pupils of the teacher who accepts realism may not be logically consistent.

c. The Pragmatic View. Nor is the pupil just a ' behaving organism ' (the phrase of Professor William James), not even if this organism be endowed with the capacity for an undetermined and original response to a specific situation. This conception of the pupil is that of pragmatism. It has the advantage over naturalism and realism of recognizing the unpredictable factor in the behavior of the pupil which makes of him an individual who counts for something in the creation of values in the world. And yet even the pragmatic conception of the learner lacks an essential element. As the idealist sees it, the learner is not only an individual, he is also a person. Organisms may have individuality, but our pupils have personality. The term individuality refers particularly to the differences that distinguish one being from another, but personality refers to the state or quality of being a self, or a conscious center of experience. Persons have individuality, but so do lower animals and inanimate objects. Only human beings are persons, with the capacity to formulate, feel, and follow ideals of conduct. Pragmatism emphasizes individuality, not personality. A teacher who

accepts pragmatism may not always be consistent with it in his attitude toward his pupils. And let it be said too that a teacher who accepts idealism may not always exemplify his philosophy in his attitudes toward his pupils.

d. *The Idealistic View.* Personality has ultimate worth, that is, we
know and can think of nothing higher or more valuable than selfhood,
or personality. Respect for personality in feeling and behavior is as
lofty a virtue as we know. It is the virtue which, if practiced, would
solve our human problems. In a sense it is true that civilizations make
personalities, but in a larger sense it is true that personalities make
civilizations. They are in the front and, for better or for worse, lead
civilizations. This is true of lower as well as of higher types of civilizations. No civilization or culture of a people surpasses that of its
greatest leader. Under the wrong sort of leader past values may be lost.

One of the marvels of our experience is that which we know as the
growth of personality. The growth of the physical organism is marvelous enough, and the more we know of it the more we are led to marvel
at it. But the growth of the person, or the spirit, in man is even more
marvelous. A correct psychology leaves us no less amazed than does
physiology. The person seems endowed with unlimited capacities for
growth in the attainment of knowledge and wisdom, in the production
and enjoyment of the beautiful, and in the acquisition of the ideal virtues of understanding, sympathy, coöperation, forgiveness, and self-
sacrifice.

The learner should really be thought of as a finite personality growing into the likeness of an infinite ideal. The pupil makes a personal
response to his physical and social environment. This view would appear to be both true and challenging.

In our conception of the learner we may progress from the atomic
organization of the naturalist to the selective nervous system of the
realist, then to the behaving organism of the pragmatist, and then on
to the growing, finite personality of the idealist. In our conception of
the responses of the pupil, we may progress from the mechanical reactions of naturalist and realist to the creative response of the pragmatist
and then to the personal, chosen, response of the idealist.

e. *The Environment as Spiritual.* The environment of the person
to which his chosen responses are made may be properly regarded as
spiritual. By this it is meant that the social environment exists for a
purpose and that the physical environment exists for a purpose. If the
environment is purposeful, it may properly be regarded as spiritual.

The reason why the social environment may be regarded as purposeful is that the individuals composing it have purposes, that different social and political groups have purposes, and that the course of development of human society seems to be realizing the purpose of developing higher types of individual and social living. If this result is actually being accomplished through the weak efforts of man, it is easy to infer that the cosmos, whose offspring man is, is purposeful too. For purpose to exist in the part, it is logical to suppose that purpose exists in the whole which explains the part. But as purpose in the part implies the finite personality having the purpose, so may purpose in the whole imply an infinite personality. There are admittedly gaps in this argument, as there are bound to be gaps in any argument which builds a conception of the whole from a knowledge of the part. If these gaps do not disturb us unduly, we may pass to the conception of the pupil as a finite personality growing through our tutelage into the likeness of an infinite personality, whose thought and purpose the world embodies. And thus the environment of the pupil may be sensed as spiritual.

This spiritual environment of man, or this spirit whose thought and purpose are embodied in the environment of man, becomes an adequate conception of the origin of man. The progress of man in self-realization, in the victory of mind over matter, in the knowledge of his world, in the more equable distribution of the physical goods of life, in the recognition of the common man, in the more peaceful communities of human society, all indicate a measure of freedom of man in achievement. And the fact that no limit seems to be set to man's capacity for achievement, that he never fully realizes his ideal, that there is always more to know, to enjoy, to be, and to become, suggests that the spirit of man is fitted for ever more living and not for ceasing to be. Man is never as wise, as artistic, as social, or as ethical as he seems capable of becoming. This is as true of societies as of individuals. These things intimate, although they do not demonstrate, ceaseless living as man's goal.

Summing up our conception of the learner in the light of all these things, our philosophy dares to suggest that the learner is a finite person, growing, when properly educated, into the image of an infinite person, that his real origin is deity, that his nature is freedom, and that his destiny is immortality. This idealistic conception of the learner in no wise minimizes the fact that our pupils, like ourselves, are often ignorant, negligent, unaesthetic, wilful, perverse, enslaved by bad habits, and far removed from their proper estate. Such conditions, however, only accentuate the necessity and importance of education. They do not mean man is uneducable. They only mean he is not yet educated, indeed, never will be completely educated — that is what his immortality portends.

The learner becomes the educated person. The educated person is not just a complicated mechanism, not just a set of conditional reflexes, not just another, though higher, animal, not even a cultivated vocationalist. He is a cultivated personality, ever becoming more cultivated and more of a person. His vocation (his skill) whereby he earns his living is but one of his characteristics. He is himself a cause and is not ruled by causes alone. The unfulfilled ends of his being are the increasing knowledge of the truth, increasing wisdom in the application of his knowledge to the problems of living, increasing enjoyment of persons and things worthy of love and appreciation, increasing realization of a proper organization of mankind on the earth, increasing fulfilment of an unconditional obligation to know and to do the right, and increasing reverence for the spiritual realities of existence. We are not meaning to deny that there are material, physical, and practical aspects of man's existence on the earth. We mean only to affirm that all these things find their true fulfilment in the ideal ends of living. Man cannot live without bread and he cannot live humanly and spiritually by bread alone.

It remains to observe that not all learners conform to one philosophical type, neither do their teachers. As there are different types of philosophy, such as naturalism, realism, idealism, pragmatism, and others, so are there different types of pupils and teachers. Not that any person is exclusively and consistently a representative of any one type of philosophy, but that each person is likely to belong dominantly to some one type. The kind of philosophy we represent depends partly on our inherited disposition, partly on the training and experiences we have had, and partly upon our choices, based upon reflection, of ideals to follow.

This is not the place to enter upon a description of the different leading philosophical types of pupil and teacher, but at least a few words may be included about the idealistic pupil and the idealistic teacher.

f. The Idealistic Pupil. The idealistic pupil is characterized by that admirable trait, the will to perfection. Whatever he does, he does as well as he can. He is ambitious to deserve honors in scholarship. He wants to grow in knowledge and wisdom, to appreciate the aesthetic things in life, to deserve approbation, and to be a worthy person. He seeks to cultivate social responsiveness and responsibility and those skills and techniques necessary for effective action. He strives for perfection because the ideal person is perfect. His motives may be misunderstood by some of his fellows but he is not disturbed thereby and goes on his straight course the best he can. He has the secret satisfaction of having aimed high and striven hard. This type of pupil is not a trouble-maker for teacher or parent or police officer, though at times he may exhibit the defect of his quality and become fanatical, ecstatic, or visionary.

g. The Idealistic Teacher. The idealistic teacher, like the idealistic pupil, pursues the method of perfecting and the ideal of a cultivated personality. The things that are dear to him are self-consciousness, self-direction, self-activity, selfhood, inner spiritual growth. He tries to be the right sort of person himself and to develop the right sort of personality in his pupils. The infinite and the eternal, though he does not fully comprehend them, mean more to him than the finite and the temporal. His mind seems to rise naturally to the heavenly places. Plato and Emerson inspire him. He is much interested in understanding others through social intercourse. He feels the need for his pupils even as they feel there is something satisfying about him, as though he answered their deepest questions and satisfied their highest cravings. For the right sort of teacher to find himself needed is stimulating. Thus, teacher and pupils grow together as he awakens the dormant powers in younger selves. The sense of companionship in spiritual growth is dear to him. He is a life-sharer. Bare facts, barely expressed, are not enough for him. He wants the feeling for the facts, the realization of their meaning and significance. Naturally, the personalities of literature and history are important to him. Men make circumstance as well as being made by it. Hero-worship has a place, since we grow into the likeness of the persons we admire.

Having great respect for the personalities of his pupils, the idealistic teacher does not tell them the final, but only the possible, answers to their questions. Rather, he stimulates them to find their own answers. They develop by their own effort. He does not seek to impose his views on his pupils. They are left free to find their own views under guidance and stimulation. He respects their own personality and intelligence so much that he will not seek to change their views to conform to his own. But he will try to help each pupil see any

weakness in his position, with a view to its correction. Being an idealist and holding that idealism conserves the real values of all other
types of philosophy, he is willing that the inherent dialectic in any
philosophy should work itself out to its logical conclusion. But he
recognizes that not all students will become idealists, and so he tries
to be understanding and tolerant. It may well be that infinite time
will be necessary to permit all minds to come to the knowledge of
what the universe is and why it is so.

This section is entitled " The Learner and His Learning." We
have now considered the learner, as well as one type of teacher he
may have. Concerning his learning, we may ask, "*What* should be
learned? " This we will undertake to answer in section 2 which deals
with the curriculum. *How* should we learn? This question will be
considered in section 3 on method. *Where* should it be learned? This
is the problem of section 4 on society. *Why* should it be learned?
This will occupy us in section 5 on objectives.

2. The Curriculum

What shall we teach? What shall pupils learn? Teaching and
learning are correlative terms, like parent and child, state and citizen,
masculine and feminine. That is to say, one of these cannot exist without the other. When there is no learning, there has been no teaching.
And where real teaching is, in contradistinction from ' going through
the motions,' there too is learning. There is no teacher without a
learner, and no learner without a teacher. Of course, one may teach
himself, and discover himself.

 The irreducibles in the teaching process are the teacher, the learner,
the thing taught and learned, the method used, the locale (where),
and the time (when). Of these the teacher and the learner are the
most important. And of these two, the teacher is engaged only for
the sake of the learner.

a. Meaning of the Term. Yet the things taught and learned are
not unimportant. These things are known as ' the curriculum.' The
term itself, derived from the Latin, means ' a little racecourse.' The
corresponding term derived from the Greek is ' encyclopaedia,' or
' circle of instruction.' Both terms suggest that the process returns
upon itself and so is complete, as though a panorama of reality were
envisaged.

In our own day the term curriculum is used to refer both to the
subjects studied and also to the experiences undergone or the activities

engaged in. But the so-called 'experience curriculum' or 'activity curriculum' is a question rather of method used than of subject matter, and as such will engage our attention in the following section. In this connection we have to avoid the superficial conception that activities are only physical and not mental.

Today there appears to be a real tendency both to group specific subjects in the curriculum into larger units, such as, 'general science,' 'the social sciences,' etc., and also to utilize 'the activity program,' which, of course, is separable from the philosophy of pragmatism out of which it grew. The term 'extracurricular activities,' although applied to activities which are commonly held to be very important, suggests a contrast between the curriculum as subject matter and the other varied interests of pupils in and out of school.

b. Importance of the Curriculum. Though not so important as learner and teacher, the curriculum as subject matter taught has strategic import. Dr. Stanley H. Rolfe, superintendent of schools, Newark, New Jersey, says:

> Schools exist and are publicly supported because citizens believe that a planned program of education is necessary for the adequate development of boys and girls, the future citizens of America. The school's curriculum determines to a great extent in what direction pupil growth and, in fact, society will move. Therefore, curriculum development and improvement are the most important tasks educators can undertake and, in an era of rapid change, must be accepted as a continuous responsibility.[1]

c. Determination of Curriculum Content. In determining the content of the curriculum it is important in a democratic society to proceed democratically and to utilize the experienced judgment of the teaching personnel as well as that of the so-called educational expert. There should be the coöperative pooling of experience and knowledge. Such procedure shows practical respect for the personal views of the teachers who have to transform the truths studied into the living experience of pupils.

In determining the content of the curriculum, regard should be had for three things: the ability and needs of children, the legitimate demands of society, and the kind of universe in which we live. The ability and needs of children are suggested by psychology, the legitimate demands of society are suggested by sociology, while our conception of the kind of universe in which we live is a matter of our philosophy,

---

[1] *New York Times,* January 12, 1941.

concerning which there is as little or less unanimity of opinion than in psychology or sociology. Inasmuch as psychology and sociology are growing sciences and human societies themselves differ and undergo changes, and since interpretations of the universe have always varied, it is evident that a universal or fixed curriculum is out of the question.

d. Objectives of the Curriculum. What the curriculum should undertake to give is, as the Greeks and the Romans saw, a rounded view of man in his world, a taste for the best things in life, and the ability to take one's own practical part in the world. These three things are really interrelated. A somewhat complex statement will describe the aim in the construction and use of the curriculum: The chosen subject matter should teach pupils to know the facts and opinions they need to know in order to feel and act as they need to feel and act; to feel as they should feel about the values of living in order to think and act as they should; and to do the useful, proper, and right things in order that they may think and feel as they should.

e. The Ideal-Centered School. The connotations of these statements are too broad for us to assent to the notion that the school should be 'child-centered,' for there are also society and the world to consider. Neither should the school be conceived of as 'society-centered,' because any given society is not what it ought to be and is itself undergoing constant change. The school should really be centered in certain ideal conceptions of what man and his society should be in view of the kind of world in which he really lives. But the kind of world in which man conceives himself really to live is a matter of his philosophy. So in the last analysis it is our philosophy that determines what the center of our school work should be. That is to say our schools are, should be, and cannot escape being, idea-centered or ideal-centered. The other philosophies have their own ideas, and, in the social sense of the term, their ideals. Our philosophy has its ideas, and in the ontological as well as social sense, its ideals.

These ideas or ideals of ours are the ones that the nature of man, truly understood, requires for its completion. They are the ones that the story of man in the earth reveals as the expression of his nature. And they are the ones that appear best to harmonize with the kind of world in which we live. A list of such ideals for our schools in the American democracy would certainly include some of our precious concepts, such as, 'government by consent of the governed,' 'the pursuit of happiness,' 'the general welfare,' 'civil liberty,' and 'the appeal to reason.' Some of these stress the individual aspect of experience and some the social. Perhaps all of them might be subsumed under the ideal of self-realization, not forgetting that self-realization is for society as well as for the individual and includes adjustment to the cosmos in worship.

The educated person is indeed, as he has been called, a cultivated vocationalist, but more, he is a cultivated human being. Man is not just another animal. He transcends the realm of nature in both his conceptual thought of it, in his artistic ideals, in his sense of an un-conditioned obligation, and in his mystical religious experiences. He is ruled in part by purposes and not solely by antecedent causes and present stimuli. More than any other creature is he ruled by the thought of the absent in space and the remote in time.

f. Three Parts of the Curriculum. In accord with the nature of man as a being who thinks, feels, and wills, the curriculum he studies may be grouped into three parts — the sciences, the fine arts, and the practical arts. The sciences teach us to know, the arts to do. An art engaged in primarily for its own sake is a fine art; one engaged in for the sake of what it leads to is a practical art. Thus, the writing of a poem for the sake of the satisfaction involved in such self-expression is a fine art. Being the mayor of a city for the sake of eliminating corruption and giving the citizen an honest and efficient government is a practical art.

Among the sciences disclosing the intellectual nature of man, we may name physics, chemistry, biology, geography, mathematics, astronomy, psychology, and sociology. These all are the product primarily of man's intelligence seeking to know certain phases of our environment. The scientist has the passion for discovery and the will to know. Science is man's organized and verifiable knowledge. It is obtained by the use of the scientific method, that is, observation, supplemented in certain subjects by experimentation, induction, and deduction. As facts become known they are classified and organized as a basis for further discovery.

As illustrations of the fine arts we may mention drawing, painting, sculpture, architecture, the various forms of poetic and prose literature, and the rhythmic temporal art of music. In their production and appreciation these all manifest the emotional nature of man, his feeling for form, his discriminating taste. Of course the artist has knowledge of social and economic conditions, of the past of his art, and of the trends in style, and he has the will to execute.

Among the thousand practical arts of man we may mention agriculture, lumbering, manufacturing, trade, all the industrial arts, such as carpentry, plumbing, printing, and such political arts as the making of war, the concluding of peace treaties, and the forming and governing of states. All these reveal man as an active agent, having a will to change and improve conditions. In all his achievements man uses his intelligence either in selecting means to chosen ends or in determining which ends to choose. And, too, his accomplishment engages his interest in the process.

In the event that a record is made of man's achievements, we have history. The events which are recorded are not the history, the record is the history, which partakes of the nature of science to the extent that its contents can be verified, and of the nature of prose literature to the extent that provable facts are supplemented by the imagination.

The point to notice is that the curriculum in each of its three branches is a revelation of the nature of man. The sciences, the fine arts, the practical arts, are all the effects of the responses of man to his environment.

We have to note that though the subject matter of learning appears to be a manifold because of the many sciences and arts, it is really a unity, because they each and all reveal the nature of man in relation to his environment. Though with diverse elements, in this sense the curriculum is one.

g. The Essential Studies. We have to raise the question as old as teaching itself, " Which are the essential studies, and why? " From the foregoing it is clear that to become fully human the student must in time familiarize himself with the scientific method and with some of the sciences: one dealing with man's inorganic environment, like physics or chemistry; one dealing with his organic environment, like biology; and one dealing with his human environment, like psychology or sociology. He will need also to appreciate one of the arts, like literature or music, and even try his hand at the production of something artistic and beautiful. And he will need to become himself a skilful agent at some one of the arts (teaching is an art too) and to know the record of man's chief accomplishments in the past. Thus the individual learner himself becomes one who knows, who feels, who acts. And still, in addition, the student will acquire for himself by his experience and observation, perhaps also by systematic study under guidance, a total view of the world. This will be his philosophy of life and will give him a certain sense of cosmic adjustment, or religion.

The total curriculum is the work of man, it is the effect of the interplay of man and his world, it is a social product, it has become a social heritage. Each new generation can add to its social inheritance only as it knows and appreciates it. To omit this acquaintance is to begin back in time where the race began. We seek to assimilate the social inheritance that we may humanize ourselves and that we may contribute our mite, if possible, to the ongoing march of civilization. " Be ashamed to die," said Horace Mann to his little band of students at Antioch College, " till you have achieved some victory for humanity."

h. The Mutual Fitness of Man and His Environment. Strange, is it not, that man's environment, whether physical or social, whether inorganic or organic, seems fitted to prod his curiosity, to stir his imagination, to impel him to action? Ours is a world that is fitted to be known, to be felt and enjoyed, and in which man may enjoy the activity it engenders. It is as though in our sciences, nature were speaking to man; in our fine arts, nature were inviting man to shape her materials to finer forms; and in our practical arts, nature were impelling man to action as the price of survival and progress. In all our study it is as though some spirit in nature were calling to the spirit in man. Maybe nature is just that, the content of space lasting through time with a view to challenging the powers of man. At least that is the effect, and it may be the purpose. Effects are read as purposes when either chance or necessity seems inadequate to account for them. The mutual fitness of man and his environment would seem too striking and marvelous a phenomenon to be explained by chance. The intelligence, feelings, and choices of man, all in cases seeking the ideal, seem too transcendent in their reach and scope to be the product of a blind necessity. The more appealing and reasonable view would seem to be that as man is personal, so nature is really a medium of the personal, and is one means by which the spirit of nature speaks to the spirit in man. As Tennyson has it:

> God is law, say the wise, oh soul, and let us rejoice,
> For if He thunder by law, the thunder is still His voice.

Our conclusion at this point must be that as the studies of the curriculum are a revelation of the spirit in man, so also are they a revelation of the spirit in nature. For this reason we may with propriety call the environment of man spiritual.

i. Results of the Use of the Curriculum. What we need is teachers who can sense the presence of the eternal in the temporal; who, with

Kepler, " can think the thoughts of God after Him "; who, with the poet, Edward Young, can feel " the course of nature is the art of God "; who, with the philosopher Hegel, can think the universal reason in all things; who, with Schopenhauer, can discern a universal will in all existence. Such teachers can properly awaken the sense of the eternity asleep in every finite being.

From this standpoint it does not so much matter, as Emerson said, " what you study as who your teachers are "; the really important thing is that the subject studied should contribute to the growth of the personal spirit of the student. His studies should enlarge his personality by increasing his knowledge, cultivating his taste, forming his character, and developing his skill. Of course he should be in harmony with nature (naturalism), should conform to the laws of our universe (realism), should be able to solve the necessary problems of life as they arise (pragmatism); but mainly he should develop his personality — his real self — in a universe that is personal. He takes an interest, he sets himself to learn, he is self-active, he wins his sense of adjustment to his world, he feels himself growing, he appreciates the great possibilities of the ages, he learns to respect others as himself, and he feels himself at home in his world. The natural evils of life he traces to man's lack of adjustment to his physical world. The moral evils of life he traces to man's abuses of his freedom, to man's ignorance, to his wrong choices. He knows it takes the Maker of man a long time to educate man in the right use of his precious birthright of freedom. He is not impatient, yet ceaseless in effort. He does not shut his eyes to injustice, yet is optimistic. As Browning has it in *Epilogue*,

> One who never turned his back but marched breast forward,
>   Never doubted clouds would break,
> Never dreamed, though right were worsted, wrong would triumph,
> Held we fall to rise, are baffled to fight better,
>   Sleep to wake.

The curriculum is the racecourse. But the race is never finished and the course never ends. That is the kind of growing life man is set to lead in our kind of universe.

3. The Methods of Teaching

a. Meaning of Method. The term ' method ' means, in general, the way of doing anything. The way actually used may be good or bad, but some way is inevitable. It is not a question of using method or not using method, in case anything at all is to be done, but it is always in order to inquire which method of doing this specific thing is better or best.

The term 'method' in education means an orderly procedure in teaching. Usually the method or combination of methods used can be identified, even though the teacher is entirely unconscious of the question of method. A principle of method often half-consciously followed is, 'teach others as others taught you.'

The purpose of using the best possible method in education is to improve the effectiveness of the procedure. Such improvement may be tested by the pleasure of the teacher and the students in the process of teaching and learning, though not all pleasures are the same and some are preferable to others. Certainly the teacher should be happy and the pupils should be happy, but both teacher and pupils should find their happiness in doing the things that their judgment and experience show are worthy of doing.

The list of methods available to teachers is legion. Many of these are associated with distinguished names. We will review some of these historic methods used and described by noted persons, gaining thereby the assurance that there is no one best universal method but that the choice of the method to be used depends on several conditions, to which later reference will be made.

b. Some Historic Methods. We begin with the *Socratic* method. Socrates, the moralist, who drank the fatal hemlock in 399 B.C., used the method of questioning. But not every teacher today who asks questions is using the Socratic art. The mother of Socrates was Phaenarete, who followed the occupation of midwife. Socrates facetiously remarked that he followed the occupation of his mother, except that he was an intellectual midwife and assisted ideas to the birth, some of which amounted to nothing. The art of Socrates consisted in leading youth to induce and frame definitions of concepts, such as virtue, temperance, courage, justice, and wisdom. Often a Socratic conversation ended in the confusion of contradiction, or in the defense of the opposite view from that with which the interlocutor began. Illustrations are found in the *Meno* and *Theaetetus* of Plato. Teachers of ethics, using the common facts of moral experience, may still follow to advantage the Socratic art.

Plato, the aristocrat, was a pupil of Socrates, the plebeian. The Socratic conversation became the Platonic *Dialectic.* The dialectical method of Plato was similar in procedure to that of Socrates, but differed in reaching a philosophical conclusion. Socratic concepts became Platonic *ideas* which are eternal verities. The idea of *the good* is supreme, giving both existence and knowability to all things. Plato's theory of ideas and his dialectical method are found, *inter alia*, in the *Republic*, his greatest dialogue. Teachers of philosophy, or metaphysics, still make use of the Platonic method of *dialectic*, and seek by the understanding of concepts to reach a knowledge of the ultimate reality.

Aristotle, the logician, was a pupil of Plato. He learned from Plato the art of dialectic and from Socrates, through Plato, the art of definition and of forming concepts. Aristotle was generally regarded till the seventeenth century as the author and finisher of our logical faith. So eminent a critic of the logic of Aristotle as Francis Bacon understood it only by half, the deductive half. Really Aristotle was a user of both the inductive and deductive methods of reasoning and formulated both. He wrote a work on the constitutions of some one hundred twenty-eight Greek city states, including that of Athens, before writing his more general *Politics*. By the inductive method we proceed from concrete facts to a general conclusion. By the deductive method we proceed from the general proposition to particular conclusions. These two methods are two aspects of one method of reasoning. The mind in reasoning is constantly going back and forth between particular and general, between the concrete and the abstract. Scientists and teachers and students of science still employ the method of Aristotle and indeed cannot avoid it. Not that God made man and left it to Aristotle to make man rational, but that rational man in studying his world both induces and deduces.

The weakness in using the deductive method of Aristotle is that it is based on the principle of contradiction, that is, *either–or*. A proposition is either true or false. Man is either good or not good. But the truth may be actually found in the synthesis of contradictory predicates, as when one says, man is both good and not good, good in some respects, not good in others. This finding of truth in the synthesis of opposites will meet us later in discussing Hegel.

Meantime we must say the method of Aristotle, both induction (synthetic) and deduction (analytic), remains as a part of the basis of all method in thinking and discovery.

Socrates, Plato, and Aristotle were all intellectualists, though Aristotle recognized the fact that man has a will, ' with power on his deed.'

Intellectualism is the Greek emphasis, presupposing that ignorance is the radical defect of man, an ignorance that can be removed by instruction. Teachers have generally followed the Greek tradition. The Hebrew consciousness is different. It is more voluntaristic, presupposing that wilfulness and wickedness are the radical defect of man, a wilfulness and wickedness that require a change of heart, a new motivation as the basis for a new mode of living. Jesus is called ' the Great Teacher.' He used all the methods familiar to teachers, such as storytelling, questioning, engaging in activities. But his essential method was that of association with his learners (called ' disciples ') as they " went about doing good." Beneath his teaching was his mode of life which he shared with his intimate followers. In contrast with the Greeks, teaching as life-sharing while engaged in individual and social service was a new emphasis. It is the method which Christian missionaries at home and abroad have found most effective in winning followers of ' the Way.' It is the preferred method when what is desired is a fundamental change in attitude and disposition, leading to a new character. It is the method especially suited to the spread of religion as a way of life. Sadly unfortunate is it that the Greek tradition has largely captured the teaching of Christianity and ideas about deeds have largely usurped the place of the deeds themselves.

It is not possible to review in detail the methods used and advocated by all the great thinkers and teachers. Time fails us to speak of the keenly analytic medieval schoolmen; of Descartes, the rationalist, and his method of proceeding from the simple (i.e., to him, the most general) to the complex (i.e., the concrete detail) ; of Spinoza, the absolutist, and his geometrical method of presenting philosophical arguments; of the great Immanuel Kant and his critical method of distinguishing the *a priori* and the *a posteriori* elements of experience, or what the knower and the world known each supply to human knowledge. But we must refer, however briefly, to the methods of Hegel, Pestalozzi, Herbart, Dewey, and Kilpatrick.

Hegel revived the dialectic method of Plato and revised the logic of Aristotle. Hegel thought he saw the ideas, or essences, of Plato in process of forming the world of nature, man, and society. And the truth he thought he found not in *either–or* but in *both–and*. When two propositions contradict each other, each being based on a fragment of experience, the truth is in the whole, in the synthesis of the two. Thus we have thesis, or position first taken, then the antithesis, or the contradiction of the first position, and finally synthesis, or the combination of the two in a complete view. This method of the reconciliation of opposites, which Hegel thought to be descriptive of the world drama, is good not only in controversy but also in all inquiries looking for the whole truth in the midst of diverse opinion.

Going back a few years in time from the panlogism of Hegel to the naturalism of Rousseau, we find the source of much that is best in modern educational method. Rousseau was himself a child of nature, a lover of the external world in its pristine state. He would have his ideal pupil, Emile, taught by the 'natural' method as he conceived it. This method consists in discovery for oneself, not in being told; in learning from one's own experience, not from that of others; in undergoing the consequences of mistakes, and so coming to avoid them. Rousseau made the mistake of not recognizing the importance of educating in a social environment. This he did because he was so much out of sympathy with the aristocratic society of his day. But, even so, from Rousseau derives our psychology of the child and his learning.

Pestalozzi, the Swiss educational reformer, was inspired by Rousseau to turn theory into action. He is sometimes eulogized as the 'Father of Modern Elementary Education.' He was a great experimenter in the fields of agricultural and industrial education as well as in the training of teachers. He advocated the sense-basis of all instruction and learning by engaging in activities. He was inspired by that handbook of much modern progressive education, the *Emile* of Rousseau. He in turn led Herbert Spencer, who knew Pestalozzi's work indifferently well, to formulate in his essay on *Intellectual Education* certain general principles of procedure, such as, " from the simple to the complex," " from the concrete to the abstract," and " from the empirical to the rational." These familiar principles are useful, if they are understood correctly and applied with a knowledge of what is ' simple ' to the mind of a child. Pestalozzi mistakenly thought that a syllable was simpler to a child than the word and the word than the sentence. Really the minds of children move from simple wholes to complex parts and then back to now integrated wholes. The principles should also be read in reverse, from the complex to the simple, from the abstract to the concrete, and from the rational to the empirical. By so doing we supplement the inductive by the deductive procedure. The Pestalozzian methods are applicable to intellectual instruction. They do not apply particularly in the acquisition of skill or in the formation of character, which require performance under supervision, though Pestalozzi himself cultivated both skills and character in his young charges.

Two of the greatest disciples of Pestalozzi were Froebel and Herbart. Each saw something different in the master, and developed it. Both the motor and the sensory bases of learning were manifest in the work of Pestalozzi, though neither clearly distinguished from each other nor clearly related to each other. Froebel saw the motor element in Pestalozzi's work, and Herbart the sensory. The method of Froebel lies at the basis of the practice of the kindergarten which he established. It consists in learning by doing in a social setting. Plays, games, and songs help the children to grow like plants in a garden. His pupils engaged in manual constructive work for educative purposes, not for vocational ends. He held that in constructive activities man could himself create and likewise acquire a sense of companionship with the Creator. Though he applied his methods only to the pre-school period of life, he held them to be applicable throughout the educative process.

Herbart was as intellectualistic as the Greeks. He thought ideas caused feelings and feelings and ideas caused acts. 'The complete circle of thought' begins with the idea and ends with the act. As we think, so are we in feeling and in conduct. The great thing then in the Herbartian method, as formulated by the immediate followers of Herbart, is the right handling of ideas. There are five essential steps in the familiar Herbartian method: (1) The preparation of the mind of the class by the teacher for the work to follow. This is done by the recall of old familiar ideas and by a clear statement of the purpose of the lesson. (2) The presentation of the new material analytically, step by step, idea by idea. (3) The comparison of the ideas presented for the detection of any similarities or dissimilarities. (4) The generalization growing out of the comparison which states the essential truth of the whole lesson. And (5) the application of this general truth to new problems and situations. This method of instruction is strictly intellectual. It has done yeoman service in the past in the training of teachers in normal schools. It introduced system into much unordered classroom work. In many cases, unfortunately, what was meant to be ' formal ' in the sense of correct became ' formal ' in the sense of nonvital. The method is still usable and is often used where it is desirable to communicate a body of organized knowledge with a measure of understanding and appreciation, as in those subjects in which Herbart was especially interested, such as mathematics and the grammar of the classical languages.

About the turn of the twentieth century, Dr. John Dewey became an independent critic of the Herbartian method and rejected Herbart's intellectualism. Instead, he developed a form of voluntarism which makes acts primary and ideas secondary. The philosophy of Dr. Dewey has been called pragmatism, because of its theory that truth is due to the successful working of ideas, or experimentalism, because of its theory that only by experimenting can we find out which ideas work best. There are six steps [1] in the Dewey method based on these principles. The first is the actual experience or activity in which the pupils are engaged. The second is the location and formulation of the problem arising in this activity. The third is the gathering of data pertinent to the problem. The fourth is the formation of an hypothesis to solve the problem. The fifth is the testing of this hypothesis by observation, experience, or experiment. The last is the organization of the results obtained by this procedure into a system as a basis for further discovery. This method is like Herbart's in having in it both induction and deduction, but is unlike Herbart's in beginning with acts instead of ideas. Rousseau and Froebel and the scientific method used by Darwin (Dewey was born in 1859, the year in which Darwin's *Origin of Species* appeared) are among the special antecedents of the Dewey method. It is especially valuable in making discoveries for oneself and in giving a sense of reality to one's work.

Growing out of Dr. Dewey's views is the project method advocated and popularized by Dr. W. H. Kilpatrick. A project is some useful activity carried through to its conclusion in as natural a setting as possible. The project is selected by an individual for himself or it may be a group project. Thus, a house may be built, a town laid out, a fire-engine constructed, in the course of which much is learned about materials, tools, and community living, as well as about the formal subjects of arithmetic and language. The project method has shown itself very useful in teaching young children who are most interested in what they themselves do. The results in the acquisition of the fundamental tool subjects are fairly satisfactory, and the cultivation of initiative and social coöperation is noteworthy. Critics of the project method find it leaves gaps in organized knowledge of subjects, that it may neglect portions of the inheritance of the race, and that it does not allow for knowledge for the sake of knowledge.

---

[1] See the revised edition of *How We Think*.

Thus we have reviewed some of the main methods used in the history of education and we draw the obvious conclusion that different methods have their characteristic uses. There is no one-best method suited to all subjects at all times for all purposes.

c. Other Methods. This conclusion would be emphasized if we went into similar detail with other useful and available methods of teaching. The list would be long, such as the lecture method, often used but not always acceptably by college and university professors; the forum or discussion method, particularly useful in democratic inquiry; debating a question, more useful in sharpening wits and in learning to handle material effectively and readily than in discovering truth; the informal conversational method, which is most valuable when at least one party to the conversation knows the subject; reciting what has been learned, which is useful in the exact fixation of material; correspondence, which is invaluable if one corresponds with an institution that has someone like an Erasmus or a Spinoza in it; imitation, in learning how to write or paint; the laboratory method of experimentation, for purposes of discovery or demonstration; storytelling, for the entertainment of young children or the vivid portrayal of truth; dramatics, for learning the art of acting, or for the forceful presentation of conflicting ideas; the natural method in teaching languages, which is useful in learning to speak the language but not so useful in learning grammar and linguistics; the use of objective tests, such as the true and false, completion, matching, which are of great value in securing exact grading of work done; the object-lesson, which at its best uses the senses and shows the importance of observation; visual and auditory aids such as the stereopticon, radio and movie which may make materials most vivid, though some pupils may be left intellectually inert; (television is in the offing, which brings the actual remote scene or occurrence near) ; observation trips, to see objects and events in their actual setting; reports of committees, useful to the committee assembling the data, but often not well presented to the class; reports by individuals to seminars, which usually benefit the individual more than the seminar; and many more. To every act of teaching in every situation there is an appropriate method.

d. The Determinants of Method. Which method, then, shall we use? What are the determinants of the method to be used? Consider the age of the pupils, their interests, the size of the class, its maturity, its preparation, the purpose of the lesson, and then use the method that you can use best under those circumstances. The youthful David could not meet the giant Goliath in the armor of the veteran Saul. Each teacher must slay the giants of ignorance, error, ugliness, and evil in his own best way. We should not be in bondage to any one method. We should not blame ourselves unduly if we cannot use successfully what others recommend. The tests of method are whether we are getting good results and whether the students on the whole enjoy the process. A large class may mean storytelling, or lecturing, or group projects, or committee reports. If the purpose is to convict of ignorance, Socrates will do; if to transmit, Herbart will do; if to discover, Dewey will do; if to cultivate pupil initiative and spontaneity, Agassiz will do. As a tool of democracy, the coöperative solution of problems is desirable.

e. *Teaching Pupils, not Subjects.* We overdo methodology. Adapt yourself to the situation, use well the method you adopt, get your subject liked, get yourself liked. It is not enough to know method. We must know our pupils and our subjects, and we must be likable people.

The main thing to remember and to practice is that we teach pupils, not subjects. In the sentence, " The teacher teaches the boy geography," ' geography ' is the direct object of ' teaches ' and ' the boy ' is the indirect object. This is good grammar but bad pedagogy. The boy, in the teacher's mind, should be the direct object of the teaching, and geography the indirect object. Think of Walter Raleigh as a boy studying geography, and being fired by it.

The objective of all method in teaching is the cultivation of the personality of the pupil. Our task and privilege as teachers is to know our students, their needs, their interests, their outlooks, and to assist them in finding, integrating, and stabilizing themselves. To lift a material body we may need to be below it, to lift a human spirit, we need to be above it, in knowledge, taste, love, maturity, and character. Our personalities count most in the work of cultivating personalities. It is a great art to be able to suggest to an individual something to read or to do that will develop, reconstruct, or cultivate his personality. Goethe said of his old teacher of art, Baumgarten, " Under him we learned nothing but became something." Froebel was a wandering spirit in search of himself until he met Grüner in Frankfurt, after which " the fish was in water." The truly great teacher has the deeds and the words of eternal life. His pupils whom he has assisted to a rebirth of intelligence, taste, or character, rise up and call him blessed, a teacher not by the book or by the method so much as " by the grace of God." Here is a reality that cannot be bought with a price but it can be acquired by any normal soul who is in touch with the springs of greatness in man, nature, and the cosmos. Short of it, we are purveyors; with it, we are coöperators with the creative spirit of all life.

4. School and Society

Where shall we educate? In a social milieu. Why there? It is the best place. What may we expect if we rightly educate there? A transformed society, composed of transformed individuals. But unless it is done everywhere, it cannot prove to be most effective anywhere.

a. The Economic Interest of Society in Schools. The practical interest of society in education is shown in the establishment of schools supported by public taxation. The item of expenditure for schools is second in amount only to that for war. There is constant economic conflict between those who would expand the offerings of the schools and those who would contract them. Various educational bodies see the need for expansion, while various taxpayers' associations demand contraction, or at least no further expansion. Just now (1941) there is great need for more vocational training in the skills required for national defense. Educators call for expansion of educational facilities, while taxpayers' associations want the existing facilities utilized to meet the new vocational needs. Educational administrators do need to be careful to expend wisely and get the full benefit of the public money without waste or extravagance. Society expends money on schools for the preservation of its own type and for its own progress.

b. The School is a Mirror of Society. The kind of schools a given society has is a reflection of the existent society. In totalitarian countries we have totalitarian schools; in democratic countries the schools are about as democratic as the countries themselves. The totalitarian state allows in theory no other institution to compete with itself. Russia has probably been most drastic in eliminating all competition between the state and other institutions of society, such as the family, private schools, the economic life, recreations, and the church. The schools in Russia illustrate the totalitarian principle at work in the making of Soviet comrades. Germany has had great difficulty in bringing its races and religions into line with Naziism. Germany's schools reflect only the Nazi philosophy of life. Italy has a Fascist government and a people homogeneously religious. Italy's schools are both Fascist and religious.

It is natural that a given society should make its schools in the image of itself. The schools do not first make society but society first makes the schools, and then the schools in turn help make society. The schools do not stand alone in the making of society or in the education of the young. All the forces and influences that exist, of which the school is one, help make society, and all of society helps educate the young.

c. Varying Conceptions of Progress. Each responsible society regards itself as making progress and regards other types of society with a critical eye. Conceptions of progress vary with different types of society, each type tending to regard its own model as superior. Among the totalitarian groups, progress is held to consist in following ' the leader ' in thought and action, in eliminating opposition to him, and in spreading his ideas and power. Among the more democratic societies, the conception of progress includes the making of the blessings of the few more widely available and the increasing recognition of the common man, including his inalienable right to " life, liberty, and the pursuit of happiness."

Other conceptions of progress may be held. Each type of society will interpret these according to its own standard. Among these conceptions of progress are growth in freedom, or the practice of self-government; the increasing victory of the spirit of man over material forces, involving both knowledge and use of the powers of nature; man's increasing mastery of himself, involving rational self-control of his passional nature; the ever-wider realization of the values of life, both personal and social, such as health, knowledge, art, character, vocation, justice, coöperation, and religion; man's control over the conditions of living, involving economic independence and the sense of security; and man's developing adjustment to reality, involving a more adequate philosophy of life. All of these conceptions of progress tend to widen man's perspective and to make him less dependent on time, place, and circumstance.

Societies are constantly changing. When the changes are in any one or more of the directions indicated by these conceptions, we have progress. When, on the other hand, the changes are away from these ends, we have regress. There is no such thing as uniform progress by all society. We do not have society, except as an abstract noun; we have societies. And each branch of society has its own rate and direction of change. We should not think of progress in any social group as a cyclic return upon itself, nor as a steady ascent, nor as a spiral staircase, but rather as a zigzag course, now up, now down, but on the whole, upward.

The brief record of most civilizations is that they were born, grew, flourished, decayed, and died. So with Egypt, Assyria, Babylon, Greece, Rome. This would be a depressing story except for the fact that the values wrought out by a given civilization are preserved and transmitted. These values may be political, literary, artistic, scientific, religious, or philosophical.

Societies put into their schools what those societies want to be and to become. The school is a given society shaping itself to its own future. The school is reactionary, conservative, liberal, or radical according to the social group it represents.

What makes progress? What are the antecedent conditions of progress? Why is society usually in a flux? It appears to be a fact that the great ages of mankind are unstable, that they are periods of conflicting forces and ideas. So it was in the age of Pericles, of Augustus, of the Medici, of Elizabeth, and of Louis XIV. The stable ages have not been the greatest ages. This fact should not lead us to the hasty and incorrect conclusion that all instability is a good. We must anticipate change and prepare to make it for the better. In times of great social change, it is important to stress those things that do not change, lest the sense of perspective be lost.

d. Four Theories of Progress. Progress has been traced to four different things. The Marxists trace it to economic conditions and the class struggle between capital and labor. Along with this economic interpretation of history is likely to go a second emphasis on the action of masses of people who are moved by the same set of conditions and ideas and who produce their own leaders as effects of the mass movement. A third view is that great men are the cause rather than the effect of mass movements and so are the main forces in the making of progress. The first and second views, implying economic determinism and dialectical materialism, reduce men in their movements to the level of things and adopt a kind of fatalistic attitude toward the destiny of man. The third theory of the great man is close to the facts according to such interpreters as Carlyle and Emerson, who regard history as biography. But this theory leaves the great man unaccounted for, unless we pass on to the fourth theory and see the great man himself as an expression of some immanent purpose in the world. This underlying principle of cosmic personality would then be the real explanation of progress. It gives us a spiritual, as distinguished from a material, interpretation of history. The great man becomes the voice of the spirit of truth silently thinking in things, an outward manifestation of the inner nature of being. The spiritual nature of reality of which great men are the temporal embodiments would then be the ultimate explanation of social progress. All things and persons embody and manifest the power and quality of Spirit according to their capacity.

  e. Five Ways in which the School Can Improve Society. What can the schools do to aid social progress? Though the schools are themselves the creation of society, the schools in turn become to a certain degree causes of social progress. Specifically, there are at least five things the schools can do to aid in improving society.

  (1) The first of these is to *suggest lines of future social growth.* Our teachers of the social sciences as well as the teachers of literature are in a position to do this very thing. It takes some insight and hindsight and foresight to do it. But it can be done. To do so helps prepare the mind of youth to see and to take their own part in social change. The trend just now in the democratic countries would seem to be away from individualism toward socialization. Following the present world war, we may expect in the democracies of the world a more equitable distribution of the material goods of life, a more flexible interchange of values between all social and economic classes, less regard for social caste and class, greater recognition of the rights of minorities and small nations, and more interracial understanding, sympathy and coöperation. These generous expectations would be frustrated by a totalitarian victory or by conservative reactions within the victorious democracies.

  (2) Our schools can, and in a measure do, *educate for leadership and followership.* Professor William James held that the function of education in a democracy was to enable us to select our leaders. Future leaders are now being trained in our schools. Too frequently the school does not recognize the future leader. Among such misfits in school, history lists the following: Darwin, Linnaeus, Napoleon, William Seward, Patrick Henry, Isaac Newton, Samuel Johnson, Jonathan Swift, Wordsworth, R. B. Sheridan, Robert Fulton, Heinrich Heine, George Eliot, Walter Scott, John Hunter, Hegel, Lord Byron, Huxley, Schiller, James Russell Lowell, Oliver Goldsmith, Wagner, Goethe, H. W. Beecher, W. C. Bryant, Emerson, Pasteur, Thackeray, Shelley, Daniel Webster, John Adams, Gladstone, Coleridge, James Watt, David Hume, Herbert Spencer, Pierre Curie, Ibsen, and Froebel.

  Such instances show the danger of school uniformity and standardization. In medicine there must be diagnosis before prescription. So our schools need to be on the alert to detect the potential leader. He may be the nonconformist. He is sure to be a variant from type. Having discerned the leader, it is enough to give him freedom in following his bent and assist him in his way with aid and comfort.

The good follower is critical, intelligent, and independent. He may himself in some situations become the leader. Most of us are followers in the unusual situations in life, though we may be inconspicuous leaders in many of the usual situations of life.

Having in mind the need for leaders and followers, the school should help pupils to think and act for themselves, to be self-reliant, to cultivate spontaneity and initiative, to command and to obey. We cannot cultivate responsibility in pupils without placing responsibility on pupils.

(3) The schools can and should *express appreciation for right social emphases and criticism of misplaced emphases.* It is a question of good judgment and taste in social matters. We have to avoid not only psychoses, neuroses, and complexes but all forms of bias in judgment. Just now (1941) the judgment that democracies are inefficient and autocracies are efficient requires reëvaluation; also, the judgment, to the extent that it exists, that some races are superior and some are inferior; also, the judgment, to the extent that it exists, that America can live unto itself alone, that our complacency about our provincialism should not be disturbed. Some well-placed emphases just now are social coöperation; refusal to be regimented in thought; and our free institutions, such as freedom of speech, of assembly, of movement, of the press, of worship, and freedom from seizure and search and imprisonment without fair trial. The school can be a medium for the cultivation of right social attitudes and the condemnation of wrong social practices. Those practices are wrong which are repugnant to the common sense and conscience of the mass of mankind. Democracy should always be on trial in its own eyes. It cannot successfully represent democratic ideas abroad if it practices undemocratic ideas at home.

(4) *The school can assist in handling social problems in a scientific way.* This is one of our greatest needs in securing social progress. Just now there is a question whether we should have 'democratic propaganda.' The phrase is self-contradictory. If it is propaganda, it is not fair to all sides, and so is not democratic. If it is democratic, it is truthful and fair to all sides, and so is not propaganda. Democracy requires no factitious aids. It is the truth and the truth alone that makes the mind of man free. " Let there be light " was the first creative act. We require the light of knowledge on our social problems, such as economic depressions, our divorce rate, the effects of a given foreign policy. In

the light of knowledge right-minded people can act rightly. It is ignorance and prejudice that we have to fear. Our research men are largely products of our schools, colleges, and universities. The intellectual may not be a good administrator, but he is a good investigator. For a good investigator it is necessary that all bias and prejudice be removed, that the open mind be maintained, that facts be gathered and weighed, that generalizations be not hasty, and that all conclusions be tested. A good scientist hews to the line of truth only, and lets the chips fall where they may.

(5) *The school can assist in transmitting the established values of the past.* This in a measure it usually does. Education is transmission, but not transmission alone. The progress we desire in society should be based on the established values of the past. Otherwise, we have revolution, with its attendant chaos. The preservation of the established values of the past provides a stabilizing influence in times of change. Among the values we may regard as established in the experience of the race are the importance of physical vitality; the knowledge of facts; the production and appreciation of works of beauty; the worth of honesty and integrity; social justice between individuals, classes, races, and nations; inventiveness and skill in the manipulation of tools; and the sense of cosmic adjustment. On a basis such as these values provide, an intelligent and wise society can go on to any degree of socialization.

f. An Ideal Social Order. Mankind has not yet arrived. It may never fully arrive in this time and place. But it is in process of arriving, here a little and there a little. There seems to be some pattern in the nature of things by following which man may more fully arrive. " The best is yet to be," as Browning sings. Democracy has been described as religion applied to politics, and ' the kingdom of heaven ' has been described as democracy applied to religion. There is an ideal social order for man. This ideal nowhere fully exists on the earth. But it haunts the imagination of man. It is real in the sense of subsistence, if not existence. It is real in the sense that perfect circles are real. This ideal order consists of all those values that social man should realize in the earth. The political state exists to help conserve and mediate those ideal values. Believing that such an ideal is real and that man can realize it is a great stimulus to improve actual conditions. Viewed in a large way, the mission of man is to make the ideal actual. Human society is, or should be, interested in that type of education which brings these unchanging and eternal values into the changing and temporal lives of men. These ideals, viewed impersonally, are Platonic; viewed personally, they are Hegelianistic of the right.

Each given society has social problems of its own. These immediate problems are the starting points for progressive action. The general formula for progress in world society at the present time (February, 1942) would seem to be a wider application of the principles of democracy. But this very principle is at the basis of the world war. The totalitarian states have taken up arms against it. The war on democracy has been their major objective. But, however the war eventuates, the principles of democracy will remain to encourage and inspire human action. The really tragic thing is that the totalitarian states believe in war, prepare for it, and begin aggression. The democratic states believe in peace, prepare for it, and appear weak at the outset of aggression. There seems little likelihood that the totalitarian states will accept the principles of democracy at any time that can now be foreseen. The only solution would seem to be a victory by force of arms for the democracies, after which the enforcement of peace on the aggressive nations of the world. It is paradoxical to maintain peace by force, but in a world in which powerful nations believe in war this is the only way. An armed victory over the democracies of the world by the despotic states means intellectual and physical bondage. The human spirit, having tasted of liberty, will always be restive under such restraint.

It is a tragic thing that the democracies, to win in a struggle with the despotisms, must voluntarily surrender some of their liberties. By so doing they adopt, temporarily, the very methods they oppose. The reason for this is that the ways of democracy are the ways of peace, not of war, and when the necessity for survival by war comes, democracies must recast themselves and become outwardly, for purposes of defense, what they are not at heart. The immediate objective of democratic society today is to win the war. The next objective will be to insure the peace of the world. Each is a stupendous undertaking.

The school can make its contribution to each of these objectives — to the first by developing the skills requisite for successful defense and attack in warfare (attack is the best defense), and to the second by keeping alive the ideals of peace even while practicing war.

g. Some Next Steps. The school as an institution may represent society at its points of growth. Just now in American society there are at least three major points of growth. These three may all fall under the concept of social justice or respect for personality. One of these points is the relation between the economic classes in our society; another is the relation between the different races in our society; and the third is our relation to the other nations of the world.

Our schools can practice interclass, interracial, and international ideals. Class distinctions based on wealth or privilege have no place in democratic schools. Racial animosities, hatred, and prejudice should not creep into the American school. Foreigners or those of foreign blood in our midst should not as such be suspect but should be treated with courtesy, justice, understanding, and sympathy. All derogatory epithets and references to other races or nations should be eliminated. It is important that our schools be real oases of democracy in the desert of a world war. In peace or war our schools should be miniature democratic societies at their best, with freedom and individual initiative for all, with a measure of self-government, and with respect for ideals loyally held wherever found.

There is danger lest in a national emergency we take too short a view of the total situation. The long-range vision is essential if we would keep our perspective true. There is no 'wave of the future' that will finally engulf the democratic ideal. In the hearts of the masses of mankind, democracy is alive, is mighty, and will prevail. On this point we may quote Thomas Mann:

> I wish to give the word ' democracy ' a very broad meaning, a much broader one than the merely political sense of this word would suggest; for I am connecting it with the highest human attributes, with the ideal and the absolute; I am relating it to the inalienable dignity of mankind, which no force, however humiliating, can destroy.
>
> . . . .
>
> We must define democracy as that form of government and of society which is inspired above every other with the feeling and consciousness of the dignity of man.
>
> . . . .
>
> Education is an optimistic and humane concept; and respect for humanity is inseparable from it.[1]

Accepting and practicing this faith, our schools can help fashion the democratic society of tomorrow.

---

[1] Thomas Mann, *The Coming Victory of Democracy*, pp. 17, 19, 25. New York: Alfred A. Knopf, 1938.

5. The Objectives of Living and Learning

We have now considered the essential views of an idealistic philosophy of life and their presence in our conception of the learner, the curriculum, method, and society's school. It remains to consider our final and culminating topic: the objectives of living and learning. Here we shall need to present and stress the values of life as idealism conceives them. The objectives of living and learning should be the realization of the values of life. What are those values?

a. What is the Highest Good in Life? The term ' values ' refers to those experiences that are most worth having. But which are these? Here we face at once the philosophic question concerning the highest good (*summum bonum*) in life. What is that? The Epicureans say pleasure, though the founder of this philosophy, Epicurus, himself (d. 270 B.C.) said rational pleasure. Plato and Aristotle said the highest good was happiness, which was to be found in the exercise of the rational powers of man. The author of the Fourth Gospel found it in ' eternal life ' which came from the knowledge of God and His revelation. Jeremy Bentham, socializing the view of the Epicureans, said it was " the greatest good (pleasure) of the greatest number." A modern ethical theorist, Thomas Hill Green, under Hegelian inspiration, finds the highest good in ' self-realization,' a concept requiring a social as well as a personal application, and involving the maximum fulfilment of man's capacities in all desirable directions.

The list of views concerning the highest good of man could be considerably extended but this list is enough to show us one thing, viz., that any formulation of the values of living is dependent on some view of human nature. The Epicureans emphasized man's emotional nature, Plato and Aristotle emphasized man's rational nature, John's Gospel emphasizes man's spiritual nature, Bentham recognized man's social nature, and Green emphasized man's potential nature. We shall have to follow these leads in determining the values of life and try to build our conception of human values on our analysis of the requirements of human nature.

However, it should be noted at the outset that human nature is not a fixed quantity, it is not unchanging, it is most flexible, most adaptable. " Human nature is always the same," is a gross misstatement, except when taken in the sense of the native propensities, drives, or inclinations. All men experience hunger, thirst, need for shelter and a mate. Even these native drives vary in different individuals. Those religions that stress ' conversion ' acknowledge thereby that man's nature can be changed. If human nature were not subject to change there would be no occasion for education. We might in that case as well speak of educating sticks and stones as of educating man.

b. The Requirements of Human Nature. Having in mind then the basic elements of human nature upon which to build our account of the values of living, we have to note that man has a physical body; that his acts have significance for others and himself; that he needs to labor in order to live, or else live undesirably on the fruit of the labors of others; that his activities may come to be enjoyed on their own account or for their own sake, and so acquire aesthetic quality; that his emotional life finds completion in another life of the opposite sex and so gives rise to the family; that he needs intelligence in order to guide his activities aright; that his power to think outruns his power to know and so develops a speculative interest; and that he feels himself and thinks of himself as a part of a vast cosmos which calls for some kind of adjustment to it in one's philosophy or religion or both.

From this sketchy but recognizable account of man's nature we can determine those experiences which have value for him, that is, those experiences which fulfil the needs of his nature and bring him a sense of satisfaction and well-being.

Because he has a body, one of his basic values is health. Because his acts have a significance for his own growing personality, another basic value is character. Because his acts have significance for others, another basic value is social justice. Because he needs to earn in order to survive, and not be a parasite, another basic value is skill. Because his activities may acquire aesthetic quality, another basic value is the production and enjoyment of works of art. Because his emotional life finds its completion in union with another of the opposite sex, another basic value is love. Because he needs intelligence to guide his activities aright, another basic value is knowledge. Because he can think beyond the limits of his knowledge, and so develop a speculative interest, another basic value is philosophy. And because he has thoughts, feelings, and perhaps activities in relation to the whole cosmos of which he is a part, another basic value is religion. Here then is our list of the values of human living, the realization of which constitutes our true objectives of living and learning: health, character, social justice, skill, art, love, knowledge, philosophy, and religion.

It may be objected that not all men are or can become philosophers. But we must recall the statue of Rodin called " The Thinker," which the sculptor first called " The Poet " or " Maker." It has universal significance. Man is willy-nilly a thinker. The difference is that some men are more systematic and technical in their thinking than others, but all men in the course of the experience and observation of life acquire a set of views which to them is the intellectual account of how things are in our world. The thinking of these views is our philosophy. The practical acceptance of these views concerning the truly real, or of other views which we have been taught, and the consequent behavior based on them, whether social living, or ritual, or prayer, or worship, or mystic communion, is our religion. These all are needed for the completion of man's being. These all constitute the objectives of man's learning and living. These are our immediate objectives and, in the broadest sense of the term ' practical,' these are our practical objectives.

c. Are Values Cosmic or Only Human? It is a proper but difficult question to raise whether these values are only human or also cosmic. Are these values newly created as man experiences them in the temporal order or are they already realized completely in some superhuman eternal experience? Here philosophies differ. Naturalistic philosophies (including realism and pragmatism) say the former. Idealistic philosophy says the latter, viz., that all human values are but temporal expressions of an eternal order which has value in itself. This eternal order is spiritual in character and changeless in nature. It is the world of essential ideas and ideals. It is the world of the Platonic ideas, the deity of Aristotle, the Jehovah of Moses and the Hebrew Prophets, and the Heavenly Father of Jesus.

When religious faith is put out of the question, and the pure light alone of bare reason, common sense, and experience are brought to bear, the idealist answers deliberately and affirmatively that his ideal world is the most real world, that it exists in its own eternal way, that the eternal world is the only adequate, ultimate explanation of the existence of the temporal changing world and its values, and that man's progress consists in realizing more and more the eternal values in the temporal order. The evil, ugliness, and error of man's way are traceable to his finitude, his weakness, and his wickedness. But if he were not finite, weak, and capable of wickedness, he would not be man and he would be incapable of that growth which makes him an educable being. There could be no finite, temporal order at all for man apart from change, ignorance, error, ugliness, and the power to choose the evil. Life, rightly understood, is just the development of man toward the infinite pattern of perfection. All man's tragedy and all his brief satisfactions are due to his disharmony and harmony with the infinite spiritual order, resulting from his poor or good adjustments, which themselves may be collective, or individual, or both.

d. Why Values Are Said to be Cosmic. But how can reason, common sense, and experience support this idealistic view? The very word ' idealistic ' has at times the connotation of the visionary, the illusory, the fantastic, the unreal, ' the tender-minded ' (James), ' the genteel tradition ' (Santayana).

The answers have the merit of simplicity. Reason says something cannot come out of nothing. But if there were no infinite reservoir of ideal values, the finite values of man would really have come out of nothing. To say that they ' emerge ' only raises the prior questions of " How could they? " and " Why did they? " Reason says life from life, mind from mind, personality from personality. If we have life, mind, personality, the universe which explains us must have life, mind, and personality.

Common sense realizes that life at its best lives by ideals. Not all is lost, if honor remains. The ship may sink, but its captain wants its flag to go down waving. Hope is held to be the anchor of the soul. The truth is mighty and will prevail. Truth crushed to earth will rise again. Faith in the ideals of mankind must be preserved. In patience we possess our souls. In these and many other similar views the common sense of mankind testifies untechnically to the influential reality of ideals.

But ' experience '? Here we have the testimony of the real mystics. Isaiah, Jesus, Plotinus, St. Augustine, St. Theresa, Martin Luther, Swedenborg, George Fox, Wordsworth, Tagore, Rufus Jones, and many others whose ' inner light ' for them is sensed as a real divine light, and not psychopathia. In ' explaining ' these experiences, psychology does not explain them away. On this point let us quote the distinguished scientist and surgeon, Alexis Carrel.

But nobody should ask whether mystical experience is true or false, whether it is autosuggestion, hallucination, or a journey of the soul beyond the diversions of our world and its union with a higher reality. One must be content with having an operational concept of such an experience. Mysticism is splendidly generous. It brings to man the fulfilment of his highest desires. Thus strength, spiritual light, divine love, ineffable peace. Religious intuition is as real as esthetic inspiration. Through the contemplation of superhuman beauty, mystics and poets may reach the ultimate truth.[1]

---

[1] Alexis Carrel. *Man, the Unknown.* New York: Harper & Brothers, 1935.

True it is that reason, common sense, and experience all combined do not demonstrate the truth of the idealistic view of the universe. But they make it reasonable for many to accept idealism. And no competing philosophy demonstrates the falsity of idealism or the truth of its own position. We are all here in a similar position, that of accepting as reasonable what cannot be demonstrated as true.

Of course, if we adopted the pragmatic position and held that philosophy best which in the long run worked best on the whole, we could with James accept theism, or with Dewey reject theism. But that would not help us much till we raised the proper prior question, " Which view is true? " Or, " Which view *has* worked better? " And, " By what criterion of truth has it worked better? " In the last analysis intellectually honest people believe what seems reasonable to them to believe, all things considered; so we have different philosophies, and we are willing in tolerance to have different philosophies. Of course, idealists think that the values represented in the other philosophies are really and properly conserved and guaranteed in idealism, which as yet anti-idealists naturally do not see.

e. Immediate and Remote Objectives. Education is not simply growing, it is growing toward a goal. It is not simply an on-going process, it is a process going on toward an objective. The immediate objective is the realization of the values just enumerated. The remote objective, the absolute goal, is likeness to the spiritual order of the universe. Education in the final analysis is the upbuilding of humanity in the image of divinity.

As the ultimate goal is infinite, the whole process of time is involved in approaching it. This is the prophecy of man's immortality, man as individual and man as society. The conception of a surviving and continuing human fellowship, ever growing toward an infinite ideal of social understanding, sympathy, and coöperation, is that of " the blessed community," of which Royce writes. This lofty conception of education as the growth of individual and social man toward an infinite personal ideal provides the finest possible motivation to teachers and pupils alike. It calls upon all that is within us to realize as fully as possible all that is without us. It will take all the time there is for the infinite fully to fill the finite, and the finite can have no richer objective for itself than to realize the infinite. That is what the finite is for and what it is about.

To some readers these views may seem verbalizing and vaporizing; to others they will appear as suggestive of the meaning of the world that is too deep and rich and full for any adequate expression in words, but which poets may intuit, music may hint, and the feelings remotely sense. Thus Wordsworth writes:

> I have felt a Presence that disturbs me
> With the joy of elevated thoughts.

And Richard Strauss, after a serious illness, composed his tone poem, *Death and Transfiguration.*

f. A Hierarchy of Values. Because there are immediate objectives and an ultimate objective, it is theoretically possible but actually difficult to arrange the values of living in a hierarchy. The criterion would be the contribution that each value makes to the realization of man's absolute goal, his likeness to the spiritual order. The application of the criterion necessarily is freighted with a considerable degree of subjectivity. We might put good health at the bottom of the hierarchy, and yet esteem it highly as a basic value for all the others, enhancing the richness of each and all of them. At the top of the scale would come worship as bringing man into conscious relation to the infinite spirit of the universe. Next to worship would come character in the individual and justice in society as indicating the will of man toward the eternal right. Next would come the production and enjoyment of the beautiful as revealing the infinite perfection. Next would come knowledge as the thinking of the thoughts embodied in the structure of the universe. And then the skill requisite to one's economic independence, which is related both to personal character and to social justice, and which should bring man into sympathy and harmony with the creative spirit of the universe.

It hardly needs to be said, because it is so obvious, that these values are all interrelated. The body and the mind and the different functions of the mind all constitute one unity. The ideal suggests the integrated individual in an integrated society growing in the image of the integrated universe. The individual and society are not yet integrated because the finite and the temporal express only inadequately the infinite and eternal.

g. Historic Review of Educational Values. In an earlier paragraph (p. 183) reference is made to the varying concepts of the objectives of living or the values of life as expressed by some of the great philosophers. At this point, for the sake of comparison, some other famous answers to the same question will be reviewed. It will be noted that the list as already given includes the values suggested by those to be presented in the following pages and includes some values not present in any of these others.

In sonorous prose, like the blowing of his own organ pipes, the English Puritan poet, John Milton (d. 1674) formulated the objectives of education as follows:

> I call therefore a complete and generous education that which fits a man to perform justly, skilfully, and magnanimously all the offices both private and public of peace and war.[1]

Milton has been called a humanistic realist because he emphasized the knowledge of things to be acquired through the study of the classical writers. This definition, however, shows him to be also a social realist, as it emphasizes equipment for rendering high service to society. Surprising to note, Milton does not here include what he clearly states elsewhere, viz., the religious objective of learning, or, in his phrase, " to regain to know God aright." The objective of health may be implied as foundational, but the aesthetic element, which Milton himself so keenly felt, is not included.

John Locke (d. 1704), the English psychologist and also, like Milton, a ' social realist ' in part, presupposed health, he himself being a physician, and added, in the order of their importance, virtue (character), wisdom (in the conduct of worldly affairs), breeding (good manners), and, finally, learning. Locke writes:

> That which every Gentleman (that takes any care of his Education) desires for his son, besides the Estate he leaves him, is contain'd (I suppose) in these four things: *Virtue, Wisdom, Breeding,* and *Learning.*[2]

This list omits religion, though Locke discusses it in relation to virtue, beauty (" I am not for poetry," says prosaic Locke), and skill, the latter being a vocational emphasis Locke's aristocratic type of education would not recognize.

Pestalozzi (d. 1827), Swiss educational reformer, lover of the people, " father of modern elementary education," was influenced by the naturalistic theories of Rousseau. He writes:

> Sound education stands before me symbolized by a tree planted near fertilizing waters. . . . In the new-born child are hidden those faculties which

---

[1] John Milton, *Tractate on Education*, p. 9. (Edward E. Morris, editor). London: Macmillan Co., 1911.

[2] R. H. Quick, *Locke on Education*, p. 115. Cambridge: Cambridge University Press, 1892.

are to unfold during life. The individual and separate organs of his being form themselves gradually into unison, and build up humanity in the image of God.[1]

Pestalozzi himself slights the aesthetic objective, though his musical disciples did not. Though not practical in the conduct of his affairs, he recognized the importance of being so. His especial emphases are ethical, vocational, social, and spiritual.

Herbart (d. 1841), the philosophical realist, maintained that the objects of our knowledge exist independently of any mind that knows them. He was one of the many disciples of Pestalozzi, seeing in his master mainly the use of sense-impression. Herbart's table of objectives is as follows:

Knowledge	Sympathy
Of the manifold (Science)	With humanity (Ethical)
Of its law (Philosophy)	With society (Institutions)
Of its aesthetic relations (Art)	And with the relation of both to the Highest Being (Religion) [2]

The most notable omissions of Herbart are health and skill. Being classically minded, he did not consider the latter as liberalizing.

Froebel (d. 1852) was a mystical idealist. Lacking adequate philosophical training, he relied on intuitive insight. He made the religious experience of the unity of all things his main objective, writing:

Education consists in leading man, as a thinking, intelligent being, growing into self-consciousness, to a pure and unsullied, conscious and free representation of the inner law of Divine Unity, and in teaching him ways and means thereto.[3]

This profound philosophy Froebel would apply to all stages of education. He founded the preschool institution known as the kindergarten (garden of children). Called by Thomas Davidson " the prince of educators," Froebel omitted no one of the objectives we have cited, though he did not stress the physical. Particularly he saw in the acquisition of skill a way of coöperating with the Creative Spirit.

Huxley (d. 1895), the agnostic naturalist, conceives ' harmony with nature ' to be the objective of education. His famous and oft-quoted

---

[1] F. P. Graves, *A History of Education in Modern Times*, p. 137. New York: Macmillan Co., 1913.

[2] J. F. Herbart, *The Science of Education*, p. 133. (Translated by Henry M. and Emmie Felkin.) Boston: D. C. Heath & Co. (n.d.).

[3] Friedrich Froebel, *The Education of Man*, p. 2. New York: D. Appleton & Co., 1887.

definition of a liberal education [1] includes physical, intellectual, emotional, and moral elements but intentionally omits the spiritual and, perhaps unintentionally, does not refer to devotion to the common good, though Huxley himself lived a devoted life. This essay on a liberal education omits the vocational emphasis, a dichotomy which we should not care to make today.

Herbert Spencer (d. 1903), like Huxley, belongs with nineteenth-century naturalistic thinkers. Over a century ago Spencer made his notable pronouncement: " To fit us for complete living is the function which education has to discharge," and made his careful analysis of what the ' activities ' (note the word) of life are. These he found to be, in the order of their importance:

1. Those activities which directly minister to self-preservation; 2. Those activities which, by securing the necessaries of life, indirectly minister to self-preservation; 3. Those activities which have for their end the rearing and discipline of offspring; 4. Those activities which are involved in the maintenance of proper social and political relations; 5. Those miscellaneous activities which make up the leisure part of life, devoted to the gratification of the tastes and feelings. [2]

Spencer, being an agnostic like Huxley, regarded the knowledge of science as having most value for man. He intentionally omits spiritual activities. His somewhat cavalier attitude toward the fine arts, placing them last in his scale of values and allowing them to occupy only the leisure part of life, probably deserves the criticism it has received. Spencer was more interested in the science of the fine arts, like music, than in the fine arts themselves.

Bertrand Russell (b. 1872) is a philosophical realist who has given special attention to the problem of education. He finds [3] the four objectives of education to be: vitality, intellectuality, sensitivity, and courage. Here we find recognition of the physical, intellectual, emotional, and ethical aspects of experience. The spiritual is omitted.

Contemporary philosophical realism of which Bertrand Russell is a representative, has close affinities with the naturalism of Spencer and Huxley. Both naturalism and realism accept the scientific view of life as final, and so both omit religious experience. There is really no

---

[1] C. Alphonso Smith (editor), *Selections from Huxley*, p. 55. New York: Henry Holt & Co., 1912.

[2] Herbert Spencer, *Education*, p. 18. New York: A. L. Burt Co. (n.d.).

[3] See his *Education and the Good Life*. New York: Boni & Liveright, 1916.

conflict between the views of science, as science, and the facts of man's religious experience. It is scientific to recognize the facts of religion. Conflicts have arisen between scientific and theological views. But theology is not religion, it is an intellectual interpretation of the meaning of religion. Religious people make a mistake if they oppose the findings of science; scientists make a mistake if they deny the actualities of religious experience. Logic does not require a scientist to be non-religious himself or an opponent of religion in others; it may require him to oppose certain views held by some religious people. Logic, on the other hand, does not require religious people to oppose science as organized and verifiable knowledge, though it may require them to oppose certain views of some scientists who, passing beyond science, make statements as true which are only matters of faith and opinion. It is not religious to deny facts, it is not scientific to deny faith. These comments on the objectives of learning according to naturalism are necessary for our understanding of the issues involved.

In accepting the views of science as final and as not recognizing a place for religious experience in the life of man, naturalism and realism are alike. Their difference lies, as we saw earlier, in the emphasis which realism in its theory of knowledge places on the independence of the object known.

When the object known, so far from being independent of the knower, is held actually to be modified in some practical way by the finite knower of it, we have pragmatism. This philosophy has dropped its historic idealistic background and has accepted the presuppositions of naturalism. As illustrating the objectives of learning and living according to pragmatism, we may take certain views of Dr. Dewey. These views fall under the two concepts of ' social efficiency ' and ' the valuable phases of life.' [1]

' Social efficiency ' as the aim of education means both industrial competency (vocation) and good citizenship. By ' industrial competency ' is meant the ability to earn one's way and to manage economic resources usefully. Good citizenship is civic efficiency. It covers many traits, such as, being an agreeable companion, being effective in politics, the making of scientific discoveries, the production and enjoyment of art, the capacity for recreation, and the significant use of leisure time. The term ' culture,' broadly understood, is synonymous with social efficiency.

---

[1] John Dewey, *Democracy and Education,* Chap. IX, 2, and Chap. XVIII, 3. New York: Macmillan Co., 1916.

The valuable phases of experience are five in number, viz., the executive, the social, the aesthetic, the intellectual, and the ethical. The executive phase of experience here is like ' industrial competency ' above. The intellectual phase of experience implies interest in some form of scientific achievement. The terms ' social,' ' aesthetic,' and ' ethical ' carry their usual meanings.

In looking over these objectives we have to note that though Dr. Dewey accepts health as one of the values of education and life, he does not amplify his views on this fundamental subject (see the short paragraph on p. 134 of *Democracy and Education*). His interpretation of the intellectual element in life is rather in terms of a method of acquiring knowledge than of a body of acquired knowledge. His identification of culture and social efficiency tends to detract from the privacy and individuality of culture — aspects which are really presupposed in any practical uses to which culture may be put. To be socially efficient is not enough; we must also be ourselves. And Dr. Dewey omits the spiritual ideal as it is commonly understood, and reinterprets it as natural, human, and social.[1] There are no transcendent ideals in Dr. Dewey's present philosophy, no " light that never was on sea or land."

In the interest of completeness, the familiar ' seven cardinal objectives ' should be included in our review. These are: mental and physical health, family and civic adjustment, vocational preparation, leisure-time activities, training in the three R's, and ethical development. In this list only by constructive interpretation do knowledge, philosophy, and religion appear. As given, this list could be taken as an expression of a secular philosophy of life. A very much better statement is that of the Educational Policies Commission.[2] The objectives are here reduced to four: self-realization, human relationships, economic efficiency, and civic responsibility. There is no objection to this statement, if we include enough under ' self-realization,' especially health, art, science, philosophy, and religion. There can be no self-realization without the additional three objectives also.

h. Idealism, Naturalism, and Pragmatism Compared. We have now presented our own conception of the objectives of living and learn-

---

[1] See his *A Common Faith*. New Haven, Connecticut: Yale University Press, 1934.

[2] Educational Policies Commission, *The Purposes of Education in American Democracy*, p. 47. Washington, D. C.: Educational Policies Commission, National Education Association, 1938.

ing and have contrasted the same with the views of some outstanding figures in the history of education. We should probably all agree that the unifying great objective is the realization of the ideals of human nature, but we should differ in the statement of what those ideals are. It should be noted that idealism acknowledges the positive ideals for which naturalism, realism, and pragmatism stand but rejects certain of their negative conclusions. To all of them idealism adds the realization of the spiritual order of the universe, and the consequent supreme value of personality as revealing this spiritual order. It agrees with Plato that despite his imperfections and with his potentialities, " man is a creature of heavenly, not of earthly, growth." Our objective is the understanding, appreciating and realizing sense of the spiritual nature of all existence, and our personal growth in the likeness of that nature.

In comparison with idealism, both naturalism and pragmatism appear as truncated philosophies. Idealism accepts Spirit, and accepts nature and man as really spiritual in character. Thus idealism is synthetic in character. Naturalism accepts nature and reduces man to the stature of nature and denies spirit. Pragmatism accepts nature as the neutral arena of man's activities, accepts man as a creative, not mechanical, though still natural, agent, in whose experience all values center, and denies spirit.

The contrasting emphases in the three philosophies may be presented as follows:

Naturalism [1]	Pragmatism [2]	Idealism
NATURE	MAN	SPIRIT
or	or	or
naturo-centric	anthropo-centric	theo-centric
Body	Mind	Soul
Senses	Creativity and growth	Spirituality
The actual	The practical	The ideal
Might	Using intelligence	Absolute right
Survival	Acting socially	Making sacrifice
Organism	Individuality	Personality

Seeing the strength of each of these positions, some philosophers have embraced pluralism, holding that reality cannot be reduced to unity or even duality. William James is a modern example of plural-

---

[1] This includes all forms of realism except ' religious realism,' which developed in the second quarter of the twentieth century.

[2] Dewey's type.

ism. Seeing the contrast between naturalism and idealism, some philosophers have embraced dualism, maintaining an ultimate division in
all reality. Thus did Zoroaster, Manichee, and Descartes. Other
philosophers, seeing the difficulties in dualism, and recognizing the natural and ideal as opposite aspects of a unified experience, have become
monists, reducing all reality to unity. Some have reduced the ideal to
the natural (naturalism), as did Democritus, Lucretius, Hobbes, and
Santayana. Others have elevated the natural to the ideal (idealism).
These include Fichte, Hegel, T. H. Green, and Josiah Royce. In our
own judgment humanism, centering in man, is better than naturalism,
because humanism saves man's creativity; and idealism, centering in
spirit, is better than pragmatism, because in addition to creativity,
idealism saves both the absolute mind and the human personality.

We have already over-run our limits of space and yet there remain
important questions which students of this text will ask. We will
briefly indicate them, and suggest the answers.

What is the relation of nature to the absolute mind? Nature is a
vast but not infinite self between the self of man and the self of the
absolute. It, like man, is a manifestation in space and time of the
absolute thought and purpose. It does not exist solely to serve man
but a part of nature is the arena for man's activity.

Why this particular natural evolution? Evolution as a descriptive account of how worlds, plants, animals, and man have come about
is a one-way irreversible process, like a serial story, revealing a plot and
a meaning. With unfolding evolution the significance of new forms
becomes greater. In a nonidealistic universe there would be change
but not evolution as the enlargement of meaning in space and time.

Does ' absolute mind ' = God? The term ' absolute mind ' is philosophical, the term God is religious. Philosophy is man thinking, religion is man worshipping. Philosophy and religion are related but not
identical. Theology is akin to philosophy of religion. The term ' absolute mind ' to an objective idealist is a real synonym for the term God.
But many religious persons have other conceptions of God, and have
an intellectual right to their conceptions.

Does idealism as a philosophy = religion? No. Idealism is a certain intellectual account of the world. It provides only one possible
basis for religious worship. Primitive animism, Cartesian dualism,
various forms of anthropomorphism, and certain modern forms of realism provide other possible bases. Pragmatism of the Jamesian type
may accept God as an hypothesis.

Is ' spiritual ' synonymous with religion? No. To hold that the universe is spiritual in character is an ontological view. To be religious is a matter of man's attitude toward the spiritual order of the universe. To be ' spiritual-minded ' might be synonymous with being religious.

What are the reasons for man's finiteness, weakness, evil? Man is finite because the infinite can manifest its nature only in finitude. The infinite cannot give birth to another infinite. Two finites are consistent with each other. There cannot be two infinites.

Man's weakness is part of his finitude. The flesh is not pure spirit, though it may be ruled by the spirit. The weakness of the flesh is the opportunity for the development of strength of character, which is one of the goals of human living.

The evil in man's life may be natural, like a flood, or an earthquake, and betokens man's failure to adjust himself as yet to the kind of world in which he lives. Or, the evil in man's life may be ethical, like murder, thieving, lying, and betokens man's ignorance, apathy, perversity, or wilful choice of the wrong, as illustrated by King Richard III. But all the evils of finitude are atoned for in the suffering life of the absolute.

i. The Reality of Ideals. In the light of the total philosophy of idealism, we conclude that the objective of living and learning is to develop the natural man into the ideal man. Some say that man has already been on the earth half a million years. However long, he has not yet advanced very far on the road toward the ideal. But he is advancing. It may take an aeon of time on the earth at man's present rate of advance for him to approximate even his present ideal. As he develops, he will conceive ever higher ideals. Or, an intellectual revolution, long preparing, may suddenly take place. Mankind may suddenly realize its own folly, drop it, and decide to live, as man can, more in accord with the ideal. We should not be discouraged but manfully struggle on.

Or, it may be, that man on the earth has made but little spiritual progress, that his material progress in the mechanical arts has only provided him with larger opportunity for injuring his fellows, that his ethical advance does not keep pace with his science, that he will always be at odds with himself on this earth, that one civilization after another will continue to go down under the stress of internal weakness or external might, that man rises higher only to fall lower. If so, the idealist must maintain that ideals are still the most real things in the world, that the eternal succeeds where the temporal fails, that " hereafter in a better world than this," man, having learned his lesson but imperfectly here, will learn it more perfectly there, and grow eternally in the image of the ideal. The basis for this conviction is that ideals are real and cannot finally fail. If indeed it be that naturalism is correct, that the material world will finally snuff out all the ideal hopes of man, and finally write a cipher as the equivalent of all his efforts and his achievements in art, science, morals, and religion, even so it will remain true that the ideal was better while it lasted than the natural. But if idealism is correct, this supposition cannot come to pass.

It can hardly be doubted that the reality of the spiritual provides the most lofty motivation to the efforts of man. This is because to the egoistic motives of the natural man, even those of the humanized man working for a better social order, it adds the motives of the spiritual man who accepts divine standards, labors for divine approval, and senses the divine solicitation. As Francis Thompson wrote:

> Halts by me that footfall:
> Is my gloom, after all,
> Shade of His hand, outstretched caressingly?

REFERENCES

Barrett, Clifford (editor). *Contemporary Idealism in America*. New York: Macmillan Co., 1932. Pp. ix + 326.

Brightman, E. S. *A Philosophy of Ideals*. New York: Henry Holt & Co., 1928. Pp. vii + 243.

Cunningham, G. W. *The Idealistic Argument in Recent British and American Philosophy*. New York: D. Appleton-Century Co., 1933. Pp. xiii + 547.

Froebel, Friedrich. *The Education of Man*. New York: D. Appleton Co., 1887. Pp. xxv + 332.

Gentile, G. *The Reform of Education*. New York: Harcourt, Brace & Co., 1922. Pp. xi + 250.

Hocking, W. E. *Human Nature and Its Remaking*. New Haven, Connecticut: Yale University Press, 1929. Pp. xxvi + 496.

Horne, Herman H. *The Philosophy of Christian Education*. New York: Fleming H. Revell, 1937. Pp. 171.

Leighton, J. A. *Individuality and Education*. New York: D. Appleton & Co., 1928. Pp. xi + 204.

Martz, Velorus. "Philosophy of Education," *Encyclopedia of Educational Research*, pp. 798–801. New York: Macmillan Co., 1941.

Radhakrishnan, S. *An Idealist View of Life*. New York: Macmillan Co., 1932. Pp. 351.

Royce, Josiah. *Lectures on Modern Idealism*. New Haven, Connecticut: Yale University Press, 1919. Pp. xii + 266.

Swabey, Marie C. *Logic and Nature*. New York: New York University Press. Pp. xiv + 384.

CHAPTER V

IN DEFENSE OF THE PHILOSOPHY OF EDUCATION

Mortimer J. Adler
Associate Professor of the Philosophy of Law
University of Chicago
Chicago, Illinois

I. Introduction

The reason why a volume of this sort can come into being is that there exists a variety of doctrines about education, among which there are many *apparent* oppositions. If all the oppositions were only apparent, and not real, then there would be perfect agreement in the field of educational philosophy. No one supposes that to be the case. There are real disagreements and we are obligated to do something about them. Now I say that to regard these real disagreements as merely differences of opinion — each ' thinker ' entitled to his own — is to do absolutely nothing about them. If the contributors to this volume regard themselves merely as expressing their several points of view, among which no choice can be made on absolutely objective grounds of truth and falsity, then this symposium is a vicious travesty on the very notion of *philosophy* of education.

1. Philosophy as Knowledge or Opinion

Either there is a distinction between knowledge and opinion, or everything is opinion. In the latter alternative, neither science nor philosophy has any objective status as a body of knowledge in which all men can be compelled to agree by the weight of the evidence and the demands of reason. In the former alternative, either (1) philosophy as well as science is knowledge, although the two spheres of knowledge are essentially distinct in object and method; or (2) only science is knowledge, and philosophy is opinion; or (3) there is no essential distinction between philosophy and science as knowledge. Only if the first of these three possibilities is actually the case, to the complete exclusion of the other two, can this symposium have the significance or worth to which it pretends. For if everything is a matter of opinion, this collection of different opinions is nothing more than a literary adventure in comparative "intellectual" autobiography, and the reader must be seeking entertainment when he takes up a volume of this sort, containing so many equally entertainable views; or, perhaps, he should simply be pleased to find that at least one of the contributors confirms his prior prejudices; or, perhaps, reading a volume of this sort would be like a field trip among primitive tribes differing in their fundamental myths about the world and man — the reader, like the anthropologist, content to record the diversity and never to judge.

The same results follow (even though a real distinction between knowledge and opinion be granted), if knowledge is identified with science, and opinion with philosophy, or if philosophy and science are identified with each other as knowledge of precisely the same sort. For, on the first hypothesis, philosophy is mere opinion, and although there may be genuine knowledge about education obtained by scientific research, nothing that can be said as the result of philosophical analysis or reflection, is genuine knowledge. This first hypothesis, therefore, makes this symposium no less a travesty on the philosophy of education than results from supposing *everything* to be a matter of opinion. And, on the second hypothesis, this volume must become unintelligible to any reader who is acquainted with the literature of scientific research in the field of education. The several essays composing it are certainly not that sort of thing: They are not the reports of *investigations* of observable phenomena; they are not records of *measurement* and *correlation;* they do not conclude with statements of empirically verifiable *findings,* which can be tested by other investigators using the same method to gather the same sort of data. I do not mean that these essays may not contain knowledge of the sort indicated, but I do insist that they all contain *more* than that.

The whole question is about what this *more* is. If it is not scientific knowledge, what is it? It must either be philosophical *knowledge,* essentially distinct from the scientific knowledge that these essays also contain, or it must be mere opinion. If the writer or reader takes the latter alternative here, he is reduced to the same position which has already been rejected. If he takes the former alternative, he admits a real distinction between science and philosophy as different types of knowledge, essentially distinct in object and method. And he cannot avoid taking one of these two alternatives because the actual content of the essays composing this volume is *prima facie* evidence that there is something more here than scientific knowledge. Anyone who knows anything about the nature of scientific knowledge knows that a ' symposium' in the science of education would not present a picture of fundamental disagreements about principles and conclusions, but rather merely a variety of compatible and supplementary researches dealing with the same or related problems. It is this very difference between a collection of scientific researches and a symposium of philosophical essays which leads most people to think that science is knowledge and that philosophy is opinion. That such an inference is shallow and erroneous does not alter the point, namely, that both the writers and readers of this volume must recognize its distinctive character as a *symposium* on the *philosophy* of education. Acknowledging this, they must further acknowledge that philosophy is a sphere of knowledge or suffer the consequences of reducing this whole enterprise to a travesty upon its name and purpose.

2. Criteria of Philosophical Inquiry

The criteria for judging the several contributions to this volume must be the critical standards appropriate to philosophical inquiry, whereby truth is distinguished from falsity. This means, furthermore, that there cannot be many equally true, though opposed, philosophies of education. With respect to education, as with respect to every other matter which the philosopher considers, there can be only one set of true principles and conclusions. To say this is to say there is only one true philosophy of education, only one body of philosophical knowledge about education, and not a variety of equally entertainable ' systems,' each with its own arbitrary ' postulates ' and ' definitions.' In this field, as in any other, the philosopher must proceed from principles evident to all, and from real, not nominal, definitions, to conclusions validly drawn. This does not mean that those who endeavor to do philosophical work cannot make errors; otherwise, how would there be so many false philosophies of education? It means only that philosophical truth is demonstrable — much more so than scientific findings are, and even more than the sort of mathematical conclusions which depend upon postulates, as in various modern geometries. It means that every error which is made in the philosophy of education can be shown to be false, and must be rejected when it is so revealed. And, above all, it means that those who accept the obligation of being philosophers must accept nothing which has not been seen or been proved to be true, and reject nothing which has not been conclusively shown to be false.

No part of what is *strictly* the philosophy of education is either a matter of faith or of opinion. Although philosophy differs from science in both object and method, it is like science in this fundamental respect — that every one of its propositions is true only in the light of experienced fact and in terms of the canons of rational procedure. Like science, it differs not only from opinion, but also from dogmatic theology which proceeds in terms of a higher light than reason or experience can provide — the light of *supernatural* faith, the gift of God who has revealed Himself to men. In short, philosophy, like science, is *knowledge* and, as knowledge, is entirely *natural*. The principles of religious education cannot be *established* by the philosopher. They ultimately rest upon religious (supernatural) faith, and are matters properly for the theologian. I shall return subsequently to the problem of religious education as that presents itself to the philosopher.

Although I must hold that there is only one true philosophy of education, because no other position is compatible with the conception of philosophy as knowledge rather than as opinion, I cannot say, *for the same reason,* that what I am here going to offer as an account of the philosophy of education is *the* true *one.* I would not be offering it, of course, if I did not think it true, but whether it is true or false depends upon whether it does or does not satisfy all the criteria relevant to a critical judgment on philosophical work. Each reader must ultimately decide that for himself. My only insistence at this point is that these criteria must be the same for all; or, to put the matter another way, I am saying that unless all of the collaborators in this enterprise, both writers and readers, initially agree upon standards of judgment appropriate to philosophical discussion, any further argument among them becomes meaningless.

3. Limitations of Present Discussion

I recognize the paradoxical situation in which we find ourselves at this point. This initial agreement is required to make our discussion intelligible as philosophical argument, and yet one of the most profound disagreements among writers in the field of education is on the nature of human knowledge itself, on the distinction between knowledge and opinion and the relation of philosophy to science. Most of my colleagues in this volume disagree with what I have said about there being only one true philosophy of education, true on objective grounds and with a certitude that exceeds the objectivity and certitude of mathematics or science. Precisely because they deny what I affirm, they do not face the difficulties I face in undertaking the task of contributing to this volume. They are willing to present what they have to say as their opinion, their point of view about education, or their ' system of philosophy ' — a doctrine consistently developed from certain assumptions, but only one among a possible many, and ultimately better than the others only for those who *voluntarily* make the same assumptions. I am not willing to proceed on such terms, nor can I regard a symposium so constituted as having any philosophical worth whatsoever. How, then, can I take part? Where shall I begin?

The perfect solution would be to *demonstrate* the propositions I have affirmed about the nature of human knowledge, and about the status of philosophy (including the philosophy of education). But that is impossible within the spatial and other limitations imposed upon the several contributions to this volume. In the first place, it would take a volume as large as the present one to give a technically adequate rendering of the theory of knowledge; and in the second place, if that account were being offered to readers unversed in the technical intricacies of philosophy, the rhetorical expansions necessary to make it intelligible would require many times the space. I am not willing to *pretend* that something has been shown when I know it has not. I cannot, therefore, begin at the proper beginning. How, then, can I consider myself as entering into argument with those of my colleagues with whom I disagree, since our initial disagreement is about the very criteria in terms of which the argument is to be judged, and since to argue the points relevant to this initial disagreement would require nothing less than an adequate exposition of the whole theory of knowledge, involving a great deal of metaphysics, as well as logic and psychology?

a. Distinction between Genuine and Apparent Disagreement. The only solution is a very imperfect one, indeed. The diversities of doctrine to be found in a volume of this sort may be due to the fact that what is being considered by different writers is not the same or that, even when the subject matter appears to be the same, the methods of inquiry are different. Now, genuine disagreement can occur between two men only if they have a common subject matter and share a common method. Thus, if two men use the word ' education ' to denote quite different things, they can disagree only *apparently,* not *really,* when they make conflicting statements about education. And this is certainly true also if they approach what is apparently the same subject matter by different methods, for, if their methods are fundamentally different, so must their objects be, and hence the subject matter can be the same only *apparently.* Real differences in subject matter (as, for example, the difference between the science and the philosophy of education) must be accompanied by differences in problem or differences in method. To the extent, therefore, that the other members of this symposium employ a method different from mine or consider a different problem, our subject matters differ and there can be no genuine disagreement between them and me. The reader is in no way obligated to choose between us, for there will be no opposition between truth and falsity; there will be only an aggregation of supplementary statements, each of which must, of course, be judged as true or false in terms of the criteria appropriate to the context of subject matter and method in which such statements occur.

To the extent, however, that the members of this symposium deal with the same subject matter according to the same method, there can be genuine disagreement among us, but then it must also be true that we all accept the same criteria of judgment concerning what is true and false, for the criteria are involved in the very definition of the method by which we together undertake the consideration of a common subject matter. It is thus shown that genuine disagreement is possible only among men who initially agree about the criteria of judgment concerning the true and the false, because genuine disagreement can occur only within the framework of a common subject matter and method, which framework itself imposes the criteria of judgment.

This solution is imperfect for two reasons. In the first place, the same difficulties which prevent me from beginning with an adequate account of the nature of human knowledge, also prevent me from making clear at once all the possible distinctions of subject matter and method which may explain the diversity of nondisagreeing doctrines in this book. This, in the second place, imposes a great burden upon the reader, for all the critical discriminations must ultimately be made by him. He must decide, in every instance, whether two writers are treating the same subject matter, dealing with the same problems, and employing the same methods. If they are not, he must be able to see how the two treatments are related to one another; if they are, and if, in addition, they disagree, he must know the criteria by which to judge the issue between them. It goes without saying that he must judge, but it needs to be repeated that he cannot judge properly unless he employs the appropriate standards.

b. .Scope of This Exposition. In terms of this solution, I shall proceed as follows. I shall first try to define the subject matter of the philosophy of education by formulating the questions to be answered by the philosopher and contrasting them with questions which are not for

him to answer. I shall then propose some of the answers which a philosopher can demonstrate and indicate in what manner they can be
demonstrated. Finally, I shall consider the relation of such answers,
constituting the philosophy of education, to other questions and answers
which lie beyond the philosopher's scope; and in so doing I hope to
indicate the relation of the philosophical to other approaches — differing both in subject matter and method. In the course of this procedure,
the philosophical method should become exemplified for the reader,
even if it is not explicitly discussed; and this, together with an explicit
definition of the subject matter considered by a philosopher of education, should enable the reader to determine the extent to which this contribution and the others join issue in genuine disagreement. If the
reader is able to make this determination, I am sure that he will also
understand the method of philosophy and employ the appropriate criteria for judging the issue.

I must call attention to two other things about my procedure.

(1) Any subject matter which is conceived in terms of a set of problems can be broadly or narrowly defined. This is not true of every subject matter the philosopher considers, such as metaphysics or ethics, for
these subject matters are objectively constituted and determine the
range of problems which must be considered. But the philosophy of
education is, strictly speaking, not an objectively constituted subject
matter. It is rather like the philosophy of law or the philosophy of art
— constituted by a set of problems which require us to cross the boundaries of such objectively constituted subject matters as ethics and politics, or metaphysics and psychology. And in every case of this sort,
the philosopher is at liberty to conceive his subject matter broadly or
narrowly, according as he includes or excludes certain problems appropriate for consideration. He is not at liberty, of course, to include
problems which are not philosophical, but he can exclude genuinely
philosophical problems in the interest of restricting the scope of his
inquiry. I shall, therefore, try to indicate what I think is a *useful*
limitation in the scope of the philosophy of education and why I think
so. I cannot quarrel, of course, with anyone who, with good reason,
chooses a broader or narrower definition of the subject matter — so long
as it remains properly philosophical. This is a point the reader must
remember in comparing the various essays, in so far as he deems them
to be philosophical in the same fundamental sense of common method
and subject matter.

(2) I said before that I shall propose answers which can be demon-

strated, and indicate *how* they can be demonstrated. *I did not say that I would present the actual demonstrations.* Just as a demonstrative exposition of the theory of knowledge is impossible within the limitations of this symposium, it is impossible, for the same reasons, to demonstrate even the few points I shall make in the philosophy of education. A demonstration cannot be achieved unless it rests upon the solid ground of evident *or* self-evident truths. Now if the readers of this book, as well as my colleagues in this enterprise, affirmed the primary (i.e., indemonstrable) truths of metaphysics and ethics, and all the conclusions, demonstrated therefrom, about the nature of man and the conditions of a good human life, we could proceed to a quick and satisfactory demonstration of the major propositions in the philosophy of education. But if that were the case, there would be no need for this symposium at all, for among men who know the truths of metaphysics and psychology, of ethics and politics, there is not likely to be disagreement about any of the major tenets of educational philosophy. The very existence of this symposium, therefore, indicates that we are living in a community of scholars which is a community in little more than the barest externals of communication. So far as genuine philosophical disagreements about education occur in this volume, they will be seen to arise from disagreements on much more basic matters, matters anterior to the discussion of education — the problems of metaphysics and psychology, of ethics and politics. It is too much to expect these basic issues to be argued — and I mean *really argued* — by any of the contributors to a volume of this sort. The philosophy of education, like the philosophy of law or the philosophy of art, can be adequately formulated only at the very end of philosophical inquiry, after all the basic (and objectively constituted) philosophical subject matters have been thoroughly treated. The reason is obvious: These branches of philosophy are not objectively constituted subject matters; rather they are sets of problems which crosscut all the basic subject matters. How, then, is it possible to give demonstrative solutions of these problems except in terms of all that is philosophically prior? And since the writers and readers of this book probably disagree more than they agree about the prior fundamentals, the writers should not pretend to give, nor the readers expect to get, demonstrations.

In the very nature of the case, a book of this sort cannot be satisfactory to anyone who really wishes to know the truth in the philosophy of education, for that depends upon almost the whole of philosophy. There is no short-cut worth taking. If anyone has not the time, patience, or willingness, to study philosophy in its entirety, let him resign himself to being ignorant of the philosophical truths about education; or let him be honest enough to admit that if he holds one philosophical position, as opposed to another, he does so on authority or by prejudice. What I have just said applies not only to the readers of the present volume, but to its writers and its sponsors, for we should all agree that if philosophy is worth considering at all, it deserves to be properly considered, and we must all honestly admit that it cannot be well considered in this way. Whether a good book on the philosophy of education can be written for a contemporary audience I do not know, but I sorely suspect its impossibility, for the simple reason that if it could be written, it would not have to be, and if it has to be, it cannot be well done. In any case, I have now sufficiently apprised the reader of the doubts and difficulties which beset me as I proceed to take part in this undertaking.

II. The Problems

I am here concerned to indicate the questions about education which are for the philosopher to answer, and to distinguish them from those which are beyond the sphere of his special competence. This is important to do because the existing literature which is called " philosophy of education " reveals the lack of such distinction: Problems which are not philosophical are treated as if they were, and men who are not philosophers try to solve philosophical problems. In either case, confusions of subject matter result and critical standards, standards of competence, become obscured. Everyone today would be shocked if a theoretical chemist did not know the difference between a problem for chemical research and the problem of running a drug store, or if a practicing pharmacist did not realize that he had to have the special competence of a theoretical chemist before he tried to solve the latter's research problems. In the field of the natural sciences we do acknowledge the significance of distinctions in subject matter and types of problems; we do recognize the requirements of technical competence for distinct intellectual tasks. It is unfortunate that, in our time, philosophy is not similarly respected either by the general public or by the ' scholars.' And this is particularly true in such fields as the philosophy of law or the philosophy of education in which the subject matter is constituted by a set of problems which can be solved only in the light of prior philosophical knowledge. Not all legal problems are philosophical; nor is technical competence in law sufficient for answering all questions about law, for some of them are truly philosophical. The same can be said for the problems of education: Only those which can be answered in terms of prior philosophical knowledge are philosophical; and the possession of such knowledge is indispensable to solving them. Technical competence as an educator, or practical experience in the work of education, is not enough.

1. Theoretical and Practical Problems Distinguished

The first step to be taken in defining the limited sphere of the philosophy of education rests upon the distinction between theoretical and practical problems. A theoretical question is one which asks about the nature of things, about what is the case in any realm of existence or phenomena. A practical question is one which asks about what should be done, about what men should do in any realm of action or production. This distinction is currently made in other ways: We speak of questions of fact or questions of value, we speak of descriptive and explanatory formulations vs. normative. The answers to theoretical questions describe or explain the facts; the answers to practical questions set up the norms or define the values which determine what men should do, for they are the standards whereby we discriminate between a better or worse choice in any case in which we face alternatives, and every practical problem is ultimately constituted by alternatives between which we are free to choose. If there were no alternatives between which we could freely choose, we would have no practical problems. The denial that men have free will — in this precise sense, that they can make genuine choices between alternatives — completely destroys the sphere of the practical as a domain of genuine problems worth thinking about.

The ultimate problems of education, like those of law and medicine, are practical. They are questions about what should be done to educate a man — one's self or another. This does not mean, of course, that purely theoretical questions cannot be asked about education. The history of education, for example, is strictly theoretical knowledge about education, for it answers countless questions about what *has been done* by men in their effort to solve the practical problems of education. It describes the institutions and practices of education in different cultures, at different times, under different conditions. Similarly, the history of the philosophy of education is theoretical, because it answers questions about the general policies men have formulated for setting up educational institutions and directing educational practices.

But the policies themselves, precisely because they are policies, are not theoretical, but practical, and the general principles on which they are founded constitute the philosophy of education as a set of answers to the most general practical questions which can be asked about what is to be done educationally.

It may be objected that there are still other *theoretical* questions about education than those which can be answered by an historian, whether of contemporary or past practices. The correlation of certain educational procedures with their educational effects can be measured; all sorts of measurements can be made of what goes on in the schools, educationally or administratively. But clearly the knowledge thus gained by empirical researches, metrical or otherwise, is *scientific*, not philosophical. We must grant, at once, that if there is a genuine *science* of education, it is a theoretical, and not a practical, science, for all of its problems are exactly like the problems of any of the other natural or social sciences. This is an extremely important point; for if the ultimate problems of education are practical, it follows necessarily that such problems can never be solved in terms of scientific knowledge alone, though science may be of secondary or minor utility in helping to solve them. Educational practices are guided by general policies, and these policies in turn can be intelligently formulated only in terms of basic practical principles. Scientific knowledge, whether it be specifically the science of education or any of the other natural or social sciences, can never by itself direct educational practices or determine the formulation of educational policies for the simple reason that such knowledge is purely theoretical. *It is descriptive or explanatory; it is not normative.* Anyone who understands the method of science, the methodology common to all the investigative sciences, natural or social, knows that by such method no questions of value can be answered, no norms determined. (The methods of testing establish norms or standards only in the sense of averages, or the modes of *normal* distribution. This is theoretic knowledge, which can be *interpreted* practically, but the interpretation is not accomplished by scientific research or method.) Thus we begin to see, not only the distinct sphere of the philosophy of education, as answering questions unanswerable by science, but also the need for a philosophy of education — for without it there could be no certain determination of the basic practical principles underlying the policies which direct actual day-to-day educational practices.

But it may still be objected that it has not yet been shown that philosophy can be practical knowledge, or that the philosophy of education does answer distinctively practical questions. That philosophy includes both theoretical and practical knowledge, whereas science is exclusively theoretical, can be shown, briefly, by the fact that the theory of the good, and the definition of the good of anything, is philosophical. We know that the nature of the good in general, or of the types and order of goods, are matters incapable of being investigated by scientific method. We know, furthermore, that every practical problem involves the good, for every choice is between a better and a worse object, or course of action, or policy. Hence, we are faced with this dilemma: *Either* there is no knowledge, but only opinion, about what the good is in general, or what is a good life or a good society, in which case, of course, there is no practical philosophy; *or* there is such knowledge, as distinguished from opinion, and this is practical philosophy, its two major branches being ethics (concerned with the good life) and politics (concerned with the good society). If we take the latter alternative, we shall be able to define the philosophy of education as answering certain practical questions subordinate to those of ethics and politics. If we take the former alternative, then there is no knowledge at all which answers practical questions, and educational policies are at best guesses or opinions without any foundation in demonstrably true principles; in which case, a book on the philosophy of education is not worth writing or reading.

One objection remains, namely, that the philosophy of education may be both theoretical and practical. That it is practical follows from the existence of ethics and politics as branches of practical philosophy, and the recognition that philosophical questions about what should be done educationally are subordinate to questions about the conduct of life or the constitution of society. It may be said, however, that there are some theoretical questions about education which the philosopher answers, as, for example, *what education is,* and *what causes are operative in the process of education.* There is some truth in this point, but its full significance requires analysis. Education itself, as something which goes on in the world, can be viewed either theoretically or practically. Viewed theoretically, education may be regarded as a process taking place in the course of human development. Viewed practically, we see that this process is not *purely natural,* for it seldom, if ever, takes place without one man purposely employing skills and other means to help another man become educated. The production of an educated man is no more natural than the production of any other work of art, a shoe or a statue, if by a *purely natural* process we mean one in which the exercise of human art is not one of the efficient causes. Now, of course, the definition of education as the process whereby one man helps himself or another to form good habits is itself a piece of theoretical knowledge; and so is the proposition that the arts of teaching or learning are indispensable as efficient causes in this process. But these two items of theoretical knowledge about education — both philosophical truths — show us at once that education is fundamentally a practical affair, because it is not purely natural, because it is an artistic enterprise.

2. Definition of Education

I shall subsequently defend the definition of education I have just given as the only true definition which can be given. Let me restate it, now more precisely than before: Education is the process by which those powers (abilities, capacities) of men that are susceptible to habituation are perfected by *good* habits, through *means artistically contrived,* and employed by any man to help another or himself achieve the *end* in view (i.e., good habits). I say that this definition can be proved to be true, and that the full statement of the proof will answer many fundamental questions in the philosophy of education. But that is a matter reserved for subsequent discussion. Here I am concerned only to use the definition in order to formulate the problems of educational philosophy. It may be thought that I am thus involved in circular reasoning, for am I not saying that we shall first use this definition to determine the problems, and then, after proving it, we shall find that it helps us solve these very problems? Yes, but it should also be obvious that no one can define the problems of educational philosophy without first defining education itself, and that if only one true definition be possible, and that one be proved true, no vicious circularity is involved in the process. This will become apparent to the reader as he observes the use to which the definition is put.

a. Practical Aspects of Education. In the first place, let me call attention to the fact that the definition, as its italicized words indicate, makes the problems of education practical, in three ways. (1) They are concerned with the good, for education aims to form not any sort of habits but only good habits, traditionally analyzed as the virtues. (2) They are artistic problems, problems of how to use means for producing certain desirable effects as ends. (3) They are ethical problems in so far as they require us to consider the virtues and to understand their role as means in achieving the ultimate end of life, happiness; and they are political problems in so far as they require us to consider the responsibility, not simply of one man to another, but of the community to its members, with regard to helping them become educated.

When, in these three ways, I say that the problems of education are practical, I am talking about the problems which any man faces when he undertakes to educate himself or another, or to say what the community should do to educate its members. I am not talking about the problems of the science of education, or the history of education (both of which are purely theoretical — concerned with knowing what has happened or how it is happening now). I am talking about the problems of education itself, concerned ultimately, not with knowing, but with actions to be taken. If such actions are to be intelligently directed, there must be knowledge of the ends to be sought and the means to be used. The range of practical problems in the field of education, therefore, includes questions about the ultimate ends of the whole process and about the means in general. These, as we shall see, are the basic problems of the philosophy of education, and in solving them it is *practical* because it directs action. In fact, the answers to these questions, constituting the philosophy of education, are the only practical *knowledge* in the field of education, for no other practical judgments which educators can make have the certitude of knowledge.

b. Education as a Coöperative Enterprise. In the second place, let me comment on the fact that the definition makes the process of education an artistic enterprise. I shall assume that everyone understands what it means to say that shoemaking or house-building, the writing of poetry and the painting of pictures, are artistic enterprises. Shoes and houses, poetry and pictures, do not happen naturally. They are things made by man, in the production of which definite skills or techniques are at work, and this is the fundamental meaning of *art*, the skill or technique which a man has for making things. An artistic enterprise is, therefore, a process in which human art is an indispensable efficient cause for the production of a certain effect — the product being aimed at.

It is necessary to go further, however, and see precisely what sort of artistic enterprise education is. All human arts are not the same. We are all acquainted with the familiar division of the arts into fine and useful (according as the product is something enjoyed or used), and into free and servile (according as the product is an immaterial thing, such as a poem or a piece of music, or a transformation of matter, such as a shoe or a house, or even a statue). But, for our purposes, the only important distinction is that between the operative and the coöperative arts. The operative arts are those by which something is produced that would not happen in the course of nature without human intervention. These arts are completely productive in the sense that they are an indispensable cause of their products, whether the product be a shoe or a statue or a poem. In contrast, the coöperative arts are not completely productive, for they *only assist* nature in the achievement of the product at which they aim. Thus, for example, the arts of agriculture and medicine are coöperative: Without human intervention, the earth produces its vegetation, and the living body possesses health and sustains itself against the forces of disease. Neither the farmer nor the physician is *absolutely* needed. But the arts of agriculture and medicine, coöperating with natural causes, make the desired result more likely and achieve it in ways and under circumstances which more regularly satisfy human needs. The physician's technique is a skilful way of coöperating with natural causes to sustain health and cure or prevent disease. When we understand this distinction between operative and coöperative art, we see at once that the various arts of the educational enterprise — among which, of course, the arts of teaching and learning are preëminent — are clearly coöperative, and not, as shoe-making or picture-painting, completely productive. Take the case of knowledge, which is one of the virtues, or good habits, at which education aims. The human mind naturally tends to learn, to acquire knowledge, just as the earth naturally tends to support vegetation. The arts of learning and teaching merely assist in the cultivation of a mind by coöperating with its natural processes of knowing, just as agricultural techniques assist nature in the production of vegetables. What is here seen to be true of knowledge as a good habit is equally true of every other good habit which men can form, for in every case men possess natural capacities which tend naturally toward certain developments, and the arts of education, the arts of human cultivation, merely coöperate with nature to achieve the desired result — a good habit rather than a bad one.

    c. Implications of Coöperative Basis of Educational Procedures. In the third place, we must consider several consequences which follow from the conception of the educational arts as coöperative. One is the relation between education as an artistic enterprise and education as an ethical and political affair. In both cases, the problems of education are practical, but the ethical and political problems of educational philosophy concern the ends to be achieved, either by a single man in his own life or by a community with regard to its members, whereas the artistic, or *technical*, problems of educational philosophy concern the means in general to be used, their variety and order.

A further consequence is the relation between education as the process in which a man *helps himself* to form good habits and education as the process in which one man is helped *by another* or *by the community* in which he lives. It may be asked whether, if the educational arts are coöperative, education must not always be the latter sort of process, that in which a man is helped by others. Can a man educate himself? Certainly, it must be true that a man is able to learn, to form every sort of good habit, without the aid of others, for if this is not the case, then the educational arts are not coöperative but completely productive. But when a man learns in this way, the process may be entirely natural or it may be facilitated by certain skills or techniques of learning by which he coöperates with his own natural tendencies toward habit formation. Only in the latter case should we speak of the man as educating himself, for in the former the learning is entirely natural, and where no art intervenes, we cannot properly speak of education. But certainly self-education, thus conceived, is either nonexistent or very rare. Man is a social animal. Most of the habits formed in childhood are formed under tutelage or direction of some kind. The very skills of learning, by which a mature man may educate himself, are usually habits which others help him form in his youth. We can conclude, therefore, that probably no man has ever completely educated himself — not that it is impossible, but that it is unlikely in the normal social development of human life. It would appear that self-education usually follows education-by-another, for two reasons: (1) In infancy and childhood, habit formation is usually under the direction of adults; and (2) the skills of learning, indispensable to self-education as an artistic enterprise, are themselves usually products of education-by-another. The only sort of learning which is excepted from this discussion is the type I have called purely natural, and as such, it is not education at all — neither self-education nor education-by-another. It is highly doubtful whether there is much learning of this sort. It would have to occur in early life, since once some art of learning is possessed, a man no longer learns naturally; yet, as we have seen, in early life most learning is education-by-another.

3. Major Divisions of Education

These considerations lead us, finally, to the major divisions of the educational process as defined.

a. Self-Education and Education-by-Another. The first division has already been mentioned, self-education and education-by-another, but it is necessary to clarify this distinction by making three further points. (1) All learning is of two sorts: It is either learning by discovery, without the aid of others in respect of the matters being learned, or learning by instruction, with the aid of others in respect of the matters being learned. Now, as we have seen, learning by discovery may, in turn, either be natural learning, totally without the benefit of art, or it may be self-education, in which some art is employed coöperatively by a man to facilitate the natural process. Learning by instruction is always education-by-another. Here it is important to observe that teaching is an art always used by one man with respect to another. No one teaches himself, even when he educates himself by using some art in his learning, for he who teaches must possess actually whatever the person being taught possesses only potentially and hence is able to learn. This being so, a man cannot teach himself, for then he would already have to possess actually what he is about to learn, which is impossible. Moreover, in every case in which one man is taught by another, the primary activity of learning is on the part of the man who is taught. *Otherwise, teaching would not be a coöperative art.* Thus, we also see that learning by instruction should be conceived as *aided discovery.* (2) Not every way in which one man causes learning in another is teaching. I shall use the word ' stimulation ' for every way, other than teaching, in which one man is the cause of learning in another. Here it is important to observe that what I have said about teaching does not hold for stimulation. A man need not actually possess the knowledge or other habits which he succeeds in stimulating another to acquire. Hence, although a man cannot teach himself, he can, in a sense, stimulate himself to learn. We now face the very difficult problem of whether to classify learning-by-stimulation as education-by-another or as self-education. If we consider stimulation, in all its forms and varieties, as one of the educational arts, along with teaching, then learning-by-stimulation, as well as learning-by-instruction, is education-by-another. But if the stimulation one man gives another is not artistically contrived, and if it is not intended as an aid to that other's learning, then, it seems to me, we should regard the stimulation as an accidental cause and classify the resultant learning as learning by discovery, whether that be a purely natural process or one of self-education. Education-by-another (i.e., learning under instruction or stimulation) must always be a process artistically planned and intentionally executed by that other. In the absence of educational artistry and intention on the part of others, all learning is by discovery. I trust it is not necessary to explain that the other need not be a man living and present; it may be a man, either dead or absent, who operates causally through books or other media of communication or influence. (3) Learning by discovery, especially self-education, may be joined with learning by instruction or stimulation (education by another) in every phase of the educational process. Neither excludes the other; on the contrary, both are usually involved in every field of learning, although at different stages or in different kinds of learning one or the other may predominate. There is only one further qualification here: It is impossible for a man to learn *the same thing* both by discovery and by instruction, for with respect to an *identical* item to be learned, discovery and instruction necessarily exclude each other as *proximate* efficient causes (although each may, *in any case,* function as auxiliary to the other). But this is not true of stimulation (in contrast to instruction), for with respect to a given item one man may stimulate another to learn by discovery. In fact, stimulation is only effective educationally if it is completed by the work of discovery on the part of the individual stimulated. Hence we see that when education-by-another is by instruction, self-education is either excluded entirely or subordinated as an auxiliary, but when it is by stimulation, self-education dominates the process.

   b. Types of Habits Established by Education. The second division is in terms of the types of habits which are the proximate ends of the process. The basic division of habits is into intellectual and moral, according as they are habits of knowing and thinking, on the one hand, or habits of desiring and acting, on the other. Thus, intellectual and moral education are divided, the one aiming at the intellectual, the other at the moral, virtues. But intellectual education can be further subdivided, according as the habits aimed at are habits of knowledge or of art. A habit of knowledge is a habit of knowing *that,* whereas a habit of art is a habit of knowing *how.* Because every art is an intellectual virtue, every sort of artistic education is intellectual. There are as many subdivisions of artistic education as there are types of art, but principally there are three: (1) physical education, which cultivates the most basic arts, the arts of using one's own body well as an instrument; (2) vocational education, which cultivates all the useful arts, whether simply productive or coöperative; and (3) liberal education, which cultivates a special sort of useful art, the liberal arts, the arts of learning itself, the arts of thinking well, of using language well, and so forth. It is difficult to classify that part of education which aims at the habit of any one of the fine arts: Certainly, it is intellectual education, but whether it is vocational or liberal is almost impossible to decide, except in particular cases when all the relevant circumstances are known. If we now call *speculative* that part of intellectual education which aims at habits of knowledge (either practical or theoretic knowledge), in contrast to *artistic* education, we can see at once that speculative education is usually auxiliary to artistic education, in so far as it is necessary to know *that* in order to know *how*. This is obviously the case in most of the learned professions, such as law or medicine, preparation for which must combine the speculative and the vocational types of intellectual education. We can also see the artistic education, of one sort at least, is almost indispensable to speculative education, for some degree of competence in the liberal arts is prerequisite to speculative education at every stage; though not to the same degree, liberal education is also auxiliary to vocational education. Finally, we can at least see, though we cannot here discuss, the problem of the relation of moral to intellectual education, a relationship which may be expressed in terms of the dependence of intellectual education of any sort on the possession of moral virtues, and the dependence of moral education upon the possession of intellectual virtues, especially speculative habits of knowledge and the habit of the liberal arts.

c. Individual Differences in Relation to Education. The third division is in terms of various attributes of the person being educated. In the first place, it should be noted that we are here considering only human education, not the training of brute animals. That men and animals are radically distinct in essence, differing absolutely in kind, not relatively in degree, is a proposition I shall discuss later; it is of paramount importance to the philosophy of education. Strictly speaking, brutes can be trained or conditioned, but they cannot be educated, for education, whether by one's self or by another, is always a work of reason, and brutes are irrational. In the second place, the human person, as the subject of education, may be normal or abnormal, and the abnormality may be either in excess or deficiency of the median quantities with respect to intelligence and other temperamental characteristics. There are also variations in the external and accidental circumstances of the person to be educated: his sex, his economic status, his social background, etc. But most important of all is the division in terms of age. The subjects of education are either immature persons (whether infants, children, or adolescents) or they are mature (adults). Education is the business of a whole human life; it is not exclusively the occupation of the young. It begins with birth and ends with death. When we fully understand all the conditions of infantile and adolescent education, on the one hand, and adult education, on the other, we must realize that adult education is the most important of all the temporal phases of education; the education of youth is at best a beginning, and it can only be at its best when it pretends to be nothing else but preparatory for adult education. While it is true that the immature, precisely because their immaturity consists in deficiencies of habit and experience, *need* education more than adults, it is also true that the mature, precisely because their maturity is constituted by ampler experience and by stable habits, can *profit* by education more genuinely than children. No philosophy of education which restricts itself to the education of the young can be adequate; worse than that, it will be distorted and misleading because the ends of education can only be defined in terms of an educated man; they cannot be properly defined in terms of a child merely in the process of becoming a man.

   d. Institutional or Noninstitutional Education. The fourth and last division turns on whether education-by-another is institutional or noninstitutional. Institutional education may be of two sorts: either by institutions which are primarily created for educational purposes, such as schools, colleges, universities, and adult education institutes of various types; or by institutions which serve purposes other than education, such as the home or the church. This does not mean that the home and the church are not genuinely educational institutions, but only that they are not exclusively such; whereas, in contrast, what I shall call educational institutions (schools, colleges, etc.) have no other function than to educate. That is the sole end which their existence, personnel, and administration serve. This holds true even in the case of universities which claim to be devoted to research and the advancement of knowledge, as well as to teaching, for the advancement of knowledge is meaningless except as increasing the scope and substance of what men can learn. By thus distinguishing exclusively educational institutions from all others involved in education, we are enabled to distinguish the professional educator, whether teacher or administrator, from all other persons, such as parents or writers, who may also be engaged in the work of educating others.

Educational institutions can be divided in many ways, of which I note these four: (1) according as they are privately endowed and operated, or maintained by state subsidies and politically controlled; (2) according to the character of the subjects being educated, i.e., whether normal or abnormal, immature or mature; (3) according to the primary educational aim of the institution, whether moral or intellectual, and if intellectual whether speculative or artistic, and if artistic, whether liberal or vocational, and so forth; and (4) in the sphere of intellectual education, according to the level of the institution with respect to the age of the persons being educated and the proportionate gradation in the substance of what is being taught, i.e., whether elementary, intermediate, or advanced. So much for the types of institutional education. Education-by-another which is noninstitutional may take a variety of forms, but they are difficult to classify exhaustively. Suffice it to mention the cultural agencies which the community is able to provide its members: books and libraries, radio programs and lectures, periodical literature, various types of vocational apprenticeship, and last, but not least, the law as promulgated, administered, and enforced. In addition, of course, there are such incidental operative causes as friends, or any individual who is helpful to another educationally.

4. The Scope of Educational Philosophy

These four divisions of the educational process enable us to indicate the full scope of the philosophy of education.

In the first place, educational philosophy cannot be restricted to the consideration of education-by-another. The ends of education, which are the ultimate principles of educational philosophy, must be conceived in such a way that they hold equally for self-education and education-by-another.

In the second place, in considering education-by-another, the philosopher must not confine himself to institutional education, and certainly not to those peculiar institutions which are exclusively educational; and if this be so, how much more is it true that educational philosophy is neither principally nor exclusively concerned with the work of the elementary or even the secondary schools. All educational institutions, from the lowest school to the university, are only one way in which the means of education are organized and become effectively operative. The philosopher of education is concerned with the means in general, and not with any mode of the means, except in relation to other modes. I wish to emphasize this point because so much of what currently offers itself as educational philosophy not only is not philosophical in method, but also is not properly philosophical in the scope of its subject matter, for it consists largely in a discussion of the extremely limited aims of and the means peculiar to educational institutions, especially the public school system at the elementary and secondary levels. It addresses itself only to professional educators; it is even written in a peculiar technical language, which is called 'pedaguese' and is almost totally unintelligible to anyone who has not 'done time' in a school of education.

The most important phase of the educational process is that which can and should take place in adult life, when a mature individual is responsible for carrying on his own education, whether that be, in mode of causality, self-education, or education-by-another. Certainly adult education-by-another is noninstitutional for the most part. Hence the philosophy of education, properly conceived in scope, must address itself to any intelligent adult who, first of all, is responsible for accomplishing the completion of his own education since it can never be completed in youth or in educational institutions of any sort; who, secondly, as a parent or an elder, may be directly or indirectly responsible for the education of youth; and who, as a citizen, shares responsibility for the educational policies of his community, for the establishment and administration of its educational institutions. Concerned with the ends of education and with the means in general (and their relationships), the philosophy of education has nothing to say to professional educators over and above what is addressed to any intelligent adult.

There are, of course, many problems which belong peculiarly to professional educators. These problems appear at various levels and in various types; but none of these problems is philosophical, as I shall subsequently make clear. That so much current discussion is of these peculiar professional problems is due not only to the fact that the method and character of philosophical knowledge is unknown or disregarded, but also to the fact that, in America today, we are blinded by a romantic adoration of the child. We thus come to suppose that the most important problems of education concern the rearing of children, and we exaggerate the importance of the educational institutions which deal with children. But clearly the beginning of anything is not as important as the end, and the beginning can only be well thought about in terms of the end. The end of education is the educated man; in a sense, therefore, the whole process of education is one of overcoming the deficiencies of immaturity. Our interest in children should be in them as potential adults. In this light, the educational institutions which deal with children and youth should, at every stage, be working to help the young cease to be immature and become adults. The significance of this point will be recognized only by those who realize how much of contemporary schooling is devoted, by explicit policy, to preserving all the undisciplined waywardness, all the inchoate habits, of childhood.

In the third place, the philosopher of education can discriminate among educational institutions according to the level of their preparatory operations, although he must always consider the education of youth as merely preparatory to adult education, and all education-by-another, whether or not institutional, as preparatory to self-education. The work of some of these institutions must be regarded as preparatory to the work of others; and the work of some can be regarded as terminal, so far as institutional education goes. Excluding, for the moment, the institutional care of subnormal persons, and considering only intellectual, not moral, education, we can see the reason for a tripartite division of educational institutions into schools (elementary and secondary), colleges, and universities. The first of these divisions is preparatory to further institutional education; the second is both preparatory and terminal; the third is terminal. To understand this, it must be remembered that no educational institution completes the process of education. University education is terminal only institutionally. By doing the fundamental work of liberal education (the formation of habits of liberal art), the college is preparatory to the speculative and vocational education of the graduate and professional divisions of the university; but it is also institutionally terminal, in so far as a person who is trained in the liberal arts *needs* no more institutional education to undertake the noninstitutional completion of his own education. And the schools, disregarding any difference between elementary and secondary institutions, are preparatory for liberal education. I am aware that there are many problems here, largely raised by the fact that there are many individuals who, for one accidental reason or another, receive institutional education only on the first level, and perhaps not even all of that. There are other problems concerning the determination of the age periods for these different levels of institutional education, concerning the relation of vocational education to liberal education at various age levels, and of both to speculative education, but they are not capable of philosophical resolution and, therefore, the philosopher should refrain from discussing them. I shall comment on this point presently.

In the fourth place, because he knows the distinction between the moral and the intellectual virtues, particularly with respect to the aetiology of these types of habit, the philosopher knows that educational institutions cannot be primarily responsible for moral education. Institutionally, the primary responsibility for moral education lies in the home and the church and in the law-making and law-enforcing functions of the political community. Noninstitutionally, moral education depends upon the ministrations of elders, other than parents, and of friends. So far as educational institutions go, moral education is accomplished by them secondarily and only in so far as (1) they are communities which, as such, can, by rule-making and rule-enforcement, regulate the conduct of their members; (2) the professional educators who compose the personnel of such institutions are elders who can advise and direct conduct, or otherwise stimulate the growth of moral habits; (3) strictly intellectual education (especially liberal and speculative), which is the primary work of educational institutions as places of teaching, is auxiliary to the formation of moral virtues.

There are here two further questions for the philosopher to consider: One concerns the relation, in general, between moral and intellectual education, not only as to division of responsibility for each, but also as to their functional or causal interdependence; the other concerns the whole matter of religious education which is, of course, both moral and speculative, but in both respects rests upon supernatural knowledge, the ultimate source of which is Divine Revelation. The philosopher of education cannot, of course, make any essential determinations with regard to the ends or means of religious education; but he must certainly ask whether the education of a man can be completed, morally or intellectually, without religious education. In so far as he knows, by strictly philosophical knowledge, that God exists and that man is divinely created with an immortal destiny, he knows, negatively, that the whole of natural (as opposed to supernaturally founded) education is fundamentally inadequate for the perfection of man. He knows *negatively* that the highest type of natural knowledge, metaphysics, is inadequate with respect to the very questions the metaphysician is able to answer *in part*, namely, the nature of God and the nature of man; he knows, at least, that another kind of knowledge is *possible*, supernatural knowledge possessed through the gift of faith, and that in this supernatural knowledge lies the possibility of more complete answers to these ultimate questions; hence, in knowing that wisdom is the highest of the speculative virtues, he also knows that natural wisdom, which is the highest end of intellectual education, is not, by itself, a complete or sufficient end for anyone who aims at the perfection of the human intellect. Again, negatively, he knows that the natural moral virtues may not be sufficient for the conduct of life, in so far as he can entertain the possibility that, without the grace of God, human weakness makes the attainment of even the natural moral virtues unlikely. These items of negative knowledge enable the philosopher to discuss the relation of secular to religious education only in the most general terms. He cannot solve any of the difficult practical problems which confront a secularized society, such as ours, in which church and state are separated, and in which there is a variety of religions, each of which should claim to be the only true one, or at least operates, in fact, as if that were the case. But at least he recognizes that an educational philosophy can be *adequate practically* only if it is subalternated to moral theology.

5. Ends and Means in Education

In the fifth place, and finally, the several divisions of the educational process which it has been necessary to make (according to the type of agent operative — one's self or another; according to the type of habit aimed at; according to the character of the subject to be educated; according to the type of agent other than one's self which is causally operative — the various sorts of institutional and noninstitutional agencies), enable the philosopher of education to formulate basic questions about the variety of the means in general, their relation and order to one another. So far as his effort is to determine the ultimate ends of education, which are the ultimate principles of educational philosophy, the philosopher need pay no attention to these major divisions of the educational process. The *ultimate* ends of education are the same for all men at all times and everywhere. They are absolute and universal principles. This can be proved. If it could not be proved, there would be no philosophy of education at all, for philosophy does not exist unless it is absolute and universal knowledge — *absolute* in the sense that it is not relative to the contingent circumstances of time and place; *universal* in the sense that it is concerned with essentials and abstracts from every sort of merely accidental variation. Similarly, it must be said that educational means *in general* are the same for all men at all times and everywhere. If the *ultimate* ends of education are its first principles, the means *in general* are its secondary principles, and the scope of the philosophy of education goes no further than this — *to know these first and secondary principles in an absolute and universal manner.* To aim at knowing less than this, or to regard this as unknowable, is to deny that there is any philosophy of education; to aim at knowing more than this, without realizing that one ceases to function as a philosopher in so doing, is to confuse the philosophy of education with other subject matters and methods, or to confuse one's self by trying to solve, philosophically, problems which cannot be philosophically solved.

As I have already indicated, there are several types of problems about the means *in general:* (1) the enumeration of what they are and the definition of each; (2) their functional relationships; (3) their order to one another in various modes of coördination and subordination. With respect to the last two sorts of problems, the various divisions of the educational process become significant in two ways. On the one hand, the division of education into moral and intellectual (and intellectual into speculative and artistic, and artistic into liberal and vocational) defines different parts of the total process by reference to one or another type of good habit (or virtue) as the exclusive end of that part; and this enables us to consider the type of means which can be best employed for achieving that type of end. On the other hand, the division of education according to the type of agent causally operative (whether one's self or another, and if another, whether that agency be institutionalized or not, and if institutionalized, what sort of institution) gives us a classification of means in terms of aetiological considerations, and this enables us to determine how the means should be related to one another in any part of education or in the process as a whole — for they either exclude one another or they can be coöperative in various modes of coördination and subordination. Thus, for example, we know that, in intellectual education, the means in general are the exercise of one's own powers and the coöperative activity of others helping one in the exercise of his own powers. This reveals, at once, the most fundamental truth concerning the means in general — that there is never any learning without the exercise of one's own powers, for the second of the two fundamental means named above is always a coöperative agency and not a completely productive one. The second type of fundamental means is, therefore, always subordinate to the first, whereas the first can be independent of the second. The second can, moreover, be further subdivided according as the activity of the other agent is mediated (by the recorded word) or direct (as in personal confrontation); whether mediated or direct, the coöperative activity may take the form of teaching, in the strict sense, or the form of stimulation (which includes every other sort of guidance).

Analysis, which I shall not state here, is able to show that these means are differently related in moral and in intellectual education. In moral education, coöperative activity which is both direct and stimulative is better than that which is mediated and doctrinal, whereas in intellectual education, teaching is always better than stimulation, and it can be equally effective as mediated or as direct activity. Moreover, self-education is much more indispensable in moral education than in intellectual education. When the difference between artistic and speculative education in the intellectual sphere is considered, analysis also shows that the ordering of the means in artistic education is, in part, like their ordering in moral education. The sharp distinction, with respect to the ordering of means, is, therefore, between the extremes of moral and speculative (intellectual) education, with artistic (intellectual) education occupying a middle ground and resembling each extreme in part.

Since my present aim is not to expound the philosophy of education, but to define its subject matter by a precise delimitation of its scope of problems, much that I have so far said must be taken as it is intended — illustratively, for the purpose at hand. Were I expounding the philosophy of education, all of these points (and others not indicated) would require much more precision of analysis as well as adequate demonstration. In the next section of this essay, I shall try to suggest the analytic and demonstrative mode of exposition, but I shall not be able actually to do more than suggest what it is like — and even then only for the ends, and not for the means — because precision of analysis and adequacy in demonstration is impossible within the confines of this volume. In this section, two steps remain to complete the definition of subject matter. Of these, the first task is to state the criteria for distinguishing those practical problems about education which are philosophical from those which are not; and the second task is to distinguish between the ethical and political dimensions of the basic problems.

6. Principle, Policy, and Practice

I have already implicitly indicated the criteria for distinguishing the problems of educational philosophy from all other problems relevant to education. In the first place, they are essentially practical, whereas the problems of educational science and history are essentially theoretic. But not all practical problems about education are philosophical. So, in the second place, we distinguish between those which are capable of being solved *absolutely* and *universally*, in the sense already suggested, and those which can be solved only *relatively* and *contingently*. Since solutions of the latter type are practical judgments having, at best, the status of probable opinions, and since practical philosophy, like theoretic, must consist of knowledge and not opinions, however probable, the only practical problems about education which are philosophical are those which can be solved by practical judgments which have the status of knowledge. These problems have already been identified. They concern the ultimate ends (what the processes and activities of education *should* always and everywhere aim at) and the means in general (what activities or devices are available for attaining each of the recognized aims, how these devices are related, and in what order they are to be used — or, in general, what means *should* be employed).

So much is already clear. It is necessary, however, to understand these problems by contrast to other practical problems which are definitely not philosophical. In every field of practical activity, in law and medicine just as in education, there are three distinct levels of practical thinking and problem solving. They are ordered according to the degree of their proximity to or remoteness from action itself, and according to the kind of practical judgment which can be made at each of these degrees. The practical problem which is proximate to action itself is always a question about what to do *in this case here and now*. The type of practical judgment which answers questions of this sort is *singular:* It applies only to the case at hand. The immediate object of such a judgment is a particular action to be performed under these unique circumstances. When it is verbally expressed, though it often is not so expressed, it takes the form of a *decision*. On the second level, in the direction of greater remoteness from action, is the practical problem of what to do, not in this particular case, but in a whole class of cases, constituted by a set of contingent circumstances considered in general. The type of practical judgment which solves problems of this sort is *general:* It applies to more than a single case; it applies to a type of case, or a class of cases all of which conform to a certain pattern of generalized contingencies. Particular actions now become the remote object of such general practical judgments, which, when verbally expressed, as they frequently are, take the form of *rules,* statements of general *policy.* On the third level, most remote from action, is the practical problem of what to do *in any and every case.* Such problems completely abstract from every contingent circumstance, whether uniquely singular or generalized for a class of cases. They regard only the *essential* factors in the practical situation, disregarding accidental variations in the human agent and disregarding the contingent circumstances which are accidental variations in the conditions of his action. The type of practical judgment which solves problems of this sort is *universal:* It applies to every case. When verbally expressed, such judgments take the form of statements of *principle,* the principles being practical in the same sense that rules and decisions are, for they are all judgments directive of action, either proximately or from afar.

For brevity of reference, let me name these three levels, in the order indicated, as the levels of *practice,* of *policy,* and of *principle.* The whole analysis can be briefly summarized as follows:

Level	*Problem About*	*Type of Judgment*
Practice	This case	Singular: Decision
Policy	This class of cases	General: Rule
Principle	Every case	Universal: Statement of principle

Now with respect to everything practical, we must distinguish the order of execution from the order of intention or thinking. Thus, in practical thinking we must begin with the ends first, with the ultimate ends, and then, in successive steps, determine the means in general, then particularizations of these means, and finally we must decide on the singular means here and now to be employed. In the order of execution, however, action starts always with the choice of these singular means here and now and only through many stages do we attain the ultimate ends which were first determined in the order of intention. Hence when we say that the ends (and the means in general) are the first (and second) principles in the practical order, we mean they are first (and second) in the order of practical thinking, not in the order of execution or action itself. This shows us two ways of viewing the three levels we have distinguished. From the point of view of thinking, the level of principles is first, and the levels of policy and practice are second and third, because until principles are determined, policy cannot be formed by general rules, nor can singular decisions be made intelligently in the light of general policy. From the point of execution, the level of practice is first in the sense that the immediate action is the first thing attained after a decision to act has been made. It is the first step taken, the proximate means. By taking many such steps we gradually achieve more generalized results, which reflect the successful execution of a policy, and finally we may attain to the complete result, the full realization of the ultimate ends, and this reflects the successful execution of our principles.

At every stage of execution, of course, the means may be regarded as the proximate ends of action, but the true ends, the ends which are not means in any sense, are reached only in the final stage of execution. The ultimate ends are always potentially present in the means, for the means are the ends in the process of being realized. Thus, the ultimate ends are potentially involved in the general means (on the level of principles) ; and, in turn, the universal means, or the means in general, are potentially involved in the particularized means (on the level of policy) ; and these, in turn, are potentially involved in the singular means (on the level of practice). Thus, we see how, in the order of thinking, we pass progressively from the universal determinations of ends and means to particularized and singular determinations of means, in order to decide how to act in this case for the sake of achieving our ultimate ends, however remote; whereas, in the order of execution, we pass from the least complete realization of the ultimate end (in the singular means in which it is most potential) through various stages in which it is more and more completely actualized.

These considerations being understood, it will now be clear that the philosophy of education treats only of problems which are on the highest, or universal, level in the order of practical thinking about education. Problems of policy and problems of practice cannot be philosophically solved, for on both of these levels the problems are constituted by accidental factors and contingent circumstances. That is why, strictly speaking, the practical judgments which solve such problems are only more or less probable opinions, not knowledge, for it is never possible to be certain that an exhaustive enumeration of accidents or contingencies has been made. But the philosophy of education, which is practical knowledge, must abstract from every accident and contingency, and hence it considers human education only in terms of what is essential to human nature, and the essential conditions and causes of human development or habit formation. To say that problems of policy and practice cannot be philosophically solved does not mean that the philosophy of education, which solves problems of principle, is not practical. If by practical thinking we understand thinking directive of action, either from afar or proximately, then educational philosophy is practical thinking about educational problems, for it is indispensable to an intelligent formulation of educational policies and to an intelligent application of these policies in actual practice. Unless we know the principles which underlie them, our policies can be no better than rules of thumb or merely empirical, trial-and-error procedures; and unless our decisions concretize policies, which are particularizations of principles, they are entirely unenlightened and arbitrary.

It must also be clear that even a perfectly formulated philosophy of education would not by itself suffice for the direction of education, for it must always be supplemented by practical judgments on the levels of policy and practice. In the light of the principles, rules must be intelligently formulated and decisions intelligently made in order that the practical knowledge which the philosophy of education can offer may have its effects in guiding action. Although the philosopher of education cannot solve these problems which arise from the consideration of contingent circumstances, generalized or singular, the educator must do what he can to solve them by forming the best opinions he can in the light of all the available evidence. It is here that the experience of the educational practitioner becomes useful; for it is not by philosophical analysis, but in the light of ample practical experience that one is able to make sound judgments in matters of policy. Here, too, all the theoretical knowledge about education which is afforded by the science and the history of education becomes useful to the practitioner who, using it judiciously in the light of his own experience, particularizes philosophical principles into rules of policy for this or that kind of case. (It should be noted that the science and the history of education remain essentially theoretic knowledge even when used by the practitioner in the making of practical judgments on the level of policy. Furthermore, it is doubtful whether such purely theoretic knowledge would be practically useful to him except in the light of his own experience as a practitioner.) On the lowest level of practical thinking, in the making of a decision in this particular case, it is primarily practical experience and the practitioner's careful inspection of the detailed circumstances of the case in hand which help him to make a sound practical judgment.

All of this can be summarized by saying that the philosopher of education moves on the same level as the philosopher of law or the political philosopher: He formulates the principles of education, but he determines no policies and makes no decisions. The legislator and the statesman formulate rules of law and governmental policies, and in doing so they must consider the *kind* of society they are regulating, in so far as it differs from other societies in a variety of general accidents or contingencies. In doing this they are aided by their own practical experience and by social science and history, as well, of course, as by legal and political philosophy. Whoever, in any community, assumes the task of formulating its educational policies, considering not man and society in their essential natures, but these men and this society in their contingent types, functions as do the legislator and the statesman, not as the philosopher. Finally, there is the judge, who applies rules of law to particular cases, and the official who executes governmental policies by deciding on this or that singular course of action. These men must be primarily men of experience, though of course they should be informed or directed by policy and principle. Here the analogy is with every man who is obligated to make educational decisions, whether concerning his own education or the education of another entrusted to his charge.

This analogy helps us to see one further point about the philosophy of education. In political philosophy, two questions must be distinguished. The first asks, " What is the best form of government, absolutely speaking? " Here one tries to determine the political ideal, and in doing so must abstract from every variable or contingent circumstance and consider only the essence of man and of human society. The second asks, " What is the best form of government, relatively speaking? " That is, what form of government is best for men and societies typified by these contingent circumstances or other specified situations? Now it is obvious that the best form of government, absolutely, may not be best relative to this type of society. If the typical circumstances are inferior, the best form of government relatively will be an inferior form, absolutely speaking. Hence we see that the best form of government absolutely is that form which is best relative to a society typified by the best circumstances. The political philosopher must solve these two problems in the order named. His first task is always to define the political ideal; only after that is done can he determine the various approximations to it, each of which may be best relative to some typical set of inferior conditions.

There are, however, two important qualifications concerning his solution of the second problem. In the first place, he can never be sure that he knows every grade of approximation or every set of contingent circumstances to which an approximation of the best must be relatively adapted; hence, his solution of the second problem is on the borderline between philosophical knowledge of principles and the sort of highly probable opinion with which practical men form policies. In the second place, the solution of the problem of what is best relative to a certain contingent type of society must never be confused with the statesman's judgment concerning the type of this particular society and the best governmental policy proportionate thereto; for the political philosopher, in so far as he deals with contingencies at all, moves only in the realm of possibilities, whereas the statesman is always concerned with the actual case even when he considers it as a case of a certain type, in order to see it in the light of a philosophical consideration of possible types.

The educational parallel is perfect. The philosopher of education is primarily concerned with the educational *ideal*, with answering the question: " What is the best education *absolutely,* that is, for any man according to his essence? " This is the problem he solves by defining the ultimate ends and the means in general, as the absolute and universal principles of education. But the philosopher of education must also consider a second problem, the one concerning various approximations of the ideal, answering the question: " What is the best education relative to this type of man or relative to this type of society, the types of men and society differing accidentally from one another according to a variety of general contingencies? " As in the case of political philosophy, this second problem, unlike the first, cannot be perfectly solved, because whenever one deals with accidents and contingencies, the enumeration of the relevant factors is always imperfect, and the resultant classification of possible types is both insecure and somewhat arbitrary. Strictly speaking, the realm of the accidental and the contingent is the domain of potential infinity, both with respect to addition and division. Hence this second problem is on the borderline between philosophical knowledge and the sort of highly probable opinions which constitute the educational practitioner's judgment when he forms a policy for this or that type of situation. Nevertheless, it is important not to confuse the educational philosopher's consideration of approximations to the ideal, relative to an analyzed variety of possible conditions, with the practitioner's judgment concerning what is the best policy relative to this type of man or society. The importance of the borderline problem, considered in one way by the philosopher and in another way by the practitioner, is that it mediates between the ideal and the real, by applying the ideal to what *can* be actual (the variety of contingent possibilities), on the one hand, and by viewing the real as an actualization of one type of possibility, on the other.

7. Ethical and Political Problems of Education

The problems of the educational philosopher have now been sharply distinguished from the problems of the educator (whether on the level of policy or of practice). They have also been divided in two ways. The basic division is in terms of the two questions: " What is the best education absolutely? " and " What is the best relatively? " The other division is subordinate because, with respect to both the ideal and the variety of possible approximations thereto, consideration must first be given to the problems of the ends (or first principles) and of the means in general (or secondary principles). Only one further division remains to be made. The problems of educational philosophy can be viewed in either the ethical or the political dimension. Thus, in the ethical dimension we are concerned with what is the best education for man, according to the essence of human nature, and what is the best education for men of different accidental types. In the political dimension we are concerned with what are the educational obligations of society to its members; and here we must consider, first, the ideal society and, then, the variety of possible approximations thereto; and in each case we must consider the educational obligations of a society to its members, first, according to their essential, or common, humanity and, second, according to types of accidental or individual differences.

Two things become obvious at once. (1) In the light of the basic political truth that the political community, and all its institutions, is not the end of human activity, but a means toward the happiness or well-being of its members, we see that the political problems of education are concerned with the means, and then only with their organization or disposition. The ends of education are always properly determined by the nature of man, taken essentially or in accidental varieties, and never by political considerations. Whenever political considerations influence the determination of the ends of **edu-**

cation, we know that they are being improperly determined and that we are dealing with some form of political corruption. (2) Since the ends are the first principles and the means are secondary principles, the problems of educational philosophy are primarily ethical and only secondarily political. Furthermore, the ethical dimension is not limited to a consideration of the ends but also treats of the means without regard to their social organization; the political dimension is limited to a consideration of the means and only from the point of view of their social organization.

It is clear, therefore, that all the basic problems of educational philosophy must first be solved in their ethical dimension before political questions concerning the obligations of a state to its members can be treated. Certain qualifications must, of course, be added to this conclusion. On the one hand, it must be remembered that political justice, the virtue of a good citizen, is one of the virtues included in the scope of moral education; hence, there is a sense in which, considering the education of the individual man essentially, we must regard him as a political agent and so refer a part of his education to the service of the political community as an end; but, in so doing, we must always remember that service of the state is only an intermediate end. He who serves the common welfare ultimately works for his own welfare. He does not serve the state, deified as an end in itself. On the other hand, it must be said that when we consider the political obligations of a community to its members, we must determine them by reference to the ultimate ends of education. This is not inconsistent with the conclusion reached above, for the ultimate ends having been ethically determined, the political problem can be solved by reference to them, but the solution itself deals with the social organization of the means.

This concludes my account of the problems of educational philosophy (both in themselves and in their distinction from other practical problems with regard to education) which must be solved by the practitioner, not the philosopher. I now turn to a brief exposition of the way in which the philosopher solves the problems which belong to him alone.

III. The First Principles

1. General Nature of Principles of Education

In contemporary educational discussion, the chief confusions result from a failure to distinguish questions of principle from questions of policy. With respect to a question of principle, there can be only one right answer, for such questions can be answered demonstratively by philosophical knowledge. When, therefore, current controversialists are opposed concerning principles, they cannot both be right. On the other hand, men who concur in the same principles may reasonably differ in policy, for judgments of policy are not solely determined by the principles but also by the view that is taken of the practical exigencies which constitute the type of contingent situation for which the policy is being made, and such judgments depend upon a command of the facts and a judicious interpretation of them in the light of educational experience. For a critical understanding of the positions and oppositions in contemporary educational discussion, it is absolutely necessary to separate issues concerning principles (which, being philosophical, can be resolved) from the competition of policies, all of which may have some merit — but only, of course, in so far as they are based on the right principles.

Let me make this point concretely by using names to symbolize the basic opposition in educational discussion today. Let us consider the issue between every variety of Deweyism (every shade of ' progressive education '), on the one hand, and the position of President Hutchins and the advocates of the St. John's curriculum (every type of ' classicism '), on the other hand. This is an extremely complex opposition, and it will be misunderstood by anyone who tries to simplify it. In the first place, it involves an issue on the level of principles which can be formulated as follows: Either the principles (i.e., the ends) of education are relative and variable, changing with the type of culture, the type of society, and many other contingent factors, or the principles of education are absolute and universal, sanctioning the same ends for men living in different cultures or societies. Moreover, this issue concerning first principles entails an issue concerning second principles, or the means in general: For those who say that the ends are absolute and universal will also say that the means in general can be enumerated, related, and ordered, whereas those who say the ends are relative and variable will deny that any adequate or final account of the means in general can be given.

The issue is clear-cut as stated in terms of principle, but when we move to the level of policy we find that the policies proposed by the opposing parties seem to have some ends in common and often seem to share the same view of the general means. Whether such agreements are apparent or real can only be determined by the closest analytical examination of how the opponents understand the ends or the means to which their words refer. Thus, for example, the fact that both parties seem to acknowledge that intellectual skills, the skills of learning and thinking, are an end of education does not mean that both understand the liberal arts in the same way, or that they agree about the place of liberal education in relation to other educational ends, or that they make the same estimation of the means to be employed in achieving the ends of liberal education, or that both regard the liberal arts (the arts of using symbols of every sort) as constituting an educational objective which is the same for all men at all times and everywhere, always having the same relation to the other basic objectives of education.

Differences in educational policy will thus have two sources: first, a fundamental opposition with respect to the ends, and second, in consequence, a different understanding even of such ends as both parties appear to affirm. But there are other sources of opposition with respect to policy. Considering the conditions of a democratic society, such as the United States, existing in a world such as the present, the opponents make conflicting judgments in answer to a vast set of practical questions about what is to be done here in America today: judgments concerning the obligations of the public school system, concerning the relation of vocational to liberal education at various levels of our educational institutions, concerning the distribution of equal education to all, concerning the role of educational institutions with respect to moral education in view of the decay of home and church as the other institutions charged with this responsibility, concerning the place of adult education in the total scheme, and so forth.

Quite apart from the political dimension of the problem of policy, and attempting to particularize the means in general, the opponents make quite opposite judgments in answer to the many questions about educational procedure, its content or curriculum, its methods or devices: judgments concerning the need for discipline, both moral and intellectual, vs. the need for spontaneity and individual impulse; concerning a prescribed curriculum vs. a system of electives; concerning the motivation of students and how it is to be achieved; concerning the relative importance of actual experience and book-learning at various levels; concerning the limitation of what can be achieved in any educational institution as compared with the scope of noninstitutional education in the years of maturity; concerning the precise content of the curriculum of studies at various institutional levels and also in adult life; concerning the role of the teacher, his authority, his methods, his functions as teacher and as stimulator or guide, the relation of the living teacher to the great teachers of the past, represented by books; concerning the relation of nonsymbolic intellectual techniques to the symbolic skills; concerning the project method vs. other ways of requiring the student's intellectual activity as indispensable to the learning process; concerning the treatment of students of unequal ability and varying temperaments, both with respect to curriculum and teaching methods, and so forth.

Now in all these issues of policy, and many others not enumerated, we must distinguish two sorts of opposition: Either (1) they follow necessarily from disagreement about the principles of education (the ends and the means in general) or (2) they arise quite independently of agreement or disagreement about the principles. In the former alternative, the disagreement may either take the form of the basic issue about the existence and character of the principles (whether absolute and universal or relative and variable) or it may take the subordinate form of a divergent understanding of a given end or a given means. In the latter alternative, the disagreement may arise from an indefinite number of factors upon which practical judgments about policy depend — the promptings of diverse practical experience, unequal emphasis upon this or that area of relevant fact, differing estimates of the probabilities with respect to competing claims that this way is more effective than that, differing evaluations of the relative importance of apparently conflicting objectives, and so on. Whatever such causes be, the opposition of educational policies is not resolvable philosophically in so far as the opposition arises *independently* of questions of principle. *Such oppositions can only be resolved by educational experiment.* The discussion of such issues is worth while only to the extent that it clarifies the practical alternatives and suggests ways of submitting the divergent points of policy to empirical testing.

It is of the utmost importance to remember that the discussion of such issues is not philosophical, that the right practical judgment in answer to all such questions simply cannot be made by the philosopher of education. In the discussion of conflicting educational policies, the philosopher of education can go no further than such conflicts in policy can definitely be shown to result from disagreement about principles. He can contribute to the resolution of conflicts in policy in only two ways: Either (1) by demonstrating that one line of policy necessarily follows from the true principles, whereas another is incompatible with the true principles rightly understood, or (2) where two or several policies are seen to be compatible with the true principles, he may be able to show that one is probably better than the rest as a particularization of the principles for this type of situation. In both cases, he must make evident the connection between principles and policy, but only in the first alternative can he achieve the certitude of philosophical knowledge (by demonstration); in the second, he must be content with a probable judgment, because here he considers not merely the connection between principles and policy, but the fitness of the policy, as a particularization of principles in relation to a typical set of contingencies. These two alternatives, it will be remembered, conform to the distinction, already made, between the philosophical determination of the educational ideal (answering the question, " What is the best education absolutely? ") and the philosophical consideration of approximations to the ideal (answering the question, " What is the best education relative to this or that type of situation? ").

2. Outline of a Complete Exposition of Educational Philosophy

In the light of everything that has been said, we can now see that a complete exposition of the philosophy of education would include: (1) a demonstration that the first principles of education (the ends) are absolute and universal, (2) a demonstrative analysis of these ends in detail, their number, their order and relation to one another, (3) a demonstration that the secondary principles of education (the means in general) are absolute and universal, (4) a demonstrative analysis of these means in detail, their number, their order and relation to one another, (5) a demonstrative analysis of the relation between the means in general and their ends, (6) a demonstrative critique of educational policies so far as these, in whole or in part, are incompatible with the true principles rightly understood, and (7) a less than demonstrative analysis of the variety of educational policies which particularize the principles for different possible types of contingent situations, attempting to say which sort of policy is probably best relative to a given set of possible contingencies.

Anyone who knows anything about the stringent requirements of adequate demonstration or demonstrative analysis will appreciate at once that the philosophy of education could not be thus expounded briefly or easily for one who has to run while he reads. It is preposterous to expect any of the essays in this volume to expound the philosophy of education — if what is being asked for is genuinely philosophy (i.e., demonstrative knowledge) and not just loose talk about contemporary issues in which questions of principle and of policy are intricately confused. It would take a volume of this size, or more, to state the philosophy of education demonstratively (on the first six points) and then to develop it in the direction of policies (on the seventh point). And even that would assume an audience who did not need instruction in all the prior philosophical subject matters upon which the solution of problems in educational philosophy depends — such theoretical subject matters as metaphysics and the philosophy of nature and of man, such practical subject matters as ethics and politics. A treatise on the philosophy of education should not attempt to compress the whole of philosophy, theoretic and practical, within its borders, for philosophical knowledge cannot be compressed without distortions and deficiencies, and a good order of philosophical exposition requires that separate treatments be devoted to each of its objectively constituted subject matters before any attempt is made, in the light thereof, to treat the subject matters constituted by problems which depend for their solution upon all the prior subject matters.

3. First Principles of Education as Absolute and Universal

These things being so, I will attempt only one thing more in the last few pages of this essay. I will try to show *what is involved* in the demonstration of the first of the seven points aforementioned, namely, that the first principles of education are absolute and universal. Note that I do not say I will expound the actual demonstration. The demonstration in full would require the reduction of the conclusion, through many sets of premises, to evident *or* self-evident truths which can be affirmed without demonstration. A philosophical demonstration does not rest anywhere upon postulates or assumptions. A given conclusion may depend upon premises which are not self-evident, and these, therefore, must in turn be proved, and so on until we come to premises which can be demonstrated in terms of strictly indemonstrable axioms, truths known immediately without demonstration. By this standard, to demonstrate the conclusion (that the ends of education are absolute and universal) would require the employment of much anterior philosophical knowledge, both theoretic and practical. More than that, to be rhetorically effective for a contemporary audience it would require the philosophical demonstration that philosophical demonstration is possible, that is, that there are evident *and* self-evident truths. I shall not here elaborate upon the distinction between *evi-*

dent and *self-evident* truths beyond saying (1) that both are inde-monstrable, (2) that evident truths are *synthetic* judgments of exist-ence whereas self-evident truths are *analytic* judgments of essential necessities, (3) that evident truths are indispensable for all inductive or *a posteriori* proofs but not for deductive or *a priori* proofs, and (4) that self-evident truths are indispensable in both sorts of philosophical dem-onstration.

The demonstration that there are self-evident truths, such, for in-stance, as the law of contradiction, can be accomplished only by an indirect mode of argument, by a *reductio ad absurdum*. I shall content myself here with a single form of this argument, applicable to the matters at hand. I say: *Either* there are self-evident truths at the foundation of philosophical demonstration, *or* there is no such thing as philosophical knowledge, and philosophy is either mere opinion or identical somehow with scientific knowledge, which does not rest on self-evident truths. If anyone takes the second horn of this dilemma, he is obligated to admit that he is denying the existence of philosophy as a body of knowledge, independent in its foundations of all of science. It follows, of course, that he denies the possibility of a philosophy of education, which is neither mere opinion nor identical with the science of education. Hence, one must either admit that there are self-evident truths, such as the law of contradiction, or deny the possibility of a philosophy of education, conceived as an autonomous body of knowl-edge. I could go further, and by means of other *reductio ad absurdum* arguments show that the denial of this self-evident truth (that nothing can both ' be ' and ' not be ' in the same respect, or that the same propo-sition cannot be both truly affirmed and truly denied), must result in the view that all scientific knowledge is at best a set of pragmatic fictions, and ultimately in the denial of the possibility of intelligent discussion among men aiming at significant agreement or disagreement. To do this effectively would take pages, and therefore I can proceed with the matters at hand only by addressing myself to those who are willing, *pro tem*, to entertain the possibility of philosophical knowl-edge — the demonstration of every philosophical conclusion by reduc-tion to evident *or* self-evident truths. For the sake of brevity here, I have not developed the other aspect of the argument, namely, the *induc-tive* demonstration of philosophical conclusions by reduction to *evident* truths; even in these cases, the law of contradiction is always indis-pensable; hence, no philosophical demonstration can take place unless there is this self-evident truth, though this by itself is never sufficient.

One other point should be noted. I have chosen to indicate the demonstration of the proposition which is central to the issue about principles in contemporary discussion. The Deweyites and progressives flatly deny what I am here affirming, and affirm, on the contrary, that the ends of education are relative and variable. Since the problems of education are practical, and since in every sphere of practical thinking, the ends are the first principles, it should be clear that from the resolution of this issue about the status of the ends, many consequences will follow with regard to the solution of all subordinate problems. In fact, I would say that every genuinely philosophical issue, between the educational opponents I have named, is crucially affected by whether the ends are absolute or relative, universal and necessary, or particular and contingent. But, even more than that, it will be seen, I think, that those who say the ends are relative and variable also necessarily maintain that there are no self-evident truths and that neither philosophy in general nor the philosophy of education in particular is a body of autonomous knowledge. In short, a complete demonstration of the thesis that the ends of education are absolute and universal would show not only the possibility but also the actual existence of the philosophy of education. That will not be shown, of course, because what I am now about to do is very far from a complete demonstration.

The conclusion I am trying to prove can be stated in the following manner: The aim of education should be the same for all men (i.e., everywhere and always, in every mode of society, every condition of life, etc.). This proposition is identical in meaning with the proposition that the ends of education are absolute and universal, for what any practical process aims at are its ends; hence, to say that education always and everywhere (for all men) aims at the same thing is to say that it has the same ends. The words ' absolute ' and ' universal ' are thus seen to mean just what is signified by the words ' the same for all men.'

Furthermore, as we have seen, in any sphere of practical thinking, the ultimate ends are the first principles; hence, if the ultimate ends of education are absolute and universal, so too are the first principles of that practical thinking about education which is educational philosophy. It will be noted, furthermore, that the proposition to be proved is practical rather than theoretic in its mode: It says what should be done, what education should aim at. To say that education *should* always and everywhere aim at the same objectives is equivalent to saying that its ultimate ends, truly determined, *are* absolute and universal. Here we see an equivalence between what looks like a theoretic statement and a practical statement; but any statement of *what ends are* is only apparently theoretic, as its conversion into the practical form (what *should* be aimed at) reveals.

Finally, let me say that in speaking of the ultimate ends of education I am restricting my view to education as one phase of human activity among many others. The ultimate end of every phase of human activity, considered without differentiation, is happiness. The reason, then, why I do not say that happiness is the ultimate end of education is because that would fail to discriminate educational activity from political activity, domestic activity, the activity of every other human art, for all these aim ultimately at happiness, though each has an end or ends peculiarly appropriate to itself. Hence we must regard the ultimate ends of education not as final ends, without qualification, but as final only with respect to education as a special process and activity distinct from government, domestic management, etc. It follows, of course, that the ends which are final specifically for education, like the ends which are final for other special activities, must in turn be means to that which is the ultimate end of every and all human activity, namely, happiness. And it should be understood, as well, that if the ends of education are absolute and universal, so is the ultimate end of human life. Human happiness, truly conceived, *is* the same for all men, which, as we have seen, is another way of saying that what all men *should* aim at, as the complete objective of their lives, is the same.

The conclusion to be proved being clear, I shall now state the premises which are proximately probative of it. Here is the syllogism:

Major: Good habits (virtues) are the same for all men.
Minor: Education should aim at the formation of good habits.
Conclusion: Education should aim at the same objectives for all men (or, what is equivalent, the aim of education should be the same for all men).

Now, neither the major nor the minor premise is self-evident; hence we must proceed with their demonstration. From this point on we have two independent lines of proof, one converging on the major premise, the other converging on the minor. Let us consider the proof of the minor first.

The proof of the minor premise seems to involve the following propositions: (1) That men are born with various capacities which are undeveloped, (2) that in the course of life, human growth involves — more than certain physical developments — the development of native capacities for various kinds of activity, such intellectual activities as knowing and thinking and artistic production, such moral activities as desiring, willing, and social coöperation, (3) that the development of these various capacities for operation are habits formed by activities appropriate to the different sorts of capacity, (4) that habits can be either good or bad according as they conform to or violate the natural tendency of each capacity toward its own perfection, (5) that the betterment of men consists in the formation of good habits, i.e., the development of their capacities by good rather than bad habits, and (6) that education should aim at the betterment of men. By combining the last two propositions (5 and 6), we get the conclusion: Education should aim at the formation of good habits.

We are now required to examine the premises which enter into this conclusion. The two crucial premises are definitions, one the definition of education in its minimum terms, the other the definition of *good* with respect to habit.

The definition of education, in these minimum terms, is indisputable. This can be shown in a series of dilemmas. First, either education is a process whereby men are *changed*, by themselves or others, or it is not. Here the latter alternative is self-evidently impossible, for the meaning of education is absolutely incompatible with the denial of change. Hence we have the second dilemma; men can be changed by education *either* for better *or* for worse. This second dilemma is intelligible however " better " and " worse " be defined, whether there are objective (absolute and universal) standards of good and bad in human life, or only subjective (relative and variable) standards. Furthermore, there is no choice between the alternatives as stated, for both are equally possible: It is possible for education to change men for worse, as well as for better. But when we realize that education is a practical process, we realize that it cannot be defined except in terms of its end, or what it *should* do. Only if education were entirely natural could we define it in terms of what it is. That being so, our dilemma becomes a choice between saying that education should aim to change men for better or that it should change them for worse. Clearly the latter alternative is impossible, for all men, however else they differ in conceiving education, think of it as something good; and what aims to make men worse cannot be so regarded. Nor can it be said that good education is defined as education which aims at making men better, and bad education as education which aims at making men worse, for if education is itself understood as something good, then the phrase ' good education ' is redundant and the phrase ' bad education ' is strictly self-contradictory. Whatever makes men worse intentionally cannot be regarded as education at all, any more than a law which is intentionally unjust can be regarded as a law, for it is nothing but a disguised expression of tyrannical force. So just as a bad law is a law in name only, so bad education is education in name only. This excludes, of course, the circumstances in which education, rightly intended for human betterment, accidentally and unintentionally fails in execution. Hence we see that the definition of education as a process of human betterment, as activity which should aim to make men better, is self-evidently true. The foregoing discussion is not a demonstration of this definition; it is merely an explication of its basic terms ' education ' and ' betterment,' which, when understood, enable us immediately to understand the truth of the definition.

Thus is established the sixth proposition in the series which I enumerated as relevant to the minor premise. But the minor premise was that education should aim at the formation of good habits. In order to pass from the truth of the definition (sixth proposition) to the truth of the minor premise, it is necessary to show that human betterment consists, in part if not wholly, in the formation of good habits. The first five propositions enumerated are directed to the definition of the good, as opposed to the bad, with respect to human habituation. Now we have a choice in procedure. ' Good habit ' is a term in the major premise as well as in the minor. Hence we can establish the definition of *good* as to habit either in the context of proving the major, or of proving the minor. I shall take the former course, for reasons that need not be given. The proof of the minor is thus temporarily completed. I say *temporarily*, for its real completion depends on the analysis of good habits. For the time being, then, we shall regard human betterment as depending on the formation of good habits, and if it can be so regarded then it is clear that education should aim at the formation of good habits if it should aim at human betterment. The first five propositions enumerated have served the purpose of making this point intelligible, but they are neither self-evident nor proved. That must be accomplished in the proof of the major premise. Unless it is, the minor premise depends upon unverified assumptions about the possibility of a demonstrable distinction among habits as *good* and as *bad.*

I turn, therefore, to the proof of the major premise, and here we face two tasks: First, to show that all men have the same natural capacities; second, to show that for every capacity or power which can be habituated there is a natural basis for distinguishing between good and bad habituation. If these two things can be shown, the whole of the major premise will follow necessarily — that good habits are the same for all men. I shall undertake these two tasks in the order named.

(1) The conclusion to be proved (that all men have the same natural capacities) must first be interpreted. It does not mean that all men possess each of these capacities in the same degree, to the same extent. All of the facts of individual difference with respect to every measurable human ability are quite compatible with the proposition to be proved — that the fundamental abilities are the same for all men essentially, that every being born a man is born with the same set of powers, however limited in degree, or however much held in abeyance by pathological conditions, such powers may be. The proof is accomplished in the following syllogism:

Major: All individuals having the same specific nature have the same natural powers or capacities.

Minor: All individual men have the same specific human nature.

Conclusion: All individual men have the same natural powers or capacities.

Now neither of these two premises is, strictly speaking, self-evident. Each must be proved. I shall return presently to what is involved in their proof, after I have accomplished the second task with equal brevity.

(2) What is to be proved here is the definition of a good habit as that development of a power or capacity which conforms to the natural tendency of that power or capacity. This proof depends upon the conception of the good of anything which can be perfected (which has potentialities capable of being actualized) as the actualization of its potencies. And this, in turn, depends upon the metaphysical conception of the good as convertible with being: Anything has as much goodness as it has being. Hence if a thing is naturally constituted by capacities to be developed, its ultimate good consists in their develop-

ment, for thereby it has more actual being. Habits as developments of powers are perfections in so far as they increase and complete the being of the thing. But so far we can only say that whatever has powers subject to habituation is perfected by the formation of habits, without distinction among habits as good or bad, for any habit appears to be the actualization of a power, the development of a capacity. It is necessary, therefore, to go further and show that each power is itself a natural being, albeit an accident of the substance possessing it, and because it is natural can only be perfected by one mode of development. To do this, we must understand the metaphysical truth that every determinate potency is a tendency toward a certain actuality. Hence every natural power of man, being a determinate potency, tends toward a certain mode of actualization, a certain development. Now human habits without qualification are the development or actualization of human capacities for operation or activity, but habits are good only if they are developments conforming to the natural tendency of the power they develop.

This last point must be understood in a twofold manner. (*a*) In the case of the intellect itself, which, as a power of knowing, naturally tends toward the possession of truth as its perfection, the habit of knowledge is good by reason of conformity to the natural tendency of the cognitive power, and the habit of error is bad by reason of violation of that tendency. If the intellect were indifferently a power of knowing and not-knowing, possession of truth and possession by error would be indifferently good as actualizations of the cognitive power. Knowledge (possession of truth) is a good intellectual habit only because the intellect is a power of knowing, not a power of not-knowing. (*b*) In the case of every human power, other than the intellect itself, the natural tendency of the power is toward that actualization of itself which conforms to reason. This follows from the subordination of all human powers, in their exercised acts, to reason itself. Hence, in the case of every power there is a natural tendency which habit can violate or to which it can conform; and in conforming, the habit is good; in violating, it is bad. Clearly, then, a man is not bettered simply by habit formation, for if the habits be bad they impede the development of his total nature by violating the tendency of his powers to their own perfection. In short, human nature, partly constituted by its natural potencies at birth, is bettered or perfected in the course of life only through the formation of good habits.

All of the analysis in (2) above (the definition of a good habit), can now be summarized in a single proposition: Every human capacity which can be habituated tends naturally toward a certain development and so, for each power or capacity, good habits are those which conform to the natural tendency of the power they develop. If now this proposition be combined with the conclusion of the syllogism in (1) above (all men have the same natural capacities), we are able to prove the major premise of the original syllogism. Thus:

Major: Every human capacity can be determined by habits which are good by conformity to the natural tendency of the power being habituated.

Minor: All individual men have the same natural powers or capacities.

Conclusion: All men are capable of having the same good habits.

This conclusion can be converted into the proposition: *Good habits are the same for all men.* This was the original major. Now if we combine that with the original minor — *Education should aim at the formation of good habits* — we get the conclusion which was to be proved, namely, *the aim of education should be the same for all men, or the ends of education are absolute and universal.* (In the light of the reasoning which establishes it, this conclusion is equivalent to the truth that the moral and intellectual virtues are the ends of education.)

The proof is completely *indicated,* but the demonstration is far from being completed. I can show its incompleteness easily by now enumerating some of the propositions which are involved in the proof of the original major premise — propositions which are either demonstrable and must be proved or which are self-evident but require their evident truth to be explicated. I say ' some ' because the enumeration is far from exhaustive; but it will do to indicate how much remains to be proved before this demonstration can be completed. (1) Corporeal substances exist; (2) corporeal substances are constituted as compositions of matter and form; (3) corporeal substances differ essentially or accidentally, according as they are individuals of different species (have diverse specific natures) or as they are numerically distinct individuals having the same specific nature; (4) the essential distinction of substances is an absolute distinction in kind, without intermediates; (5) the distinction between living and non-living substances is an essential distinction; (6) living substances have vital powers which are essentially distinct from the potencies of inanimate things;

(7) man is essentially distinct from all other living things; (8) the essential distinction between man and brute as species in the genus animal is that man is rational and brute is irrational; (9) only man can know intellectually and only man has free will; (10) man has all the vital powers possessed by other living things (plants and brutes), and in addition has powers not possessed by them, i.e., intellect or reason, and will; (11) the vital powers of animals can be developed by the modification of instinctive determinations, but only human powers can be habituated; (12) habit is the modification of a human power resulting from its rational and free exercise; (13) all men are of the same species, i.e., they have essentially the same nature, and differ *inter se* only in accidental respects, i.e., in such traits as complexion, weight, height, etc., or in the *degree* to which they possess characteristically human abilities, abilities common, *in some degree*, to all; (14) all men have the same vital powers, for the vital powers any living thing possesses are determined by its specific nature; (15) a vital power is a determinate potency and as such is a nature having a tendency toward a certain definite actualization; (16) the good is convertible with being; (17) the good of any imperfect thing (anything composite of potency and actuality, or matter and form) consists in the actualization of its potencies; (18) in the case of human powers, the actualization of potency is good only if it conforms to the natural tendency of that power to its own perfection.

Of these eighteen propositions, only two are self-evident, the 3rd and 16th. All the rest are demonstrable and can be proved. And of these, the 1st, 5th, 7th, 8th, and 13th are conclusions which must be demonstrated inductively. (Though some self-evident truths and some *deductively demonstrated* conclusions will occur in the a posteriori proof of these five propositions, the proof here must also rest upon certain evident truths known by *intellectual observation* of existing facts.) The remaining eleven propositions can be deductively proved. But in neither case does the work of demonstrating these sixteen propositions belong to the philosophy of education. These propositions are truths in metaphysics, the philosophy of nature and the philosophy of man (which will be recognized by the readers of this book as ' faculty psychology '). All of this knowledge is necessarily presupposed by the philosophy of education. It would not be difficult to prove, in terms of this presupposed knowledge, that the ends of (specifically human) education are absolute and universal. That, at least, should be clear from the foregoing indication of the demonstration as running backwards to its ultimate roots in theoretic philosophy. But, unfortunately, even more must be presupposed for a full understanding of what has been proved. For good habits are virtues. And the virtues are both constitutive and generative means with respect to the ultimate end of all human activity, happiness. Hence to understand what it means to say that the ends of education are the virtues requires that one understand: first, the relation of the virtues to happiness; then, the relation of the virtues to all other goods constitutive of that whole of goods which is happiness; then, the division of the virtues into two groups, intellectual and moral; then, the analysis of both sorts of virtue, with respect to their kinds, their order to one another, and their aetiology; and finally, the relation of all the virtues *inter se*. All of this knowledge, being concerned with human goods to be sought, is practical and belongs to ethics.

IV. CONCLUSION

Let me, in conclusion, repeat the definition of education which I gave in the beginning, asserting then that it could be demonstrated. It was: Education is the process by which those powers (abilities, capacities) of men that are susceptible to habituation, are perfected by *good* habits, through means artistically contrived, and employed by any man to help another or himself achieve the end in view (i.e., good habits). In so far as this definition implies that education should be the same for all men (i.e., should aim at the same ends), its truth is proved by the establishment of the proposition that the ends of education are absolute and universal. To do that, as we have seen, requires the whole of theoretic philosophy, and this is presupposed by the philosophy of education. The definition also requires us to understand what the several ends are and how they are related to one another, for it is not sufficient to know simply that they are absolute and universal. Such understanding would involve the complete analysis of the virtues, in themselves, in relation to happiness, to other goods, and to each other. At this point, the whole of ethics is presupposed. And if we examine the definition one step further we see that it calls upon us to understand the means in general, and the social organization and employment of these means, in the process of education-by-another whereby the community cares for its members. At this point, a great deal of political philosophy is presupposed. Hence by examining the definition of education, which has been central to this whole analysis, we learn two sorts of things: first, the reasons why the philosophy of education presupposes almost all of theoretical philosophy, and most of practical philosophy; and second, that a complete understanding of the definition, through demonstration of its truth and demonstrative analysis of its parts, would be equivalent to solving the first five of the seven problems which I enumerated earlier as constituting the whole of the philosophy of education. All that would remain, then, would be two problems concerning educational policy, neither of which is philosophical in the strict sense, but merely an application of philosophy to the discussion of problems which concern educational practitioners.

I should like to add only two further comments.

(1) Those who say that the ends of education are relative and variable are obligated (if they wish to proceed as philosophers and rationally support what they assert) to disprove, or prove the contraries of, most of the propositions I have indicated as involved in the proof that the ends are absolute and universal. They can agree, of course, with the minimal definition of education as betterment, but they must deny that man is specifically (i.e., essentially) distinct from brutes if they think there is nothing specifically different about human education, in contrast to animal conditioning. They must deny that all men have the same essential nature; that, having the same nature, they all possess the same vital powers; that the goodness of habits is determined by reference to the natural tendency of these powers. Otherwise they will not be able to maintain that what is essentially good for some men is not essentially good for others; and this they must maintain if they are to support their claim that the ends of education, directed toward human betterment, are relative to a wide variety of contingencies.

(2) I regret that this essay may be unsatisfactory to many who are genuinely seeking enlightenment about the philosophy of education. I trust they will appreciate my reason for writing a defense of the philosophy of education rather than an exposition of it. I trust, also, that they will find that the analysis I have given of educational problems (as theoretic or practical, as philosophical or concerned with policies) helps them to clarify the intricate confusions in so much of contemporary discussion. At least they should learn some of the central issues about the philosophy of education, as well as the issues in it. That no adequate demonstrations have been completed is a fact better acknowledged than hidden; for that fact itself, when its causes are

understood, says a great deal about the presuppositions of educational philosophy. If space had not been wanting, I should have wished to indicate the analysis of the virtues, as the several ends of education, as I did indicate the proof that the virtues, as ends, are absolute and universal; for the ethical knowledge, which educational philosophy presupposes, is of the greatest importance to all persons engaged in the work of education. In this last connection, I take the liberty of recommending to the reader of this essay an essay of mine which tries to do what I regret not having been able to do here — a dialectical or inductive demonstration of the fundamental truths of moral philosophy, concerning happiness, the virtues, pleasure and other goods, and the relation of the individual to the common good. This essay first appeared in *The Review of Politics*, 1941 (Vol. 3, Nos. 1, 2, 3), under the title " A Dialectic of Morals," and (under the same title) is now published by the editors of the Review as a separate booklet.

REFERENCES

Historical Sources

ARISTOTLE. *Ethics.*
——. *Politics.*
NEWMAN, JOHN HENRY. *Idea of a University.* New York: Longmans, Green & Co., 1912. Pp. xxii + 527.
——. *On the Scope and Nature of University Education.* New York: E. P. Dutton & Co., 1915. Pp. xlvii + 261.
PLATO. *Meno.*
——. *Protagoras.*
——. *The Republic.*
ST. THOMAS AQUINAS. " De Magistro " (in *QQ. Disp. de Veritate*, Q. 11).
——. *Summa Theologica*, I–II, QQ. 1–97.
WHEWELL, WILLIAM. *Of a Liberal Education in General.*

Contemporary Sources

ADLER, MORTIMER J. *How To Read a Book.* New York: Simon & Schuster, 1940. Pp. ix + 398.
——. " Education in Contemporary America," *Better Schools*, II (March–April, 1940), 76–80.
——. " Can Catholic Education Be Criticized? " *Commonweal*, XXIX (April 14, 1939), 680–83.
——. " Liberalism and Liberal Education," *Educational Record*, XX (July, 1939), 422–36.
——. " The Order of Learning," *Moraga Quarterly*, XII (September, 1941), 3–24.
——. " The Crisis in Contemporary Education," *Social Frontier*, V (February, 1939), 140–45.
BARR, STRINGFELLOW. " The Ends and Means of General Education," *Proceedings*

of the Fifty-third Annual Convention of the Middle States Association of Colleges and Secondary Schools (November, 1939), pp. 41–53.

BUCHANAN, SCOTT, " A Crisis in Liberal Education," *Amherst Graduates' Quarterly*, February, 1939.

BYRNS, RUTH KATHERINE, and O'MEARA, WILLIAM. " Concerning Mr. Hutchins," *Commonweal*, XXXII (May 31, 1940), 114–16.

FITZPATRICK, EDWARD A. " Central Concepts of a Philosophy of Education in Relation to Public Education," *American School Board Journal*, CII (June, 1941) 29–31, 82.

HUTCHINS, ROBERT M. *No Friendly Voice.* Chicago: University of Chicago Press, 1936. Pp. viii + 196.

——. *The Higher Learning in America.* New Haven, Connecticut: Yale University Press, 1936. Pp. 119.

——. " Education for Freedom," *Harper's Magazine*, CLXXXIII (October, 1941), 512–26.

PEGIS, ANTON C. " The Catholic Contribution: The Role of Reason in Education for Democracy," *Proceedings of the Congress on Education for Democracy*, pp. 198–209. Columbia University, August, 1939.

PIUS XI. Encyclical Letter, *The Christian Education of Youth.* 1930.

SLAVIN, ROBERT J. " The Essential Features of the Philosophy of Education of St. Thomas," *Proceedings of the American Catholic Philosophical Assn.*, December, 1937, pp. 22–38.

WHITEHEAD, ALFRED N. *The Aims of Education.* London: Williams & Norgate, 1929. Pp. vi + 247.

CHAPTER VI

THE PHILOSOPHY OF CATHOLIC EDUCATION

WILLIAM McGUCKEN, S.J.
Professor of Education, Saint Louis University
Saint Louis, Missouri

I. INTRODUCTION

To understand the philosophy of Catholic education it is necessary to understand — not necessary of course to accept — the Catholic philosophy [1] of life which has its roots deep in the past. When Christianity came on the world scene, the revelation of Christ brought a completion of the Old Law; but not that merely, it also came as a completion, a correction often, of the thought of Greco-Roman civilization. The philosophy of Aristotle and Plato, for example, had an extraordinary influence on early Christian thought and thinkers. To the making of Christian philosophy many minds contributed: Aristotle and Plato, Augustine and Aquinas, and the great galaxy of philosophers and theologians of all ages aided in clarifying and defining the Christian view of life.

The essentials of Christian philosophy are found in the New Testament and the early writings of the Fathers of the Church. Augustine of Hippo and the American Catholic of today differ not at all with regard to essentials. Thomas Aquinas and the other medieval schoolmen, dispute though they did over the accidentals of that philosophy, were yet at one in basic principles. Through all the centuries from Augustine to Aquinas to Suarez and Bellarmine to Newman and Chesterton and Pius XII there is seen a uniform pattern of the Christian philosophy of life, startling by reason of its uniformity. From that philosophy of life is derived the philosophy of Catholic education.

To many moderns it is not an acceptable philosophy. But even if it be not accepted, the Catholic may ask that a sincere effort be made to understand what it is all about. Idiom and language may be

---

[1] 'Catholic' or 'Christian' philosophy is not used in M. Gilson's sense. (*The Spirit of Medieval Philosophy,* chap. 1. New York: Charles Scribner's Sons, 1936.) It is used here for convenience to designate all the philosophical-theological bases of the Catholic outlook on life.

251

strange, yet the philosophic mind investigating, let us say, the strange ideologies of the Australian bushmen will find these no barrier to understanding. Indeed it may well be worth the effort. Here in the United States Catholics have 273 universities, colleges, and institutions of collegiate rank with 128,844 students; 2,235 high schools and 350,190 pupils; 7,794 elementary schools with an enrolment of 2,114,-037. It would seem to be desirable to know why Catholics have these schools, and what philosophy underlies the education there given.

II. Philosophic Bases of Catholic Position

Scholastic philosophy is theocentric. Catholic life and thought and education have God as their basis. Arnold Lunn, the English convert, once said petulantly, " The answer to the educational problem is a monosyllable — God." This cornerstone of scholasticism is apt to prove irritating to the modern secularist who either ignores God or relegates Him to lower case. Secularism and naturalism, so characteristic of many American philosophies of education, make it exceedingly difficult for the modern mind trained in these philosophies to understand the Catholic position on this important matter. It is important to note that God, whose existence is proved by human reason, is not the undying energy of the physicist, not the vague impersonal being of the deist, but He is a personal God, who has created man, upon whom man is dependent and to whom, therefore, man has certain duties and obligations. Without God, the Catholic maintains there is no ultimate purpose in life, no ultimate purpose in education. For God made man, according to the words of the penny catechism, " to know, love, and serve Him in this life and be happy with Him forever in the next."

1. God

One of the five proofs [1] that Saint Thomas gives for the existence of God is based on the argument from contingency, that is, there are contingent beings in the world about us, beings that have not the reason for their existence within themselves; they depend for their existence on some other force. Eventually we must come to some being upon which they all depend. Ultimately we come to a noncontingent

---

[1] The *quinque viae* are found in the *Summa Contra Gentiles* and in the *Summa Theologica*. For a further explanation of them cf. E. Gilson, *The Philosophy of Saint Thomas Aquinas*, chaps. iv and v. (St. Louis: B. Herder Book Co., 1939.) Also R. P. Phillips, *Modern Thomistic Philosophy*, Vol. II, chap. ii. (London: Burns, Oates, & Washbourne, 1935.)

or necessary being, a being that is not dependent but independent. This necessary, self-existent being we call God.

Since God is the First Cause, He must be infinite and must contain in Himself in an infinite degree all the qualities and perfections He has caused. Among these are intellect and will. God therefore is infinitely wise and infinitely powerful. In other words, He is a personal God. This fact of facts, the existence of a personal God, is of supreme importance for any program of education. For education deals with the formation of the whole man, body and soul, intellect and will. In the area of character education, for example, the Catholic would hold that any character-training program that left God out of consideration would be not merely inadequate but utterly false.

2. The Nature of Man

Verbs of teaching govern two accusatives, the person taught and the thing taught. Now obviously a great deal of our philosophy of education depends upon our view of the person taught, in other words, upon the nature of man. Obviously, those who hold that the child is composed of a material body and an immortal soul will differ *toto coelo* from those who hold that the educand is merely a machine or a physico-chemical combination, or a bundle of S–R bonds or a product of the cosmic evolutionary process. That is the reason why we have *philosophies* of education, not a philosophy of education.

Scholastic philosophy, basing its proofs on rational grounds,[1] holds that:

a) Man was created by God. Since God is infinitely wise and infinitely good, He must have created man for a purpose. That purpose is man's happiness, a happiness to be realized only perfectly in God.

b) Man is composed of body and soul, united in essential unity. Thus it is not the mind that thinks, it is the person, John Smith, that thinks. It is not the body that feels, it is again John Smith that feels.

c) The soul of man is immaterial, spiritual, that is, intrinsically independent of matter, although necessarily united to the body to form a composite.

d) Man has an intellect, that is, he is capable of understanding, of forming judgments, of drawing conclusions.

---

[1] For these proofs cf. G. J. MacGillivray (editor), *Man*. (New York: Benziger Bros., 1932.) Or C. C. Martindale, *Man and His Destiny*. (London: Burns, Oates, & Washbourne, 1928.)

e) Man has free will, the ability to make a free choice. I ought, therefore I can, although I need not. Free will does not imply that we act without a motive. Nor does it imply that all human acts are free. In an individual's day there may be very few fully free acts.

f) Because of his intellect and free will man is essentially different from the highest form of brute life. Man is an animal, but a rational animal. No mere animal thinks or wills.

g) Since the soul of man is immaterial or spiritual, it can be destroyed by God alone. Only annihilation can blot it out of existence; and to annihilate belongs solely to God. On the other hand there is in human nature everywhere and at all times a craving for perfect happiness, so universal that it can only have been put into human nature by the Author of that nature itself. Since this perfect happiness is unattainable in this life even by those who keep God's law, we can have no reasonable doubt of the immortality of man's soul. Otherwise, we have a natural human craving that never can be fulfilled.

h) There are certain human acts which are of their very nature good and deserving of praise, and therefore independent of all human law; other actions are of their very nature, that is, intrinsically, bad and deserving of blame. The scholastic holds that there is a norm to determine the good act from the bad act.

If there be no norm to determine what actions are good and what are bad, then indeed man is a weathercock, carried now in this direction now in another, according as whim or the influence of his fellows or his environment is most prevalent. Even though he desire to be moral, unless he has a yardstick with which to measure the good and the bad, morality will be beyond his reach.

Scholastic philosophy teaches that there is such a yardstick, such a norm of morality, one eminently usable; namely, man's rational nature taken in its entirety. Consequently, the scholastic would hold that those actions that are in conformity with man's rational nature are good, those that are not in conformity with man's rational nature are bad. What does reason teach us about man's nature? First, that it is composite, made up of body and soul. Second, that man's nature is social by its very essence, that is, intended by its Creator to live in society. Third, it is contingent, that is, not independent, not responsible for its own being and existence, but dependent on its Creator, God. From this it follows that man has duties to himself, to his neighbor, to his God. He must so live his life that the higher part of him, the spiritual, be not made subordinate to the organic. Consequently, drunkenness is in itself evil, because it is not in conformity with man's rational nature, rather it places the soul and its powers in a subordinate position to the animal appetites. Secondly, he has duties to his fellow man. Certain of these duties are in conformity with his social nature, as a member of domestic society, the family; as a member of civil society; as a member of world society. Therefore, assisting one's neighbor, playing the good Samaritan, supporting one's children, and obeying parents are things good in themselves because in conformity with man's social nature. On the other hand, dishonesty, lying, stealing, and murder are intrinsically wrong because they run counter to man's social nature. Thirdly, man's contingent nature indicates clearly man's duties to God. Therefore blasphemy, irreverence toward God are things bad in themselves. Worship and service of God are good because in accord with the contingent nature of man. Suicide is an evil thing in itself because man, as a contingent being, has no dominion over his own life.

Difficult as it may be to indicate all the duties of man to God, his neighbor, and himself, this is nevertheless simplicity itself compared to the attempts made by some of the character educators who put before us a changing norm of morality. In the scholastic system there is a yardstick, fixed and unchanging, suitable for all ages and all countries. Granted that it may be hard in certain circumstances to determine what is lying, what is dishonesty, the fact remains that in the scholastic system lying and dishonesty are evil things. Further, there is a hierarchy of values. If there be a conflict between man's duties to God and to his neighbor, the inferior right must cede to the superior. First things come first. Charity is a good thing, but if giving away one's possessions means impoverishment of one's dependents, right order would show that this was not a good thing. Man's duties are first to his own household.

3. Educational Implications of the Foregoing

Quite independently of any dogmas of faith, or any calling on truths known through revelation, the scholastic can formulate a definition of education:

Education is the organized development and equipment of all the powers of a human being, moral, intellectual, and physical, by and for their individual and social uses, directed towards the union of these activities with their Creator as their final end.[1]

---

[1] T. Corcoran, S.J., *Private Notes*. Dublin, n.d.

Anyone who accepted Aristotle's or Aquinas' teaching about the nature of man would concur in that definition, be he Catholic or Calvinist, Jew or Gentile. Indeed there was a time in the history of the world when this was the only definition of education. Until the nineteenth century, all education was religious and God-centered, if we except the brief interlude of the Encyclopedists and the French Revolution which had little immediate influence on school practice. President Hutchins, in the *Higher Learning in America*, says that in the modern world, theology, the principle of order in the medieval university, cannot be an integrating force in education and as a consequence the modern man is obliged to go to metaphysics to draw education out of its disorder and chaos. Yet Mr. Hutchins knows very well that metaphysics necessarily deals with the existence and nature of God. With the metaphysical principles of which President Hutchins speaks — which Professor Adler has clearly enunciated — the Catholic will readily concur. His only difficulty is that they do not go far enough. For the Catholic bases his theory of education not merely on metaphysical principles, he must also take into consideration the facts about man and his destiny made known to him through revelation. In fact, he would argue that the metaphysics of Aristotle and Aquinas need completion by the theology of Aquinas.

It is not merely because President Hutchins rejects theology that Catholics disagree with him, no matter how greatly they may admire the lucidity and sanity of his theory. But even his philosophy or metaphysics can be questioned — not because it is false — it is not — but because it has no *roots*. In the literal sense of the word it is *une philosophie deracinée*. It is a de-Christianized philosophy or metaphysic. M. Gilson says:

I call *Christian, every philosophy which although keeping the two orders* [i.e. the natural and supernatural] *formally distinct, nevertheless considers the Christian revelation as an indispensable auxiliary to reason.*[1]

Mr. Hutchins rejects revelation, not because he wants to, but because a naturalistic, secular world will have none of it. When he quotes Aquinas, he quotes an Aquinas that never existed. For Aquinas did not merely reëdit Aristotle, he added to Aristotle's metaphysics those corrections made known to him through Christian revelation. In a Christian philosophy, the supernatural must descend as a constitutive

---

[1] *The Spirit of Medieval Philosophy*, p. 37. Charles Scribner's Sons: New York, 1936.

element not, of course, into its texture which would be a contradiction, but into the work of its construction.

In an article in the *Journal of Higher Education* discussing the new program at Saint John's College, Adam Alles claims that the restoration of medieval metaphysics is not enough; there must also be a restoration of medieval theology, which he sneeringly calls ' mythology.'

Our second thought reminds us that medieval metaphysics or theology [*natural theology?*] was accompanied by a mythology [*theology*] and that whoever wants to reclaim medieval theology [he means *metaphysics* or *natural theology*] must also reclaim medieval mythology [*theology!*]. On the theoretical [*metaphysical*] side God was thought of as the creator and sustainer of the events of nature; on the mythological [*theological*] side He was thought of as having taken on human form. . . . This is the great fact of the incarnation and God's supreme revelation to man. Around it centered medieval thought. Therefore, whoever desires to reclaim medieval metaphysics must also recapture medieval mythology. [Again, *theology*.] He cannot take medieval theology [*metaphysics* or *natural theology*] and leave its mythology [*theology*], because that theology [*natural theology*] makes sense only in the light of the mythology [*theology*] on which it is based. . . . The Catholic church has been fully conscious of this fact; that is the reason why she has kept her mythology [*theology*] intact. . . . Under no conditions, therefore has the Catholic church ever compromised on that mythology [*theology*].[1]

Despite Mr. Alles' contemptuous use of the term mythology in speaking of the sacred science of theology, despite his confusion in applying the term theology to what is evidently metaphysics or that branch of metaphysics known as natural theology, there is a certain half-truth in what he says *mutatis mutandis*. Not that metaphysics is dependent on theology. On the contrary, as Mr. Adler said so finely and truly at the Conference on Science, Philosophy, and Religion, held in New York, September 10, 1940:

Metaphysics is valid knowledge of both sensible and suprasensible being. Metaphysics is able to demonstrate the existence of suprasensible being, for it can demonstrate the existence of God, by appealing to the evidence of the senses and the principles of reason, and without any reliance upon articles of religious faith.[2]

---

[1] Adam Alles, " Whither Education," *Journal of Higher Education*, XI (October, 1940), 371–378.

[2] Mortimer Adler, " God and the Professors," *Vital Speeches*, VII (December, 1940), 101.

Metaphysics is autonomous; it does not stand or fall on facts discovered by theology. Nevertheless, the truths of philosophy are made clearer, more certain by revelation. Certain facts pertaining to man and God would never be known except for revelation. The scholastic holds that the candlelight of reason shows us the fact of God's existence so clearly that only the wilfully blind could fail to see it; nevertheless to glimpse the richness and fullness of the concept of God, especially the wondrous sweep of the divine attributes, there was needed the effulgent beaconlight of revelation. So, too, with regard to man's nature. Reason here can tell us much; it can never tell us all about man; it can never tell us that man was raised to a supernatural life, that he fell from his high estate and was restored in wondrous manner by the Son of God.

To quote Mr. Adler again:

What is known by faith about God's nature and man's destiny is knowledge which exceeds the power of the human intellect to attain without God's revelation of Himself. . . .

Religious faith, on which sacred theology rests, is itself a supernatural act of the human intellect and is thus a divine gift.

Because God is its cause, faith is more certain than knowledge resulting from the purely natural action of the human faculties.

Sacred theology is independent of philosophy, in that its principles are truths of faith, whereas philosophical principles are truths of reason, but this does not mean that theology can be speculatively developed without reason serving faith.

There can be no conflict between philosophical and theological truths, although theologians may correct the errors of philosophers who try to answer questions beyond the competence of natural reason, just as philosophers can correct the errors of theologians who violate the autonomy of reason.

Sacred theology is superior to philosophy, both theoretically and practically; theoretically, because it is more perfect knowledge of God and His creatures; practically, because moral philosophy is insufficient to direct man to God as his last end.[1]

It is necessary then to examine the theological postulates — annoying though it may be to the modern mind that distrusts theology — upon which the Catholic theory of education rests.

---

[1] *Loc. cit.*

III. THEOLOGICAL BASES OF THE CATHOLIC THEORY OF EDUCATION

1. Man has a 'Supernature'

Christianity is meaningless without revelation. The Catholic Church teaches that revelation is possible and that a revelation has taken place. Revelation is the act whereby God speaks to men through Himself or through His messenger, making a statement the truth of which He guarantees. It is not an interior emotional experience; it is a statement of truth made to man in a definite place at a definite time, by a personal God who is outside and distinct from the recipient.[1]

Among these truths, revealed to man by God, is that of a supernature, or of a supernatural life of grace, as it is called. Confusing theological controversies have obscured the very meaning of the supernatural. Some writers on education confuse it with ' other-worldly.' Yet ' other-worldly ' and supernatural are not synonymous. ' Other-worldliness,' it is true, implies a supernatural viewpoint, but it is by no means identical with supernatural. Neither does it mean mystical nor magical nor ' ghostly.' The reason for this confusion is largely owing to the fact that the modern world has lost its interest in its Christian heritage, has whittled down the meaning of supernatural until it has ceased to have any clear meaning at all.

The teaching of the Catholic Church is that not only did God create Adam with his human nature, consisting of a human body and an immortal soul, but He also gave him that to which man has no right, a higher kind of life, a supernature, implying a supernatural life of grace and a destiny of supernatural union with Him. This life is not merely an improved human nature. It is something distinct from, superadded to human nature. The natural life, man's body and soul with all their faculties, remain intact even when the supernatural is added. The natural, moreover, would not be destroyed even if the supernatural life itself should be lost.

2. The 'Fall of Man'

Now the supernatural life of grace was given to Adam conditionally, namely, on the condition of fidelity to a special command. This command was disobeyed and therefore God withdrew His special gift of supernatural life, and left Adam on the merely natural level. Such is

---

[1] George D. Smith, *Faith and Revealed Truth*. London: Burns, Oates & Washbourne, 1929.

the teaching of the Church on the ' Fall.' The Fall means simply the rejection and loss of the supernatural life. Adam was the head of the line; if he had kept his inheritance of supernature, all his descendants would have come into the world with it. But he, the responsible representative of the race, rejected the gift of God; therefore all the sons and daughters of Adam are born without that special life of grace God intended them to have. This in brief is the Church's dogma of original sin. Human nature was not *depraved* because of Adam's sin, as Calvin held, but *deprived* of this supernatural life of grace.

Calvin believed in the Fall, but unlike the Catholic, he regarded man as essentially depraved by reason of the Fall. Hence, the doctrine of total depravity, which originated with Calvin, and its fatal consequences to education. Rousseau did not believe in the dogma of original sin; it is doubtful if he believed in any dogma; he regarded nature as essentially good. The Calvinistic doctrine of total depravity was too much for this romantic sensualist. Therefore, he threw out the whole thing: fall, original sin, redemption, Christianity. Two men, Calvin and Rousseau, are responsible for the world's failure to accept the Catholic *via media;* that nature, by reason of Adam's sin, is deprived and wounded, but not depraved; that deprivation is made up for us by a restoration through the second Adam; for " by his wounds we are healed."

3. The Restoration of Man

It is the Church's teaching that it was not God's will that this deprivation should be final. In God's plan this restoration was to take place through a second Adam, one who was to stand like the first Adam as the representative of the human race, with whom we could be incorporated or united through bonds of solidarity. For this office of Second Adam, God chose His own Son, the Second Person of the Blessed Trinity, who took upon Himself our human nature. Through His Incarnation, Life, Passion, Death, and Resurrection, He gloriously atoned for Adam's sin. God's plan was that all men should incorporate themselves with the Second Adam, and thus, united with the very source of supernatural life, since He is God, be in a state even better than if merely restored to the position lost to them through Adam's sin.

The liturgy of the Church shows this whole teaching in striking fashion in the ancient prayer that the priest says at Mass, as he pours water into the wine which is to be consecrated, thus symbolizing the union of our human nature with the divine nature of Christ:

O God who through creation has wonderfully ennobled human nature and still more wonderfully re-created it, grant that by the mystery of this water and wine we may be made partakers of His divinity who in our humanity did not disdain to share.

4. Difficulties of Moderns

Nothing is more irritating to the modern than this dogma of the supernatural, a dogma that cannot be proved by anthropology, history, psychology, or any other human science. Yet nothing is more certain than this, that all traditional historic Christianity is inextricably bound up with it. It cannot be demonstrated by human reason; it requires God's revelation to bring to our knowledge this fact that man is supernaturalized. This traditional teaching of Christendom, which the Catholic Church teaches today as she did in the fourth century, gives point and focus to the life and practice of that Church, explains her attitude toward the things of eternity as opposed to the transient pageant of this world, brings out in bold relief her hierarchy of values.

This may be far from clear to the modern; indeed, it may sound like the veriest nonsense. Yet it must be insisted that the Catholic position is utterly unintelligible unless this primary fact of the supernatural life be recognized. The Catholic takes the existence of the supernatural on the word of God and the teaching of the Church; it is part of the very air that he breathes. Unacceptable the supernatural may well be to the 'modern mind'; it may be regarded as the nadir of irrationality to admit even the possibility, still more the fact, of a divine revelation of the existence of the supernatural. Yet once the Catholic starting point of a supernatural life and man's supernatural destiny is recognized, then with unerring logic follows the Catholic position on the whole educational question.

5. Christianity Based on the Dogma of 'Fall'

It must be evident to one who knows anything about history that revelation — prescinding for the moment whether it be true or false — and theological speculations concerning revelation have played a tremendous part in the theory and practice of education in the Western world. If there had been no revelation made to man by God, or if man had not imagined such a thing, then the whole history of civilization and education would have been vastly different from the present record. Either there was in human history such an event as is succinctly spoken of in Christian theology as the 'Fall of Man,' or for thousands of years men mistakenly believed there was such a fact. Not only does Christianity base its doctrine and practice upon that fact, but our whole civilization and, consequently, education depend upon it.

No reputable historian could deny that the main factor in the building of our western civilization has been Christianity. Now, unless this fact of the ' Fall of Man ' — or, if you will, the dogma of original sin — be admitted, Christianity simply collapses like a pricked balloon. It not only becomes an antiquated superstition; it becomes, in a very literal sense of the word, nonsense. For without the Fall, there would be no need of the Incarnation and Redemption, the two cardinal points of Christian belief.

6. Educational Theory Dependent on View of ' Fall '

Two moderns of widely different antecedents, with antipodal philosophies, Friedrich Foerster, the devout Lutheran educator, and Bertrand Russell, the modern skeptic, both have come quite independently to the same conclusion, namely, that in the last analysis all theories of education are dependent on the views taken of the dogma of original sin. For every theory of education hinges on the precise nature of the educand. What is the nature of the material with which we are dealing in our educational work? What is there inherent in the nature of the child that enables us to indulge in wild Utopian dreams about the effect of education on the human spirit? Or are these dreams as fantastic as the palaces of Xanadu? Is there some essential obstacle in human nature that prevents us from even thinking high thoughts about the possibilities of education?

7. Catholic Attitude toward the ' Natural '

With the Catholic emphasis on the supernatural, the question may well be raised: What is the Catholic attitude toward nature? Does the supernatural exclude the natural? Saint Thomas gives the answer. God is the beginning and end of creation; God's goodness and beauty are the absolutes to which all natural beauty and goodness are relative;[1] the symmetry Aquinas advocates is the symmetry demanded by a supernatural end. The supernatural completes the natural; *gratia perficit naturam*, grace *perfects* nature. For the Catholic is neither Manichee nor Puritan.

Nature was not corrupt, even despite the cataclysmic effects of the Fall; it was merely wounded. Hence in education as in life, there was

---

[1] See G. Vann, *On Being Human*. New York: Sheed & Ward, 1934.

no repression of legitimate human desires merely for the sake of repression. Marriage was a good thing as was merriment and song and laughter. The humanism of the Catholic is the humanism of Christ, a Christ that suffered the little children gladly for of such is the kingdom of Heaven, a Christ that consorted with publicans and winebibbers and attended as an honored guest the marriage-feast at Cana. All flesh was sanctified, in the Catholic sense, since the day that the Word was made flesh and dwelt amongst us.

8. Catholic Theory of Education Unchangeable

There has been acrimonious debate within the Catholic Church at various periods of history as to what the child should be taught, but the attitude of the Church in this matter of the child's nature has never changed. Every child born into this world is regarded as a child of Adam. Therefore, he comes into the world with Adam's inheritance, a lowlier estate because deprived of supernatural life than would have been his had it not been for the fall of Adam. Through the life, passion, death and resurrection of Christ, the Son of God, every one of the descendants of Adam can be restored to his rightful heritage as a child of God. The whole business of the Church is for this purpose, to give this new life to all the sons of men, to keep it alive and growing, bringing forth fruits. So, too, the educational work of the Church is precisely for that purpose. Her whole educational aim is to restore the sons of Adam to their high position as children of God, citizens of the kingdom of God.

The encyclical of Pius XI merely reëmphasizes these ancient truths:

Education consists essentially in preparing man for what he must do here below in order to attain the sublime end for which he was created. . . .

It must never be forgotten that the subject of Christian education is man whole and entire, soul united to body in unity of nature, with all his faculties, natural and supernatural, such as right reason and revelation show him to be; man, therefore, fallen from his original estate, but redeemed by Christ and restored to the supernatural condition of adopted sons of God. . . .

Hence, the true Christian, product of Christian education, is the supernatural man who thinks, judges, and acts consistently in accordance with right reason illumined by the supernatural light of the example and teaching of Christ; in other words, to use the current term, the true and finished man of character.[1]

---

[1] Pius XI, *Encyclical on Christian Education.*

9. The Supernatural, the Basis of the Catholic System

The key of the Catholic system is the supernatural. Not only Catholic theology, but Catholic practice, the Catholic attitude toward life, and most of all, Catholic education are insoluble mysteries if we exclude an understanding of the supernatural. The Church holds that she is divinely commissioned by Christ to carry on His Work, to do what He did. " I am come that you may have life, that you may have it more abundantly." The Church continues that work, bringing this supernatural life to men who have not yet received it, surrounding it with safeguards that it may not be lost, restoring it once more to those who perversely cast it aside. The same is true of her educational system. Her primary purpose in establishing schools, kindergartens or universities is not merely to teach fractions or logarithms, biology or seismology, grammar or astronomy — these subjects are subordinate to her main purpose to inculcate the " eminent knowledge and love of Jesus Christ our Lord," a knowledge so intimate, a love so strong that it will lead necessarily to a closer followng of Christ. Other-worldly? Yes, if you will; for strange as it may seem, the Church considers religion as more important than fractions. If it came to a point where a choice must be made between endangering faith by learning fractions or keeping the faith and not knowing fractions, there is only one answer.

Not, of course, that there is an essential conflict between fractions and the supernatural life, but man can create a factitious conflict. Let us suppose, for example, that the Nazis should conquer America, should establish a monopoly of schools, forcing all in its schools to accept the pagan ideology of Rosenberg with its cult of the state. To such a school no Catholic child could go, even though it meant that the child would grow up illiterate.

10. Catholic Hierarchy of Values

Since so much time has been spent elaborating the Catholic concept of man's nature, a concept derived from psychological dualism that man's nature is a unit, though composite, made up of body and soul, possessing intellect and free will, derived too from ethical theory with regard to man's origin, nature, and destiny, man's duties to God, his neighbor, and himself, the unchanging norm of morality based on man's composite, social and contingent nature, a concept of man's nature illuminated by revelation to include the supernatural, with all in theological science that is connoted by that term, it clearly follows that there is a certain hierarchy of values in Catholic education. Supernatural values, if the supernatural exists, are obviously of more importance than the natural; spiritual values of greater import than the bodily; and eternal of more significance than temporal.

IV. Objectives of Catholic Education

The ultimate objective of Catholic education can be stated very simply. In the words of Pius XI:

> The proper and immediate end of Christian education is to coöperate with divine grace in forming the true and perfect Christian, that is, to form Christ Himself in those regenerated by Baptism. . . .
> For precisely this reason, Christian education takes in the whole aggregate of human life, physical and spiritual, intellectual and moral, individual, domestic, and social, not with a view of reducing it in any way, but in order to elevate, regulate, and perfect it, in accordance with the example of and teaching of Christ.
> Hence the true Christian, product of Christian education, is the supernatural man who thinks, judges, and acts constantly and consistently in accordance with right reason illumined by the supernatural light of the example and teaching of Christ; in other words, to use the current term, the true and finished man of character. For, it is not every kind of consistency and firmness of conduct based on subjective principles that makes true character, but only constancy in following the eternal principles of justice.
> . . . The true Christian does not renounce the activities of this life, he does not stunt his natural faculties; but he develops and perfects them, by coördinating them with the supernatural. He thus ennobles what is merely natural in life and secures for it new strength in the material and temporal order, no less than in the spiritual and eternal.[1]

With this ultimate aim of Catholic education, there never has been, there can be no change. Given the Church's teaching about man's nature, and supernature, and man's supernatural destiny, it is impossible to see how there could be any change. Into this ultimate aim every type of Catholic educational institution must fit from kindergarten to graduate school; otherwise it has no right to be called a Catholic school. For no matter how poor the intellectual training it imparts, no matter how badly equipped academically the teachers may be, that school is a Catholic school which holds fast to its philosophy of supernaturalism. This is not to say that the school, *qua* school, must have as its specific

[1] Pius XI, *Encyclical on Christian Education.*

concern the moral virtues as opposed to the intellectual virtues; that controversy will be referred to later.

Education is not confined to the school. There are other agencies concerned in the training of the child, the home and the Church to mention but two. Thus religious education, moral education, training in citizenship, courtesy, character education, even intellectual training, are not exclusively the perquisites of the school; they could not be. But the Catholic Church insists that each Catholic agency, the Catholic home, the Catholic school, place first things first, but that does not necessarily mean that the Church intends that character training, religious training and the rest should be the exclusive function of the school. It may well be doubted, however, whether character training, religious formation, can be imparted without a solid intellectual foundation. Some element of knowledge, varying in amount with the stage of development of the child, must enter into the formation of habit which is the basis of good character education and even of religious education. Obviously, habits cannot be properly established in a human being without his having some intellectual grasp of the motives upon which habits are based, of the standards by which their value is judged. Objectives of conduct are not attained by irrational, mechanical drill.

1. Objectives of the American Catholic Elementary School

Dr. George Johnson of the Catholic University has stated what he regards as the aim of the Catholic elementary school.

> The aim of the Catholic elementary school is to provide the child with those experiences which are calculated to develop in him such knowledge, appreciation, and habits as will yield a character equal to the contingencies of fundamental Christian living in American democratic society.[1]

American Catholics believe that America's tradition of democracy, her splendid struggle to achieve that democracy are of right taught every Catholic child in the elementary school together with his rich colorful Catholic heritage. In addition, of course, there must be training in the skills necessary to enable him to take his place as a useful citizen in America. To prepare the child to lead an intelligent Catholic life in contemporary American society it is necessary to impart training in processes that are needed for American Catholic citizenship.

---

[1] *National Catholic Educational Association Bulletin,* XXII (November, 1925), 458 ff.

Further it is necessary to hand on the tradition of Catholicism and American democracy in such a fashion that knowledge will develop into an appreciation of that Catholic and American background. In a word, the elementary school aims to impart those knowledges and skills, habits and appreciative attitudes that will fit the child to be an intelligent practical Catholic, a good citizen, a good member of society, including the various groups to which he belongs, family, working group, neighborhood, and the like.

2. Indoctrination

The Catholic educator does not hesitate to teach the rules of grammar, the multiplication tables, spelling, and the like. The child is given no choice in these matters. So, too, with regard to patriotism, love of country — a very noble Christian virtue — truths about God and God's law, he does not wait for the child to discover these important truths for himself, he helps him to discover them. As E. I. Watkin says,

[This is] the justification of a religious education — no imposition of ideas upon the unreceptive and recalcitrant, but simply the showing what is actually there and what otherwise they might not see. For not only are individuals intellectually or spiritually colour-blind or sufferers from astigmatism; entire groups, races or epochs display particular faults of vision, which require correction by reference to a complete body of truth handed down through the ages and taught universally.[1]

3. Objectives of the American Catholic Secondary School

The high school in America is a completion of education for some and a preparation of further education for others. The theory of universal secondary education, about which there probably is among Catholic as among other groups wide divergence of opinion, has brought about a multiplication of secondary schools and an amazing increase in the secondary-school population which unquestionably have produced a lowering of intellectual standards through adaptation of the curriculum to the needs of the students. Yet taking it as it is, the Catholic secondary school in America must find its objectives within the frame of reference that is common to all Catholic institutions — the supernatural. Therefore, its aims are a further and richer development of those knowledges and skills, habits and appreciations that will fit the pupil to be

[1] E. I. Watkin, *The Bow in the Clouds,* p. 8. New York: Macmillan Co., 1932.

a) an intelligent human being according to his capabilities;

b) an intelligent, practical Catholic, with all that these terms connote;

c) an intelligent, good American citizen;

d) an intelligent, helpful member of society and of these particular groups of which he is or will be a member — the family, professions, vocations, etc.

Therefore, the Catholic high school must cultivate in its pupils an intelligent appreciation of Catholicism and of the traditions of American democracy so as to bring about these ends.

It may be noted that ' intelligent ' is emphasized throughout in the above statement. This does not mean that the Catholic school is indifferent to character, or supernatural virtue, but it must be insisted as the writer has said elsewhere that:

A school is set up by a community to perform certain functions that it, and it alone, can perform. In addition, it aids other agencies, notably the family and the Church in other functions that are common to it and to them. Now those who conduct a secondary school must have a hierarchy of values. For example, good moral character is more important than proficiency in grammar; good citizenship of greater value than ability to appreciate a play of Shakespeare. For the Catholic secondary school, development of the Christian virtues is obviously of greater worth than learning or anything else. Therefore it follows that the secondary school cannot be indifferent to these higher values. Since the pupils in the Catholic secondary school are not disembodied intellects, still less merely higher types in the animal kingdom, but children of God, redeemed by Christ our Lord, a Catholic school would fail wholly if it did not consciously strive to impart training in Catholic character.

But it must be remembered that these higher values, Christian citizenship, Christian character, supernatural virtues, are not the exclusive concern of the school. The school alone cannot secure them unaided. Surely it is conceivable that virtues can be developed by young people who never went to high school. Mere literacy of itself or the possession of a high-school diploma is no guarantee of either virtue or citizenship. But if the school does not attend to intellectual training at all, is not concerned with the fact that its students are not mastering grammar or reading or whatever may constitute the high-school curriculum, then it is not merely a poor school; it forfeits the right to be called a school at all, even though it may be successful in developing the virtues of a Christian character.

The Catholic secondary school has the specific function of training for intellectual virtues. Yet as a Catholic institution it must always recognize that since it is concerned with the whole pupil, intellectual training is not enough, nor is it ever the most important thing in the life of the child. It is even possible that under certain circumstances it must forsake or abandon temporarily its specific purpose, and turn to the more important business of training for the moral virtues.

Examples may help to clarify this point. The specific purpose of a shoe factory is to make shoes; yet a Christian shoe manufacturer will necessarily admit that development of Christian virtue is more important. If shoemaking interfered with Christian virtues, shoemaking would have to cease. But in that event, he would cease calling his establishment a shoe factory. A library is a place to serve readers with books; yet in time of war the librarian and his staff might have to use the building for housing the wounded. If this were to be a permanent arrangement, quite obviously it could no longer be called a library. So, too, with our high schools. If a great moral or physical disaster were imminent, we might conceivably have to give up the work of intellectual training of our students and devote our efforts for the time to the exclusive development of the moral virtues. But, I maintain, there is no necessary incompatibility between virtue and learning. A good secondary school will use its intellectual training as a means to the well-rounded development of the characters of its pupils. One can say that if a secondary school fails to insist on intellectual training, it fails also in character training.

The purpose then of the Catholic high school, as I understand it, is to develop Catholic boys and girls along intellectual lines, to turn out intelligent Catholic citizens with an appreciative knowledge of their heritage as American citizens and an appreciative knowledge of their Catholic heritage. Only in the Catholic school can this appreciative knowledge be fully secured. If it be true — and we know that it is true — that our concept of democracy is based on the dignity of man, then it is only in the Catholic school that the proper dignity of man can be learned, because only there will youth learn that man has dignity because he is created by God to His image and likeness, only there will he learn of the high estate to which he has been called — a son of God, redeemed by Christ our Lord.[1]

4. Objectives of Catholic Higher Education

Higher education in America includes everything from the college of liberal arts to the graduate school, from a school of medicine to a college of agriculture. The confusion and bewilderment of aim so characteristic of American higher education, the utilitarian, anti-intellectual elements that there prevail, which makes Mr. Hutchins despair of hoping for anything but triviality, mediocrity, and chaos from the present American educational system, are unfortunately all too true of most Catholic institutions. Nevertheless, despite this lack of solidity and

---

[1] William J. McGucken, " Intelligence and Character," *The National Catholic Educational Association Bulletin*, XXXVI (May, 1940), 10–12.

standards, the Catholic college and university have retained their supernatural viewpoint.

Naturally enough Catholic institutions have imitated the externals of college and university here in America; perhaps necessarily so. Nor do they cease by that fact *qua* Catholic institution to be any the less Catholic, just so long as they hold fast to their philosophy of supernaturalism, so long as they realize they are training not merely for time, but for eternity, although possibly inefficient *qua* institutions of higher education.

The traditional purpose of the university is

a) the conservation of knowledge and ideas and values;

b) the interpretation and transmission of knowledge and ideas and values;

c) the quest of truth through scholarly research;

d) the preparation for professions not by mere *ad-hoc* training in techniques but by intelligent and thorough training in the principles underlying the professions.

5. Idea of the University in its Origins

This was the idea of the university from its origin. True, historically the character of the university was determined by the idea of knowledge which its age valued, by the type of man it intended to produce, and by the economic, social, political, and religious conditions of the nation and age in which it found itself. The oneness of learning, which in an earlier day united all the universities irrespective of their accidental differences, no longer exists. In the Middle Ages, theology or philosophy, rooted in Christianity, was that principle of unity. The Reformation shattered the common faith that united Christendom and the universities of Christendom, without, however, removing theology from its place at the summit of the tower of learning. But in the eighteenth century, theology was dismissed as a poor slattern by the men of the Enlightenment. The principle of unity where such a principle existed now became philosophy, not indeed the ancient Christian philosophy of the schoolmen, but a philosophy that was contemptuous of all revealed truth, hostile to all supernatural values. In the nineteenth century, philosophy gave way to naturalism; the experimental method became the ruling spirit in the secular university. The scientific method is the sole possession that is common to all modern universities.

Science, however, and the scientific method — excellent though they are in their proper sphere — cannot alone help the university to fulfil that function which is proper to it, namely, an interpreter and guardian of values. It is because of this that confusion has overtaken the modern university. It has failed properly to guard and hand on the heritage entrusted to it. Pragmatism has ruled the university and in the mad scramble to turn out statisticians, business men, social workers, laboratory technicians — all excellent professions, as who shall deny? — the university has forgotten that it must train its sons in human values first before it attempts to impart techniques.

6. A Non-Catholic View

Howard Mumford Jones, a non-Catholic writer, says in this connection:

What is the source of this confusion? Let us contrast the Catholic and the non-Catholic traditions in liberal education. Roughly speaking the problem of values does not arise in the Catholic educational tradition, or if it does arise, it does not arise in the same way. The Catholic university may be objective in matters of pure science, but in the humanities it is not unpartisan and it does not try to be. The core of the Catholic system is theology, theology in turn conditions Catholic ethics and Catholic philosophy; and the Catholic point of view in the interpretation of history and literature is unmistakable. Indeed it is precisely because the church does not desire to intrust the question of values to irreligious hands that Catholic institutions of higher learning exist. There is a definite point of view which if it avoids dogma, implies doctrine; and consequently Catholic education in the humanities has a certainty with which one may quarrel, but which in contrast to the confusion of mind among non-Catholic professional educational leaders is admirable.[1]

No doubt many who heard Professor Jones' lecture at the University of Chicago misinterpreted his words to mean that the Catholic university is hampered by Pope and dogma. Many were perhaps naive enough to believe that Catholic universities receive bulls from Rome at the beginning of September mapping out their course of instruction for the coming year. Unfortunately, no such delightful practice exists.

7. The Function of the Catholic University

The precise function of the Catholic university was defined in imperishable prose in Cardinal Newman's sermon on " Intellect the In-

---

[1] William S. Gray (editor), *General Education: Its Nature, Scope, and Essential Elements*, pp. 43–44. Proceedings of the Institute for Administrative Officers of Higher Institutions, Vol. VI. Chicago: University of Chicago Press, 1934.

strument of Religious Training." All of it deserves careful reading in the light of the present confusion.

Here then, I conceive, is the object of the Holy See and the Catholic Church in setting up universities; it is to reunite things which were in the beginning joined together by God, and have been put asunder by man. Some persons will say that I am thinking of confining, distorting, and stunting the growth of intellect by ecclesiastical supervision. I have no such thought. Nor have I any thought of a compromise, as if religion must give up something, and science something. I wish the intellect to range with the utmost freedom, and religion to enjoy an equal freedom; but what I am stipulating for is, that they should be found in one and the same place, and exemplified in the same persons. I want to destroy that diversity of centres, which puts everything into confusion by creating contrariety of influences. I wish the same spots and the same individuals to be at once oracles of philosophy and shrines of devotion. It will not satisfy me, what has satisfied so many, to have two independent systems, intellectual and religious, going at once side by side, by a sort of division of labor, and only accidentally brought together. It will not satisfy me, if religion is here, and science there, and young men converse with science all day, and lodge with religion in the evening. It is not touching the evil, to which these remarks have been directed, if the young man eat and drink and sleep in one place, and think in another: I want the same roof to contain both the intellectual and moral discipline. Devotion is not a sort of finish given to the sciences; nor is science a sort of feather in the cap, if I may so express myself, an ornament and set-off to devotion. I want the intellectual layman to be religious and the devout ecclesiastic to be intellectual.

This is not matter of terms, nor of subtle distinctions. Sanctity has its influence; intellect has its influence; the influence of sanctity is the greater in the long run; the influence of intellect is the greater at the moment. Therefore, in the case of the young, whose education lasts a few years, where the intellect is, there is the influence. Their literary, their scientific teachers really have the forming of them. Let both influences act freely. As a general rule, no system of mere religious guardianship which neglects the reason, will in matter of fact succeed against the school. Youths need a masculine religion, if it is to carry captive their restless imaginations, and their wild intellects, as well as to touch their susceptible hearts.[1]

The Catholic university can, indeed should, be singularly free from prejudice, although it may be freely granted that it is not always so. Catholic and secular educators alike may be swayed by passion, emotion, prejudice, propaganda. The Catholic university welcomes research and scientific investigation; the only thing it has to fear is preju-

[1] *Sermons on Various Occasions.* Sermon I.

dice. A secular professor trained in naturalism may enter upon his research with certain definite prejudices. For example, here is a professor of psychology who is sure there is no spiritual soul, although he has no evidence for that conviction. His research is conditioned by blind irrational prejudice. The Catholic professor, trained in metaphysics, enters his laboratory with no such bias. For the materialist, the soul, immortality, spirituality, God are anachronisms. For the Catholic scientist they are ever present realities. They in no way hamper the research of the Catholic scientist or historian or philosopher. On the contrary, the Catholic scholar welcomes every scientific discovery wherever found. The experimental naturalist too often fears the truth, seems dominated by theophobia. If the Catholic is dogmatic — and some Catholics are dogmatic — so too is the materialist with his absurd dogma denying the existence of all dogma, refusing even to consider the possibility of the existence of the spiritual.

The Catholic university, as all universities, is devoted to the pursuit of truth, has an obligation to further and deepen the intellectual life of its students, to raise the cultural standards in the community and region wherein it is situated. For the Catholic university above all, the thing of ultimate importance is not here but hereafter. This world has genuine value only in so far as it leads to the next.

The university must hold fast to its primary function — the imparting of wisdom and the discovery of truth. Conservation and conservative are terms closely allied. The university should be conservative in the etymological sense; it is the guardian of the culture of the intellectual world. While in no wise unfriendly to new discoveries, it should be unwilling to pick up its academic robes and run pell-mell after every pedagogical pied piper that pipes in the marketplace. It is not progress for the university, even in a democracy, to lower its drawbridge for the howling mobs clamoring for admittance under the leadership of the apostles of service.

8. Values in a University

The university must have a standard of values. The rejection of values has been the great tragedy of the modern university, as it has been of the modern world. If there be no standards, if there be no abiding values, then indeed we must accept the gospel of despair. Material things have values — bread and circuses, pennies and footballs, jobs and games, but surely they are not the primary concern of the university. The university deals with things of the mind; education is an intellectual and spiritual process which has to do with the opening of the windows of the human mind, the enrichment and ennobling of the human soul. Therefore, the university must place humane values, spiritual values, above material values; training of men in thinking is of more importance than training in techniques.

For the Catholic university there is another grade in the hierarchy of values. Above the material, above the spiritual, there exist supernatural values, values known through revelation. The Catholic university from its coign of vantage in the ancient Church has a view not merely of the world but of the superworld as well, not only of the facts in the natural order but of those in the supernatural order also, those facts that give meaning and coherence to the whole of life. And while it is true that it is the province primarily of the faculty of theology to impart knowledge of the supernatural, to investigate and promote research on revealed truth, nevertheless in a Catholic university there should always be on the part of all the faculties an awareness of these supernatural facts and values.

A university that is a static institution is bound to decay. It must give evidence that a life-giving principle is at work. This will be shown in the men that it sends forth to the world, intellectual leaders of the generation, to whom the university has handed on the burning torch of knowledge and wisdom. The university itself must promote the quest for truth, advancing the frontiers of knowledge by its research, its experimentation. The university is not a fortress, not a mere treasure-house of knowledge; it is in a very real sense an army in battle array, capturing now this outpost, now that, from the enemy, ignorance, while breaking new paths into unexplored fields. A university that simply hands on its knowledge and does not set its students aflame with enthusiasm to spread that knowledge has signally failed in its mission.

Since the Napoleonic era the principle of integration has scarcely existed in the university. It is this lack of integration that President Hutchins and Norman Foerster particularly deplore. Each discipline in the modern university is virtually autonomous. Philosophy where it raises its trembling head is sent back to its lair by the lord of the intellectual world, science. But how can this integration be accomplished in the modern university? Will the Hutchins solution of metaphysics be satisfactory?

9. Catholic Principle of Integration

For the Catholic university, there is a principle of integration — not an eclectic metaphysics, but the metaphysics of Aristotle and Aquinas. In Newman's phrase we are all Aristotelians, we cannot help being so " for the great Master does but analyze the thoughts, feelings, views, and opinions of the human mind. He has told us the meaning of our own words and ideas, before we were born. In many subject matters to think correctly is to think like Aristotle; and we are his disciples whether we will or no." Nevertheless, for the Catholic university this principle of integration is not merely metaphysics, but metaphysics supplemented by theology. In this the Catholic university of today is at one with the ancient University of Paris, the mother and fountainhead of all universities.

The Catholic university exists not for the sake of apologetics, not for the purpose of merely training its students for the ' other life.' In the words of Dietrich von Hildebrand,

[Catholic Universities are necessary] for the sake of the truly adequate objective knowledge, not by any means merely for the protection of the religious knowledge of the students. They are needed as the institutions where Catholic thinkers and men of science, supported by a truly Catholic environment, informed in their attitude by the spirit of Christ and of His Church, shall be enabled by a really unbiased, truly liberated and enlightened intelligence to penetrate adequately to reality and to achieve by organized team work that *universitas* which is nowadays so urgently needed. They must further be institutions in which young people may be educated to that attitude which represents an inevitable prerequisite for the learner also. A Catholic university would have no meaning, if it were nothing but a collection of Catholic men of thought and science, while following the model of the modern university in its general atmosphere. It requires the conscious production of an atmosphere filled by Christ, an environment imbued with prayer; as an organism it must in its structure and in the common life of its teachers among each other and with their students be thoroughly Catholic. The students must breathe a Catholic air and Catholic spirit which will make them into anti-pedantic, humble, faithful, metaphysically courageous men of winged intelligence and yearning, and therewith capable of truly adequate and objective knowledge. . . . Only through the existence of Catholic universities can the labours of Catholic research in the other universities be brought to full fruition. Catholic universities must create the atmosphere in which the Catholic teacher can find his way back to a true ideal of science and become conscious of the advantage for adequate knowledge which he enjoys through revelation, and of the responsibility of giving to mankind in the way of knowledge what by reason of this advantage he is capable of giving to it.[1]

V. NATURE OF KNOWLEDGE

Whether man can know anything, how he comes to know, and how true is this knowledge are fundamental to the whole educational question. Saint Thomas begins his treatise *De Magistro* with the question: " Whether man can teach another and be called a teacher or God alone? "[2] Skeptics, anti-intellectuals, rationalists, Kantians have answered all these questions in various ways. The answer given here is that of moderate intellectualism, the theory of Aristotle and Saint Thomas.

The Aristotelian-Thomist concept of knowledge is very simple. Knowledge implies three things, a knower, a thing known, and the act of knowing. The knower is assumed to have the capacity to attain to truth with certitude because his senses and his intellect under certain conditions are infallible means of truth. This supposes, therefore, that truth exists; that man can attain it under certain conditions. It does not maintain that all our judgments are veracious, all our ideas are true, all our sense perceptions are correct, only that some of them can be. Further, it assumes that man can know when he has attained the truth.

1. How We Get Our Ideas

How man comes to know is handled by the scholastics in this fashion:

a) With our senses we see, let us say, trees of various shapes and colors and sizes.

b) Imagination and sense-memory keep the concrete images of the various trees, as they exist in nature, with their determinate sizes, colors, and shapes.

c) Then the active intellect, by reason of its power of abstraction, prescinds from the various differences in the images of the trees retained in the memory, and attends to the essential features common to all trees.

d) This essence, *abstracted* from its individuating notes, immaterialized, so to speak, in the process, is presented to the cognitive intellect.

---

[1] Walter M. Kotschnig and Elined Prys, *The University in a Changing World*, p. 219 ff. London: Oxford University Press, 1932.

[2] *De Veritate*, q. xi.

e) The cognitive intellect, after this action of the active intellect, expresses the essence of the tree by means of a concept or immaterial representation of what is common to all trees.

This is the origin of universal concepts or ideas according to the scholastics. The abstract idea that we formulate of beauty, for example, is derived as follows: We see beautiful things in nature; the active intellect abstracts, the cognitive intellect cognizes and forms the abstract idea of beauty. So too with patriotism, derived from patriotic deeds or from patriotic men. When we say ' Man is mortal,' man is a universal idea, derived from our sense-experience of Tom, Dick, and Harry; of white men, black men, yellow men, red men; of brilliant men and stupid men; of kings and beggars; of Nordics and Alpines and Mediterranean types; of men who are our friends and men who are our enemies. By the power of abstraction in the human mind, we strip off the ' Tomness,' the whiteness, the brilliance, the kingliness, the ' Nordicness,' the ' friendness ' and reach the universal abstract idea of man. Nor will it do to attempt to reduce all ideas to sensations or to fusion of sense-images. We can distinguish our ideas from sensations, although it is undoubtedly true that our ideas are accompanied by sense-images, more or less vague. Gruender, in his chapter on " Thought," says:

By an idea we become aware of the nature of any object whatever, while by a sensation we become aware only of a sensible object as it appears to our senses here and now. When, therefore, we become aware of an object which has no sensible qualities, we know by that very fact that we have an idea and not a sensation.[1]

The relation between the hypotenuse and the other two sides of a right-angled triangle is an idea and not a sensation, because it is " neither hot nor cold, neither black nor yellow, etc., it simply has no sensible qualities."

Without universal ideas, science itself would be impossible; we cannot formulate a scientific law or scientific hypothesis without the aid of abstract, universal ideas. When the mathematician says, " In a right-angled triangle the square on the hypotenuse is equal to the sum of the squares on the other two sides," he is not talking about this right-angled triangle on the blackboard, not even of an imaginary right-angled triangle, but he is talking about the ' universal ' right-angled

---

[1] Hubert Gruender, *Experimental Psychology*, p. 308. Milwaukee, Wisconsin: Bruce Publishing Co., 1932.

triangle, which exists nowhere outside of his mind, but which has its foundation in reality. Of any right-angled triangle the statement in the proposition is true.

2. Being — the Object of the Mind

The object of the mind is to know what is — that is, to know being. The mind must see the universe of being — God, man, the cosmos — as a totality, with all its constituent elements in right relation to one another. Individual things must be studied, of course, but only as they fit into the total view; only then is every piece of knowledge enrichment.

This totality of view is the indispensable element. This view of education is what marks off the Catholic from most other groups. Catholics still believe that every sphere of human life is related essentially to every other. For the Catholic, the world is ordered on the principle of theocentric realism. As Sheed says:

For the theist, the matter hardly needs stating. God is not simply the supreme Being, enthroned at the apex of all that is in such wise that the universe may be conceived as so many strata of being from the lowest to the highest and God over all: if that were so, one might conceive of a true study of the lower strata which should take no account of God. But the truth is that God is at the very centre of all things whatsoever. They come into existence only because He sustains them. To omit God, therefore, from your study of things is to omit the one being that explains them: you begin your study of things by making them inexplicable! Further all things are made not only by God but for God; in that lies their purpose and the relation of each thing to all others. . . .

But the place of God in our view of the totality of things — and so of education — is not simply a matter of recognizing Him as first cause and last end and sustained in being more intimate to each being than it is to itself; there is also His revelation of the purpose for which He made man — not simply that He made man for Himself but just what this involves in terms of man's being and action. This question of purpose is a point overlooked in most educational discussion, yet it is quite primary. How can you fit a man's mind for living if you do not know what the purpose of man's life is? You can have no reasonable understanding of any activity — living as a totality or any of its departments — if you do not know its purpose. You do not even know what is good or bad for a man till you know the purpose of his existence, for this is the only test of goodness or badness — if a thing helps a man in the achievement of the purpose for which he exists, then it is good for him; if not, it is bad. And the one quite certain way to find out the purpose of anything is to ask its maker. Otherwise you can only guess. The Catholic knows that man has a Maker and that the Maker has said what he made man for. Therefore — not of himself but by the revelation of God — the Catholic knows the purpose of human life and if he be an educator he has the answer to this primary question. He may be a thoroughly bad educator — perhaps through being like many of us a born fool — but he has the first requirement.[1]

3. 'What Knowledge Is of Most Worth?'

This question the Catholic answers in straightforward fashion: religious knowledge, knowledge of God and man's relations to God as made known through reason and revelation — this is the knowledge that is of most worth. Not that Catholic schools of any type are concerned merely with knowledge of Christian doctrine. The point is academic; it is conceivable that in a more primitive civilization some Catholic schools might confine themselves almost, if not exclusively, to religious knowledge. The thing to be insisted on is that religion permeates all Catholic education from arithmetic to zoölogy, just as ideally it impregnates all of Catholic life and living. Naturally, there is no such thing as Catholic chemistry; yet in a chemistry class taught in a Catholic school to Catholics by a Catholic there will be an awareness of and a reverence for God and supernatural values. The Catholic scientist will never make the mistake of becoming so absorbed in test-tubes that there is room for no higher loyalty.

4. The Catholic Theory of a Liberal Education

Catholic education has, generally speaking — it is impossible to speak with more precision — been sympathetic to the humanist theory of a liberal education. Terence expressed the humanist ideal perhaps as well as anyone, *Nihil humani a me alienum puto*. All that is human must enter into the education that is humanistic and liberal. All that is human, all that belongs to man — the true, the beautiful, the good — all these constitute the elements of humanism in education. Not one alone, but a synthesis of all three. Not merely Greek thought and Roman thought, but Christian thought and Christian art, and modern thought and modern art and modern science as well — in so far as they are true, beautiful, good — these are the elements, often jarring because of false emphasis of one over the other, that must be harmonized to secure a liberal education.

---

[1] F. J. Sheed, "A Note on Reading and Education," *Ground Plan for Catholic Reading*, pp. 7–8. New York: Sheed & Ward (n.d.).

In the history of the world there have been surprisingly few great minds. The minds, the thoughts of these great minds, are preserved in matchless poetry and prose for our delight and edification. The traditional liberal education puts man in contact with these great minds. Most Catholics believe that humanities and those disciplines that prepare for the understanding and appreciation of the humanities must always be basic to any adequate theory of a liberal education. Not any sort of study of the humanities, surely not the gerund-grinding drudgery of the pedant, not the scientific dissection of the masterpieces of literature, but a study of literature that will show vistas of new worlds and old, that will unlock magic casements opening on sunlit seas, that will lift youth out of his narrow parochialism, remove him from the current barbarism and neopaganism of the day and make him a world citizen, at home with great minds ancient and modern. History has its contribution to make to a liberal education, a history that sees the relationship between our own age and that of a civilization that has disappeared from the face of the earth. Science and mathematics will play their part; they are the language of the contemporary world and are needed to impart experience in scientific method.

Philosophy is needed, a genuine and strenuous exercise in the art and science of thinking, a dynamic and fearless investigation of ideas and facts and things that will color all of life for the man who undergoes this discipline, and will enable him to meet problems of a modern changing world unafraid, not because he has the solutions ready-solved in a mental answer-book, but for the reason that his mind and soul have been steeled for conflict, have been anchored so sturdily that even a world tottering to ruins would find him not unprepared.

Religion must play a part in the integral humanistic training of man. Philosophy and science give only partial answers to the world riddle. Religion is needed to secure a complete view of life. If religion be banned from a liberal education, you have not merely an incomplete education, you have a maimed and distorted education.

Classical culture, Christian culture, the medieval synthesis of Thomas Aquinas, and modern science and modern thought — these are the strands that the Catholic believes must be combined somehow into unity to provide a liberal education for the youth of our day, to place him in contact with truth, and beauty, and goodness. How can integration be secured for these divergent and sometimes clashing forces? The metaphysics that President Hutchins speaks of is a partial solution; it is not a complete solution. The Catholic believes humbly and sincerely that the answer to this problem of integration is one word, a monosyllable, Christ. Christianity *is* Christ. Christianity is not the history of one nation or race or people; it is universal history, the history of the human race, the most human thing in the world. The humanism of Christ, who is also God, as the Catholic confidently believes, this is Christian humanism, integral humanism that will make a marvelous synthesis of old and new. In this framework the classical theory of a liberal education remains not a relic, however glorious of a golden past, not something static, but a dynamic force, transformed and vivified by all that is of permanent value in past and present, providing the world with a liberal education in the truest and finest sense of the word.

VI. Nature of Society

The idea of society connotes a plurality of persons united in some form of permanence with a common aim or object. Thus there are three features common to every society: plurality of persons, common aim, and authority to ensure permanence and common aim. Since man is a social being, society is natural to man, yet it must never be forgotten that he has an individual personality and dignity of his own. Therefore, education is hard put to it at times to keep a nice balance between individual and social aims.

1. State and Family

On the purely natural level there are two societies of educational import — the state and the family.

The family [was] instituted directly by God for its peculiar purpose, the generation and formation of offspring; for this reason it has priority of nature and therefore of rights over civil society.[1]

It is on this point that Aquinas, and other scholastic philosophers, part company with Aristotle. Aristotle [2] and pagan civilization generally regarded the individual as subordinate to the state. The important thing was to be a good citizen. Aristotle had said in his *Politics*, "A citizen does not belong to himself but to the state; he should be educated for it and by it." [3] Christianity changed this emphasis

---

[1] Pius XI, *Encyclical on Christian Education.*
[2] *Nicomachean Ethics*, I, ii, 8. See also Charles A. Hart, *Philosophy of Society,* especially Clare Riedl, "The Social Theory of Saint Thomas Aquinas," pp. 11 ff. Philadelphia: Dolphin Press, 1934.
[3] *Ibid.*, c. viii.

on the state by indicating man's supernatural end. This explains the importance of the individual man in scholastic thought, the reason why the state exists for man and not man for the state. This would be true even in the merely natural order. For the state exists for the common good. Although the common good, the good of society, is in general more important than the good of an individual, this does not hold when the private good is of a higher order.[1] So, too, with the rights of the family. The state may think it for the common good to require all children to attend state schools. This conflicts with the higher right of the family over the education of its children.

Part of the Supreme Court decision regarding the Oregon Act of 1922 indicates clearly that American opinion is in perfect accord with Catholic principles.

We think it entirely plain that the Act of 1922 unreasonably interferes with the liberty of parents and guardians to direct the upbringing and education of children under their control. . . . Rights guaranteed by the Constitution may not be abridged by legislation which has no reasonable relation to some purpose within the competency of the state. The fundamental theory upon which all governments in this union repose excludes any general power of the state to standardize its children by forcing them to accept instruction from public teachers only. The child is not the mere creature of the state; those who nurture him and direct his destiny have the right coupled with the high duty to recognize and prepare him for additional obligations.[2]

2. The Church

In the supernatural order, there is a third society concerned with education, the church. Since education, in the Catholic view, has a necessary connection with man's supernatural destiny the Catholic Church rightly claims that the education of her children belongs to her preëminently. Hers it is to decide what may help or harm Christian education. It is worth noting, in view of the widespread misunderstanding of the Church's position on her educational rights, that the Church has no jurisdiction over those that are not baptized, nor does she exercise any authority in matters of education over those not of her fold.

Again if the Church's position be true, her social objective in education is higher, nobler than any other. Humanity alone is not its aim,

---

[1] Cf. *Summa Theologica* II–II, q. 39, a. 2 ad 2um.

[2] Charles N. Lischka, *Private Schools and State Laws*, p. 292. Washington: National Catholic Welfare Conference, 1926.

still less a humanity without God; a realization of the brotherhood of man and the fatherhood of God, good as far as it goes, is too vague for her; citizenship and patriotism are noble objectives and are worthy of cultivation in every school system, yet citizenship and patriotism are not enough. The objective of the Church is to realize the consequences of a child's incorporation with Christ through baptism, a realization that Christ and the Church of which he is a member are *one* thing — the Mystical Body of Christ — Christ the Head, and we the members. In the light of this doctrine of the Mystical Body of Christ the social end of Christian education stands in bold relief. Information is not its aim, but formation of the whole man; better still transformation of Christians into other Christs. And Catholic schools, no matter of what type, no matter of what nature their material of instruction, all of them are engaged in this one aim, so startling because of its unity " of building up the body of Christ . . . till all attain to the full measure of the stature of Christ."

3. Democracy and Education: the Catholic View

It is well to recall Jacques Maritain's three meanings of democracy in his *The Things That Are Not Caesar's*. As his third meaning is the one most commonly used when American educators speak of democracy and education, that meaning had better be examined first. The third meaning of democracy, Maritain styles democratism:

> Democracy as conceived by Rousseau, the religious myth of democracy, an entirely different thing from the legitimate democratic regime. . . . Democracy in this sense becomes confused with the dogma of the Sovereign People, which combined with the dogma of the General Will and Law as the expression of Number, constitutes in the extreme, the error of political pantheism (the multitude — God).[1]

It is precisely this type of Rousseauistic democracy or democratism that is being urged on schools by an influential minority. For them democracy is a religion; democracy is the only absolute. And this new religion is creating a new school and a new education. Democratism is the standard by which to judge every phase of the school, methods and techniques, administration, and curriculum. If other educators insist that discipline and authority and traditional subjects still have a place in the training of American youth, the label of Fascist is at-

---

[1] Jacques Maritain, *The Things That Are Not Caesar's*, p. 227. New York: Charles Scribner's Sons, 1931.

tached to them. With this type of democracy, it is hardly necessary to state, Catholic education will have no traffic.

Democracy, however, has other meanings as Maritain points out. Democracy may mean a social tendency to procure social justice for the working classes. It is only necessary to point to the Encyclical letters from Leo XIII to Pius XII to be certain that this sort of democracy is sound Catholic doctrine, since it is based on the essential dignity of man.

Political democracy as conceived by Aristotle and Saint Thomas is that form of government exemplified in the old Swiss democracy, consecrated by Lincoln's phrase " government of the people, by the people, and for the people." This is considered by the Church and scholastics as a legally possible form of government. Not, however, the only possible form. The Church can adapt itself to any form of government, except the totalitarian state where the rights of the individual, the family, and the Church are all flouted.

Political democracy such as Americans enjoy is of primary concern to American Catholics. In 1938 the American Catholic Bishops issued a joint pastoral calling for a Catholic crusade for Christian democracy.

It is necessary that our people, from childhood to mature age, be ever better instructed in the true nature of Christian democracy. A precise definition must be given to them both of democracy in the light of Catholic truth and tradition and of the rights and duties of citizens in a representative republic such as our own. They must be held to the conviction that love of country is a virtue and that disloyalty is a sin.[1]

Experience, common sense, the sad results seen in other lands in the present critical hour for Christian civilization where political democracy has disappeared, as well as the Christian virtue of patriotism, urge Catholics in the Bishops' words " to the defense of our democratic form of government, framed in a constitution that safeguards the inalienable rights of man." This is in accord " with the American hierarchy's traditional position of unswerving allegiance to our free American institutions."

VII. Conclusion

This then represents, the writer hopes, an adequate presentation of the theory of Catholic education, of the philosophical and theological

---

[1] *Pastoral Letter of the American Bishops,* 1938.

bases upon which the Catholic theory of education rests. Despite the difficulty, perhaps the irritation, inherent in bringing in ideas such as supernatural, Incarnation, Mystical Body, the Fall of Man, it was felt essential that these ideas had to be clear if one would understand the Catholic position on education.

1. Essentials in the Philosophy of Catholic Education

It is quite clear that Catholics regard certain things as essential to the Catholic theory of education, certain things as accidental. To put it in other words, a Catholic as a Catholic is not free to accept or reject the essential postulates of Catholic education; on the other hand as an individual he may disagree — violently if need be — over the accidentals of Catholic education.

a. Nature of Man. The whole theory of Catholic education depends on the Catholic doctrine regarding man, his nature and supernatural destiny. From the Catholic concept of the nature of man follows the primary objective of Catholic education, its theory of values. Everything else is subordinate to this ultimate aim of Catholic education. Every demand that the Church makes, every disciplinary regulation is based on her supernatural viewpoint. The whole history and theory of Catholic education is unintelligible unless the Church's teaching on the supernatural be grasped.

b. Nature of Truth. Truth exists and the human mind can attain truth. Reason is capable of reaching with complete certainty the most sublime truths of the natural order, but with difficulty and only when duly trained. Therefore, the school or teachers have a right and a duty to aid the pupil to attain these truths. There are also truths of the supernatural order which the mind can never know unaided. For this, revelation is needed. The Catholic school again has the right and duty to present these truths to the child since he could never learn them unaided.

c. Agencies of Education. The school, the family, and the Church all have the right and the duty to educate in the Catholic system. Since man has a supernatural destiny, any educational system that fails to impart religious instruction is not acceptable to the Catholic. For the Catholic believes that religion is an essential part of education, since it is indispensable for right living here and for eternal life hereafter.

2. Accidentals in the Philosophy of Catholic Education

a. Curriculum. The Catholic as a Catholic is not concerned with curriculum. As a humanist he may demand training in the liberal arts; as an essentialist he may insist on a curriculum made up of traditional subjects, a curriculum that is not a ' rope of sand '; as a ' utilitarian ' he may insist on training in practical subjects. The one thing the Catholic will insist on is that, whatever type the curriculum may be, the first place must be assigned to religion.

b. Method. Still less is the Catholic *as a Catholic* concerned with method. He may advocate the outmoded method of drill; he may believe that the project method or the problem method has a place in his schools; he may insist on interest as the keystone of all educational progress; he may employ the methods of ' progressive ' education, while necessarily rejecting their underlying philosophy of naturalism; and there is no one to say him nay. Every acceptable method of learning must be based on the theory that all education is self-education. Consequently method, as distinct from techniques or mere tricks of the educational profession, must have as its aim the teaching of the child to think for himself, to express adequately his own thoughts, and to appreciate in a humane way the true, the beautiful, and the good.

c. Freedom vs. Discipline. The Catholic school, even those conducted along ' progressive ' lines, believes in discipline, but that discipline must eventually be self-discipline. Undoubtedly, Catholic schools differ among themselves in external discipline from the progressive type to the ultraconservative type that is perilously close to regimentation. Yet every Catholic school would admit that discipline is necessary. Discipline means right order. And every Catholic teacher knows that his charges are not angels, but very human beings, with all the limitations of human nature. Not a *depraved* nature certainly, but *deprived* and with the ' wounds of nature ' that need watchful guidance in order to lead him on to his last end. Regimentation may accomplish this externally, but self-discipline is the real answer, a self-discipline based on sound principles. Interest is the secret. A child will be good if he wants to be good. A child will learn fractions if he wants to learn fractions. It is the teacher's business to make him want it. That is the essence of good method, however it may be applied.

3. A Final Word

The main difficulty for the reader of all the foregoing will be his inability to see what may be called the architectonic structure of Catholicism and Catholic education. The reason is that Catholics and non-Catholics have come to talk two different languages. The background of their thought is not the same. This is true not merely in the religious sphere but in the whole of life. Hence, the difficulty of understanding the Catholic theory of education.

There are two things particularly which set off the Catholic from the non-Catholic world. There is in the Catholic a singular unity of thought that springs from his totality of outlook that is particularly irritating to the non-Catholic. The Catholic never forgets at any time or place the totality of being — God, man, and cosmos. The other provocative feature of Catholic thought may be styled other-worldliness. This is not to imply that Catholics are necessarily holier than other people; still less that they are the only people who believe in the world to come. The modern non-Catholic feels sure of what he has; he is not sure — not *so* sure at all events — of what is to come. Therefore, quite logically he emphasizes living in this world. Probably, he reasons, there is another world, but let us make this one that we are sure about a better place to live in. For the Catholic on the other hand, the idea of the world to come looms large; it makes its presence felt in a greater number of spheres. To him the thing of ultimate importance is not here but hereafter. Not, of course, that the Catholic does not recognize values in this world; he enjoys, as any other, natural truth and beauty and goodness; the glory of this world, of mountain and sea and plain; the glow that comes from family life and human friendship finds an echo in his heart; they are good and true and beautiful but they lead him on to the Creator of all these manifold delights made for him. ' The heavens announce the glory of God.'

With his philosophy of supernaturalism, the Catholic rests his case for education and for everything else in the world. Reactionary he may be, even dangerous to modern life, but at least in the light of his first principles he believes that he is consistent.

REFERENCES

CASTIELLO, JAIME, S.J. *A Humane Psychology of Education.* New York: Sheed & Ward, 1936. Pp. 254.

CHARMOT, F. *L'humanisme et l'humain.* Paris: Edition Spes, 1934. Pp. 524.

288   *THE PHILOSOPHY OF CATHOLIC EDUCATION*

Cohausz, Otto, S.J. *The Pope and Christian Education.* New York: Benziger Bros., 1933. Pp. 131.

Cunningham, W. F. *Pivotal Problems of Education.* New York: Macmillan Co., 1940. Pp. 588.

DeHovre, Frans. *Catholicism in Education.* New York: Benziger Bros., 1934. Pp. 501.

———. *Philosophy and Education.* New York: Benziger Bros., 1931. Pp. 443.

Fitzpatrick, Edward A. *I Believe in Education.* New York: Sheed & Ward, 1938. Pp. 218.

James, Fr. *Life and Religion.* St. Louis, Missouri: B. Herder Book Co., 1932. Pp. 260.

Kane, W. T. *Some Principles of Education.* Chicago: Loyola University Press, 1938. Pp. 215.

McGucken, William J., S.J. *The Catholic Way in Education.* Milwaukee, Wisconsin: Bruce Publishing Co., 1934. Pp. 131.

Mercier, Louis. *The Challenge of Humanism.* New York: Oxford University Press, 1933. Pp. 288.

Ryan, James H. *A Catechism of Catholic Education.* Washington, D. C.: National Catholic Welfare Conference, 1922. Pp. 98.

Shields, T. E. *Philosophy of Education.* Washington, D. C.: Catholic Education Press, 1917. Pp. 446.

CHAPTER VII

COMPARATIVE PHILOSOPHY OF EDUCATION

JOHN S. BRUBACHER
Associate Professor of the
History and Philosophy of Education
Yale University, New Haven, Connecticut

I. INTRODUCTION

All the preceding statements of educational philosophy commence with a more or less extended statement of principles. Application to educational problems occurs secondarily or incidentally. Perhaps in this comparative chapter it might be well to commence with what is more usual and familiar to teachers and parents, namely, problems of the processes of education themselves, and then proceed to compare the several theories or philosophies which are proposed as proper guides to the solution of these problems.

On the surface diverse educational practices are much in evidence. This family brings up its children this way; that family rears its young in another way. So too are these differences to be noted when one compares private with public schools, progressive schools with more conventional ones, or the teacher in the fourth grade with the one in the fifth or with another fourth-grade teacher. Yet in spite of the apparent multiplicity of practices, it is possible to reduce them all to two main types. Stated as simply as possible these two types are manifestations of differences as to aims, on the one hand, and differences as to means of achieving them, on the other.

The diversity of educational aims arises in the diversities of our culture. The family has one aim, industry another; the church sets another ideal and the state still another. And this is to say nothing of conflicting points of view among poor and well-to-do families, as between capital and labor, humanists and theologians, democrats and Fascists. Besides, even where there is agreement on aims, there is such a wealth of means or instructional methods at hand that there may still be a clash of views as to how given or accepted aims are to be instrumented. Some, for instance, would adopt progressive methods and others more conservative ones; some favor employing interest and others discipline.

Through the midst of such diversities of practice, how shall the parent or particularly the teacher thread his way? How can he pick his aims, his curriculum, his methods, and have some confidence in the result? For one thing, he might read history, especially the history of education. But since history affords hindsight rather than foresight, it has only limited usefulness in writing the prescription for the present and the future. For another thing, he might consult science, particularly the science of education. But science too has only a circumscribed utility. It can tell within limits exactly what the existing state of affairs *is* but it has no authority to recommend what *ought* to be done. Finally, the parent or teacher might study philosophy, emphasizing of course educational philosophy. Here he would find a discipline peculiarly competent to tell what should be done both now and later on.

What, as a matter of theory, educational philosophy has to offer the practitioner, is a subject of dispute among the schools of thought represented in the preceding chapters. For the moment, however, before comparing these theories, let us still endeavor to approach the need for educational philosophy from the point of view of one continually immersed in the practical aspects of education. It has already been noted that the chief problems that confront the parent or teacher are those of aim and those of means, notably, content and method. Some progress in their solution can be made at once by arranging these questions in the order of their importance. It almost goes without argument that the selection of curriculum and methods of instruction, being instances of ways and means, must await a decision first as to what the parent or teacher is trying to do, what he is aiming at. Responding to the question *which* aim, however, is a complicated affair.

The diary of one's thoughts on such a problem might run along some such pattern as the following. In ruminating at first, a number of specific aims might leap to mind. But which are the ones to be preferred? And what is the standard of preference? Or, in brief, what is the good? Does the cosmos afford data or ' givens ' which at once give the bearings from which to compute the aim or course of education? For instance does the cosmos have a design from which a design for education could be deduced? If so, is the design eternally the same or is it temporal and changing? Can we *know* which it is? Are there *true* aims? What is truth? Should educational aims take their character

from what we know about knowing? Going further, can a design for
education be found in human nature? Do its potentialities set the direction for education? Or does the social culture in which we live shape
these potentialities of human nature? Or is society, the state, only a
means for the realization of human personality? Can 'society' and
'state' be used interchangeably as equivalent terms?

Assume now that satisfactory conclusions have been reached on
these questions, one must still ask what kind of curriculum and what
kind of method will be adequate instruments. Indeed, should the
curriculum be conceived as an instrument at all? Or is it an end —
knowledge for knowledge's sake? Should one conceive of the curriculum as composed of subjects or of activities, attitudes, and the like?
What different theories of knowledge are involved here? What theories of learning? In what form does knowledge exist before it is
learned? How can one be sure that learning has taken place, that
knowledge has been acquired? What is the most effective way of teaching so that learning will take place, that knowledge will be acquired?
Should knowledge be transmitted by the authority of the teacher —
backed by the folkways, the state, or the church? Should knowledge
be the outgrowth of the method of experience, particularly the method
of experimentation?

The foregoing questions are just samples of a possible train of
thought that might arise in a teacher's mind when he is perplexed about
next steps in his educational endeavors. There are probably few teachers who ask themselves such questions as these. Yet, if asked the reasons why they teach as they do, few would fail to have at hand some
ready answer. But if they were asked the reasons for their reasons,
the further answers would no doubt come more slowly and with more
hesitation. How far or how long one would need to press this search
before coming to reasons that were ultimately satisfying to their owner,
would almost surely differ for different teachers. Yet, perplexing or
annoying as the quest for these reasons may be, it is the only way to a
secure confidence in the attainable objectives of the teaching one undertakes.

Indeed, it is submitted that no satisfactory answer can be found to
practical questions about the method, curriculum, or aims of the schools
till adequate answers are obtained to such underlying questions as
those already raised. Of course one can give an immediate off-hand or
common sense answer to questions of aim, method, and content. By its
very nature, however, such an answer is bound to be more or less super-

ficial. A thoroughly professional answer demands that one think through the questions which are prior to further practice. These questions inescapably involve theoretical or philosophical considerations. Such considerations, however, are not to be thought of as entirely different in nature from practical ones. Philosophical theory is really an elaboration and enlargement of the more significant and more widely ramified aspects of practice.

The foregoing chapters present the ultimate reasons which their several authors can give, in the limited space available, for carrying on the educative process as they, together with those of a kindred outlook, believe it should be carried on. Presented in this systematic fashion, they constitute different philosophies of education. Laying them down along side each other has obviously been done for comparative purposes. However, no thought is entertained in the present chapter of comparing them so as to determine which views are sound and which are unsound or to determine *the* philosophy of education which teachers should accept. The aim of this chapter is rather to contrast these philosophies at their specific points of conflict and to note their specific points of agreement so that both experienced and inexperienced teachers may better understand the problems which confront them as well as the options available for their solution.

The comparison, unfortunately, will not be as adequate at every point as the reader might wish. This is because the materials to be compared often are unequal. That is, problems covered by one contributor have not always been treated by each of the other contributors. Or, if covered by two or more, the respective expositions may be of unequal length or of considerably varying importance relative to the total exposition. Except for the restrictions of space which doubtless have forced some omissions and slighted emphases, these very omissions and emphases might speak eloquently themselves. However, in spite of these hindrances to effective comparison, the comparison must now go forward.

II. Scope of Educational Philosophy

Probing further and further back for supporting reasons has two effects that need now to be noted. On the one hand the reasons so adduced seem to become more and more remote from practice. This remoteness is associated with an increase in their theoretical character which seems to grow in almost direct proportion to their distance from the practice which they support or in which they are involved. It would be a mistake, however, to think that these reasons therefore are becoming less and less significant. As a matter of fact, and as the second effect of such searching, the further back one presses for reasons, the more fundamental and basic they are likely to be.

Not all basic or supporting reasons are of the same sort. As already noted, educational practice might be based on historical or scientific reasons, for instance, as well as philosophical. This raises the question of what is the nature of philosophical reasons, what should be included within the scope of the phrase *philosophy of education*. What is its proper content, its method of solving problems? What can the educator hope to accomplish by approaching the problems of his profession philosophically? It is different answers to these questions in the first instance which give rise to some of the differences discussed in the preceding pages. The nature of philosophy being conceived differently, the resulting philosophies themselves have inescapably been different.

1. Knowledge and Opinion

Perhaps the sharpest differences with respect to the scope of philosophy would arise over the propositions put forward in the Aristotelian position, in the statement of which more space is devoted to this problem than is given to it in any of the other expositions. According to this view the philosophy of education is concerned with knowledge rather than with opinion.[1] The distinction between knowledge and opinion is of preëminent importance. In the realm of opinion each person is entitled to his own. There it is impossible to make judgments on absolutely objective grounds of truth and falsity.[2] In the realm of knowledge just such judgments can be made. Obviously, therefore, a philosophy of education which can be proved true or false will differ widely from one which is merely grounded in opinion however well thought out. Not only that, but there can be only one true philosophy of education according to such tenets. Bold as such a claim is, it needs to be noted that Adler does not necessarily claim that his exposition of educational philosophy is this one and only philosophy. He is merely asserting that there is only one standard by which all educational philosophies are to be judged, his own included.[3]

Although in the exposition of the Catholic philosophy of education there is no expansion on the scope of educational philosophy, the position just stated would probably not be uncongenial. The Aristotelian

---

[1] *Supra,* pp. 197–200.   [2] *Supra,* p. 199.   [3] *Supra,* p. 200.

hopes to reach absolutely objective truth on strictly natural or secular grounds. If this is possible for him, it should be much more so for a Catholic who is further aided by faith and revelation. It goes without saying that a philosophy of education resting on supernatural support would be the true one and that it would be based on knowledge rather than opinion.

The other philosophies, as might well be anticipated,[1] would almost certainly find themselves definitely arrayed against stating the nature of educational philosophy in these terms. More than likely they would not draw such a sharp distinction between knowledge and opinion. The idealist, especially if he is committed to Hegelian triads, necessarily rejects statements in disjunctive form, that is, he denies that knowledge is either true or false.[2] There is thesis and antithesis, to be sure, but there is also synthesis. Furthermore, the experimentalist could hardly accept a view of knowledge founded on ' absolutely objective grounds ' for he denies absolute principles, or at least that any have yet been found.[3] In this he faithfully represents the point of view of experimentalism, which not only tolerates but welcomes competing philosophies of education. If this reduces the philosophy of education to the level of opinion, it is at least a considered attempt to be critical.[4]

2. Science and Philosophy

Merely to indicate that the philosophy of education is preoccupied with knowledge rather than opinion is not precise enough, according to the Aristotelian position. After all, the scientific study of education also is concerned with knowledge. It is necessary, therefore, to go further and point out that knowledge is of two kinds, theoretic and practical.[5] Theoretic knowledge is knowledge about the nature of things as they exist; for instance, the nature of the child to be educated. Practical knowledge is knowledge about what should be done when engaged in a course of action. What phases of a child's education should be the responsibility of the state and which are the responsibilities of the family and the church, is a case in point.

With these premises in mind, it should be clear that scientific knowledge about education is strictly theoretical. It deals with facts; it is descriptive. Limited to stating what is, it is inadequate to determine

---

[1] *Supra,* pp. 200–1.
[2] *Supra,* p. 166.
[3] *Supra,* pp. 53–54, 58–59.
[4] *Supra,* p. 39.
[5] *Supra,* pp. 206–12.

what should be. Useful as the science of education is, then, it settles
no practical problems of education. The philosophy of education, on
the other hand, since one of its major concerns is normative, is to judge
educational undertakings as to their worth or value, and is definitely
practical. But the philosophy of education, unlike the science of education, is not *strictly* practical. It is theoretical too. It not only tells
what to do (practice), but it must know what in fact is worth doing
(theory). Indeed, unless there is *theoretic knowledge* of the good, there
can be no sound practical philosophy of education. Although the science and the philosophy of education are thus to be distinguished, it
needs pointing out that they are alike in that all the propositions of
each are to be verified by experienced fact and by the canons of rational
procedure.[1] But finally, in spite of this similarity, the philosophy of
education ranks above the science of education because it is true on
objective grounds and with a certitude that exceeds the objectivity and
certitude of mathematics and science.[2]

Of the other statements in this volume, that of idealism would probably most closely approximate this further elaboration of the scope of
the philosophy of education. Although not employing the distinction
between theoretical and practical knowledge, the idealist does try to
steer the ship of knowledge between the Scylla of skepticism and the
Charybdis of agnosticism by describing philosophy as " an account of
man finding himself as an integral part of a universe of mind." [3] It
is a search for the ultimate reality or meaning of things wherein the
totality of reality and meaning is inferred from what we know of the
fragment man.[4]

Farthest from agreement with the foregoing position would be those
of realism[5] and experimentalism.[6] According to realism, the philosophy of education is seen to possess neither materials nor methods
peculiar to itself. On the contrary its methods and materials are those
of science itself, with the possible qualification that the problems of
philosophy may be somewhat more general than those of science.
While the experimentalist is not quite so categorical in identifying the
method of educational philosophy with that of science, he nonetheless
proposes that the method of science be extensively employed in solving
the ethical problems of education. Certainly one advantage on behalf
of the realist and experimentalist position is the fact that it is in har-

---

[1] *Supra*, pp. 199–200.   [4] *Supra*, p. 154.
[2] *Supra*, p. 199.   [5] *Supra*, p. 91.
[3] *Supra*, p. 140.   [6] *Supra*, pp. 43–45.

mony with the unity-of-science movement and the integration of all knowledge.

3. Theory and Practice

Finally, the Aristotelian notes that, while all problems of education are ultimately practical and while the philosophy of education is both theoretical and practical, not all practical problems in education are capable of philosophical solution.[1] If this proposition does not seem paradoxical at first glance, it must at least appear as one of the more controversial ones put forth in the delimitation of the nature and scope of educational philosophy. The key to understanding this position lies in distinguishing between three types of practical problems. Since the practical problem is one of what to do, one should be careful to note whether the recommendation is for a single particular case at hand, for a class of cases, or for all cases.[2] When the teacher is absorbed with an individual case, he must pay careful attention to all the accidental circumstances that are contingent on this isolated case. Concerning such contingencies there may well be differences of opinion. When the teacher is recommending action for all cases there can be no exceptions for the accidents of circumstance. Here one deals with universal principles. To enunciate these he must have knowledge. Where the practical problem concerns a class of cases, the teacher's judgment of what to do approximates the universal but it still has elements of the contingent inherent in it. Consequently, although the teacher is here telling what to do as a general rule or as a matter of policy, the solution of the problem is still one of opinion rather than of knowledge and at best can be expected to have only a high degree of probability.

From these premises it follows that the philosophy of education, being concerned with knowledge rather than opinion, is further concerned only with those practical problems where universal principles can be stated. It cannot provide solutions for single cases or even formulate policy for the general run of cases. To handle such cases the teacher should be armed not so much with a philosophy of education as with ample experience. Only by an empirical study of many cases can he predict the probabilities for resolving conflicts and contingencies which occur in the particular or average case. It is here that the experimental method is particularly useful.[3] It may seem that policy based on a very large number of cases would tend to approximate educational principles which state the rule for all cases. Es-

---

[1] *Supra*, p. 224.   [2] *Supra*, pp. 224–28.   [3] *Supra*, p. 234.

pecially would this seem to be the case when one notes that the educational philosopher is sometimes called upon to determine which sort of system of education most nearly approximates the ideal determined on principle. But close as the educational philosopher and practitioner approach each other at this point, the function of the one must not be confused with that of the other.[1]

The realists, and particularly the experimentalists, take no such limited view of the practical character of their educational philosophies. With them, educational philosophy must work twenty-four hours a day and seven days a week. They invoke it in the case beset with the accidents of circumstances as well as in the case free from exceptions. Furthermore, in both instances the philosophy of education is practical, not only because it tells what to do, but also because it is put to the test of experience. Experience is central. Ideas mean only their consequences in experience and their predictability or dependability is based on studying experimentally the uniformities of experience.[2] Indeed, as the experimentalist remarks, "If there is any other kind of knowledge or any other access to knowledge, some traces of them should appear in experience." [3]

III. Generic Traits of Reality

If by now the reader has been able to delimit the field of philosophical endeavor, he must next use that philosophical process to ascertain the particular bearings by which to guide the cultivation of his professional domain. In searching for the reasons which the teacher can give in support of the reasons he gives for practice, it was suggested that he might ultimately come to reasons which are basic, reasons beyond which he could not or did not care to go. In pressing for reasons of this sort, a typical answer that one finally gets is " The world just is that way " or " That is just the nature of things." In other words, there are generic traits of reality which constitute the data, the ' givens,' of the educative process. If the course of education be set in accordance with them, it can have reasonable assurance of succeeding.

1. Origin and Destiny

Concerning what is ' given ' to begin with, however, there is wide difference of opinion. As the Catholic looks about, the characteristic of the cosmos that strikes him most forcefully is the contingent nature

---

[1] *Supra,* pp. 229–30.   [2] *Supra,* p. 44.   [3] *Supra,* p. 43.

of man.[1] He has not within himself the answer to how or why he happens to be in the world he finds himself in. Therefore, the reason must lie outside himself. He must be dependent or contingent on the fiat of someone else. This, of course, is an omniscient, omnipotent, personal God. God being the origin of man, it is to the maker of man that one must go to learn what he was made for, what his destiny is. Given such a supernatural framework, the pattern of the educative process becomes imperatively clear.

Most akin to the Catholic philosophy of education at this point is that of idealism. Although not stating its conclusions in exactly the same form nor arriving at them in quite the same way, the import for education is quite similar.[2] The most striking thing to the idealist is his own ideas, his mind. Mind, however, is not just composed of ideas; it is the thinking, feeling, purposing self which everyone introspectively knows himself to be.[3] As such it is the strongest conviction of reality that he has. But, as with the Catholic, the idealist is concerned to explain the origin of mind. Realizing that something cannot spring from nothing, he concludes that mind springs from mind, and that finite mind springs from Infinite Mind. Not only that, but the finite finds its fulfilment in the Infinite, the Absolute, in a personal God. Here again, given such broad outlines of the world and man's place in it, the implications for education are very definite indeed.

The Aristotelian position of Adler is not altogether clear on this point of the ultimate ground of education. His main point seems to be that questions of origin and destiny are to be reserved for religious education where they can be dealt with more adequately. Because philosophy is knowledge and because its propositions rest on experienced fact and on the canons of rational procedure, it is distinguished from religious education whose speculative arguments proceed according to faith and revelation, a light higher than experience and reason can provide. The philosophy of education, thus, is natural, not supernatural.[4] It rests ultimately on metaphysics rather than theology. It is this distinction more than any other which sets the Aristotelian position of Hutchins and Adler off from that of Catholicism.

Since some confusion has arisen on the relation of these two educational philosophies, it may be well to dwell on them a little more at

---

[1] *Supra,* pp. 252–54.
[2] *Supra,* pp. 143–48.
[3] Cf. the experimentalist's statement, pp. 40–41.
[4] *Supra,* p. 200.

length. There has been a tendency among both lay and professional people to lump these two positions together as if there were no significant difference between them. McGucken for the Catholics, however, is careful to disown this alliance.[1] He indicates that Hutchins and Adler parallel Catholicism up to a certain point, but he regrets that they do not continue to parallel it beyond that point. Thus, both positions follow Aristotle, but Hutchins and Adler stop short of accepting the modifications made by Thomas Aquinas to accommodate Christian revelation. Although McGucken thinks Adler supplements his position with theology and quotes him to that effect, Adler tries in this Yearbook to make his position quite precise in this connection.[2] Here he specifically states that he writes a natural or secular philosophy of education. However, he recognizes that to the extent which metaphysics may reveal the existence of God and man's dependence on him, a purely natural or intellectual education is disclosed as inadequate for achieving the perfection of man. For this purpose he admits another kind of knowledge is ' possible,' that of faith and revelation. But this lies beyond philosophical knowledge, as he defines it, and therefore is not strictly a part of the philosophy of education.

2. Change and the Changeless

Realism and experimentalism confine themselves to the realm of the natural even more strictly than does the Aristotelian position of Hutchins and Adler. Questions of origin and ultimate destiny do not greatly concern them. Their quarrel is at a different point. It has rather to do with the way in which the flow of events between these two limits is characterized. Of this process of change the experimentalist in particular makes much.[3] The main problem, however, is not just the recognition of change, for other educational philosophies do at least that much, but rather the importance that is to be attached to it. This importance is brought into relief when one inquires further how education is to take its bearings if change is the ' given,' the context of its undertakings. How is stability to be achieved in the midst of change? Because the experimentalist takes change seriously as one of the generic traits of existence, he finds no fixed stars by which to guide the educative process. For him there are ' no absolute principles.'[4] In a future that is more or less uncertain, he finds whatever stability there is in his experimental method and in whatever store of already tested ex-

---

[1] *Supra,* pp. 256, 258.
[2] *Supra,* pp. 199–200, 220–21.
[3] *Supra,* pp. 59–60, 64–66.
[4] *Supra,* pp. 53–54.

perience it has been able to accumulate. Hence, the school should accustom children to change and include in their curriculum the resources they will need for the problems which will most probably occur.[1]

The realist, although he employs the same experimental method as the experimentalist, states the nature of this stability in sufficiently different terms to merit separate statement.[2] With him it is not just the uniformities in experience which give stability to the conclusions of his educational philosophy but the objective or independent nature of the reality which provoked these experiences. He is, of course, here contrasting the nature of reality with the human experiencing of reality. However, this being more particularly a problem of our knowledge about reality, it will receive more extended treatment in connection with the theory of knowledge.[3] In any event he concurs with the experimentalist on the point that the problem method in teaching is the one demanded by the nature of the situation.[4]

The other three philosophies of education react quite differently to this problem. At the very outset it must already be evident that philosophies of education like those of Aristotelianism and Catholicism, which claim to be the only true educational philosophies, must necessarily be founded on a certainty which quite transcends that of the realist and the experimentalist. This also appears in the Catholic claim that its ultimate aim of education not only has not changed in the past but can never change in the future.[5] Part of the explanation of this situation lies in the fact that these philosophies of education deal with *theoretic knowledge* and that such knowledge deals with universals and essences rather than with contingencies and accidentals.[6] When one deals with education at the level of universals or essences he has excluded from consideration all its aspects which are exceptional because contingent on the accidents of circumstance. Inferentially this must include the exclusion of change for when one deals with universals or essences of this order, he is hardly dealing with that which may change and thereby prove an exception. But change, be it noted, is not denied in the statement of this position; it is merely classed as an instance of accidental or contingent circumstance and hence less important than what is capable of absolute or certain determination.

Again, idealism takes a position much the same in effect, although stated quite differently. It, too, notes the shifting scene, even notes

[1] *Supra*, pp. 45–47.
[2] *Supra*, pp. 108–9.
[3] *Infra*, pp. 301–5.
[4] *Supra*, p. 125.
[5] *Supra*, p. 265.
[6] *Supra*, pp. 224–25.

that the great periods of mankind have been those of flux and instability,[1] but nevertheless it has its fixed points of reference by which to guide the educational process. It steers by an ideal of the social order which is " real in the same sense that perfect circles are real." [2] Obviously such ideals approximate very closely to the universals just considered. Moreover, there is a subtle steadiness to change for it is stated that whatever *e*volves in the process of evolution must have already been *in*volved.[3] While such a doctrine probably does not commit idealism to the culture epoch or recapitulatory theories of education, there is nonetheless a strong implication that no genuine novelty accompanies change. Consequently, the uncertainty and contingency, which the experimentalist feels is so real, is apparently to be ascribed to the limitations of the finite mind or, in the Aristotelian or Catholic phrase, to the accidental.

IV. THEORIES OF KNOWLEDGE

The last statement above suggests another datum, another ' given,' which the teacher should consider as an anchor for his reasons for teaching as he does. This datum concerns the nature of human knowledge. It may be quite valid to base a philosophy of education on certain generic traits of existence; but what if, as the last statement above implies, there is a difference between these traits as they are and our knowledge of them? If all our knowledge must be refracted through the lens of human experience and the human mind, perhaps the main underpinning of a philosophy of education should be an examination of the nature of this lens.

Indeed, so important is this distinction that philosophies of education might almost be divided into those which are primarily predicated on the nature of reality and those which are primarily predicated on the nature of knowing. If this division is recognized, the Catholic philosophy of education belongs in the first group for it is grounded in theology, the existence of God and His designs. Curriculum and method — the core of knowledge and its method of acquisition — are merely accidentals.[4] Here, too, belongs the Hutchins-Adler Aristotelian position which explicitly centers in metaphysics. In the other group belong the other three philosophies of education. Idealism, which is really ' idea-ism,' shows its epistemological inclination in its very title. The experimentalist philosophy of education is an off-

---

[1] *Supra*, p. 175.   [3] *Supra*, p. 144.
[2] *Supra*, p. 178.   [4] *Supra*, p. 286.

shoot of idealism, being a way of verifying or making ideas clear. Its major concern is with curriculum and method. Finally, realism locates in this group; for, though it emphasizes the thing known rather than the idea we have of this thing, it is a theory of knowing since it holds that the objects of knowledge exist independently of their being known.[1]

1. Knower and Known

It may almost be taken for granted that some sort of knowledge is possible for the human learner. None of the philosophies of education portrayed in this volume is either skeptical or agnostic on this point. Furthermore, according to the Aristotelian system, it is of the very nature of mind to learn or to know[2] and, according to the idealistic system, it is of the very nature of the world to be known, to be intelligible.[3] If these two statements can be taken as complementary to each other, there perhaps need be no further doubt as to the fundamental efficacy of a philosophy of education.

But even if this conclusion be conceded, there remains the very controversial problem of determining the nature of knowing and its significance for learning. The exposition of this point may well begin where our confidence in reality was obscured by suggesting that reality might only be what was thought to be reality. It is the idealists who have been most sensitive to this possible ambiguity. After careful examination they have concluded that all we know about the world are ideas of it. In other words, mind is the primary fact here; mind is the explainer. Indeed, " the very conception of something other than mind is itself a concept made by the mind.[4] This being the case, the schools not only should be but inescapably are ' idea-centered or ideal-centered.' [5]

The realist supports the opposite side of this controversy. He holds to the ' *principle of independence*,' that is, that the object of knowledge exists independently of its being known or studied by the student.[6] In this, he trusts the common sense point of view of the common man rather than the sophisticated reasoning of the idealist. But it is after all only a trust, for he admits that he has no direct knowledge of his principle of independence as a matter of generalized fact. His realism is just an assumption or presupposition on which he acts. His preference for it seems to stem from a stability which a regard for objectivity

[1] *Supra*, p. 93.   [4] *Supra*, p. 142.
[2] *Supra*, p. 211.   [5] *Supra*, p. 160.
[3] *Supra*, pp. 149, 163.   [6] *Supra*, pp. 93, 104–5.

is calculated to impose on education.[1] Moreover, the student, he believes, should be more concerned with the question ' what is ' than the question ' what to do.' It is not that he would deëmphasize doing or inquiry but that he would hold in higher regard the content of knowledge.[2] Consequently the good curriculum is composed of just such attested values. As such they exercise a wholesome authority, both individually and socially.

It is easy to see how one learns or comes to know his world if he is an idealist. The individual and his world both being expressions of intelligence, there is at once a common denominator for the learner and his lesson, a bridge between the two over which knowledge can pass.[3] Of course the theory that education is world building and that the world is one's own idea is admittedly highly subjectivistic — ' solipsistic ' or ' egocentric,' to recall the criticism of the realist. Serious as such name-calling may be, the idealist but takes it as further emphasis on the reality and primacy of mind as the bedrock on which to build a philosophy of education.[4]

The realist, on the other hand, has himself to thank if he has difficulty in explaining the same phenomena, for he has made a declaration of independence for the thing learned from the learning mind. However, after having set up the autonomy of the object of learning, the curriculum, he reëstablishes contact with it by finding that both it and the learner reduce to a theory of activity.[5] The bridge between the physical and psychic lies in the concept that both partake of a common nature in that they are both vibratory. It is but an instance of the well-recognized phenomenon of vibrations being transferred from one medium to another. In this fashion the realist, like the idealist, escapes any dualism of mind and matter in his theory of knowledge. Yet, unlike the idealist, the realist ends up with a thoroughly materialistic point of view. However that may be, the realist believes that he has establish " a common world of sense " which enables the philosophy of education to escape the undependable subjectivism of solipsism.

The experimentalist does not pause over that aspect of the problem of knowledge which so concerns and divides the idealist and realist.

---

[1] *Supra,* pp. 108–9, 124–28.

[2] *Supra,* pp. 120–22. Cf. the Aristotelian position where the same distinction is drawn but without the difference in emphasis, p. 214.

[3] *Supra,* p. 146.

[4] *Supra,* pp. 141–42.

[5] *Supra,* pp. 105–7.

On the contrary he launches forth on a description of knowledge as experience. Experience assumes both an organism and an environment and is the outcome of their continual interaction.[1] Furthermore, experience is not just something which is privy to the person who has it. Experience is what it is largely because of the social context in which it takes place. Indeed, if experience did not occur in a common culture it would have far less meaning than it does. One's knowledge of himself is enhanced by his knowledge of others and his knowledge of others by knowledge of himself. Since the breadth and depth of experience depend on the culture context in which it occurs, preparing the individual to participate in that culture is the main objective of education.[2] But this culture only enters into experience as it is experienced and *lived*. Furthermore, it can only be lived as the school enters into community activities, takes field excursions, has shops, and the like.

The Catholic philosophy of education does not seem to feel itself called upon to resolve the same sort of subtleties as those which perplex the preceding points of view. Instead of elaborately erecting a bridge to connect the knower and the thing to be known, the child and the curriculum, this philosophy simply assumes that the knower has the capacity for knowing the object of his studies, that is, to know being or what is.[3] More particularly the process of knowing is one wherein percepts are reduced to concepts. All the accidental differences are stripped from sense impressions till their essences stand forth clearly. These, then, are formed into concepts or immaterial representations of what is universal in sense. Supplementary to this natural knowledge is supernatural knowledge, knowledge which comes by revelation from God or His messenger.[4] This knowledge is not to be confused with subjective emotional experience nor with anything magical. If anything, this knowledge is even more dependable than that gained through the learner's senses and intellect, for it is guaranteed by God Himself.

2. Truth

The mention of the dependability of knowledge brings the discussion of reality and knowledge about reality to a focus in the concept of truth. If the student can but learn the truth, if the teacher can but moor his philosophy of education to the truth, then it would seem that at last that ultimate reason for all other reasons has been found. It is already evident in the Catholic philosophy of education that an infal-

---

[1] *Supra*, p. 41.
[2] *Supra*, pp. 62–63.
[3] *Supra*, pp. 276–78.
[4] *Supra*, p. 259.

lible knowledge of truth is possible. Under proper conditions truth can be known with guaranteed certitude.[1]

Although it does not have the advantage of a supernatural sanction, the Aristotelian position parallels the Catholic at many points in its claim for the singleness of truth. It has already been noted, for example, that it claims that there can be only *one* true philosophy of education.[2] Such a position proceeds in the first instance from self-evident truths.[3] These should be demonstrable to all by showing that any alternative propositions result in a *reductio ad absurdum*. Once granted that there are self-evident truths as a foundation for the philosophy of education, the detail of the superstructure follows without much difficulty.

This auspicious start on a more or less harmonious conception of truth is interrupted by the realist and the experimentalist, however, for both explicitly reject any truths as self-evident or a priori.[4] It follows from the realist's principle of independence — the fact that the thing known has an existence independent of the knower — that knowledge is a " disclosure of the preëxistent." [5] This being the case, truth must be the conformity of knowledge with reality. Perhaps the idealist has a somewhat similar conception of truth when he describes it as " man thinking the thoughts and purposes of this eternal order as they are embodied in our world." [6] In any event, conformity or correspondence is to be tested experimentally.

Furthermore, the experimentalist adds that no such results should be accepted by anyone unless he believes substantially similar results would be achieved by other independent and impartial inquiry.[7] Truth may be humanly contrived from what is found, but it emphatically is not a private matter. If misunderstandings arise in the endeavor to make truth a public affair, meanings are to be cleared up by finding out what their consequences are in experience. Thus, meanings, knowledge, truth, are put on an operational basis.[8] Herein, in part at least, lies the basis for the activity school and the activity curriculum.

V. HUMAN NATURE AND LEARNING

Whatever one may conclude as to the limits or methods of knowing, the foregoing discussion has clearly indicated that a philosophy of edu-

---

[1] *Supra,* p. 276.
[2] *Supra,* p. 199.
[3] *Supra,* p. 236.
[4] *Supra,* pp. 42–43, 136.
[5] *Supra,* p. 108.
[6] *Supra,* p. 140.
[7] *Supra,* p. 58.
[8] *Supra,* p. 44; cf. pp. 145–46.

cation will hardly be adequate which does not include an account of the way in which the educative process is conditioned by human nature. Human nature, from this point of view, is just as much one of the data or ' givens ' of that process as are any of the other generic traits of reality. As to the nature of human nature, the preceding philosophies of education do not so much clash as they make quite different emphases.

1. The Nature of Man

Both Catholic and Aristotelian philosophies of education insist at the very outset that although man is an animal, he is a rational animal.[1] This rationality, however, is not something which he shares with animals, differing from them only in degree. On the contrary, the difference is held to be an absolute one of kind without mediates in between.[2] The significance of this difference is that man with his rational nature can be educated while the brute without it is capable only of being trained.[3] What such a distinction would mean for inferences drawn from animal experimentation as to human learning can easily be imagined.

In addition to rationality, the Catholic claims also a supernature for man.[4] This is not just an improved human nature; it is rather something distinct from and superadded to human nature with its natural faculties. Furthermore it implies a supernatural life of grace with a supernatural destiny of union with God.

The dualism noted between man's nature and supernature is to be noted again between his body and his soul. The soul is immaterial, spiritual, intrinsically independent of matter.[5] Substituting mind for soul, the idealist comes to pretty much the same conclusions as does the Catholic.[6] He, too, holds that mind is qualitatively different from matter, that the two are simply inconvertible terms. Idealism does not even adopt the functional view that the mind is a function of the brain or even of the whole organism.

Over against these views stands that of realism with its rejection of dualism.[7] It thinks of the physical and psychical as belonging to the same continuum. In fact there are no entities that are completely devoid of experience or perhaps even of consciousness. " That which

---

[1] *Supra*, pp. 253–54.
[2] *Supra*, pp. 244–45.
[3] *Supra*, p. 215.
[4] *Supra*, p. 259.

[5] *Supra*, p. 253.
[6] *Supra*, pp. 142–45.
[7] *Supra*, pp. 111–12.

is sensed is a form of experience that can appear equally well inside or outside the human mind, mind being regarded as a manifold of such contents and their relations." [1] Vibrations like those of sound and light can be picked up and carried by neural impulses without any compromise of identity.

Closely akin to the problem of whether the difference between mind and matter or between man and the brute is one of kind or one of degree is the problem of whether human nature is essentially the same for all men. The Aristotelian position holds this to be the case.[2] Accordingly, all men, being of the same species, have the same abilities. What differences they have are only " *inter sese* " and as to accidentals. Thus, having the same abilities does not mean that all men have them in equal degree. There are individual differences, no doubt, but these are, as stated, chance or accidental. The educational significance of this emphasis foreshadows the claim of the Aristotelian stand that, therefore, the aims of education should be the same for all men, at all times, and in all places.[3]

On the whole, the idealist too accepts the thesis that human nature is always the same as to native propensities.[4] Yet he does not put his main emphasis here. Neither does he stress the great flexibility and wide individual differences of human nature. Rather does he select personality as the characteristic of chief importance.[5] Personality is " the state or quality of being a self, or a conscious center of experience." Individuality, the state of being different from others, is not enough because even the brute has that. There must be self-conscious purpose as well. The pattern according to which finite personality takes shape is that of an infinite ideal.

The experimentalist too is primarily interested in self-consciousness and selfhood. His emphasis differs, however, in that he sees the self as a social product.[6] The formation of selves only occurs adequately and significantly in interaction with a social group where one can associate with other more or less mature selves. It is through reciprocal, mutual relation of ' self and other ' that selfhood is built and such essential characteristics as agency and responsibility emerge. As ingredients for this process, human nature provides a certain initial endowment of intelligence and susceptibility to action. As these issue forth in experience and as experience accumulates, a certain organization or inte-

---

[1] *Supra*, p.111.
[2] *Supra*, p. 242.
[3] *Supra*, p. 244.
[4] *Supra*, pp. 181–82.
[5] *Supra*, p. 154.
[6] *Supra*, pp. 40–41.

gration takes place which is called character, mind, or soul, according to the angle from which this unity is viewed.[1]

On the matter of intelligence as an aspect of human nature the experimentalist has an especial point to make. While the other philosophies of education apparently treat it merely as a matter of innate endowment, experimentalism goes further and notes a sociological as well as a biological component of intelligence.[2] Differences in achievement between races or nations, often attributed to differences in native intelligence, turn out to be really differences in culture. In other words, the same original capacity can produce either civilization or barbarism depending on whether or not it has been reared in a rich cultural matrix. It is but one further instance for reëmphasizing, as the experimentalist does, the fundamentally social quality of human nature.

2. Theory of Learning

Pursuing human nature from the psychological angle a bit further, it appears that only one of the preceding philosophies of education gives extended consideration to a theory of learning apart from a theory of knowledge. This is experimentalism. Perhaps the other philosophies hold learning theory a matter for the science of psychology of education. At any rate, the feature that impresses the experimentalist most is the close connection between living and learning.[3] The child learns what he lives. Thus, if it is a feeling that is to be learned, he must actually *feel* it. Indeed, he will only learn it to the extent he actually does *live* it or *feel* it. Stated differently, one learns his responses and he learns his responses only as he accepts them as his own appropriate responses to the situation at hand. Stated still differently, what one learns he builds at once into character.

3. Will

Obviously such a theory of learning lays considerable store by the fact that the responses that are learned are the ones that the learner 'accepts' or 'chooses' as his own. This emphasis on 'choice' in philosophies of education could be stated as an emphasis on 'will.' The experimentalist, however, prefers not to call it this for fear that the word 'will' might be misleading.[4] There has been a tendency in some quarters to reify the concept of will and give it standing as an inde-

---

[1] *Supra*, pp. 71–72.
[2] *Supra*, p. 57.
[3] *Supra*, pp. 63, 66–71.
[4] *Supra*, p. 52.

pendent entity that does the choosing and this the experimentalist wants
to avoid. While the experimentalist emphasizes will as a phase of
learning, the other philosophies, notably idealism,[1] the Aristotelian,[2]
and the Catholic,[3] mention it in conjunction with the old problem of
the freedom of the will which they espouse. This, of course, is particularly important in moral education. In this connection the Catholic
is especially eager to make clear, first, that his acceptance of this doctrine does not imply that human nature acts without a motive and,
second, that by no means are all acts free.

4. Original Sin

Touching on free moral acts brings up one final aspect of human
nature as a possible ' given ' by which educational philosophy may
have to steer and that is whether human nature is fundamentally good,
as Rousseau held, or whether it is fundamentally bad, as Calvin maintained. The Catholic philosophy of education, the only one to take a
stand here, holds with neither of these views.[4] It heartily endorses the
doctrine of the ' fall of man ' as the very cornerstone of Christian education but its account of human nature differs from the other two.
According to it, man's nature was originally composed of natural and
supernatural elements. When the ' fall ' occurred, it did not render this
nature utterly corrupt. Nature was merely injured; its supernatural
character was put in jeopardy. This was atoned for in the life and
death of Jesus and through Him man's inheritance has been restored.
Hence, the ideal of Catholic education is " the supernatural man who
thinks, judges, and acts consistently in accordance with right reason
illumined by the supernatural light of the example and teaching of
Christ; in other words, to use the current term, the true and finished
man of character." [5]

VI. EDUCATIONAL VALUES

While some philosophies of education seem more concerned with the
data of reality and others with the data of knowing, all have a major
interest in the data of ethics or value theory. It is clearly the basic
consideration in formulating the aims of education and through them
of determining the curriculum, in formulating methods of instruction,
and in selecting other ingredients of the educative process. But how

[1] *Supra,* p. 148.
[2] *Supra,* p. 245.
[3] *Supra,* p. 254.
[4] *Supra,* pp. 259–62.
[5] *Supra,* p. 263.

does one know what is valuable, in what order things shall be held valuable, and what specific values or aims shall be set up for education? Here again the several philosophies of education take various stands.

1. Theory of Value

With the experimentalist value arises, as does experience, in the interaction between the organism and the environment.[1] Any action or tendency to action denotes an inclination, a desire, a wish, or a want. The good, simply defined, is what satisfies these cravings. But what satisfies one man's craving will often not satisfy another's. Hence one must go further with the exposition of the good. In addition to having the backing of an individual's senses, the good must also be supported by a significant number of others as well, especially those whose opinion about the good is respected.[2] Again, the good may be obscured because there are two or more competing goods, or because different people may disagree as to what is the good. In such cases, one must have resort to thought and its consequences in action in order to judge between these different conceptions. Some people reserve the word value for such a judgment about the good. The defensible good is the valuable. In making such judgments, the experimentalist always bears in mind what will be best for the greatest number in the circumstances under which the need for judgment arises.

The educational realist thinks of value largely in terms of interest or motivation.[3] He recognizes two kinds of interest or value, the one immediate and intrinsic and the other mediate or extrinsic. No learning situation is without either one or the other type. In the case of immediate or intrinsic interest studies are valued as ends. They are valued in and of themselves. In the case of extrinsic interest there is no such immediate appeal of studies. These must be motivated or valued because they are mediate to something else which does have immediate or intrinsic appeal, as for example, a professional career. In such a case values are instrumental and closely akin to the experimentalist point of view, although they are here stated somewhat differently.

The Aristotelian arrives at his conception of the good quite differently. Here the good lies in the direction of the development of a native power or capacity.[4] If one has abilities that can grow, then for

---

[1] *Supra*, pp. 52–53.   [3] *Supra*, pp. 102–4, 136.
[2] *Supra*, pp. 47–50.   [4] *Supra*, pp. 242–43.

those abilities to develop into their full stature is the good. Find out what the purpose or design of a power is, and the good must be the realization of that end. Thus, the mind has a natural tendency to learn. For it to learn or acquire knowledge, therefore, must be good. Or, in other words, knowledge is one of the virtues or good habits at which education aims.[1] The good is proportioned by the extent to which potentialities have been actualized. Stated differently, this means that the good is convertible with being. A capacity or power has as much goodness as it has achieved development.

The Catholic philosophy of education states its theory of value only slightly differently.[2] In this theory some things are of their very nature good. They do not derive this quality from any human legislation; they are just intrinsically good. So, too, with that which is to be rejected as the bad. The criterion for judging whether something is good or bad is to determine whether it is in conformity with man's rational nature. Reason indicates that this rational nature is both body and soul, that it is essentially social, and that it is dependent on God for its existence. These characteristics are detailed because the order of their mention aids in establishing a hierarchy of value. Thus, for instance, sports in school, because they minister to the body, must be subordinated in importance to intellectual studies, which enrich the soul.[3] Or again, intellectual studies like mathematics must be made secondary to the study of religion and one's duties to God.[4]

The idealist's statement of value seems to partake of several of the preceding ones for he holds value to consist of " those experiences which fulfil the needs of his nature and bring him the sense of satisfaction and well-being." [5] In this he speaks of satisfaction as the experimentalist does; but he speaks of the fulfilment or development of native needs or powers as does the Aristotelian and the Catholic. However, he probably leans toward the latter. For him education is not just a matter of development or growing; there must be movement toward a goal, a goal where value is already realized in infinite, eternal form.[6] Human educational values are therefore but " temporal expressions of an eternal order which has value in itself." This ideal exists nowhere among us fully but it is the duty of man and education to try to actualize it.[7] Where educational values conflict, the hierarchy of values will take

---

[1] *Supra*, p. 211.
[2] *Supra*, pp. 253–55.
[3] *Supra*, pp. 273–74.
[4] *Supra*, pp. 264–65.

[5] *Supra*, p. 182.
[6] *Supra*, pp. 183, 185.
[7] *Supra*, p. 178.

its order from the degree to which such values aid in the realization of this absolute goal.[1]

2. Moral Education

While dwelling on the problem of educational value it may be well to put in a word for that special instance of it, namely, moral education. On the whole, theory here follows the same lines as that already laid down for value in general. But there is the question of moral sanction which perhaps has not been adequately covered. What is the obligation of the pupil or teacher to choose the good? In the Catholic philosophy of education this is quite clear.[2] In making man, God must have had some purpose. Since man's existence is contingent upon God, man owes him certain duties. These duties are defined by God's purpose. Indeed, without God as the fountain-head of goodness there can be an adequate and ultimate purpose neither in life nor in education.

The idealist's view on this point is not very different from the Catholic, and yet different enough to be mentioned. He finds the sanction for moral education in a moral world order.[3] Acts in harmony with this order have a survival value. Those inconsistent with it are self-destructive. The experimentalist, fairly close to the idealist but even farther away from the Catholic than the idealist, finds the obligation for moral conduct in social experience.[4] Solutions to moral problems which prove to afford the greatest good for the largest number come to have social approval. When such solutions become apparent, the moral obligation arises coincidentally and ' naturally ' out of the human relationships which ushered in the solution. In this view the realist also would no doubt concur.[5]

3. Aims of Education

Educational aims and educational values naturally have a close affinity. Some values are the incidental outcome or result of education but the values of chief concern in this connection are the ones men deliberately seek to achieve through education. In considering educational aims it will be well for the reader to ponder them not only in the light of theories of value but also in the light of theories of reality, knowledge, and human nature as well. With this in mind it will be well to remember, too, that educational aims may be stated specifically or

[1] *Supra,* p. 186.
[2] *Supra,* p. 252.
[3] *Supra,* pp. 149–50.
[4] *Supra,* pp. 49–50.
[5] *Supra,* p. 127.

generally. The more specifically they are stated, the more numerous they become. Limitations of space forbid anything more than a comparison of the general, fundamental aims of the philosophies of education presented in this Yearbook together with only the briefest mention of specific objectives.

The basic aim of the Catholic philosophy of education stands out at a number of points. Declared simply, it is " to know, love, and serve Him [God] in this life and be happy with Him forever in the next." [1] This must be the case, for it is the purpose God had in mind in creating man. Elaborated somewhat, the educational mission of the church is announced to be " to restore the sons of Adam to their high position as children of God." [2] Elaborating still further, the aim of Christian education is put forward as " to coöperate with divine grace in forming the true and perfect Christian, that is, to form Christ himself in those regenerated by baptism." [3] Citizenship and patriotism are recognized as social aims of Catholic education but subordinate to a realization of " the brotherhood of man and the fatherhood of God." Yet even this last is not precise enough. Rather " the objective of the church is to realize the consequences of a child's incorporation with Christ through baptism, a realization that Christ and the Church of which he is a member are *one* thing — the Mystical Body of Christ." [4] Finally, it must be realized that the aim of education so stated is immutable, eternal. This supernatural ideal of education dominates the elementary, secondary, and higher grades of schools, each of which has its own particular contribution to such objectives as knowledge, skill, habit, and appreciation, or as citizenship, vocation, family, and church life.

In the Aristotelian position three levels of aims are noted. At the first and highest level is the ultimate aim of all human activity.[5] This is happiness. But since happiness is the end of *all* activities — domestic and political, as well as educational — it is necessary to distinguish the aims of education in particular. Here at the second level, are the ultimate aims of education. They are ultimate, but only for education. In relation to happiness they are only a means. The ultimate aims of education are the first principles of the philosophy of education. Moreover, so stated, " the aim of education should be the same for all men (i.e., everywhere and always, in every mode of society, every condition of life, etc.)." [6] This is equivalent to saying, of

[1] *Supra,* p. 252.
[2] *Supra,* p. 263.
[3] *Supra,* p. 265.
[4] *Supra,* p. 283.
[5] *Supra,* pp. 238–39.
[6] *Supra,* p. 238.

course, that the aims of education are absolute and universal. Finally, at the third level are the proximate ends of education.[1] These being more specific in character will only be hinted at in outline. They are two in number, intellectual habits and moral habits — habits of knowing and thinking and habits of desiring and acting. Intellectual habits, as ends, may be further subdivided into habits of knowledge and habits of art — habits of knowing ' that ' and habits of knowing ' how.' The arts as proximate ends of education may be further subdivided into such as the liberal, vocational, and fine arts.

Since for the idealist " the final test of the value of any . . . educational system is the effect it has on individual personality," [2] it follows that the main aim of education is to perfect the ideal of cultivated personality.[3] Perfection, of course, means " finite personality growing . . . into the likeness of an infinite personality." [4] More particularly " the values of human living, the realization of which constitutes our true objectives of living and learning [are]: character, social justice, skill, art, love, knowledge, philosophy, and religion." [5]

As might be expected, the experimentalist, dominated as he is by the importance of the group culture and the need for experimentation in a world that is continually undergoing change and whose future is always more or less contingent, sets up educational aims which are appropriate to these premises. " The culture thus is the first great task of education. . . . The original and primary aim in education, so felt by responsible parents and teachers in every previous age, has been that the child shall increasingly learn to live the life of the group and to accept appropriate responsibility in connection therewith." [6] It is not enough, however, to aim to live this culture as it is at any given time. The times are changing at an ever accelerating rate. Education must, therefore, also " prepare our youth to live amid conditions yet to come, amid conditions now unknown to us." [7]

With these two main aims of the educational experimentalist, the educational realist would no doubt be in agreement. He, too, wants the schools to conserve and transmit the verified knowledge of the group; and he also wants children to have training in the methodology by which this attested knowledge is obtained.[8] What he mistrusts in the experimentalist's position is that methodology will receive a dispropor-

---

[1] *Supra*, pp. 214–15.
[2] *Supra*, p. 147.
[3] Cf. p. 157.
[4] *Supra*, p. 155.

[5] *Supra*, p. 182.
[6] *Supra*, pp. 62–63.
[7] *Supra*, p. 65.
[8] *Supra*, pp. 121–24.

tionately greater emphasis than it deserves. It is the realist's special pride that he keeps these two educational aims properly balanced.

VII. School and Society

1. Respect for Personality

It may seem amiss to have expounded the aims of education before giving more than incidental attention to the social dimension of an educational philosophy. This must certainly seem the case to the many who think that the controlling purpose of education is to be deduced from the social structure in which the school operates. In spite of this claim, no one of the educational philosophies expounded in this Yearbook adopts this point of view. On one ground or another each holds that the individual is the primary end of education and that the claims of society or the state are to be subordinated to him. This is perhaps the most striking instance of unanimity of viewpoint among the diverse philosophies of education presented in this volume.

Even though the experimentalist and the realist stress the acquisition of the group culture as an aim of education, this is in order that the individual may achieve adequate selfhood or personality. Indeed, the realist makes respect for the demands of the individual equal with those of society;[1] and the experimentalist lists first among his half dozen most fundamental philosophical principles that "each person is to be treated always as end and never merely as means."[2] The idealist too subscribes to this Kantian dictum. Because he can think of nothing higher or more valuable than personality, the effect on personality, as already noted, is the ultimate test of any social system.[3] Moreover, it is the core of the idealistic teacher's method.[4] Sustaining this unanimity of viewpoint, the Catholic places the individual ahead of the state in educational importance because his end is supernatural while that of the state is purely natural.[5] But he would hold to this priority of worth even if he considered nothing more than the natural order alone. How important the individual is may perhaps best be realized from the Aristotelian position of Adler, for on this point Adler appears to depart widely from Aristotle himself. Aristotle held that the individual should be educated not only by the state but *for* the state. Adler on the other hand holds that, while the individual is to be

---

[1] *Supra*, pp. 131–33, 138.
[2] *Supra*, p. 54.
[3] *Supra*, pp. 147, 154.
[4] *Supra*, p. 157.
[5] *Supra*, pp. 281–82.

educated as a good citizen and hence with reference to the ends of the state, the state is only an intermediary end and not an end in itself.[1] The ultimate end of education is an ethical rather than a political question. In other words, the relation of the state to education is one of means and not ends.

2. Democracy and Education

In view of this strong emphasis upon the individual as the main end of the educational process, little of importance remains to be said about the part of democracy in a philosophy of education. Respect for personality *is* the democratic theory of education. It will be difficult to achieve, however, the experimentalist believes, unless underlying economic problems are solved in its favor.[2] Where opportunity is predicated on the system of production and distribution of goods, this system will have to hold democratic ends in view if the corresponding philosophy of education is to prevail. Besides clearing economic privilege from the path of democratic education, the idealist would also extend respect for personality into respect for national and racial minorities as well.[3]

In placing respect for personality as the central theme of democratic education, the main stress is on individuality, on freedom. There is, however, a social dimension which must not be overlooked merely because it is relegated to the position of means. The realist is especially fearful that the emphasis on freedom will lead to excesses. He therefore insists in putting at least equal weight on the authority of socially tested experience.[4] Yet, although authority is set as a counterweight to freedom in democratic education, it is not supposed to contradict it but rather to complement it.

The experimentalist states this social dimension as the effort of the members of society to manage society coöperatively on the basis of the experimentalist's theory of values.[5] Just how far such a conception of democracy would be acceptable to the Catholic is in doubt because the experimentalist does not indicate how far he would extend such coöperative management. If he would include every phase of the school — techniques of instruction, curriculum, organization, and administration — then the Catholic would reject it.[6] He does not believe that these educational procedures should be predicated on the dogma of the

---

[1] *Supra,* pp. 231–32.   [4] *Supra,* pp. 125–27, 131–37.

[2] *Supra,* pp. 80–82.   [5] *Supra,* pp. 54–56.

[3] *Supra,* p. 180.   [6] *Supra,* pp. 283–84.

'sovereign people' which in the extreme amounts to political pantheism. In short, he rejects democracy as an absolute, as a religion. Doubtless he would also reject the idealistic statement that democracy is religion applied to politics and that the kingdom of heaven is democracy applied to religion.[1] Nevertheless, he holds Catholicism and democracy compatible if democracy be limited to the sphere of government by a majority vote of the free equal citizens of the state. Yet even with this qualification Catholicism shows neither exclusive nor enthusiastic preference for democracy, declaring that it is only one among several legally possible forms to which Catholicism can adapt itself.

3. The State and the School

Regardless of the political form which society takes, there is still one further aspect of the relation of school and society which deserves mention. This is the scope of the responsibility of the school. The experimentalist not only thinks that the school should enable the immature to participate in the group culture but he also urges that the school make an active effort to improve the culture.[2] While the idealist would probably concur in this program, he has grave doubts that the school should take the initiative in reconstructing the social order.[3] On the contrary he sees the school as a reflection of the kind of society in which it is maintained. So, it is reactionary, conservative, liberal, or radical, according to its economic, political, and social context.

Not only does the school not have chief responsibility for the direction of social progress, but some philosophies of education maintain that it is not to be the sole educational agency of society. Other institutions share this responsibility with the school. Notably these are the home and the church; but the economic and political community are not to be overlooked in this regard.[4] Catholic educational philosophy is particularly insistent on this point.[5] It is especially opposed to the view that the schools of the state should have any monopoly of education. On this point it asserts that the family has a higher right than the state in determining the education of the child. And anterior to both the state and the family is the right of the church in matters educational. This follows from the fact that the church is a society of

---

[1] *Supra*, p. 178.
[2] *Supra*, p. 40.
[3] *Supra*, pp. 173–75.

[4] *Supra*, p. 220.
[5] *Supra*, pp. 266, 281–82.

the supernatural order and that education is necessarily connected with man's supernatural destiny.

VIII. Conflict, Communication, and Coöperation

This comparison of educational philosophies commenced by raising such practical questions as what aim, what curriculum, what method should the teacher adopt. These questions, it was seen, cannot be answered till more basic questions have been raised. Thus, what is the good; what is the true; what are the realities of nature and human nature? On examination it turns out that there are virtually no generally accepted answers to these basic questions. There being no agreement at the base of the thought structure of education, it should occasion no surprise if there is diversity of practice in the superstructure of the aim, content, and method of education. Different premises lead to different conclusions. But must premises be different? Can it not be decided at the outset which premises are sound and which are unsound so that all or much of the subsequent confusion can be eliminated? Much depends on one's attitude toward diversity. It is an ultimate datum of existence? Or can difference be resolved in some inclusive unity?

If the former be the fact, little further need be said. The whole Yearbook has been an exposition of these differences. To the extent that progress depends on the expression of difference of point of view or to the extent that freedom is the demand of difference to express itself, the Yearbook has amply justified itself. Perhaps one could stop right here if each of the preceding philosophies were to set up schools of its own, like the Catholic parochial system, for example, where its tenets could operate unchallenged. This, however, is far from being the case. The more usual situation is one in which teachers of different philosophical commitments must work side by side in the same school system. The critical problem is, how can such teachers collaborate in their common endeavors? Indeed, how can they even communicate? When differences crop out in the management of the school, how shall these differences be arbitrated?

The Aristotelian has a ready answer for these questions. He at once takes the view that there cannot be a profitable exploration of our differences unless at the outset we agree on certain fundamentals. Coöperation, in fact just bare communication without coöperation, depends on our holding certain things in common at the start. Language is an excellent illustration. If we do not speak the same language or if we speak the same language with different meanings, coöperation or communication is rendered proportionately difficult or even impossible.[1] It is an easy step from here to the main point of the Aristotelian doctrine, namely, that we must also agree at the outset on what is to be accepted as proof of truth and falsity, as to what is knowledge and what is mere opinion.[2] Unless we agree on such matters, he would further say we cannot adjudicate our differences of opinion so that educational policies can be formed. A concrete illustration, in fact, is right at hand. How can a symposium like the current Yearbook be read unless there is some common denominator by which the various chapter numerators can be weighed and compared? Unless there is, the Aristotelian is ready to doubt the efficacy of a symposium such as this.

The principle enunciated here is no doubt sound enough. The discussion of our conflicts and disagreements must take place within a common frame of reference or there is no hope of arbitrating their merits. But how can such a common frame of reference be agreed upon? The Aristotelian makes this difficult at the very outset by stating that there is only *one true* philosophy of education [3] and by addressing himself only to those who are willing to agree with him ' pro tem.' [4] However, the fact that one need only agree with him pro tempore is an important gesture in the direction of further communication. There is an assumption that the reader could understand the argument without necessarily accepting it. The Catholic, for instance, invites the reader at least to try to comprehend what he is driving at even if the reader ultimately decides that he cannot agree with it.[5] The realist expresses this same aspiration for a common frame of reference through commendation of the unity-of-science movement.[6] Perhaps the experimentalist goes further than any of the others. He lays it down that the more individuals and groups study their common problems honestly and carefully, the greater is the likelihood that they will reach common results.[7]

With these sincere and promising gestures in the direction of a basis for better communication and coöperation between people holding diverse philosophies of education, it would seem as if a Yearbook such as this should put more stress on points of agreement than on those of disagreement. The fact is, however, that at present the points of conflict are much more obvious and numerous than those of concurrence.

---

[1] Cf. *supra*, p. 287.
[2] *Supra*, pp. 197–202.
[3] *Supra*, pp. 199–200.
[4] *Supra*, p. 237.

[5] *Supra*, pp. 251–52.
[6] *Supra*, p. 124.
[7] *Supra*, p. 54.

Moreover, one must be very cautious about agreements for they may so easily turn out to be apparent agreements rather than real ones. In spite of these drawbacks, it is submitted that the avenue to broader understanding and greater mutuality of coöperation is to start with such real or apparent agreements as may be found and to expand from there.

Such a point of departure has already been noted in references to preceding chapters. This is the uniform agreement of all these philosophies of education on the ultimate worth of individual personality.[1] What this conception covers and the reasons assigned in support of it will doubtless vary from view to view. But with such a consensus as a start, it might well be possible to formulate an educational program to which all could lend a very high degree of support.

If this seems too simple or limited an example, another might be posed in the definition of education given by the authors of four of the preceding chapters. The definitions, being more inclusive, present a more complex problem. Let the reader examine the following and try to identify each before verifying its authorship.

Education should be thought of as the process of man's reciprocal adjustment to nature, to his fellows, and to the ultimate nature of the cosmos.[2]

Education is the organized development and equipment of all the powers of a human being, moral, intellectual, and physical, by and for their individual and social uses, directed towards the union of these activities with their creator as their final end.[3]

Education is the process in which these powers (abilities, capacities) of men which are susceptible to habituation, are perfected by *good* habits, by *means artistically contrived,* and employed by any man to help another or himself achieve the *end* in view (i.e., good habits).[4]

Any adequate educational program will thus be concerned to help each individual child grow up from his state of initial dependence into full participation in the richest available group life, including in a democratic country a full share in the active management of group affairs. Such an adequate program will besides go on further to an active effort to improve the group culture.[5]

Of course there are clues which betray the authorship of each of these definitions. Yet in spite of this fact there is a striking degree of similarity in expression. Doubtless much of this similarity is due to the

[1] *Supra,* p. 315.
[2] *Supra,* p. 140.
[3] *Supra,* p. 255.
[4] *Supra,* p. 209.
[5] *Supra,* p. 40.

generality of each statement. As generalizations, each carries a very compact and concentrated cargo of meanings. Expanded into the detail of a whole chapter, each releases all the disagreements noted earlier. Nevertheless, it cannot be overlooked by those genuinely interested in promoting coöperation and communication that these general statements offer a common starting place for enlarging the areas of mutual understanding and defining more precisely the next points of attack.

How successful one can hope to be in resolving this age-old problem of unity and diversity or, as Plato called it, the problem of the one and the many, is very difficult to say. However, if in addition to setting forth differences of viewpoint, this Yearbook can aid ever so little in reducing conflicts, in promoting communication, and in increasing coöperation, it will have been eminently worth while.

INFORMATION CONCERNING THE NATIONAL SOCIETY FOR THE STUDY OF EDUCATION

1. PURPOSE. The purpose of the National Society is to promote the investigation and discussion of educational questions. To this end it holds an annual meeting and publishes a series of yearbooks.

2. ELIGIBILITY TO MEMBERSHIP. Any person who is interested in receiving its publications may become a member by sending to the Secretary-Treasurer information concerning name, title, and address, and a check for $4.00 (see Item 5).

Membership is not transferable; it is limited to individuals, and may not be held by libraries, schools, or other institutions, either directly or indirectly.

3. PERIOD OF MEMBERSHIP. Applicants for membership may not date their entrance back of the current calendar year, and all memberships terminate automatically on December 31, unless the dues for the ensuing year are paid as indicated in Item 6.

4. DUTIES AND PRIVILEGES OF MEMBERS. Members pay dues of $3.00 annually, receive a cloth-bound copy of each publication, are entitled to vote, to participate in discussion, and (under certain conditions) to hold office. The names of members are printed in the yearbooks.

Persons who are sixty years of age or above may become life members on payment of fee based on average life-expectancy of their age group. For information, apply to Secretary-Treasurer.

5. ENTRANCE FEE. New members are required the first year to pay, in addition to the dues, an entrance fee of one dollar.

6. PAYMENT OF DUES. Statements of dues are rendered in October or November for the following calendar year. Any member so notified whose dues remain unpaid on January 1, thereby loses his membership and can be reinstated only by paying a reinstatement fee of fifty cents, levied to cover the actual clerical cost involved.

School warrants and vouchers from institutions must be accompanied by definite information concerning the name and address of the person for whom membership fee is being paid. Statements of dues are rendered on our own form only. The Secretary's office cannot undertake to fill out special invoice forms of any sort or to affix notary's affidavit to statements or receipts.

Cancelled checks serve as receipts. Members desiring an additional receipt must enclose a stamped and addressed envelope therefor.

7. DISTRIBUTION OF YEARBOOKS TO MEMBERS. The yearbooks, ready prior to each February meeting, will be mailed from the office of the distributors, only to members whose dues for that year have been paid. Members who desire yearbooks prior to the current year must purchase them directly from the distributors (see Item 8).

8. COMMERCIAL SALES. The distribution of all yearbooks prior to the current year, and also of those of the current year not regularly mailed to members in exchange for their dues, is in the hands of the distributor, not of the Secretary. For such commercial sales, communicate directly with the University of Chicago Press, Chicago 37, Illinois, which will gladly send a price list covering all the publications of this Society and of its predecessor, the National Herbart Society. This list is also printed in the yearbook.

9. YEARBOOKS. The yearbooks are issued about one month before the February meeting. They comprise from 600 to 800 pages annually. Unusual effort has been made to make them, on the one hand, of immediate practical value, and, on the other hand, representative of sound scholarship and scientific investigation. Many of them are the fruit of co-operative work by committees of the Society.

10. MEETINGS. The annual meeting, at which the yearbooks are discussed, is held in February at the same time and place as the meeting of the American Association of School Administrators.

Applications for membership will be handled promptly at any time on receipt of name and address, together with check for $4.00 (or $3.50 for reinstatement). Generally speaking, applications entitle the new members to the yearbook slated for discussion during the calendar year the application is made, but those received in December are regarded as pertaining to the next calendar year.

5835 Kimbark Ave.   NELSON B. HENRY, *Secretary-Treasurer*
Chicago, 37, Illinois

PUBLICATIONS OF THE NATIONAL HERBART SOCIETY

PUBLICATIONS OF THE NATIONAL SOCIETY FOR
THE STUDY OF EDUCATION

PUBLICATIONS

PUBLICATIONS

Twenty-ninth Yearbook, 1930, Parts I and II—*Report of the Society's Committee on Arithmetic.* Part I—*Some Aspects of Modern Thought on Arithmetic.* Part II—*Research in Arithmetic.* Prepared by the Society's Committee. F. B. Knight, Chairman. Bound in one volume. Cloth.. 5.00
Paper... 3.25
Thirtieth Yearbook, 1931, Part I—*The Status of Rural Education.* First Report of the Society's Committee on Rural Education. Orville G. Brim, Chairman. Cloth...... 2.50
Paper... 1.75
Thirtieth Yearbook, 1931, Part II—*The Textbook in American Education.* Report of the Society's Committee on the Textbook. J. B. Edmonson, Chairman. Cloth........ 2.50
Paper... 1.75
Thirty-first Yearbook, 1932, Part I—*A Program for Teaching Science.* Prepared by the Society's Committee on the Teaching of Science. S. Ralph Powers, Chairman. Cloth 2.50
Paper... 1.75
Thirty-first Yearbook, 1932, Part II—*Changes and Experiments in Liberal-Arts Education.* Prepared by Kathryn McHale, with numerous collaborators. Cloth......... 2.50
Paper... 1.75
Thirty-second Yearbook, 1933—*The Teaching of Geography.* Prepared by the Society's Committee on the Teaching of Geography. A. E. Parkins, Chairman. Cloth....... 4.50
Paper... 3.00
Thirty-third Yearbook, 1934, Part I—*The Planning and Construction of School Buildings.* Prepared by the Society's Committee on School Buildings. N. L. Engelhardt, Chairman. Cloth... 2.50
Paper... 1.75
Thirty-third Yearbook, 1934, Part II—*The Activity Movement.* Prepared by the Society's Committee on the Activity Movement. Lois Coffey Mossman, Chairman. Cloth 2.50
Paper... 1.75
Thirty-fourth Yearbook, 1935—*Educational Diagnosis.* Prepared by the Society's Committee on Educational Diagnosis. L. J. Brueckner, Chairman. Cloth........... 4.25
Paper... 3.00
Thirty-fifth Yearbook, 1936, Part I—*The Grouping of Pupils.* Prepared by the Society's Committee. W. W. Coxe, Chairman. Cloth................................. 2.50
Paper... 1.75
Thirty-fifth Yearbook, 1936, Part II—*Music Education.* Prepared by the Society's Committee. W. L. Uhl, Chairman. Cloth.. 2.50
Paper... 1.75
Thirty-sixth Yearbook, 1937, Part I—*The Teaching of Reading.* Prepared by the Society's Committee. W. S. Gray, Chairman. Cloth............................... 2.50
Paper... 1.75
Thirty-sixth Yearbook, 1937, Part II—*International Understanding through the Public-School Curriculum.* Prepared by the Society's Committee. I. L. Kandel, Chairman. Cloth... 2.50
Paper... 1.75
Thirty-seventh Yearbook, 1938, Part I—*Guidance in Educational Institutions.* Prepared by the Society's Committee. G. N. Kefauver, Chairman. Cloth.................. 2.50
Paper... 1.75
Thirty-seventh Yearbook, 1938, Part II—*The Scientific Movement in Education.* Prepared by the Society's Committee. F. N. Freeman, Chairman. Cloth............. 4.00
Paper... 3.00
Thirty-eighth Yearbook, 1939, Part I—*Child Development and the Curriculum.* Prepared by the Society's Committee. Carleton Washburne, Chairman. Cloth....... 3.25
Paper... 2.50
Thirty-eighth Yearbook, 1939, Part II—*General Education in the American College.* Prepared by the Society's Committee. Alvin Eurich, Chairman. Cloth........... 2.75
Paper... 2.00
Thirty-ninth Yearbook, 1940, Part I—*Intelligence: Its Nature and Nurture. Comparative and Critical Exposition.* Prepared by the Society's Committee. G. D. Stoddard, Chairman. Cloth... 3.00
Paper... 2.25
Thirty-ninth Yearbook, 1940, Part II—*Intelligence: Its Nature and Nurture. Original Studies and Experiments.* Prepared by the Society's Committee. G. D. Stoddard, Chairman. Cloth... 3.00
Paper... 2.25
Fortieth Yearbook, 1941—*Art in American Life and Education.* Prepared by the Society's Committee. Thomas Munro, Chairman. Cloth....................... 4.00
Paper... 3.00
Forty-first Yearbook, 1942, Part I—*Philosophies of Education.* Prepared by the Society's Committee. John S. Brubacher, Chairman. Cloth................... 3.00
Paper... 2.25
Forty-first Yearbook, 1942, Part II—*The Psychology of Learning.* Prepared by the Society's Committee. T. R. McConnell, Chairman. Cloth.................... 3.25
Paper... 2.50
Forty-second Yearbook, 1943, Part I—*Vocational Education.* Prepared by the Society's Committee. F. J. Keller, Chairman. Cloth........................... 3.25
Paper... 2.50
Forty-second Yearbook, 1943, Part II—*The Library in General Education.* Prepared by the Society's Committee. L. R. Wilson, Chairman. Cloth.................. 3.00
Paper... 2.25

PUBLICATIONS

POSTPAID PRICE

Forty-third Yearbook, 1944, Part I—*Adolescence.* Prepared by the Society's Committee. Harold E. Jones, Chairman. Cloth.................................... 3.00
    Paper.. 2.25
Forty-third Yearbook, 1944, Part II—*Teaching Language in the Elementary School.* Prepared by the Society's Committee. M. R. Trabue, Chairman. Cloth.......... 2.75
    Paper.. 2.00
Forty-fourth Yearbook, 1945, Part I—*American Education in the Postwar Period: Curriculum Reconstruction.* Prepared by the Society's Committee. Ralph W. Tyler, Chairman. Cloth.. 3.00
    Paper.. 2.25
Forty-fourth Yearbook, 1945, Part II—*American Education in the Postwar Period: Structural Reorganization.* Prepared by the Society's Committee. Bess Goodykoontz, Chairman. Cloth... 3.00
    Paper.. 2.25
Forty-fifth Yearbook, 1946, Part I—*The Measurement of Understanding.* Prepared by the Society's Committee. William A. Brownell, Chairman. Cloth........... 3.00
    Paper.. 2.25
Forty-fifth Yearbook, 1946, Part II—*Changing Conceptions in Educational Administration.* Prepared by the Society's Committee. Alonzo G. Grace, Chairman. Cloth 2.50
    Paper.. 1.75
Forty-sixth Yearbook, 1947, Part I—*Science Education in American Schools.* Prepared by the Society's Committee. Victor H. Noll, Chairman. Cloth.................. 3.25
    Paper.. 2.50
Forty-sixth Yearbook, 1947, Part II—*Early Childhood Education.* Prepared by the Society's Committee. N. Searle Light, Chairman. Cloth..................... 3.50
    Paper.. 2.75
Forty-seventh Yearbook, 1948, Part I—*Juvenile Delinquency and the Schools.* Prepared by the Society's Committee. Ruth Strang, Chairman. Cloth............. 3.50
    Paper.. 2.75
Forty-seventh yearbook, 1948, Part II—*Reading in the High School and College.* Prepared by the Society's Committee. William S. Gray, Chairman. Cloth........ 3.50
    Paper.. 2.75
Forty-eighth Yearbook, 1949, Part I—*Audio-visual Materials of Instruction.* Prepared by the Society's Committee. Stephen M. Corey, Chairman. Cloth.............. 3.50
    Paper.. 2.75
Forty-eighth Yearbook, 1949, Part II—*Reading in the Elementary School.* Prepared by the Society's Committee. Arthur I. Gates, Chairman. Cloth............... 3.50
    Paper.. 2.75
Forty-ninth Yearbook, 1950, Part I—*Learning and Instruction.* Prepared by the Society's Committee. G. Lester Anderson, Chairman. Cloth................... 3.50
    Paper.. 2.75
Forty-ninth Yearbook, 1950, Part II—*The Education of Exceptional Children.* Prepared by the Society's Committee. Samuel A. Kirk, Chairman. Cloth.......... 3.50
    Paper.. 2.75
Fiftieth Yearbook, 1951, Part I—*Graduate Study in Education.* Prepared by the Society's Board of Directors. Ralph W. Tyler, Chairman. Cloth................ 3.50
    Paper.. 2.75
Fiftieth Yearbook, 1951, Part II—*The Teaching of Arithmetic.* Prepared by the Society's Committee. G. T. Buswell, Chairman. Cloth........................ 3.50
    Paper.. 2.75

Distributed by
THE UNIVERSITY OF CHICAGO PRESS
CHICAGO 37, ILLINOIS
1951